Ray P. Martin
325 Aderhold Hall
Univ of Georgia
Athens, Ga. 30607
(404) 542-4110

DEVELOPMENT, GENETICS, AND PSYCHOLOGY

Table
9.1   pg 173-174
10.1   pg. 195
10.4   pg 207
10.10   211
10.9   218
11.1   227
  12.1   255
  12.4   270
  12.6   272
  12.10   280
  12.13   290
  14.2   323
     10.1   197

          76
4.1
          77
4.1   81
  4.2   98
    5.2   101
      5.3   104
        5.4 107
          5.7 112
          6.1

DEVELOPMENT, GENETICS, AND PSYCHOLOGY

Robert Plomin

Institute for Behavioral Genetics
University of Colorado, Boulder

LEA LAWRENCE ERLBAUM ASSOCIATES, PUBLISHERS
1986 Hillsdale, New Jersey   London

Lawrence Erlbaum Associates, Inc., Publishers
365 Broadway
Hillsdale, New Jersey 07642

Library of Congress Cataloging-in-Publication Data

Plomin, Robert, 1948–

  Development, genetics, and psychology.

  Bibliography: p.
  Includes indexes.
  1. Developmental psychology.   2. Genetic psychology.

I. Title.
BF713.P57   1986   155   86-3181
ISBN 0-89859-630-0

Printed in the United States of America
10   9   8   7   6   5   4   3   2   1

This book is dedicated to John C. DeFries, Director of the Institute for Behavioral Genetics, whose intellectual stimulation, support, and standards are directly responsible for this book. We have collaborated so closely that the ideas in this book are as much his as mine.

Contents

Acknowledgments

I am grateful to Judy Dunn, who encouraged me to write this book, and to my colleagues at the Institute for Behavioral Genetics. I also thank Sandra Scarr, the premier developmental behavioral geneticist, for reading the manuscript and for her support and suggestions. The book also profitted immensely from an excellent group of students at the Institute who used the manuscript in a class and provided valuable comments. I am especially indebted to Rebecca Miles at the Institute for her excellent editorial advice.

Research involving the Colorado Adoption Project has been continuously funded since 1977 by the National Institute of Child Health and Human Development (HD-10333) and since 1978 by the National Science Foundation (BNS-7826204 and BNS-8200310). The Spencer Foundation and the W. T. Grant Foundation have also contributed generously to aspects of the longitudinal project. Other support during preparation of the book included a grant from the National Institute of Child Health and Human Development (HD-18426) and from the National Science Foundation (BNS-85-05692). The book was completed while I was a Fellow at the Center for Advanced Study in the Behavioral Sciences and I am grateful for financial support provided by the John D. & Catherine T. MacArthur Foundation.

FOUNDATIONS OF DEVELOPMENTAL BEHAVIORAL GENETICS

1 Introduction

This book is based on two simple ideas. The first is that genes are involved in change as well as continuity in development. The second is that the best way to study effects of environment on behavior is through the study of genetic influences, employing the theory and methods of quantitative genetics. These are the major themes of a new interdiscipline, developmental behavioral genetics, which applies the tools of quantitative genetics to the study of behavioral development. Over a decade ago, the integration of behavioral genetics and developmental psychology was viewed as "overdue" (Gottesman, 1974). Research in developmental behavioral genetics has just begun; nonetheless, significant advances already have been made and these have important implications for developmental psychologists.

The approach of behavioral genetics is highly empirical, an orientation that is reflected in this book. I do not attempt to argue or persuade as much as to present methods and data that I hope speak for themselves. The inductive approach of behavioral genetics appears plodding and tedious as we watch bricks being put into place one at a time, often in different parts of the building, and sometimes so far away from the building that the brick serves no purpose other than tripping workers on their way to the construction site. No foreman seems to be on the job and many of the workers are temporary. However, this has been going on for half of a century and, when we step back to look at it, it is clear that something substantial is being built. In contrast, a disturbing trend in developmental psychology is the construction of instant edifices in which the bricks are pronouncements rather than facts. These fabrications are mirages, disappearing when approached for closer examination, or facades soon blown over by the mercurial winds of fashion.

In this chapter, basic issues in quantitative genetic theory and methods are discussed. The other two chapters in this section on foundations of developmental behavioral genetics describe developmental molecular genetics and developmental behavioral genetics. Shock waves from the recent explosion of research in developmental molecular genetics are beginning to reach psychology and, eventually, developmental behavioral genetics will inherit the conceptual and methodological advances of molecular genetics. For now, developmental molecular genetics makes it clear that many opportunities exist for genetic change during development. These changes are the focus of developmental behavioral genetics, which is described in the third and last chapter in this section on foundations.

Recognition of genetic influence on developmental change as well as continuity will bring the fields of development and behavioral genetics closer together in an interdiscipline of developmental behavioral genetics. The mistaken notion that genetic influences begin prior to birth and remain immutable ever after pervades the field of developmental psychology. For example, nearly all developmental psychology texts discuss genetic influences in an early chapter, usually the chapter preceding one on perinatal influences. Developmentalists are justifiably unenthusiastic about such an apparently nondevelopmental phenomenon. We need to pry apart the close association that the adjectives *genetic* and *stable* have come to share: Longitudinally stable characters are not necessarily hereditary, nor are genetically influenced characters necessarily stable. Once developmentalists realize that genes contribute to the instability that is predominant in most realms of child development, interest in behavioral genetics will grow.

The next section indicates that developmental behavioral genetics can accomplish much more than estimating the relative contributions of genetic and environmental influences to development. Paradoxically, developmental behavioral genetics is likely to make more progress in studying environmental influences than genetic effects. In terms of genetics, we have much to learn about genetic change during development. However, most of the next steps in genetic analysis require the identification of single major genes; without single-gene effects, we cannot map genes to specific chromosomes using linkage analysis, we cannot use recombinant DNA techniques to clone genes and produce copies of gene products, and we cannot trace pathways between genes and behavior. Unfortunately, there is no example of a single gene that accounts for a detectable amount of variance in any psychological characteristic such as cognitive abilities, personality, or psychopathology.

In contrast, even during its brief existence, developmental behavioral genetic research has made significant contributions to understanding environmental influences on development. In behavioral genetics, *environmental* means *nongenetic,* that is, all influences that are not encoded in DNA. This broad definition of environment thus includes the gradients of chemical constituents in the cytoplasm of the egg as well as psychosocial experiences such as the death of a spouse in old age. The second section describes five advances in understanding environmental influences that have emerged from behavioral genetic research. Chapter 4 discusses a discovery that may be the single most important contribution of human behavioral genetics to date: Environmental variance relevant to psychological development is not shared by members of a family. Behavioral genetic research provides evidence—perhaps the best available evidence—for the importance of environmental influences on development. At the same time, this research consistently makes the point that the relevant environmental factors are not shared by children growing up in the same family. That is, children in the same family share no more similar relevant environmental experiences than do children taken at random from the population. Other topics in this section include genotype-environment interaction (chapter 5), genotype-environment correlation (chapter 6), genetic effects on environmental measures (chapter 7), and genetic effects on the relationships between environmental measures and measures of development (chapter 8).

The third and final section consists of a review of behavioral genetic research from a developmental, life-span perspective. There are chapters on infancy, childhood, adolescence, adulthood, and senescence; a final chapter provides an overview from a life-span perspective. The extensive behavioral genetic literature on cognitive abilities, personality, and psychopathology has not previously been viewed from a developmental perspective and this new vista leads to some interesting observations. Heuristically, however, the most important message conveyed by this review may be that developmental behavioral genetics is itself in its infancy. For example, there are few such studies of mature adults and only one study of elderly individuals. Needed most of all are longitudinal behavioral genetic studies, the sine qua non for the study of change and continuity in development.

As mentioned earlier, the purpose of this first chapter is to introduce fundamental concepts and methods of quantitative genetics. The most important issue, the starting point for behavioral genetic research, is variance, inter-individual differences within a population.

Variance

Behavioral geneticists explore the etiology of individuality, differences among individuals in a population. In contrast, most developmental psychologists attempt to describe and explain group differences, not individual differences. Some developmental research considers average differences between species; this is also the focus of sociobiology (Wilson, 1975) and other comparative research. Rather than comparing species explicitly, other researchers emphasize modal developmental patterns by which the human species comes to walk, talk, think, and form attachment bonds between infants and caretakers. The bulk of developmental research, however, is focused on average differences among groups within our species—groups of different ages, males and females, special groups such as premature infants, cultural groups, and, of course, experimental versus control groups. There are exceptions—for example, research on personality development and socialization involves the study of individual differences. In this section, however, I exaggerate the contrast between an individual differences perspective and a group differences perspective because, in my experience, confusion between the two lies at the source of most misunderstandings about the interpretation of behavioral genetic research.

Sometimes group differences research leads to typological thinking in which the mean of a distribution comes to be thought of as a species type. The evolutionary biologist, Ernst Mayr (1982), calls this *essentialism*, in which things are seen in in terms of their essence, as physicists view atomic particles. In biology, an essentialist looks at members of a species as representatives of a common type. In contrast, Mayr argues that biology must recognize the uniqueness of individuals within a species; without variation among individual members of the species, evolution cannot occur. Human variation is not error. Each of us is a unique genetic experiment, never to be repeated again. Human variability is not merely imprecision in a process that, if perfect, would generate unvarying representatives of the species type.

Similarly, discussions about group differences often sound as if the groups are discontinuously distributed when, in fact, significant mean differences are often observed for distributions that overlap by 95% or more. For example, one of the best documented sex differences in the cognitive realm is the superiority of females on tests of verbal ability (Maccoby & Jacklin, 1974). However, this average difference in verbal ability between the sexes accounts for only about 1% of the variance (Plomin & Foch, 1981). In other words, if all we know about individuals is their gender, we know next to nothing about their verbal ability.

Although typological thinking is not useful, developmentalists must eventually understand both means and variances, as McCall has argued (1977, 1981). However, for now it is important to maintain the distinction between the two approaches because they differ fundamentally, in terms of both description and explanation. Descriptions of modal developmental patterns are unrelated conceptually—and often empirically as well—to descriptions of individual differences in these patterns. For example, from 12 to 24 months, infants increase in height by 15% and in weight by 25% on the average. However, these dramatic average changes in height and weight are accompanied by considerable stability of individual differences, with correlations of about .70 from 12 to 24 months. Even more importantly, the causes of average differences between groups are not necessarily related to the causes of individual differences within groups. For example, the rapid average increase in mental development in infancy seems likely to be due to maturational events highly canalized at the species level, yet individual differences in infant mental development appear to be largely environmental in origin, as discussed in chapter 9.

The two perspectives differ methodologically as well as conceptually. Compared to the study of means, the study of variance is more demanding psychometrically, requires larger samples, and employs different statistics—the statistics of individual differences, which focus on variability rather than treating it as "error variance" in analyses of mean differences among groups. Fulfilling these demands opens the door to powerful analytical techniques such as quantitative genetics and causal modeling that can be used to test theories across individuals. Finally, it should be noted that data collected for the purpose of conducting individual differences analyses are just as useful for studying normative questions—indeed, such data are especially useful because they usually involve large, representative samples. However, data collected solely for the purpose of studying normative issues are not often useful for the study of individual differences.

The distinction between the normative and individual differences perspectives is particularly important for developmental behavioral genetics because confusion between the two perspectives tends to stoke the ashes of the nature-nurture controversy. Although it is fashionable to proclaim that issue dead, the mistaken divisive view that pitted nature against nurture is too frequently replaced with the equally mistaken interactionist notion that the separate effects of heredity and environment cannot be analyzed. From a normative perspective, both genes and environment are necessary for an organism to develop. From the perspective of individual differences, however, either genes or environment or both can contribute to observed differences among individuals.

Mixing the two perspectives is also responsible for some misguided antipathy towards behavioral genetics. For example, discovery of genetic influence on individual differences in a population has mistakenly been assumed to imply innateness—hard-wired, species-wide genetic determination that is impervious to environmental influence. To the contrary, finding that differences among children for a trait are to some extent due to genetic differences among the children rather than to their differences in experience says nothing about the origins of species-wide tendencies or the extent to which environmental factors could affect the trait. It merely means that genetic differences among children are to some extent responsible for the differences we observe among children in a particular population with that population's mix of genetic and environmental differences. Change the mix and the answers change. At the extreme, a trait that is entirely explained by genetic influences could be dramatically affected by a novel environmental intervention. In this sense, behavioral genetics is descriptive, it considers "what is" in a population rather than "what could be" or "what should be."

In summary, the distinction between an individual differences perspective and the prevailing normative perspective is critical for understanding behavioral genetics, which explores the etiology of variance, not means. It is the study of what makes people different.

Quantitative Genetic Theory

Theories in developmental psychology tend to be normative theories in the sense that they describe and attempt to explain the average developmental sequence of our species. In contrast, studies of individual differences tend to be atheoretical. However, it has seldom been recognized that quantitative genetic theory, the foundation for the methods used in behavioral genetics, is a theory of scope and power rarely seen in the behavioral sciences. It organizes and condenses already existing facts in a reasonable, internally consistent manner; it makes predictions concerning phenomena not yet investigated; and it is testable and falsifiable. It attempts to explain developmental phenomena as well as to describe and to predict them.

To begin with, the theory provides a rationale for expecting genetic differences among individuals and for expecting these genetic differences to lead to phenotypic differences in the complex behavioral traits that interest psychologists. In this way, quantitative genetic theory organizes a welter of data on individual differences so that they are no longer viewed as imperfections in the species type or as nuisance error in analyses of mean differences between groups, but rather as the quintessence of evolution and life.

Quantitative genetic theory emerged in the early 1900s from disagreements between Mendelians who rediscovered Mendel's laws of inheritance and so-called biometricians who felt that Mendel's laws derived from experiments with qualitative characteristics in pea plants were not applicable to complex characteristics in higher organisms, traits that are nearly always distributed quantitatively on a normal bell-shaped curve. Quantitative genetic theory was born when Ronald Fisher (1918) put the finishing touches on the resolution to the dispute. The essence of quantitative genetic theory is that Mendel's mechanism of discrete inheritance also applies to normally distributed complex characteristics if we assume that many genes, each with a small effect, add up to produce observable differences among individuals in a population. If more than three or four genes affect a trait, the observed distribution cannot be distinguished from a normal curve. For example, a trait influenced by two alleles at each of three loci yields 27 different genotypes. Even if the alleles at the different loci equally affect the trait and there is no environmental variation, seven different phenotypes will be observed and will appear to be distributed as a normal curve.

The fundamental point of quantitative genetic theory is that polygenic differences among individuals can lead to phenotypic differences. The theory also recognizes that environmental influences can contribute to observed variance among individuals and observed covariance between relatives. Normal behavioral variation does not involve simple, single-gene mechanisms that are unaffected by environmental variation as do genetic diseases such as galactosemia, phenylketonuria (PKU), and Huntington's disease; nor is it like measles or the plague, which are matters of exposure rather than disposition. More appropriate medical analogies are those, such as diabetes or cardiovascular disease, that show polygenic and environmental influences.

By specifying the expected genetic and environmental components of covariance among relatives, quantitative genetic theory points the way to methods to disentangle these genetic and environmental influences. The theory specifies the degree of genetic resemblance expected for different types of family relationships. For example, parents and their offspring are 50% similar genetically in that they share half of all segregating (varying) genes that have additive effects—that is, genetic effects that sum linearly in their effect on the phenotype and thus breed true. If parents and their offspring do not resemble each other for a particular measured trait, additive genetic variance cannot be important for that trait. Because parents share family environment as well as heredity with their offspring, parent-offspring resemblance does not prove the existence of genetic influence. Adoption designs separate the influence of heredity and the influence of family environment by studying resemblance between "genetic parents" (biological parents) and their adopted-away offspring and between "environmental parents" (adoptive parents) and their adopted children.

Siblings also share 50% of the additive genetic variance on the average. In addition, they share 25% of the nonadditive genetic variance due to dominance (interactions among alleles at a locus), although they share next to nothing of nonadditive genetic effects caused by interactions among alleles at different loci (epistasis). Assortative mating, phenotypic correlations between spouses for a particular trait, increases additive genetic variance for that trait and also increases genetic resemblance among first-degree relatives. Half-siblings, who have only one parent in common, share only 25% of the additive genetic variance. Most interesting are identical twins, who are identical genetically for all additive and nonadditive genetic factors.

All of these familial relationships involve shared environment as well as shared heredity. However, the theory points to ways in which the influences of heredity and environment can be separated. As mentioned in the case of parent-offspring resemblance, resemblance between genetic relatives adopted apart reveals genetic influence and resemblance between adoptive relatives reflects the influence of family environment. In addition, comparisons of the resemblance for types of relatives differing in genetic relatedness can also be used to assess genetic influence. For example, if a trait is influenced by heredity, full siblings should be more similar than half-siblings, even when both are reared in the same family from birth. The most widely used tool in the armamentarium of human behavioral genetics is the twin method, which compares the degree of resemblance for identical and fraternal twins. These methods emanating from quantitative genetic theory are discussed in greater detail in the next section.

Because the research activity generated by these methods sometimes over-shadows the theory of quantitative genetics, it is necessary to emphasize that a powerful theoretical foundation underlies this research activity. In my view, its recognition and identification of both genetic and environmental influences makes quantitative genetic theory the best available theory of environmental influence.

What other theories of the environment do we have in developmental psychology? Learning theory describes processes by which children may learn from their experience, although we have much to learn about learning during development, especially in terms of its relation to attention, motivation, and emotion. Moreover, learning theory consists of general descriptive laws; it is difficult to use learning theory to make specific predictions about who will learn what.

Some theories of development emphasize specific features of the environment thought to be of developmental significance. Most notably, Freud felt that the parent-child relationship is of primary importance. He suggested that parent-child interactions involving feeding, weaning, and toilet-training are especially influential. After decades of research, it is clear that, contrary to Freud's assertions, these parent-child interactions have little effect on development (e.g., Schaffer, 1971). Although Piaget emphasized the importance of the processes of assimilation and accommodation in relation to experience, his theory does not specify the features of environment critical for development, with a few exceptions such as the importance of peers in overcoming egocentrism.

In addition to general theories of Freud and Piaget, researchers interested in specific domains of development have, of course, considered sources of environmental influence. Often, however, no theory is specified, perhaps because the likely environmental factors appear so obvious. For example, the most obvious feature of the language-learning environment of infants would appear to be parental language and teaching. However, research to date has not found consistent or substantial relationships between these aspects of the language-learning environment and individual differences in language acquisition (Hardy-Brown, 1983; Hardy-Brown & Plomin, 1985). In terms of cognitive development in infancy, some environmental correlates have been identified (e.g, Gottfried, 1984) and attempts have been made to formulate theories of environmental action (e.g., Wachs & Gruen, 1982).

Quantitative genetic theory can provide a boost to environmental research because it provides a novel way of thinking about and studying environmental influences. As indicated in the second section of this book, behavioral genetic research has been primarily responsible for discovering that environmental influences that affect psychological development are not shared by members of a family. Furthermore, consideration of nature as well as nurture opens new vistas for studying gene-environment transactions during development, which is the focus of several chapters, including the discussion in chapter 6 of a general theory of developmental gene-environment transactions proposed by Sandra Scarr. In summary, quantitative genetics consists of a powerful theory and set of methods for studying environmental influences, genetic influences, and their developmental interaction because it recognizes the potential contributions of both nature and nurture.

Methods of Quantitative Genetics

The three basic methods used in human behavioral genetics are family, twin, and adoption studies. Before describing these, methods for nonhuman animal research, single-gene analyses, and chromosomal analyses are mentioned. The goal of this section is to provide the minimum background needed to understand the application of these methods in developmental behavioral genetics as described in the remainder of the book. More complete discussions can be found in behavioral genetic textbooks (e.g.,. Cattell, 1982; Dixon & Johnson, 1980; Ehrman & Parsons, 1981; Fuller & Thompson, 1978; Hay, 1985; Plomin, DeFries, & McClearn, 1980; Vale, 1980).

Nonhuman Behavioral Genetic Methods

The scope of this book is essentially limited to human developmental behavioral genetics, even though the methods used in nonhuman animal research are more powerful. Humans are far from an ideal species for genetic analyses: Their generation time is long, experimental control is next to impossible, and selective breeding is out of the question. However, the difficulties in studying humans are a disguised blessing in that, in contrast to studies of nonhuman animals, we are forced to work with naturally occurring genetic and environmental variation. Nonetheless, developmental behavioral genetics would certainly profit from greater interplay between animal and human research.

The two major methods used in animal research are strain studies and selection studies. Strain studies compare inbred strains in which animals have been bred brother to sister for at least 20 generations; this intensive inbreeding makes each animal within the strain virtually a clone of all other members of the strain. In genetic research, mice are the most extensively studied mammalian organism next to man; over 100 inbred strains of mice are available. Because inbred strains differ genetically from one another, genetically influenced traits will show average differences between inbred strains, whereas differences within strains provide estimates of environmental influence. Such studies have been instrumental in showing that genetic effects are ubiquitous in animal behavior, including learning and temperament. Finding strain differences is so common that comparisons between two inbred strains are no longer publishable. More

powerful methodologies, particularly the diallel method of complete intercross-
ing in which several inbred strains and all possible hybrid crosses are compared
simultaneously, are *de rigueur* because they yield much more information than
do comparisons of only two strains. Heterogeneous stocks, deliberately outbred
animals derived from crosses among inbred strains, are also useful because they
incorporate much of the genetic variability of the species.

 Selection studies provide the clearest evidence for genetic influence: If a trait
is heritable, you can select for it, as animal breeders have known for centuries.
The largest and longest selection study of mammalian behavior in a laboratory
involved 30 generations of mice selected for open-field activity (DeFries,
Gervais, & Thomas, 1978). Selection was bidirectional—that is, both high-
active and low-active lines were selected. A control line was also maintained,
and each of these three lines was replicated. After 30 generations of selective
breeding, there is no overlap between the activity of the low and high lines and
a 30-fold difference in activity is observed. The high-active mice now run the
equivalent total distance of the length of a football field during two, 3-minute
test periods, while the low-active mice sit on the sidelines.

Single-Gene and Chromosomal Effects

In addition to being restricted to human behavioral genetics, this book is also
limited to a discussion of quantitative genetic research. A quantitative genetic
approach, in that it considers the influence of many genes as well as environmental factors, is necessary to study normal variation in the development of
complex behaviors. Although 1637 single-gene disorders have been catalogued
in the sixth edition of McKusick's (1983) *Mendelian Inheritance in Man*, single
genes do not account for significant variability in complex traits. This statement
does not contradict the fact that many single-gene mutations that seriously
disrupt the normal developmental course have been discovered. For example,
Huntington's disease, a single-gene neurological disorder recently mapped to
chromosome 4, is discussed in chapter 13. Although its effect on IQ is dramatic,
only 1 in 20,000 adults is affected; thus, this genetic disease, as dreadful as it is,
does not contribute significantly to the normal distribution of adult IQ scores.
Another example is a single-gene recessive disorder, phenylketonuria (PKU).
Children with a double dose of the recessive allele are unable to metabolize
phenylalanine so that it builds up to amounts that are damaging to the developing
brain. This results in severe retardation unless the child is given a diet low in
phenylalanine. Similar to Huntington's disease, only about 1 in 20,000 children
is afflicted with PKU. However, approximately 1 in 50 children is a carrier of
one of the recessive alleles for PKU, and some evidence exists that these carriers
may have slightly lower IQs than normal homozygotes (Bessman, Williamson,
& Koch, 1978). Even so, the PKU gene does not contribute a detectable amount

of variability to the normal IQ distribution. A recent review of the field of developmental behavioral genetics emphasizes single-gene approaches and also provides an excellent discussion of basic genetic principles and evolution (Scarr & Kidd, 1983). Powerful techniques are available for isolating single-gene effects through the use of linkage analysis (Conneally & Rivas, 1980), especially in light of the recently discovered ability to detect highly polymorphic markers with restriction enzyme techniques, as discussed in chapter 2.

As yet, no single-gene effect has been found to account for a significant portion of variance for any normally distributed psychological characteristic. This should not be surprising considering the complexity of such characteristics. Molecular genetic research with bacteria, paramecia, nematodes, and *Drosophila* makes it clear that many genes affect the simplest behaviors (Plomin, DeFries, & McClearn, 1980). For example, at least 40 genes are involved in normal swimming in bacteria and over 100 genes are involved in the structure of the eye of fruit flies. Any one of these genes can seriously alter swimming or visual behavior. An example closer to home is the human brain. It has been estimated that the adult brain contains 100 billion neurons, each with approximately 1500 synapses, and that at each synapse there are a million receptor molecules including over 30 classical neurotransmitters and 200 other neuropeptides (Cowan, 1979; Snyder, 1980). Even though these neurotransmitters and neuropeptides are directly coded by DNA, there is little likelihood that the activity of any neuron or group of neurons is significantly determined by a single major gene. In summary, any one of many genes can disrupt development, but the normal range of behavioral variation is likely to be orchestrated by a system of many genes, each with small effect, as well as by environmental influences.

Chromosomal anomalies have a similar relationship to variance. Although obvious chromosomal abnormalities occur in 1 of 200 live births, no chromosomal anomaly accounts for a detectable amount of variance in the normal distribution of behavioral characteristics. For example, Down's syndrome, a trisomy of chromosome 22, is the single most important cause of major mental retardation, accounting for 10% of institutionalized mentally retarded individuals. However, the incidence of Down's syndrome is only 1 in 700 births, even though it is by far the most common of the classic chromosomal anomalies. For this reason, chromosomal anomalies scarcely put a bump on the normal distribution of psychological traits. Advances such as new banding techniques that can identify small fragments of chromosomes (Sanchez & Yunis, 1977) and identification of "fragile" sites on chromosomes (e.g., Turner & Opitz, 1980) will undoubtedly reveal more relationships with behavioral development. Nevertheless, until we are able to assess genome-wide DNA variation directly, investigations of complex, polygenically and multifactorially determined psychological traits will require the methods of quantitative genetics.

Family Method

As indicated earlier, quantitative genetic theory makes predictions concerning familial resemblance for different types of relatives. Because family members share family environment as well as heredity, the family design cannot disentangle genetic and environmental influences. However, family studies provide upper-limit estimates of genetic influence, as explained later.

Resemblance among first-degree relatives primarily reflects additive genetic variance, the component of genetic variance that "breeds true." Nonadditive epistatic genetic variance does not result in resemblance among family members. Thus, if epistatic genetic variance is important, as some suggest that it is (e.g., Lykken, 1982), correlations for first-degree relatives can be low even though genetic variance contributes substantially to phenotypic variance in the population.

Twin Method

Most behavioral genetic research has employed the twin design. The twin method compares correlations for identical twins and fraternal twins because the two types of twins differ dramatically in terms of genetic relatedness. Identical twin partners are genetically identical to each other, whereas fraternal twins are about 50% similar, on the average, for segregating genes. Assortative mating would raise the fraternal twin correlation and nonadditive genetic variance would lower it. If heredity affects a trait, the roughly twofold greater genetic similarity of identical twins will make them more similar phenotypically than are fraternal twins. If identical and fraternal twin correlations do not differ, then heredity is unimportant for the trait.

As in any experiment, potentially confounding effects must be considered. In the twin design, even though twin partners of both types live in the same family, it is possible that identical twins experience more similar family environments than do fraternal twins. If this were the case, some of the greater observed similarity of identical twins might be due to greater similarity of their experiences. This possible confounding effect has been examined and, so far, does not appear to represent a major problem for the twin design (Plomin et al., 1980).

Adoption Method

The adoption method is generally recognized as the most powerful human behavioral genetic design because it includes genetically related family members who are adopted apart and thus do not share family environment, and compares the resemblance between these relatives with that between genetically unrelated family members who are adopted together and thus do not share heredity. Resemblance between adopted-apart relatives reveals the impact of heredity, whereas similarities between adopted-together family members point to the influence of family environment.

Selective placement, in which adoption agencies match adoptive parents to the biological parents of the adoptees, introduces a possible confound that will inflate estimates of both family environment and heredity. Fortunately, the extent of selective placement can be assessed and its effects on genetic and environmental estimates are understood (DeFries & Plomin, 1978).

Heritability and Environmentality

The foregoing discussion of behavioral genetic methods is oriented toward detecting significant genetic and environmental influences. For example, genetic influence would be implied by significantly greater correlations for identical twins than for fraternal twins or by significant correlations for adopted-apart relatives. In addition to evaluating statistical significance, these methods can yield estimates of effect size, that is, the amount of variance explained by heredity and by environment. These components of variance are referred to as heritability and environmentality.

For example, an observed correlation of .20 for first-degree relatives would imply that 20% of the variance in the trait is due to genetic and environmental influences shared by first-degree relatives. (The familial correlation, not the square of the correlation, is at issue because the correlation represents the proportion of variance that covaries between family members rather than the extent to which one family member's score can be predicted from the other family member—which would require the square of the correlation; see Jensen, 1971, for details.) If the observed correlation were due solely to genetic similarity (as it would be in the case of adopted-apart first-degree relatives), the correlation would represent the proportion of phenotypic variance that is due to half of the genetic variance because first-degree relatives are only 50% similar for segregating genes. Thus, doubling the correlation estimates heritability, the proportion of phenotypic variance that is due to genetic variance. When family members share family environment as well as heredity, doubling the correlation for first-degree relatives provides an upper-limit estimate of heritability—heritability can be no greater and it could be much less, even zero, if family environment is responsible for the observed resemblance between family members.

With the twin method, heritability is estimated by doubling the difference between the identical and fraternal twin correlations because the difference estimates roughly half of the genetic variance (Falconer, 1981). Assortative mating would raise the fraternal twin correlation and nonadditive genetic variance would lower it; the identical twin correlation would be unaffected because identical twins are genetically identical. Because genetic influence is deduced from the difference between correlations for identical twins and fraternal twins, assortative mating would lower estimates of genetic influence and nonadditive genetic variance would inflate them. As discussed in chapter 4, the twin method can also be used to estimate shared family environment, the component of environmental variance that makes family members similar. This component of variance is estimated as the extent to which the identical twin correlation exceeds the genetic variance (i.e., twice the difference between identical and fraternal twin correlations). For example, if identical and fraternal twin correlations are .8 and .5, respectively, shared family environment would be estimated as 20%, that is, 20% of the total variance would be due to shared family environment.

In the adoption design, the correlation for adopted-apart relatives directly estimates familial resemblance due to heredity. As mentioned above, the observed correlation for first-degree relatives adopted apart estimates the proportion of phenotypic variance due to half of the genetic variance. The most dramatic evidence for genetic influence comes from adoption studies involving identical twins adopted apart—their correlation directly estimates the proportion of phenotypic variance due to genetic variance because they are identical genetically. These studies are reviewed in chapter 12. Just as important is the flip side of the adoption design: genetically unrelated individuals reared together in the same adoptive family. The correlation for pairs of such individuals adopted together directly estimates the proportion of phenotypic variance due to shared family environment, as discussed in chapter 4.

In general, quantitative genetic theory posits that variance not explained by heredity is due to environment. Thus, if heritability is 30%, environmentality (i.e., nongenetic influence) accounts for 70% of the phenotypic variance. Of course, some of the nongenetic variance involves error of measurement. Most behavioral geneticists prefer to work with observed variability, which includes a component of variance due to unreliability. It is possible to correct measures for unreliability of measurement, thereby boosting all familial correlations as well as estimates of genetic influence. With scores uncorrected for error of measurement, we address total variance; when we correct scores for unreliability, we address total true variance. However, unless estimates of unreliability are quite good, attempts to correct quantitative genetic parameter estimates for unreliability can easily go astray. Better than statistically adjusting the parameter estimates for unreliability of measurement is to use more reliable measures.

Another preliminary issue concerns the reliability of estimates of genetic or environmental influence. In general, compared to most research in developmental psychology, larger samples are needed to attain reasonable statistical power. Power considerations vary for different designs and for the estimation of different parameters. When a simple correlation can be used to estimate such parameters, power considerations are the same as for any correlation. Power is a function of the effect size and the sample size (see Cohen, 1977). For example, the expected effect size (i.e., correlation) for separated identical twins (chapter 12) is about .50 for personality measures. In this case, a sample of only 23 pairs would provide 80% power to detect a significant genetic effect ($p < .05$, one-tailed; Cohen, 1977). In contrast, the expected correlation for adopted-apart first-degree relatives is only about .20, and a sample size of 160 pairs would be needed to yield 80% power to detect a significant genetic effect. From this perspective, designs based on second- and third-degree relatives require huge samples because the expected genetic effect size is so small.

As mentioned earlier, the correlation within pairs of genetically unrelated individuals adopted together directly estimates the importance of shared family environment. The same power considerations apply to this correlation. For example, if pairs of unrelated children reared together were studied in order to estimate the total impact of shared family environment for a particular trait, a sample of 50 pairs would provide 80% power to detect a significant effect of shared family environment that accounts for 35% of the variance (i.e., a correlation of .35 for unrelated children reared together). However, a sample of over 600 pairs would be needed if we wished to have 80% power to detect a significant effect of shared family environment that accounts for as little as 10% of the total variance, that is, a correlation of .10 for adoptee pairs.

Many designs, however, are based on the difference between two correlations—for example, the difference between identical and fraternal twin correlations or the difference between correlations in nonadoptive and adoptive families. In this case, larger samples are needed because the standard error of differences between correlations is much greater than the standard error for a simple correlation. For example, twin studies involving self-report personality questionnaires typically find identical twin correlations of about .50 and fraternal twin correlations of .30 (chapter 11). A sample of over 200 pairs of identical twins and over 200 pairs of fraternal twins would be needed to detect a significant difference between correlations of this magnitude with 80% power. With samples of 50 pairs of each type of twin, a researcher would have only 32% power to detect a significant difference, which means that a true difference between correlations for identical and fraternal twins will not be detected two out of three times with samples of this size. The same considerations apply to estimates of genetic influence based on the difference between correlations in nonadoptive and adoptive families, although even larger samples would be needed because the expected magnitude of correlations is lower than in the twin design. Model-fitting approaches, discussed later, can provide greater power, especially when data from several designs are combined.

Combining Family, Twin, and Adoption Methods

The family, twin, and adoption methods each has its own particular problems; convergence of results from the different methods provides the strongest evidence. During the past 2 decades, behavioral geneticists have moved toward combining family, twin, and adoption designs in order to incorporate as much information as possible in their analyses. For example, the longitudinal Colorado Adoption Project combines the family and adoption designs by studying resemblances between biological parents and their adopted-away offspring, adoptive parents and their adopted children, and matched nonadoptive parents and their natural children (Plomin & DeFries, 1985).

One method that was first considered only a decade ago combines the family and twin methods. When identical twins grow up and have their own separate families, interesting relationships are available for exploration. For example, in families of male identical twins, nephews are as closely related genetically to their uncle as they are to their father; cousins are as closely related as half-siblings.

When data from several designs are analyzed together, interpretation of results becomes more difficult. This is one of the reasons why behavioral geneticists are increasingly employing structural models and model-fitting approaches.

Structural Models and Model Fitting

Structural models—also called biometrical models, causal models, and path models—are superior in several ways to simple comparisons of correlations: They permit analysis of all data simultaneously, they make assumptions explicit, they permit tests of the relative fit of the model, they provide for the calculation of standard errors of estimates, and they allow tests of different models. Modeling basically involves fitting a series of over-determined simultaneous equations in order to estimate genetic and environmental parameters that best fit observed familial correlations (Jinks & Fulker, 1970).

The mathematical procedures for solving an extensive series of simultaneous equations are complicated. Path analysis, originally developed by Sewall Wright (1931) to solve problems of quantitative genetic inheritance, is useful for deriving expectations in structural modeling work (Li, 1975). Loehlin (1978, 1979) provides an excellent and readable introduction to the topic.

Although model-fitting approaches are sophisticated and elegant, they have the disadvantage of being difficult to understand and they seem to resemble a black hat from which parameter estimates magically appear. We should not stand too much in awe of them or allow them to obfuscate the basic simplicity of most behavioral genetic designs. For example, the basic twin design estimates genetic influence on the basis of the difference between identical and fraternal twin correlations—if there is no difference between identical and fraternal twin correlations, there is no heritability and model-fitting approaches must come to that conclusion or there is something that is wrong with the model. Similarly, the correlation between adopted-apart relatives provides a direct estimate of the importance of genetic influence. The results of model-fitting analyses can only be used to reject certain models as untenable; as in tests of any scientific hypothesis, model fitting cannot prove that a particular model is correct. Finally, it is important not to stray too far from the basic data: Model fitting provides refined analyses of the basic data of behavioral genetic methods—the correlations derived from the family, twin, and adoption designs. Although a few relevant model-fitting results are included in this book, the emphasis is on the basic behavioral genetic data.

Interpretation of Genetic Influence

What does it mean if we find that genes influence behavioral development? As emphasized earlier, behavioral genetics only addresses variance within a population. Saying that genes influence behavior is shorthand for saying that genetic differences among individuals in a certain population to some extent are related to observed individual differences in the trait as we have measured it. It might be helpful to say a few more words about this interpretation of genetic influence in relation to issues in developmental psychology.

Process and Outcome

One issue in the interpretation of genetic influence involves the distinction between process and outcome. Developmentalists profess interest in process more than outcome, whereas behavioral geneticists are often viewed as studying outcomes in the sense that genetic influence means an influence on some measured trait. The word *process* is used in different ways. It is sometimes used to refer to mechanisms of development, the hyphen in cause-effect relationships, although developmentalists rarely attempt to move beyond correlation to consider causation. In practice, the process-outcome distinction is most often used to refer to different levels of analysis. My reading of the developmental literature suggests that both process and outcome refer to measured outcomes; however, process tends to be reserved for more basic levels of analysis. An IQ test is viewed as the prototype of an outcome measure because it involves performance on a test. However, IQ tests were designed to assess cognitive processes such as reasoning and problem solving. At the other extreme, learning is viewed as the prototype of a process. However, learning is a construct that refers to changes in measured performance over time. Although most psychologists would view measures of learning performance as more basic than performance on psychometric measures of specific cognitive abilities, to a neuroscientist thinking about neurotransmitters and neuropeptides, both types of measures would appear to be molar outcomes of complex neural processes.

In summary, I find the distinction between process and outcome unhelpful, especially when it is used to suggest that developmentalists study process, whereas behavioral geneticists ''merely'' study outcomes. The point is that quantitative genetics theory and methods equip researchers with the tools needed to explore genetic and environmental mechanisms that transact in the development of individual differences. This approach is applicable to any level of analysis, including the level of neuronal activity (e.g., Plomin & Deitrich, 1982). When we find genetic influence, this implies a developmental process by which DNA is transcribed and translated into polypeptides that then have an influence on development, a process more clearly understood than any other in psychology. Quantitative genetic studies of phenotypic variance in a population represent a reasonable first step toward understanding genetic and environmental mechanisms contributing to phenotypic variance in a population observed at any level of analysis. However, it is just a first step and leaves much to be learned about the biochemical, physiological, and experiential pathways in which nature and nurture transact during development.

Fixity and Flexibility

Developmentalists are sometimes disturbed by the idea that genes can influence behavior because they picture genes as master puppeteers within us, pulling our strings. As discussed in the next chapter, genes are merely chemical structures that code for sequences of amino acids. In this sense, there are no genes for behavior just as there are no genes for height. Genes only code for the construction of sequences of amino acids. The polypeptides formed by these sequences of amino acids are the enzymes and other proteins that are the building blocks of the organism. Some polypeptide products regulate the transcription of other genes, which is the essence of developmental change at a molecular genetic level. During development, these structural and regulatory gene products are woven together; genetic differences in this tapestry often result in differences in anatomical characteristics, such as height, as well as in behavioral traits. For this reason, most genes are likely to have effects on many different behaviors (pleiotropy) and any behavior is likely to be influenced by many genes (polygeny). This complexity makes it unlikely that simple pathways exist between genes and behavior. However, quantitative genetics allows us to take the reasonable and important first step of asking the extent to which behavioral differences, observed among individuals, are related to genetic differences among them.

This view of genetics makes it clear that genes do not determine one's destiny—genetic influence does not imply hard-wired circuits that determine a specific response. Consider alcoholism, for example. As discussed in chapter 12, behavioral genetic data suggest genetic influence on alcohol abuse. This does not mean that there is a gene or a set of genes that determines whether an individual will become alcoholic. No one becomes alcoholic without consuming large quantities of alcohol. However, most individuals in our society are exposed to alcohol and some individuals are genetically predisposed to abuse the drug, for reasons that are not yet completely understood. Because of the complexities of pleiotropic, polygenic effects, genetic influences are indeed just influences— propensities, or tendencies, that nudge development in one direction rather than another.

Viewed in this way, genetic influence is not in opposition to such developmental concepts as embeddedness and plasticity. Embeddedness connotes the concept that "the key phenomena of life exist at multiple levels of being"; plasticity refers to the "processes by which one develops one's capacity to modify one's behavior to adjust to, or fit, the demands of a particular context" (Lerner, 1984, p. 24). Genetic influence is embedded in the complexity of interactions among genes, physiology, and environment. It is probabilistic, not deterministic; it puts no constraints on what could be.

Implications of Genetic Influence

A spectre that lurks in the shadows is the concern that genetic influence counsels despair: Nothing can be done about genetic effects. As an antidote to this concern, it can be argued that the more that is known about a trait genetically as well as environmentally, the more likely that rational intervention and prevention strategies can be devised. This is especially the case as we come to realize that problems such as psychopathology and alcoholism cannot be effectively treated by means of rehabilitation or tertiary prevention in which we attempt to help people after they develop problems. Nor is secondary prevention likely to be effective, that is, trying to help people early to keep their problems from worsening; the answer must ultimately lie in primary prevention of the sort that eliminated the great plagues of the past. Nature as well as nurture contributes risk factors for the major psychological problems in our society and we need to take advantage of every lead, whether genetic or environmental, in an attempt to identify individuals at risk with the goal of preventing problems before they appear. PKU is a classic example in which discovery of the genetic basis for this type of retardation led to an environmentally mediated prevention strategy. Alcoholism is another example. The discovery of genetic influence permits identification of individuals at risk for alcoholism: If a male has a first-degree relative who is alcoholic, the man has a 25% chance of becoming alcoholic. Explaining the implications of such research could be an important "low-tech" intervention for this important societal problem.

A variant of the concern that genetics counsels despair is that genetic influence is irrelevant because psychologists are constrained to working with environmental variables regardless of the relative potency of nature and nurture. To the contrary, one hope for behavioral genetics is that it will isolate genotype-environment interactions by identifying genetically mediated differences among individuals that lead to differential responses to environmental influences. In other words, a balanced genetic/environmental approach to development can provide for a more fine-grained investigation of the environment than does an approach that only considers "main effects" that make a difference on average for all individuals. Furthermore, genetic research can point the way towards identification of powerful environmental influences. The best example is the finding that most environmental variance relevant to behavioral development is not shared by two children growing up in the same family, as discussed in chapter 4. In addition, even high heritability is informative about the environment. As emphasized in this chapter, high heritability does not imply that a trait is immutable: It only suggests that environmental influences that vary in the population do not create variability. In the face of high heritability, environmental attempts at prevention and intervention must look for novel environmental influences, factors that do not currently vary in the population. Thus, high heritability could provide justification for more innovative and experimental approaches to environmental intervention.

An implicit concern is that finding genetic influence on behavioral traits has dangerous implications. Again, behavioral geneticists merely describe "what is" in a population, not "what could be" and certainly not "what should be." The discovery that heredity is important is compatible with a wide range of social action, including no action at all. And, in accord with the old-fashioned view of a truth-seeking science, I believe that wiser decisions can be made with knowledge than without it. Furthermore, any important new knowledge is likely to make us re-think issues. This is as true for environmental research as it is for genetic research. Indeed, Scarr and Weinberg (1978) suggest that the negative effects of environmentalism should not be overlooked:

> Three decades of naive environmentalism have locked most Westerners into wrong-headed assumptions about the limitless malleability of mankind, and programs based on this premise can lead a country into a thicket of unrealistic promises and hopes. The fallacy is the belief that equality of opportunity produces sameness of outcome. Equality of opportunity is a laudable goal for any society. Sameness of outcomes is a biological impossibility. (p. 36)

Of course, it is important that the pendulum not swing from environmentalism to genetic determinism. This is not likely to happen because behavioral genetics provides a balanced approach that considers environmental as well as genetic sources of variation in behavioral development.

The essential worry about genetic influence is that it appears to go against our basic democratic principles. Are not all men (and women) created equal? When our founding fathers proclaimed that principle, they were not so naive as to think that all people are inherently identical. Even John Locke, whose treatise *Of Civil Government* played a key role in the American revolution and in educational thought, had a more balanced view of the nature-nurture question than is usually recognized. By equality, Locke clearly meant political equality, not an absence of individual differences (Loehlin, 1983). In a democracy, we do not treat people equally because they are identical—there would be no need for principles of equality if that were true. The essence of democracy is to treat people equally in spite of their differences.

2 Developmental Molecular Genetics

One reason why developmental behavioral genetics has a promising future is that it will inherit the effort, energy, and excitement of molecular geneticists' recent focus on development. The fundamental question is how we begin life as a single cell and, in a few months' time, become a complex differentiated organism with trillions of specialized cells, each with the same DNA. As one of numerous examples, red blood cells contain millions of globin molecules in contrast to undetectable levels of globin in other cell types. Most developmental biology textbooks emphasize classical experimental embryology based largely on nongenetic descriptions of morphological changes. Classical embryology contains descriptions of developmental changes in cells and tissues as revealed by microscopic examination. However, the explanation of differentiation lies in genetic molecules invisible to the microscope: Some genes regulate the activity of other genes. The goal of this chapter is to describe what is known about gene regulation, especially as it pertains to development.

At the outset it should be emphasized that the findings of developmental molecular genetics are not as yet directly applicable to developmental psychology—for example, they will not inform us about the development of cognition. A wide chasm involving different levels of analysis separates molecular genetics from psychology. Although complex organisms are being studied in the 1980s, molecular geneticists in the past have primarily studied single genes in primitive, single-celled organisms, such as bacteria, which have no nucleus (prokaryotes) and only one chromosome. It almost seems inappropriate to use the word *development* to describe bacteria that can divide into clones as often as every 20 minutes. However, some bacteria do undergo a major developmental change called sporulation that creates endospores, remarkably durable life forms with no detectable metabolism that await favorable environmental conditions to spring back to life. The lowly bacteria's sporulation has been found to require the coordinate expression of more than 50 genes; each stage of endospore formation involves the expression of many genes (Youngman et al., 1985). This typifies the complexity of developmental genetics, even in prokaryotes. Nonetheless, this focus on relatively simple systems contrasts sharply with the level of analysis in developmental psychology—lying at the other end of the continuum of complexity, and involving the behaving, developing human organism. However, as this chapter indicates, the gap is narrowing as molecular geneticists begin to turn their attention to issues related to development in mammals, including our species.

Despite the gulf between molecular genetics and psychology, knowledge of molecular genetics is useful for developmental psychologists and crucial for developmental behavioral geneticists. At the least, we would not want to violate principles known at the molecular level of analysis as we think about more complex levels. For example, in behavioral genetics, models usually are phrased in terms of structural genes, genes that code for the constituent amino acids in proteins such as hemoglobin. Genetic variation in structural genes produces alterations in the amino acid sequences such as the single amino acid substitution that produces the sickled cells of sickle-cell anemia rather than normal hemoglobin. However, the excitement of developmental molecular genetics lies not in structural genes, but in the many genetic processes that regulate the expression of structural genes, as emphasized over two decades ago by one of the founders of modern behavioral genetics (Fuller, 1964). These findings draw the attention of developmental behavioral geneticists to the changes wrought by genetic regulation.

In addition to the immediate impact of developmental molecular genetics at a conceptual level, molecular genetics in the long run will contribute to empirical advances in developmental behavioral genetics. Most notably, techniques are already available to make it possible to "gene-type" individuals in the same sense as bloodtyping. When these techniques become applicable to the study of large numbers of individuals, DNA variation among individuals can be assessed directly and related to variations among individuals in their behavior. If we are to capitalize on the stunning advances of molecular genetics described in this chapter, we will need to be able to meet the molecular geneticists halfway and to speak their language. Molecular geneticists are progressing steadily up the road toward understanding the development of higher organisms, with the new recombinant DNA technology picking up the pace dramatically.

Introduction to Molecular Genetics

The goal of the following overview of molecular genetics is to set the stage for a discussion of gene regulation, the key issue in developmental genetics. In this section, three topics are briefly described: the structure and function of DNA, the exciting techniques provided by recombinant DNA, and the newly discovered complexities in higher organisms.

Structure and Function of DNA

Physically, the DNA molecule is so tiny that its structure cannot be viewed even with an electron microscope. Conceptually, it is grand and elegant. Its simple structure contains specific instructions honed by evolution for the development of the millions of species we see around us and the hundredfold other species that no longer survive. The complexity of this task taxes the imagination. Even the tiniest life form, viruses, which take over the genetic machinery of the cells of host organisms, have several score genes involving about 50,000 base pairs of DNA. The simplest complete single-celled organisms such as bacteria—much less than 1 mm in diameter and invisible to the naked eye—contain more than a thousand different molecules including 750 different types of small molecules such as sugars and amino acids, which are the building blocks by which cells grow, and hundreds of macromolecules including proteins and nucleic acids such as DNA. The single chromosome of such organisms contains about 4 million nucleotide base pairs of DNA. *Homo sapiens* has 23 pairs of chromosomes and about 80 million base pairs in the average chromosome—a total of 3½ billion base pairs in each of trillions of cells (Watson, Tooze, & Kurtz, 1983).

One function of DNA, hereditary transmission, is the essence of behavioral genetics. However, our focus here is its other major function—the coding and regulation of proteins. Proteins form the structure of cells, the connective tissue between cells, and muscles. They also perform physiological functions as neurotransmitters and hormones. In addition, there are specialized proteins (enzymes) that determine which chemical reactions occur in a cell. Proteins consist of chains of specific sequences of amino acids from 50 to 2000 amino acids in length. The complexity of the situation can be recognized by noting that most cells have over 2000 varieties of proteins. Each amino acid in each protein is coded by a sequence of three nucleotide base pairs of DNA.

DNA, like protein, is built from smaller linked building blocks; however, the nucleotide bases of DNA are more complex than amino acids in that DNA contains phosphate and sugar groups in addition to a ring-shaped carbon and nitrogen molecule. The phosphate and sugar groups link the nucleotide bases together in long chains; this regular backbone of DNA causes it to fold in a helical form. Weak hydrogen bonds hold the two chains of DNA together in a double helix. Given the large number of these weakly bonded base pairs, the two chains of the double helix do not separate spontaneously, although they can be separated at near-boiling temperatures, a technique called denaturation that yields single-stranded DNA used in the study of DNA functioning.

Nucleotide bases of DNA have only four forms of the ring-shaped carbon-nitrogen molecule: adenine, thymine, guanine, and cytosine. These four bases can occur in any sequence along the sugar/phosphate backbone of single-stranded DNA; however, the complementary strand is limited because adenine can bond only with thymine and guanine can bond only with cytosine. Thus, if the sequence of one strand of DNA is known, the sequence of the complementary strand is also known. This complementary structure permits high fidelity replication of each DNA strand into a complete double helix: Each strand serves as the template to attract new nucleotide bases to form its complement.

By 1953, the basic model of molecular genetics was understood: DNA is transcribed by an intermediate molecule, messenger RNA, which is translated at the ribosomes into sequences of amino acids that form proteins. In higher organisms with nuclei in their cells (eukaryotes), the messenger RNA travels outside the nucleus to ribosomes situated in the cell body, a difference between prokaryotes (without nuclei) and eukaryotes that has implications for genetic regulation, as discussed later. In addition to messenger RNA, which constitutes only 5% of the cell's RNA, cells contain ribosomal RNA (about 80% of the cell's RNA) and transfer RNA (15%). Ribosomal RNA has no specificity; messenger RNA moves over the surface of ribosomes where transfer RNA molecules specific to each amino acid decode the messenger RNA and attach the appropriate amino acid specified by each triplet code.

The triplet code was fully deciphered by 1966. Given four types of nucleotide bases, there are 64 possible combinations of bases considered three at a time. Of these 64 possible "codons," 61 specify amino acids and three specify stop signals indicating the end of a gene. The first two positions of each triplet codon are unique, but the third position can "wobble" in translation. For example, a messenger RNA codon with three uracil bases in a row (uracil is the RNA equivalent of DNA's thymine base) and a uracil-uracil-cytosine codon are both translated as the code for the amino acid phenylalanine because one transfer RNA species that transfers phenylalanine to the polypeptide chain growing at a ribosome is attracted by both codes.

The triplet code of DNA is the same in all living organisms with the exception of slight differences in the mitochondria of cell bodies. Mitochondria are believed to be descendants of primitive bacterial cells engulfed by ancestors of eukaryotic organisms. The average protein involves a unique sequence of about 400 amino acids and thus requires 1200 nucleotide DNA base pairs for its coding. However, as we shall see, such "structural" genes that code amino acid sequences of proteins comprise only a small fraction of DNA.

Recombinant DNA Technology

During the past decade, the most important advance in molecular genetics has been the recombinant DNA technology described in an excellent book by Watson, Tooze, and Kurtz (1983). The critical step in this discovery was the isolation of restriction nucleases that cleave DNA at specific sites. Restriction nucleases come from certain bacteria that have the ability to fragment foreign DNA. Restriction nucleases are now available for nearly 100 DNA sites. Some recognize a specific group of four bases; most cleave a specific group of six bases (e.g., one which splits each sequence of TGGCCA nucleotide bases of DNA between the G and C bases).

This technique has made it possible to sequence DNA directly. Each restriction nuclease produces a different set of DNA fragments; the fragments can be sorted by molecular weight using electrophoresis, and a restriction map can be deduced from comparisons of overlapping fragments of different length. The first DNA sequencing required about a year to sequence 5000 bases; new techniques now permit DNA sequencing of comparable lengths in a few weeks. DNA sequencing is so fast that it is easier to sequence a protein's amino acids by sequencing DNA and then determining the amino acid sequence with knowledge of the triplet code of DNA rather than attempting to sequence the protein's amino acids directly.

Restriction nucleases also make possible the recombination of any DNA with bacterial DNA because some nucleases make cuts with "sticky" ends that anneal with other DNA similarly cut when another DNA enzyme called a ligase is used to seal together the restriction fragments. The first recombinant DNA was formed in 1973. A foreign bacterial DNA fragment cut by a particular restriction nuclease was inserted into a bacterial plasmid also cut by the same restriction nuclease. Plasmids are tiny circular DNA molecules that bacteria possess in addition to their main chromosome. These plasmids usually carry genes that code for enzymes that neutralize antibiotics. Because only the main chromosome is duplicated during cell replication, most plasmids (with the exception of a few that have the ability to incorporate themselves into the main chromosome) are not transferred hereditarily. However, plasmids are easily taken up by plasmid-free bacteria. Thus, once foreign DNA is inserted into a bacterial plasmid, it is easy to have this recombinant DNA plasmid absorbed into bacteria which then express the foreign DNA fragment.

It was quickly realized that recombinant DNA techniques made it possible for the first time to analyze DNA of higher organisms. Large numbers of different restriction fragments of human DNA can be inserted randomly into bacterial plasmids, and there is a high probability of generating bacterial clones carrying a specific human gene. This means that a particular gene need only be transcribed, not translated into a gene product, in order to be recombined with bacteria.

A round-about process to obtain many copies of pure DNA probes led to an important discovery. The normal process of forming messenger RNA was reversed to produce single-stranded DNA copies of messenger RNA. The single-stranded DNA was provided with the nucleotide bases to form its complementary half and this double-stranded DNA was inserted into plasmid and then transferred into bacterial cells. Cells producing the appropriate protein were cloned to yield a plentiful supply of messenger RNA. However, when these DNA copies were compared to chromosomal genes, it became clear that chromosomal genes in eukaryotes include far more nucleotide bases than are represented in the messenger RNA. It is now known that the "extra" DNA in chromosomal genes is involved in gene regulation, split genes, and repetitive DNA sequences, as described later. For these reasons, eukaryotic and especially vertebrate genes have turned out to be perhaps 20 times larger than expected on the basis of messenger RNA.

The major advantage of recombinant DNA technology for understanding gene regulation is that it permits the study of chromosomal DNA itself rather than messenger RNA, which does not include the codes for gene regulation. Fragments of chromosomal DNA can be recombined in host organisms to elucidate its control elements. A problem arose in that these fragments are usually too long to be stable in tiny plasmids. One attempt to resolve this problem involves the use of bacteriophage viruses rather than plasmids as vectors for recombining DNA. Bacteriophage ("bacteria-eating") viruses are viruses that multiply in bacteria. Bacteriophages can create hundreds of progeny particles in a few minutes and some recombine with bacterial DNA. Only the ends of the bacteriophage DNA are needed for its replication in bacteria so that the entire central portion of the phage DNA can be switched for recombination, although the inserted DNA needs to be about 15,000 base pairs in length. In this way, a DNA library of an entire fragmented eukaryotic genome can be established. A particular gene can be screened through the use of radioactive probes and, if identified, can be cloned in bacteriophage.

The phage insert of 15,000 base pairs is often long enough for an entire eukaryotic gene and its flanking sequences; however, some genes and their accompanying control regions are much longer. A recently developed technique can be used to clone much larger eukaryotic fragments. This procedure is called *cosmid cloning* and utilizes a special phage with "cos" sites at each end that allow chains of hundreds of DNA copies. These permit packaging much longer DNA sequences (35,000 to 45,000 bases) with "cos" sites at each end; however, cosmid cloning is less efficient than the usual phage techniques and makes it difficult to obtain cosmid libraries of an entire genome.

Even the opportunity provided by cosmids to study recombinant DNA fragments 45,000 base pairs in length is sometimes not enough. It is often useful to analyze several hundred thousand base pairs. One technique to accomplish this is called "chromosome walking" and involves cloning overlapping sets of DNA fragments; however, this technique does not work in the presence of repeated sequences of DNA which, as described later, is common in most eukaryotes except fruitflies.

The search for recombinant DNA methods to study control elements of chromosomal DNA led to the recombination of foreign genes with eukaryotic cells rather than with bacterial cells (Watson, Tooze, & Kurtz, 1983). One technique, called *transfection*, introduces foreign DNA directly into nuclei of cells using microinjection. About half of the injected cells will integrate and express the injected genes. Thus, any piece of DNA can be introduced into any cell; in this sense, recombinant DNA techniques are easier with eukaryotic than with prokaryotic cells. Foreign genes inserted into eukaryotic cells sometimes continue to respond to signals that control the expression of the gene *in vivo*.

Even better than transfection is the use of viruses as vectors for recombinant DNA because they provide many copies of the foreign DNA and have strong promoters that insure efficient expression of the gene. The virus that is used is a retrovirus, or RNA tumor virus, that consists of RNA rather than DNA. Retroviruses code for reverse transcriptase that synthesizes a DNA copy of the retrovirus RNA and also codes for enzymes that insert the DNA copy into one of the host cell's chromosomes. The host cell then transcribes its own DNA into messenger RNA in which the viral RNA has been inserted. Foreign DNA, when recombined with the virus, infects the eukaryotic cell, sometimes replicating in the cell body and sometimes integrating itself into the eukaryotic chromosomal DNA. This approach is the main hope for gene transplants in humans (Baskin, 1984).

Although recombinant DNA in eukaryotic cells has advanced our knowledge of gene regulation (as discussed in the following section), the fact that the cells used in culture have already differentiated makes it difficult to ask developmental questions. For this reason, the most exciting advance for developmentalists is the introduction of foreign genes into fertilized mouse eggs. Instead of implanting a foreign gene into nuclei of cells in culture, it is injected into the male pronuclei of fertilized mouse eggs that are then placed in the oviduct of foster mothers (Gordon, Scangos, Plotkin, Barbos, & Ruddle, 1980). This procedure can accommodate large gene segments—so far up to 50,000 base pairs—and is successful about 10% of the time. Incorporation of foreign genes appears to be random, takes place early (perhaps before the first cell division of the zygote), and remains stable. Even with large DNA inserts, as many as 100 copies of the DNA are incorporated into the mouse chromosomes. It is easy to identify the foreign DNA among the host chromosomes because a radioactively labeled copy of the foreign DNA can be hybridized to single strands of the host chromosomes.

The application of recombinant DNA methods to eukaryotes has made it clear that eukaryotic genetic mechanisms are more complex than those in prokaryotes, as discussed in the following section.

Eukaryotic Complexities

Some of the additional complexities of eukaryotic genetics are nucleosomes, repetitive DNA, clustered gene families, split genes, and transposable genes.

Nucleosomes. A distinctive feature of eukaryotic DNA is chromatin, so named because it colors with certain stains. Chromatin is now known to consist of DNA tightly complexed with proteins. Stretches of DNA bound with these proteins are called *nucleosomes*. A nucleosome appears as a bead or puff and is thought to be inaccessible to RNA transcription and thus inactive. Actively transcribed DNA is bound with histone rather than the chromatin proteins and lacks the beaded appearance. These DNA regions loop out from the more compact nucleosomes and are thereby accessible to RNA polymerase that begins the process of transcription. Change in chromatin structure is thought to be a major component of developmental differentiation of eukaryotic cells.

Repetitive DNA. Another complexity of eukaryotic DNA (with some exceptions such as *Drosophila*) is repetitive sequences, 100- to 300-base-pair sequences present in thousands of copies (e.g., Schmid & Jelenik, 1982). There are also somewhat longer repetitive sequences (700 to 1,400 bases) repeated hundreds and sometimes thousands of times. The function of such repetitive sequences is not known, although the fact that they are similarly located in different species suggests that they do serve some function. It is thought that they might code for the small RNA molecules involved in gene splicing as described later; however, the reason why so many copies are present would still be a mystery.

Clustered Gene Families. A third complexity of eukaryotic DNA is clustered gene families—clusters of nearly identical genes with spacers between the genes that are often longer than the genes themselves (Hentschel & Birnstiel, 1981). Gene families often include vestigial genes that are no longer transcribed, perhaps because other genes in the family have taken over their function.

Split Genes and Splicing. As mentioned in the previous section, when recombinant DNA methods made it possible to study DNA itself rather than messenger RNA, DNA copied from messenger RNA was found to be substantially different from chromosomal DNA, especially in eukaryotes. It was expected that some of the chromosomal DNA of a gene is involved in gene regulation and may not be transcribed by RNA. However, it was a surprise to discover that about 80% to 90% of chromosomal DNA transcribed into messenger RNA does not leave the nucleus.

This means that some complex process is required to snip out these transcribed but untranslated RNA segments and then splice together the remaining messenger RNA fragments that contain the genetic code to be translated by ribosomes once the RNA leaves the nucleus. To distinguish messenger RNA before and after splicing, the pre-spliced version is called *primary transcript RNA* or *heterogeneous nuclear RNA*. "Split genes" were discovered in 1977 when eukaryotic DNA fragments were first examined (for reviews, see Chambon, 1981; Crick, 1979). The deleted DNA sequences are called "introns" because they stay in the nucleus; the translated sequences remaining after splicing are referred to as *exons*. Nearly all eukaryotic genes have introns, often more introns than exons. Exon sizes typically involve about 150 to 300 nucleotide bases, but the sizes of introns vary widely from 50 to 20,000 bases in length. Although introns are sometimes located similarly in different species, the number and location of introns generally shows no pattern across species, which implies that the location of split genes has not been conserved in evolution. Still, split genes and splicing seem like a lot of work for an evolutionary "free ride." One hypothesis is that introns are involved in the regulation of transcription or of processing the primary RNA transcript to messenger RNA. Another hypothesis is that, in some cases, introns assemble genes for proteins with repeating structures such as the folds of the immunoglobulins and the helix of collagen. It is clear that introns greatly increase the length of eukaryotic genes and thus add to the difficulties of sequencing eukaryotic DNA.

The splicing process within the nucleus is thought to involve numerous small RNA molecules and specialized enzymes that cleave and splice the messenger RNA. Also, an exciting discovery made in 1981 is "autonomous splicing" in which RNA splices itself without the aid of enzymes (Cech, Zaug, & Grabowski, 1981). This finding might substantially alter views of RNA's capabilities.

Transposable Genes. In the 1950s, studies with maize suggested the presence of movable regulatory genes that have no fixed location but inhibit the expression of genes when they move (McClintock, 1957). In the late 1960s, the same phenomenon was observed in *Drosophila*. It turns out that these genes are transposable rather than movable: A copy of the gene is transposed and the original gene is left unaltered. In bacteria, segments of DNA called *insertion sequences* have the ability to make copies of themselves that are inserted elsewhere in the chromosomal DNA. When two insertion sequences are close together, they can transpose the gene between them to another location. The entire unit of the transposed gene and two flanking insertion sequences is called a *transposon*. It is now thought that transposable genes are a major feature of all eukaryotic DNA and may be importantly involved in gene regulation (Shapiro, 1983).

Genetic Regulation

Structural genes code for proteins; many other genes code for products that regulate expression of structural genes. This topic of gene regulation is central to developmental genetics because mechanisms responsible for short-term changes in gene expression are believed to control developmental change as well. Although this assumption might appear simplistic, a similar assumption is made in psychology: No developmental mechanisms have been proposed in psychology that produce long-term developmental changes but not short-term changes. For example, learning processes, the major mechanism by which environment is translated into experience during development, produces short-term as well as long-term changes. Nonetheless, an issue for both developmental genetics and developmental psychology is timing, why certain aspects of development occur at specific times. For example, why do children begin using two-word sentences at 18 months on the average? In developmental psychology, a purely environmental hypothesis is sometimes assumed: Parents begin to model and reinforce two-word sentences at that time. More often, an interaction between environment and maturation is assumed to be important in that the language-learning environment is effective only when the child's cognitive capacities have reached an appropriate level of maturation. As we shall see, formally similar hypotheses concerning developmental timing have been proposed in the field of developmental genetics.

Even before the functioning of DNA was understood, it was clear that the expression of genes must be regulated because the amounts of proteins can vary several hundredfold minute by minute in response to changes in the environment. The basic model of genetics and the complexities recently discovered in eukaryotes offer numerous possible mechanisms for gene regulation. The general categories in which these mechanisms are discussed are transcriptional control, post-transcriptional control, and translational control. After describing gene regulation, specific issues in developmental genetic regulation are considered.

Transcriptional Control

Researchers interested in gene regulation have focused on the first step in protein production, factors that control the rates at which messenger RNA molecules are transcribed from the DNA template. The best-studied system is bacterial beta-galactosidase, an enzyme that catalyzes the splitting of lactose into the simpler sugars glucose and galactose. Beta-galactosidase appears at high levels only when the lactose inducer is present.

The Operon Model.   The fact that some mutant bacteria, regardless of the amount of lactose present, produce large amounts of the enzyme and other mutants produce none led Jacques Monod and Francois Jacob to suggest in 1961 that an ''operator'' gene exists at the beginning of the structural gene. Furthermore, they suggested that a repressor molecule, also coded by DNA, binds with this operator gene, somehow preventing the synthesis of messenger RNA. The binding of inducers such as lactose to the repressor molecule prevents the repressor from binding with DNA, thus freeing up the DNA template for transcription. This model implies that there must be a regulatory gene that codes for the repressor molecule. The model has been shown to be essentially correct for beta-galactosidase. As is usually the case, the operator is close to the structural gene, although the regulatory gene is often far away from the gene complex involving the operator and structural gene. Together, the regulator, operator, and structural genes are referred to as an *operon*. Evidence from organisms other than bacteria suggests that the negative action represented by the operon model is a general process of regulation.

To this classical operon model has been added a "promoter" gene, a short sequence of DNA that is the place at which RNA polymerase binds to DNA to begin the synthesis of messenger RNA. The promoter gene lies between the operator gene—the site at which the repressor molecule binds—and the structural gene. For bacterial beta-galactosidase, the promoter consists of two blocks of base pairs. One block, consisting of six base pairs, is located 10 base pairs from the start of the structural gene. The other block is 25 base pairs further upstream and consists of 10 base pairs. When the operator gene is free from repression, it is thought that RNA polymerase binds to the promoter segment farthest upstream from the structural gene. The other segment of the promoter then opens up into its single strands, exposing the DNA template to RNA synthesis. Mutations in either of these DNA promoter sequences can alter the rate at which messenger RNA is synthesized by a factor of one thousand.

Other Forms of Transcriptional Control.   Positive control processes, although much less well understood than the negative action of the operon system, are also likely to regulate DNA transcription. In 1981, short segments of bases were found in viruses that turn on or substantially increase transcription of any gene near them, either upstream or downstream, even when these control bases are as far as 5000 to 10,000 bases from the gene. Similar segments, known as "enhancer sequences," have been found in DNA of other organisms including humans (Gluzman & Shenk, 1983). Although it is not known how enhancers affect transcription, it is thought that they somehow alter chromatin structure, opening up DNA and exposing it to RNA for transcription.

A control element of a different type also has been discovered recently: A methyl group has been found to be attached to the nucleotide cytosine in many cases and is now thought to inactivate genes in higher organisms (Wigler, Levy, & Perucho, 1981). About 50% to 70% of cytosine bases in birds and mammals are methylated, and it has been shown that methylation patterns, once established, continue to occur in a cell line. The search is on for enzymes that are responsible for adding the methyl group (turning off the gene) and deleting the methyl group (turning on the gene). DNA methylation is not likely to be the primary force controlling gene regulation in eukaryotes. For example, certain invertebrates show no cytosine methylation. It is generally agreed that several processes are involved in gene regulation (Razin, Cedar, & Riggs, 1984).

As mentioned in the preceding section, transposable genes are thought to affect eukaryotic gene regulation. Transposons can change the expression of target genes through insertion of promoter elements or by bringing genes under the control of new regulatory processes by transposing them to new sites. A model of developmental genetics based on transposable gene regulation is described later.

Finally, viral cancer research is becoming increasingly important in pointing to new regulatory genes. "Cancer genes" are expressed at low levels in normal cells, suggesting that cancer involves normal regulatory mechanisms gone awry. Most cancers involve over-expression or mis-expression of regulatory genes by insertion of a new promoter that enhances expression of the regulatory gene, by insertion of extra copies of the regulatory gene, or by mutation of a regulatory gene.

Post-Transcriptional Control

After the messenger RNA that codes for split genes of eukaryotes is transcribed, it is processed by specialized enzymes that delete introns and splice exons together before the messenger RNA leaves the nucleus. Splicing has implications for genetic regulation: One gene can be spliced to yield different messenger RNA molecules. For example, differential splicing produces a hormone in the thyroid gland that differs from a hormone transcribed from the same gene in the hypothalamus (Anava, Jonas, Rosenfeld, Ong, & Evans, 1982). The complexity of gene splicing and other factors that affect messenger RNA before it leaves the nucleus make it likely that other post-transcriptional control processes will be found. For example, control can be exercised in terms of the degradation of messenger RNA. In bacteria at least, the average half-life of messenger RNA is one to two minutes; in eukaryotes, considerable variability exists in the half-life of various messenger RNAs as a function of cell differentiation.

Translational Control

Gene expression might also be regulated by processes that affect the rate at which messenger RNA molecules are translated into proteins. For example, control could be exercised at a ribosome-binding site located six to eight nucleotides upstream from the codon of messenger RNA that initiates translation at the ribosomes (Shine & Dalgarno, 1974). Translational control can occur when other proteins bind with these sequences to prevent translation of the messenger RNA (Gold et al., 1981).

Another type of translational control involves the availability of transfer RNA. Different transfer RNA molecules occur in different amounts, and messenger RNA with rare codons calling for rare transfer RNA are translated more slowly.

Post-Translational Control

Another possible mechanism for controlling gene expression is post-translational modification of proteins. Although it is traditional to regard gene action as ending with the production of a protein, genes are involved in the degradation of proteins. Genetic factors can also be involved in the sorting of proteins within cells, and delivery of proteins to their proper destinations could have an effect upon gene expression.

Genetic Regulation of Development

Any of the control processes described in the previous section can regulate long-term developmental change. For example, although research on the operon model involves short-term changes in transcription, the same process can result in long-term genetic changes. Once an operator is bound by a repressor, it will not permit transcription of its structural gene until the proper inducer appears. Similarly, other mechanisms of genetic regulation affecting transcription (e.g., transposable genes), post-transcription (e.g., gene splicing), and translation can produce long-term as well as short-term changes in gene expression.

Although the process by which genes guide development certainly hinges upon gene regulation, it should be emphasized that there are no genes that code for development in the literal sense. For example, there is no separate set of genes to code for development in childhood, adolescence, or adulthood. In other words, DNA has no explicit representation of each developmental phase or of the entire organism. Rather, a series of genetic changes eventuates in developmental steps that culminate in a reproducing adult.

Also, it is safe to say that developmental regulation involves no simple, single mechanism. Sydney Brenner, who initiated developmental genetic research on the nematode, put it bluntly in a recent interview published in *Science* (Lewin, 1984):

> At the beginning it was said that the answer to the understanding of development was going to come from a knowledge of the molecular mechanisms of gene control . . . I doubt whether anyone believes that anymore. The molecular mechanisms look boringly simple, and they don't tell us what we want to know. We have to try to discover the principles of organization, how lots of things are put together in the same place. I don't think these principles will be embodied in a simple chemical device, as it is for the genetic code. (p. 1327)

For example, a thousand complex molecules must be synthesized in a specific sequence during the half-hour life cycle of bacteria. It used to be assumed that this sequential synthesis was programmed genetically, perhaps by assembling the proper sequence of enzymes as a single coordinated unit so that component enzymes would pass efficiently from one step to another. However, the developmental system is not efficient; the sequence of steps is not programmed. Interactions between substrates and DNA binding sites that control transcription of the necessary enzymes are random and dependent upon the products of earlier transcription of DNA. In other words, there is no code for the specific sequence of enzymes needed for development in bacteria—rather, it seems to be a case of "this leads to that."

An example of genetic regulation of development in a multi-celled eukaryotic organism is provided by research on the nematode, *Caenorhabditis elegans*. Although some genetic research with nematodes was begun in 1948, current interest in the nematode as an organism for the study of the genetic control of neural development and behavior was stimulated by a paper published by Sydney Brenner in 1974. The adult nematode is about one mm in length, has 959 cells with 302 involved in the nervous system, and contains about 20 times the amount of DNA found in bacteria. The nematode is the first organism for whom the entire wiring diagram of the nervous system has been worked out, and it is also the first metazoan organism for which the complete developmental fate map and timing of each cell has been determined. Genetic information about the nematode is accumulating rapidly. For example, the nematode has a total of about 2000 genes and as many as a quarter of these are essential during embryogenesis (Cassada et al., 1980). Identification of temperature-sensitive mutations that affect embryogenesis, usually interfering with the timing of cell divisions, has shown that the same gene products have different functions at different times in development (Edgar, 1980). In addition, the complete description of cell lineage in the nematode has shown that cell division does not proceed in a simple, logical sequence. Sometimes a certain sequence of cell divisions will give rise to a set of differentiated cells each of which is of a different type. Structures are often assembled from components from different cell lineages. Symmetrical structures are often constructed in an asymmetric manner.

Most exciting is the identification of genes that affect the timing of developmental events in the nematode. Because the precise timing of every cell division is known, it is possible to look for mutants abnormal in specific aspects of developmental timing. For example, one developmental mutation alters the pace of differentiation. The dominant mutation slows differentiation by causing cells to repeat the lineage of their ancestors; the recessive mutation accelerates differentiation by causing cells to express the fates normally expressed by their own descendants (Ambros & Horvitz, 1984). It is thought that such temporal genes function by specifying regulatory proteins that are expressed and act within the cells they affect; the other major possibility is that they control the levels of hormone-like substances that act throughout the organism. Although isolation of such temporal genes, discussed in more detail later, are critical for understanding genetic differentiation, it still leaves the question unanswered of what is the clock that controls such temporal genes.

The reason for this complexity is that evolution has not worried about making life easy for developmental geneticists by producing neat sequential programs. Natural selection builds upon what is available and what works. The frequency of a mutant gene increases in a population if it has a positive effect on reproductive fitness in the complex context of all of the developmental interactions among other gene products of the organism. In this sense, development is not programmed in DNA; it is the jerry-built result of millions of small experiments to sculpt an efficient and effective reproducing organism.

In this section, four topics of special relevance to development are briefly discussed: recombinant DNA in mice, coordinate gene expression, the cassette model of development, and temporal genes.

Recombinant DNA in Mice

As described earlier, it is now possible to introduce foreign genes into fertilized mouse eggs, a technique that opens up new horizons for the study of eukaryotic development. In some cases, such as a rabbit globin gene, the recombined gene is not expressed. In most cases, when expression of a foreign gene occurs, it is not tissue-specific; for example, globin genes can be expressed in muscle cells as well as in red blood cells (Costantini & Lacy, 1981).

The fact that the timing of introduction of the foreign gene can affect its expression suggests that the foreign gene has fallen under the control of the developmental program of the mouse. For example, this is the case when leukemia virus DNA is introduced (Jahner et al., 1982). When the gene is introduced early (at the 32-cell stage), it is not expressed. When the gene is introduced later (embryos 8 to 10 days old), it is expressed in nearly every cell. The major hypothesis to explain these results is that DNA is highly methylated early in development and the gene is not transcribed. Later, embryonic cells no longer methylate DNA so that a gene introduced at that time will not be methylated and its expression is not suppressed. Other work with this system suggests that the chromosomal site of integration also affects gene expression.

In some cases, normal expression of recombined genes has been found. The most notable example involves a viral enzyme, thymidine kinase. The regulatory sequence for a mouse gene that codes for a cadmium-binding protein was inserted in front of the viral thymidine kinase gene in the hope that the regulatory sequence could be turned on by introducing cadmium ions into the nuclei of mouse eggs. This proved correct in culture and then *in vivo*. The fused mouse-virus gene complex was integrated into the chromosomes of about 10% of the mice. Several mice incorporated the fusion gene into their liver DNA, and expression of the thymidine kinase gene could be induced by injections of cadmium sulfate solution. Most importantly, induced gene expression was tissue-specific and followed the normal endogenous pattern: greatest in liver, less in kidney, and absent in brain (Brinster, Chen, Warren, Sarthy, & Palmiter, 1982).

Another interesting feature of these studies is that expression of the gene may be altered in progeny. Some offspring with the fusion gene could not be induced to express the gene, and other progeny showed more viral thymidine kinase activity than their parents (Palmiter, Chen, & Brinster, 1982). Discovering the reasons for the enhancement or suppression of the gene during embryonic development could further understanding of tissue differentiation. The major possibilities being examined are changes in base sequences of regulatory regions, patterns of methylation of DNA, and changes in positions of genes.

The best-known example of recombinant DNA research in mice is the successful insertion of the rat growth hormone gene with the same cadmium-binding regulatory sequence (Palmiter et al., 1982). Each male pronucleus of fertilized mouse eggs was injected with about 600 copies of the fusion gene complex, and 170 fertilized eggs were inserted into foster mother mice. Of the 21 surviving offspring, 7 were positive for rate growth hormone. Six of these grew faster than littermates even before heavy metals were added as inducers; these mice had 100 to 800 times the growth hormone of control mice.

Recombinant DNA research using fertilized mouse eggs has just begun. However, it has already contributed to understanding eukaryotic development and is likely to lead to important advances during the next decade.

Coordinate Gene Expression

Although it is necessary to understand the developmental expression of individual genes, it is clear that genetic differentiation involves the coordinate expression of many genes. For example, the sporylation stage of bacteria involves the coordinate expression of more than 50 genes (Youngman et al., 1985). Another example of coordinated gene expression in development is the formation of red blood cells, which involves at least 17 genes on 10 chromosomes.

Although there are many more questions than answers concerning this issue, there is agreement that the topic is critical to understanding development. There is also agreement that a single gene can be integrated into several developmental programs controlled by different regulatory mechanisms. Moreover, certain regulatory elements, such as hormones, can affect several gene groups. Part of the excitement about enhancer sequences is that enhancers for different genes may be turned on by a common set of proteins, which could explain coordinate expression of many genes in the process of differentiation.

Cassette Model of Developmental Genetics

One model of coordinate gene expression in development is the cassette model (Herskowitz et al., 1980). The model is based on the concept of transposable genes: Developmental change is produced by genetic rearrangement of regulatory genes in which unexpressed "storage" DNA coding for regulators is transposed to a site where the DNA is expressed, presumably because it is adjacent to an active promoter. The DNA formerly at the site is no longer expressed. "Cassettes" in this "tape player" can be changed throughout development. Sequential cassette insertions could lead to differentiation and serve as a timing mechanism as well. For example, cassettes could code for transposases, enzymes that promote replacement of the cassette by another type of cassette. In other words, completion of one cassette initiates play of another.

Developmental research on the cassette model has primarily been conducted with one of the simplest eukaryotic organisms, the single-celled baker's yeast, whose genome is only four times larger than that of bacteria, whose generation time is a few hours, and in which foreign DNA can be introduced merely by removing the cellulose cell wall. Although some support for the model has been found in other organisms, doubt remains about its generalizability because the site of transposition often appears to be random in other organisms. Moreover, when restriction fragments from sperm DNA in the nematode were compared to DNA from juveniles, no evidence for genetic rearrangements was detected— suggesting that transposable genes, in this organism at least, are not a major source of developmental change (Emmons, Klass, & Hirsch, 1979). Similarly, as early as 1964, studies of hybridization between DNA from various adult mouse tissues and embryonic DNA suggested no difference in the DNA of embryos and adults (McCarthy & Hoyer, 1964).

Finally, the cassette model has been criticized by Leighton and Loomis (1980) as being too reductionistic:

> There is increasing uncertainty concerning the conceptual validity of the cassette model for developmental regulation. An alternate model for developmental regulation would be that the cell could be thought of as an extremely complex interactive network device. This holistic view of developmental cellular function argues that housekeeping gene functions may be interdependent and overlapping. For example, a central metabolic enzyme may have a housekeeping function in a predevelopmental cell state and a developmentally specific function in some alternate cell state. An extreme version of the network model would state that since environmental changes usually initiate developmental transitions, it is expected that the physiological adaptation and response to these changes set the new developmental state of the cell. (p. xxii)

Interest in the cassette model has been renewed by the discovery in 1984 of *homeoboxes*, DNA segments of about 180 base pairs that appear in several gene complexes important in developmental timing and that are surprisingly similar in *Drosophila*, frogs, mice, and man (Gehring, 1985). Although the several homeoboxes in the genome might be independent, it is possible that they are cassette duplicates inserted from a master cassette. Homeoboxes were first discovered as part of *homeotic* genes in *Drosophila* in which mutations can produce normal structures in the wrong places, such as legs where antennae should be. Each homeobox is transcribed and translated and these protein products may have important developmental functions. For example, homeoboxes might regulate developmental segmentation because they are found in segmented invertebrates and imperfectly segmented vertebrates including humans but they do not occur in unsegmented creatures such as the nematode. However, it is also possible that homeoboxes serve a more basic function that acts as a prerequisite for further development (Gould, 1985)

Temporal Genes

As discussed earlier, long-term developmental changes are likely to involve mechanisms that also produce short-term changes. However, an issue unique to development is timing. Developmental biologists have focused on cues from the environment, such as the location of a cell and metabolic interactions, as expressed by Leighton and Loomis (1980) in their discussion of the "network model" in which "physiological adaptation and response to these changes set the new developmental state of the cell." Genetic programming cannot be "hard-wired" in the fertilized egg because embryos can be divided into eight parts and each will give rise to complete individuals.

On the other hand, some geneticists suggest that genetic programming in development is more important than previously recognized (Paigen, 1980). Although metabolic signals are necessary, genetic programs establish a cell's capacity to respond to signals. For example, cellular responses to hormonal signals depend on which genes have entered a responsive state. In other words, mice have many cell types with the same androgen receptor protein, yet each cell type responds to androgen stimulation by activating a different set of genes.

Genes involved in developmental timing have been called *temporal* genes (Paigen, 1980). Temporal genes have been studied by identifying mutations that alter developmental sequences, especially single genes that change enzyme levels developmentally. The first and most thoroughly studied temporal gene is the so-called *Gus* locus that controls an enzyme, beta-glucuronidase, involved in glucose metabolism. In some inbred mouse strains, for example, the C3H strain, a temporal gene causes an abrupt decline in activity of this enzyme at about 12 days of age. Prior to this age, production of the enzyme is normal, indicating that the control elements and the structural gene for beta-glucuronidase are intact. Importantly, the developmental change is tissue-specific in that the temporal gene affects production of the enzyme only in the liver. The temporal gene in this case is closely linked to the structural gene, although there are examples of temporal genes that are located far away from the structural genes. Work mentioned earlier with nematodes (Ambros & Horvitz, 1984) has identified several temporal genes.

There are also temporal genes in humans, such as the gene that controls the expression of Huntington's disease, although these are difficult to study because the gene product is not known. The best-known example in humans is adult lactose intolerance. In nearly all mammals except humans, intestinal lactase that hydrolyzes lactose in milk is high at birth and then declines after weaning until something less than 10% of its peak activity remains. In humans, the enzyme often persists at high levels into adulthood, presumably as an adaptation to the use of milk as a staple food. Some adults do not show persistence of high lactase levels and are therefore intolerant to milk. It has been shown that the enzyme is the same in lactose-intolerant as in lactose-tolerant individuals and that the phenomenon involves a switch in the rate of enzyme synthesis. This suggests that adult persistence of intestinal lactase may be due to a temporal gene mutation that interferes with the reduction in lactase synthesis that occurs in adulthood in nearly all mammals and some lactose-intolerant adult humans.

The molecular mechanism by which temporal genes affect development is unknown. Because some temporal genes operate at a distance from the structural gene, it is likely that some form of molecular signaling is involved. A major unresolved issue is the mechanism by which temporal genes keep track of developmental time. Although molecular geneticists have just begun to consider developmental programming in terms of temporal genes, it has been suggested by Paigen (1980) that "genetic programming is at least an appreciable aspect of developmental regulation and quite possibly the major driving force" (p. 423). If this proves correct, it will make the task of developmental genetics considerably easier:

> Comprehending the mechanisms of differentiation will be an enormous task if it requires unraveling an intricate network of metabolic interactions that change in time and space. Instead, just as the rules of molecular genetics and the coding of protein structure are available to us without the necessity of understanding each enzyme's metabolic role, it may be possible to understand the rules of developmental programming before we fully understand the complex physiological processes of morphogenesis. (p. 466)

Developmental Molecular Genetics and Behavioral Genetics

Quantitative genetic methods can reveal all sources of trait-relevant genetic variability among individuals. Although the quantitative genetic model is usually phrased in terms of structural genes, it is just as appropriate for detecting genetic variability that arises from gene regulation in the form of operons, transposable genes, and temporal genes. It even detects trait-relevant genetic variability that arises from DNA factors such as repetitive DNA sequences whose function is not yet known.

For example, identical twins are not merely identical for structural genes. They will develop identically in terms of all genetic regulatory processes that are coded in DNA at conception. To the extent that changes in DNA expression or rearrangements are brought about by environmental factors not controlled ultimately by DNA, identical twins could differ. This is as it should be because changes of this type, although they involve DNA, are initiated by environmental factors. In this way, quantitative genetics also considers environmental variance that is clearly important in behavioral development.

In this sense, behavioral genetic studies will always remain a major step ahead of molecular genetic research. Even when the function of genetic phenomena such as transposable genes and repetitive DNA sequences is understood, we will be a long way from understanding the relationship between individual differences in these genetic systems and individual differences in behavior. In contrast, behavioral genetics begins at the "bottom line" by assessing the total impact of genetic variability of any kind on behavioral traits. Developmental molecular genetics makes it clear that many opportunities exist for genetic change during development; developmental behavioral genetics charts changes in the impact of such genetic influences during the course of development.

3 Genetic Change and Developmental Behavioral Genetics

Although the techniques of molecular genetics have not yet been applied to the study of behavioral development, the focus of the field on developmental genetic change lends credence to, and will eventually provide the foundation for, the concept of genetic change as the essence of developmental behavioral genetics. If genetic changes did not occur during development, there would be little use for the field because the behavioral genetic story at any point in development—infancy, childhood, adolescence, adulthood—would be the same elsewhere in the life span. However, developmental change throughout the life span is patently obvious, and it would be incredible if genetic effects were not involved in these changes.

The term *genetic change* in developmental behavioral genetics really means changes in the effects of genes on behavioral differences among individuals. It is in this sense that developmental behavioral genetics was described in the previous chapter as the "bottom line." It ascribes variance in a population to genetic and environmental origins regardless of the molecular mechanisms by which genetic variation among individuals emerges—in developmental behavioral genetics, genetic change is a population concept, not a polypeptide concept. This is fortunate because molecular genetic research has shown that development in eukaryotes is complex, with many possible regulatory mechanisms that seem to work in concert as rheostats rather than as simple on/off switches as in prokaryotes. These facts are likely to combine to snarl the study of genetic mechanisms interwoven in the processes of behavioral development.

Another way in which genetic change means something different in developmental behavioral genetics is that it refers to variance in a population. Developmental behavioral genetics does not speak to genetic universals—that is, that you and I share many nonvarying stretches of DNA and that we both share a large proportion of these with other primates and other mammals. No doubt some of these nonvarying genes govern developmental changes universal to all mammals and all primates, as well as to our species; molecular geneticists are primarily interested in such genetic phenomena. However, developmental behavioral genetics is limited to the study of genetic effects upon behavioral differences among individuals in a population, as explained in chapter 1.

From the perspective of developmental behavioral genetics, genetic change can be viewed in two major ways: as changes in the relative magnitude of genetic and environmental variance for a particular characteristic, and as changes in genetic covariance during development.

Developmental Changes in Heritability

Heritability is a descriptive statistic referring to the portion of observed variability that can be accounted for by genetic differences among individuals. The rest of the variance, the nongenetic portion, has been called environmentality (Fuller & Thompson, 1978). Although these descriptive statistics often raise hackles, they are merely a convenient shorthand for describing genetic and environmental components of phenotypic variance. When we say that heritability can change during development, we mean that the relative roles of genetic and environmental influences can change during development in terms of their effects on behavioral differences among individuals in the population. For example, the twin method assesses heritability by examining the magnitude of the difference between correlations for identical twins (who are 100% similar genetically) and those for fraternal twins (who are roughly 50% similar genetically for segregating genes). Thus, a change in heritability means that the difference between identical and fraternal twin correlations changes. If heritability increases during development, the difference in correlations increases because the identical twin correlation increases or the fraternal twin correlation decreases.

It should be clear that developmental changes in heritability do not implicate molecular mechanisms of change. For example, heritability could increase from one age to another even if the same genes were actively transcribed at both ages: If environmental variance declines during development, genetic variance accounts for a relatively larger portion of the phenotypic variance. Conversely, heritability could remain the same for a particular trait at two ages yet completely different sets of genes could be transcribed, for reasons discussed in the next section.

Although developmental changes in heritability are not especially informative for molecular geneticists, it could be useful for psychologists to know, for example, that variance for a trait of interest is entirely due to environmental variance early in development and then becomes increasingly affected by genetic variance as development proceeds. Although few developmentalists have considered the issue of developmental change in heritability, most would probably guess the reverse to be closer to the truth: As children develop, they experience more diverse environments and thus environmental variance will increasingly account for phenotypic variance. In other words, heritability will decrease during development. This is explicitly the view among Soviet developmentalists (e.g., Mangan, 1982). However, as we shall see in later chapters, when developmental change in heritability is found, it always occurs in the opposite direction: Heritability increases during development.

Early Studies

The earliest studies in human behavioral genetics were focused on this issue. Galton (1875) studied the life histories of two groups of twins: those in which twin partners were similar to each other early in development, and those in which the twins were dissimilar. Galton investigated the extent to which the twins' initial similarity or dissimilarity changed during development and concluded that the initial resemblance of twins was maintained throughout life. Galton was primarily interested in testing the influence of environment, reasoning that twins in a family, because they experience more similar environments than do twins in different families, should become more similar if the family environment is important. If the groups of initially similar and initially dissimilar twins were identical and fraternal twins, respectively, Galton's results would suggest that heritability does not change. However, this assumption cannot be made because identical twins are often less similar than fraternal twins early in life—for example, identical twins show larger birth weight differences than fraternal twins. If heritability increases during development and if Galton's groups each contained identical and fraternal twins, no changes in twin resemblance would be detected because identical twin correlations would increase and fraternal twin correlations would decrease.

The well-known learning theorist, E. L. Thorndike, conducted a similar study in 1905 using objective measures of specific cognitive abilities. He found that 9- and 10-year-old twins showed the same degree of similarity as 13- and 14-year-old twins. Thorndike did not believe that there were two types of twins and made no attempt to separate the twins in his study. Thus, his sample contained approximately equal numbers of identical and fraternal twins and therefore could not reveal developmental changes in heritability.

Merriman (1924) conducted the first methodologically valid twin study comparing identical and fraternal twins for IQ. However, to study developmental change, he divided the entire twin sample into two groups, those 5 to 9 years old and those 10 to 16 years old, regardless of zygosity. As in the studies by Galton and by Thorndike, he found no difference in the IQ correlations for the younger and the older groups.

Because none of these early studies considered changes in the relative magnitude of identical and fraternal twin correlations during development, they do not speak to the issue of developmental change in heritability. More recent studies that do address the issue of developmental change in heritability are discussed in later chapters.

Analyzing Developmental Change in Heritability

Rather than dividing twin samples into younger and older pairs, a far more powerful method for analyzing changes in heritability during development is hierarchical multiple regression (HMR; Ho, Foch, & Plomin, 1980). The procedure begins with the regression of one twin partner's score on the other twin partner's score, a measure of twin resemblance. Data on the twins, say identical twins, are entered in double-entry format (each twin's scores are duplicated, the score for twin partner B follows the score for twin A on the "independent variable," and B's data precede A's data for the "dependent variable") in order to equalize means and variances, which makes this regression equivalent to the usual twin intraclass correlation. Thus, a significant standardized partial regression coefficient indicates significant twin resemblance. The twins' age is added as a second variable in the multiple regression. Then another variable is constructed to represent the two-way interaction between twin score and age simply by obtaining the product of twin score and age for each individual. The multiple regression is called "hierarchical" because variance due to "main effects" (twin score and age) is removed in a first step before the significance of the interaction term is tested. (This is exactly what is done in the computational short-cut for multiple regression using discrete groups which is known as analysis of variance.) A significant standardized partial regression coefficient for the interaction term implies a conditional relationship: Twin resemblance differs as a function of age. Various procedures can be used to determine the direction of the age changes in twin resemblance (Cohen & Cohen, 1975), but the simplest is to dichotomize the sample (e.g., most and least similar twins; youngest and oldest twins) and examine the means of the four cells for the dependent measure.

This procedure can be repeated with fraternal twins and the results of the hierarchical multiple regressions for identical and fraternal twins can be compared. However, a considerably more efficient and more powerful procedure is to include data from both identical and fraternal twins in a single HMR analysis, adding a third variable, zygosity. Zygosity is a "dummy" variable indicating whether each individual is a member of an identical twin pair or a fraternal pair. As mentioned in chapter 1, the coefficient of relationship (1.0 for identical twins and .50 for fraternal twins) could be used to code zygosity. The

TABLE 3.1

Sample Sizes (Twin Pairs) Needed for Detecting Significant
Three-Way Interactions (Developmental Change in Heritability
Using Twin Data) with 80% Power and $p < .05$ Using Hierarchical
Multiple Regression[a]

b^2: The Amount of Variance Accounted for by the Interaction Effect	R^2: The Amount of Variance Accounted for by Main and Interaction Effects Together							
	.01	.05	.10	.20	.30	.40	.50	.60
.01		748	709	628	552	471	395	316
.05			143	128	112	96	81	65
.10				65	57	49	41	33
.20					29	26	22	18

[a]From Cohen and Cohen, 1975, pp. 117–120.

significance of each of the three main effects is tested first in the hierarchical analysis. The second step tests the three two-way interactions (twin score × age, twin score × zygosity, age × zygosity). For example, a significant two-way interaction between twin score and zygosity implies that twin resemblance differs as a function of zygosity—that is, heritability is significant. Of most interest is the three-way interaction (twin score × age × zygosity) which is tested in the third step. A significant three-way interaction means that heritability (i.e., twin score × zygosity) differs as a function of age. If significant interactions are found, additional analyses need to be conducted to determine whether heritability increases or decreases with age (Cohen & Cohen, 1975).

It should be noted that large samples are needed to assess developmental changes in heritability; small samples will not detect such change. Statistical power for detecting a significant three-way interaction depends on the "effect size"—the magnitude of the change in heritability during the developmental span under study—and also on the overall R^2 of the HMR as well as the sample size (Cohen & Cohen, 1975, pp. 117-120). Table 3.1 indicates the sample sizes (number of twin pairs of each type) needed to obtain 80% power to detect a significant three-way interaction (i.e., to detect a significant change in heritability 80% of the time) for reasonable combinations of b^2 (total variance explained by the three-way interaction) and R^2 with $p < .05$. For example, if the HMR yields an R^2 of .50, a three-way interaction accounting for 1% of the total variance (2% of the explained variance) requires a sample size of 395 for 80% power. If the three-way interaction explains 5% of the total variance, a sample size of 81 is needed. This means that over 80 pairs of identical twins and 80 pairs of fraternal twins are needed to detect a change in heritability that accounts for 5% of the variance of twins' scores in an HMR analysis whose overall R^2 is 50%. Despite its need for large sample sizes, HMR is considerably more powerful than arbitrarily dichotomizing samples into younger and older twins; furthermore, from a conceptual point of view, age is a continuous variable and should thus be analyzed in a continuous manner.

The HMR can also be applied to other behavioral genetic designs to explore developmental changes in heritability. For example, because resemblance of identical twins reared apart directly assesses heritability, the two-way interaction between separated identical twins' scores and their age directly assesses heritability as a function of age.

In summary, one way to conceptualize genetic change in development is as a change in heritability, and HMR is a useful procedure for such analyses. Although few studies have systematically examined this issue of genetic change, reviews of research on the major developmental epochs lead to the conclusion that, when heritability changes during development, it increases. Such research is discussed in later chapters. However, changes in heritability do not speak to the issue of the covariation of genetic effects at different points during development—that is the topic of the following section.

Genetic Correlations in Development

Developmental change in heritability is essentially a cross-sectional concept. The second concept of genetic change addresses the genetic contribution to longitudinal, age-to-age change and continuity. Age-to-age genetic correlations indicate the extent to which genetic effects at one age correlate with genetic effects at another age. To the extent that genetic variance at two ages does not covary, genetic change is implicated. Identification of genetic sources of developmental change is important because change prevails over continuity for most aspects of development. For this reason, a major task for developmental behavioral genetics is to explain longitudinal change, not just continuity. Developmental transitions—such as those seen in cognitive development in the second year, at 5-7 years, and at 11-13 years—could be due to genetic reorganization: Age-to-age genetic correlations would be expected to dip during transitional periods.

Assessing Age-to-Age Genetic Correlations

Figure 3.1 depicts a simple path diagram for a trait measured at two ages in development. The scores at each age can be analyzed in a twin or adoption study to estimate the extent to which phenotypic deviations can be explained by genetic deviations (paths h_1 and h_2) and by environmental deviations (paths e_1 and e_2). Paths are standardized partial regressions; thus, path h is $\delta^2_G \div \delta^2_P$ (the proportion of the phenotypic standard deviation due to the standard deviation of genetic effects on the trait), which is the square root of heritability ($V_G \div V_P$). Change in heritability from Age 1 ($h_1{}^2$) to Age 2 ($h_2{}^2$) was the topic of the previous section.

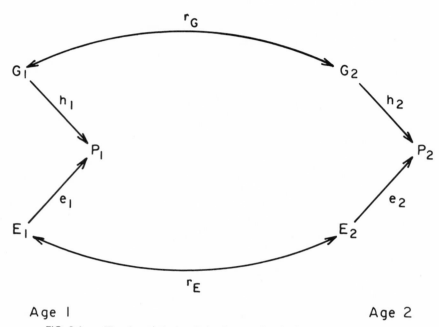

FIG. 3.1   The phenotypic correlation between longitudinal measurements of a trait can be mediated genetically ($h_1h_2r_G$) and environmentally ($e_1e_2r_E$). (Adapted from Plomin & DeFries, 1981.)

If longitudinal data are available for the same individuals at both ages, important additional information can be obtained: the genetic and environmental correlations between Age 1 and Age 2 (Plomin & DeFries, 1981). Genetic correlation is the correlation between genetic deviations (G_1) that affect the trait at Age 1 and the genetic deviations (G_2) that affect the trait at Age 2. If there is no genetic change from Age 1 to Age 2, the genetic correlation will be 1.0. That is, any genetic effects on the trait at Age 1 correlate perfectly with genetic effects on the trait at Age 2. Again, this concept of genetic change in development does not imply molecular mechanisms. For example, the same genes need not be transcribed at the two ages even if the genetic correlation is 1.0—the relevant genes at Age 2 might no longer be actively transcribed, but their structural legacy (e.g., differences in neural networks) could produce the genetic correlation between Age 1 and Age 2.

Genetic correlation refers to genetic deviations as they affect a particular trait rather than to specific genes. Genetic change is implicated when genetic deviations affect a trait at both ages but the genetic correlation between the ages is less than unity. A genetic correlation of zero means that genetic effects at Age 1 are unrelated to genetic effects at Age 2. Even if a genetic correlation between two points in development is zero, actively transcribed genes that affect the trait at Age 1 could continue to be actively transcribed at Age 2 if their gene products no longer have the same effect at that time.

Environmental correlations between two ages are analogous to genetic correlations. An environmental correlation is the correlation between environmental deviations (E_1) that affect the trait at Age 1 and environmental deviations (E_2) that affect the trait at Age 2. An environmental correlation of 1.0 means that environmental effects are shared completely at the two ages; an environmental correlation of zero implies that completely different sets of environmental factors operate at the two ages.

From Fig. 3.1, it can be seen that developmental stability, the phenotypic correlation between Age 1 and Age 2, can be mediated genetically and environmentally. Genetic mediation involves the genetic correlation weighted by the square roots of the heritabilities at the two ages, $h_1h_2r_G$. Thus, the genetic correlation between two ages could be 1.0 even though heritability is low. In other words, genetic deviations at Age 1 could correlate perfectly with genetic deviations at Age 2 even though the genetic deviations at each age make only a small contribution to phenotypic variance. Similarly, environmental mediation is $e_1e_2r_E$. If phenotypic stability is zero between the two ages, both the genetic and environmental chains of paths must be zero (except in the unlikely event that a positive genetic correlation is offset by a negative environmental correlation).

Genetic and environmental correlations are critical concepts in developmental behavioral genetics because they indicate the extent to which developmental change and continuity are mediated genetically or environmentally. For example, consider transitional periods, times in development when change is most obvious, such as the transition from infancy to early childhood. Developmentalists often think about transitional issues from a universals perspective—for example, the characteristic increase in our species' use of language from the second to the third year of life. However, as always, developmental behavioral genetics is concerned about individual differences, not normative development. From an individual differences perspective, transitional periods refer to the scrambling of phenotypic rank-orderings of individuals. For example, the correlation between receptive vocabulary at 12 months and at 18 months might be substantial, but the correlation between 18 months and 24 months might be lower given the tremendous cognitive changes that occur around 21 months of age. To what extent does genetic reorganization bring about such transitions? Answers to such questions will come from analyses of genetic correlations during development.

The concept of developmental genetic and environmental correlations is an extension of multivariate analysis (Plomin, in press, a). Rather than analyzing the covariance between two different traits at the same time in development, the covariance between the "same" trait at two different times in development can be analyzed. The basic point is that any behavioral genetic design that can estimate genetic and environmental components of the variance of a single trait can also be used to estimate genetic and environmental components of the covariance between two traits. Using the twin method as an example, instead of correlating one twin's score with the twin partner's score on the same variable, twin cross-correlations can be analyzed. A cross-correlation is the correlation between one twin's score on one variable and the other twin's score on the other variable. In the case of developmental analysis, the cross-correlation involves one twin's score at Age 1 and the other twin's score at Age 2. Everything else is similar to quantitative genetic analyses of the variance of a single trait and of the covariance between two traits (see Plomin & DeFries, 1979, for details). For example, in univariate analysis, genetic variance and environmental variance sum to the phenotypic variance; in bivariate analysis, genetic covariance and environmental covariance sum to the phenotypic covariance. In univariate analysis, doubling the difference between identical and fraternal twin correlations estimates heritability, the proportion of phenotypic variance that can be accounted for by genetic variance. In bivariate analysis, doubling the difference between identical and fraternal twin cross-correlations estimates the genetic contribution to the phenotypic correlation ($h_1 h_2 r_G$), bivariate heritability (Plomin & DeFries, 1981) or, in the case of longitudinal analysis, the heritability of stability (Plomin, in press, a).

Thus, the genetic correlation (r_G) answers some questions and the genetic chain of paths ($h_1 h_2 r_G$) answers others. If one's goal is to assess the genetic contribution to phenotypic stability in development, the appropriate term is the $h_1 h_2 r_G$ chain of paths—the genetic correlation weighted by the square roots of the heritabilities at each age, which standardizes the genetic covariance in terms of its contribution to the phenotypic variance. The genetic correlation itself is also of considerable interest in developmental behavioral genetics. As indicated earlier, the genetic correlation can be substantial even though heritabilities are low. Genetic correlation indicates the extent to which genetic effects overlap at two ages, regardless of their relative contribution to phenotypic variance. If heritabilities at each age are known, the genetic correlation can be derived by dividing $h_1 h_2 r_G$ by the product, $h_1 h_2$.

For example, suppose phenotypic stability between two ages is moderate, .50, and the identical and fraternal twin correlations for the trait at both ages are .75 and .50, respectively. This pattern of twin correlations suggests a heritability of .50 at each age. However, this does not mean that phenotypic stability between the two ages is mediated genetically—that depends on the genetic correlation. If the identical twin cross-correlation (the correlation between one twin at Age 1 and the other twin at Age 2) is .50 and the fraternal twin cross-correlation is .25, this suggests that genetic factors can completely explain the observed developmental stability: Doubling the difference between the identical and fraternal twin cross-correlations yields .50, the estimate of $h_1 h_2 r_G$. Dividing .50 by $h_1 h_2$ ($h_1 h_2 = \sqrt{.50} \times \sqrt{.50} = .50$) estimates the genetic correlation as 1.0, which means that genetic factors that affect the trait at the two ages are perfectly correlated.

In contrast, if the identical twin cross-correlation is .40 and the fraternal twin cross-correlation is .275, heredity is responsible for only half of the phenotypic stability ($h_1h_2r_G = .25$) and the genetic correlation between the ages is .50. This example implies genetic change from Age 1 to Age 2: Some of the genetic variance at Age 2 differs from genetic variance at Age 1. To the extent that genetic factors cannot account for phenotypic stability, environmental mediation is posited because $h_1h_2r_G + e_1e_2r_E = r_P$. In this latter example, the remaining half of the phenotypic stability can be attributed to environmental factors ($e_1e_2r_E = 0.25$) and the environmental correlation is .50.

Although analyses of genetic and environmental correlations will undoubtedly become a hallmark of developmental behavioral genetic analyses in the future, few longitudinal behavioral genetic studies have been conducted and little is known as yet about the extent to which genetic factors mediate change and continuity in development. In fact, in addition to the Skodak and Skeels (1949) adoption study of IQ, there are only two long-term longitudinal behavioral genetic studies. One is the Louisville Twin Study (Wilson, 1983). Analyses of the longitudinal twin data from this study have employed twin trend correlations based on age-to-age profiles. As discussed in chapter 9, the results of analyses of twin trend correlations for longitudinal profiles are generally similar to the average twin results for scores at each age, perhaps because trend correlations include twin similarity both for overall level and for age-to-age changes. Trend correlations are complex functions of heritabilities at each age and genetic and phenotypic correlations among the ages. The other major longitudinal study is the Colorado Adoption Project (Plomin & DeFries, 1983, 1985). The studies complement each other in design because the twin design provides estimates of genetic parameters for the same-aged sibling relationship of twins and the parent-offspring adoption design, from a genetic perspective, is like an "instant" longitudinal study from infancy to adulthood. Together, data from the two studies point to a surprising model of developmental behavioral genetics that is referred to as the *amplification* model. Prior to describing the amplification model, the effect of developmental genetic change on the resemblance between relatives is considered.

Developmental Genetic Change and Familial Resemblance

A fundamental tenet of genetics is that first-degree relatives share roughly half of their segregating genes. Some qualifications have long been understood. For example, siblings share half of their segregating genes only on the average—for a particular sibling pair, it depends on how many chromosomes from their mother and father they happen to have in common. Also, the statement applies only to additive genetic variance; siblings also share one-quarter of nonadditive genetic variance due to dominance. Thus, to the extent that nonadditive genetic effects are important, siblings share more than half of their segregating genes.

Parents and their offspring share only additive genetic variance; however, assortative mating can inflate parent-offspring (and sibling) genetic similarity beyond 50% (for details, see Plomin, DeFries, & McClearn, 1980).

These qualifications of the statement that first-degree relatives share 50% of their segregating genes are well known. However, recognition that genetic effects change during development leads to a new qualification; unless first-degree relatives are the same age, we would not expect their effective genetic similarity to be 50%. Twins are exactly the same age and any genetic changes that occur during development will be shared to the extent of their genetic similarity—100% for identical twins and 50% for fraternal twins. However, nontwin siblings and, especially, parents and their offspring cannot be expected to display their 50% genetic similarity unless they are studied at the same ages.

The effective genetic similarity of first-degree relatives at different ages depends upon the genetic correlation between the ages. For example, in Fig. 3.1, if one member of an identical twin pair were tested at Age 1 and the other were tested at Age 2 for a characteristic that is completely heritable at both ages, their observed similarity would not necessarily be perfect. It would depend on the genetic correlation, r_G. If the genetic correlation between the two ages is unity, observed similarity should be 1.0. However, if genetic change occurs during development, the genetic correlation will be less than 1.0. If the genetic correlation between the two ages is zero, the correlation for identical twins will be zero.

Of course, no one would test members of a twin pair at different ages. However, with siblings and, especially, with parents and offspring, it is usually a practical necessity to test family members at different ages. In this case, genetic similarity between the relatives depends on the extent of genetic change during development, as indexed by the genetic correlation. Consider, for example, the similarity between biological parents and their adopted-away infants. In the absence of selective placement, biological parents and their offspring share only genetic similarity and parent-offspring resemblance is usually described in terms of a simple path diagram as in Fig. 3.2. This usual approach assumes that developmental genetic change is unimportant. Heritabilities for the parent and offspring are assumed to be the same, and the genetic correlation between adulthood (i.e., parents) and childhood (i.e., offspring) is assumed to be 1.0.

If we are to recognize developmental genetic change, the expected similarity between parent and offspring must take into account the genetic correlation between childhood and adulthood and must also recognize the possibility that heritability differs at the two ages. A path diagram illustrating these concepts of developmental genetic change is presented in Fig. 3.3 (adapted from Plomin & DeFries, 1985). Although the diagram looks complicated, it merely combines the information in Fig. 3.2 on parent- offspring resemblance with the information on genetic correlation from Fig. 3.1. The left side is the same as Fig. 3.2: The heritabilities for parent and offspring are the same and the genetic correlation is

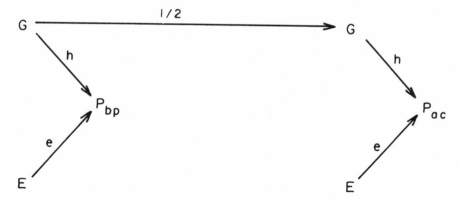

FIG. 3.2 Path diagram depicting parent-offspring similarity for biological parents (bp) and their adopted-away child (ac) assuming no genetic change from childhood to adulthood.

assumed to be 1.0. These assumptions can be made because the left side of the path diagram depicts expected parent-offspring similarity with the parent as a child of the same age as the adopted-away child. Of course, the biological parent cannot be put in a time warp and be restudied as a child—this is the reason for the right side of the path diagram. This part of the path diagram merely indicates, as in Fig. 3.1, that genetic resemblance from childhood to adulthood is a function of the genetic correlation and that heritabilities in childhood and adulthood can differ.

From the path diagram in Fig. 3.2, the expectation for the correlation between biological parents and their adopted-away children is simply $.5h^2$. From Fig. 3.3, the expectation is $.5h_Ch_Ar_G$. If heritabilities are the same in childhood and adulthood and if the genetic correlation between childhood and adulthood is 1.0, this reduces to $.5h^2$. Although children in the Colorado Adoption Project (CAP) are being studied longitudinally, the major reports to date have focused on infancy (DeFries, Plomin, Vandenberg, & Kuse, 1981; Plomin & DeFries, 1983, 1985). If developmental genetic change is important, CAP parent-offspring analyses of data on the adoptees as infants are not likely to reveal evidence for genetic influence. Significant resemblance between biological parents and their adopted-away infants has three requirements: The characteristic must be heritable in infancy, it must be heritable in adulthood, and the genetic correlation between infancy and adulthood for the characteristic must be positive. In fact, it would be difficult to detect parent-offspring resemblance unless all three factors are substantial because, in effect, they are multiplied to produce the parent-offspring expectation (i.e., $.5h_Ch_Ar_G$). For example, if a trait is 50% heritable in childhood and in adulthood and the genetic correlation for the trait is .50 between childhood and adulthood, then the expected parent-offspring correlation is .125. A correlation of this magnitude would require a sample of

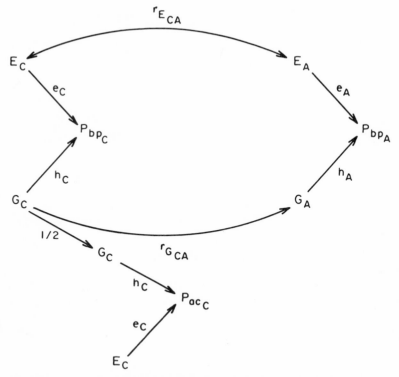

FIG. 3.3   Path diagram depicting parent–offspring similarity for biological parents (bp) and their adopted-away child (ac) taking into account possible genetic change from childhood (C) to adulthood (A) and differing heritabilities in childhood and adulthood. (Adapted from Plomin & DeFries, 1985.)

over 500 biological mothers and their adopted-away infants to detect the correlation with 80% power ($p < .05$; Cohen, 1977). The CAP sample size provides about 50% power to detect such correlations, which means that significant genetic influence of this magnitude will go undetected half of the time.

This apparent weakness of the parent-offspring design is, in fact, a strength in terms of developmental behavioral genetics: When significant parent-offspring resemblance is found, we know that the three requirements have been met. That is, heritabilities in infancy and in adulthood are significant (and likely to be substantial) and the genetic correlation between infancy and adulthood is significant (and probably substantial). In combination with data from twin studies, it is possible to estimate the genetic correlation from infancy to adulthood. Twin data are needed to estimate heritability in childhood (h_C^2) and in adulthood (h_A^2), although the CAP will eventually include enough pairs of adoptive and nonadoptive siblings tested at the same age to provide estimates of h_C^2. At the extreme, if the parent-offspring correlation for biological parents and their adopted-away infants equals $.5h_Ch_A$ for given heritabilities in childhood and adulthood, the genetic correlation must equal 1.0. This would mean that the genes that affect individual differences in the trait in infancy correlate perfectly with those that affect individual differences in the trait in adulthood. At the other extreme, if h_C^2 and h_A^2 are significant and the correlation between biological parents and their adopted-away infants is zero, the genetic correlation must equal zero. This implies that the genes that affect infant variability are completely uncorrelated with those that affect adult variability. Analyses of this type in the CAP have led to some exciting results and to the amplification model of developmental genetic change.

The Amplification Model of Developmental Genetics

In summary, genetic change during development can involve changing heritabilities and genetic correlations less than unity. These components affect expectations for parent-offspring resemblance.

All combinations of changing heritabilities and genetic correlations are possible; Fig. 3.4 depicts a few. The prevailing view among developmentalists that individual differences in infancy are not at all predictive of later variability would lead to Model A: Regardless of the relative heritabilities in infancy and adulthood, no genetic continuity exists. Moderates might go along with Model B, slight genetic overlap between infancy and adulthood, as a possibility. One of the most exciting findings to emerge from the CAP data is support for the surprising Model C, which suggests nearly complete genetic overlap between infancy and adulthood. That is, when genetic influence is found in infancy, it covaries nearly completely with adult genetic variance. Moreover, a substantial increase in genetic variance from infancy to adulthood (the right side of Model C) makes it necessary to posit an amplification model of gene action, as explained in this section.

IQ. To understand these conclusions, it is necessary to bring together the concepts discussed previously in this chapter. Using IQ as an example, the CAP infancy results (presented in greater detail in chapter 9) suggest a correlation of about .10 between biological parents' IQ and adopted-away infants' Bayley Mental Development Index (MDI) scores. Although this correlation is small, our previous discussion of the impact of genetic changes during development on parent-offspring correlations led to the expectation of correlations of this magnitude for reasonable combinations of heritability and genetic correlations. Moreover, maximum-likelihood, model-fitting approaches confirm significant genetic variance when the biological parents' data are analyzed simultaneously with adoptive parents' data and data from nonadoptive families (Fulker &

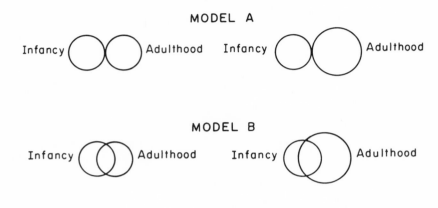

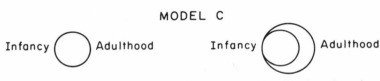

FIG. 3.4   Models of development behavioral genetics: Genetic variance in infancy and in adulthood (depicted by circles) and genetic covariance between infancy and adulthood (depicted by overlap of the circles).

DeFries, 1983). Finally, taken at face value, this implies that 20% of the variance is due to heredity, and it is rare in the behavioral sciences that we can explain 20% of the variance.

At the simplest level, significant resemblance between biological parents (who are, of course, adults) and their adopted-away infants implies some genetic continuity from infancy to adulthood. We can be more precise, however. As discussed earlier (see Fig. 3.3), the expected correlation between biological parents and their adopted-away children is $.5h_Ch_Ar_G$, which means it is the usual 50% weighted by the heritabilities in childhood (h_C) and adulthood (h_A) and the genetic correlation between childhood and adulthood (r_G). To estimate the genetic correlation, we need to employ estimates of heritabilities in infancy and adulthood. The heritability of adult IQ is usually taken to be about 50% (Plomin, 1985; Plomin & DeFries, 1980). What is the heritability of Bayley MDI scores in infancy? It is at this point that the data from the Louisville Twin Study become critical. They yield a heritability estimate of .13 (Wilson, 1983).

These data indicate that heritability increases from infancy to adulthood, from about .15 to about .50, which moves us into the right side of Fig. 3.4. We can use these results to estimate the genetic correlation between infancy and adulthood. If the correlation between biological parents and their adopted-away infants is .10, the genetic correlation is .73:

$$.10 = .5h_Ch_Ar_G$$
$$.10 = .5(\sqrt{.15})(\sqrt{.50})r_G$$
$$r_G = .73$$

Estimation of a high genetic correlation between infancy and adulthood does not depend upon this particular combination of values. Heritability of Bayley MDI scores in infancy could be .10, .20, or even .30, and the estimate of the genetic correlation would nonetheless be substantial. If the correlation between the biological parent and adopted-away infant is greater than .10, estimates of genetic correlations will be even greater. If the parent-offspring correlation is lower, the genetic correlation will be lower; even if the parent-offspring correlation is .05, however, the genetic correlation will be between .25 and .50 for infancy heritabilities between .10 and .30. A model-fitting approach to these data generally confirms these conclusions, although when the effects of assortative mating for IQ are taken into account, estimates of genetic correlations are slightly lower (DeFries, Plomin, & LaBuda, submitted).

The reason why these estimates of genetic correlation are so high is that heritability in infancy is low. Given significant resemblance between biological parents and their adopted-away infants, this small amount of genetic variance in infancy must covary substantially with genetic variance in adulthood. This is why the right-hand side of Model C in Fig. 3.4 was selected as best fitting the facts of increasing genetic variance and substantial genetic correlation from infancy to adulthood.

The estimate of genetic correlation for IQ from infancy to adulthood for IQ is so great that it poses a problem: How can the genetic correlation be nearly 1.0 when genetic variance increases so substantially from infancy to adulthood? This question is what led DeFries (personal communication) to pose the amplification model of developmental genetics: Genes that affect IQ make only a small contribution to phenotypic variance at first, but their effects are amplified throughout development. Suppose, for example, that genetic differences among infants are responsible for differences among them in the formation of dendritic spines during the first few years of life and that complexity of dendritic spines is related to information- processing capability. At first, these structural differences do not have a chance to cause functional differences because so little information has been processed at that point. Gradually, the functional differences are amplified as more and more information is processed by children. If we were to measure differences in categorization ability early in childhood, the genetic differences among children due to the complexity of dendritic spines would contribute a negligible amount of variance to observed variability among the children in categorization ability. The differences snowball as development proceeds, so that a study of the children when they are older will show more genetic variance. Yet the genetic correlation between the two ages is near unity because the genetic portion of observed variability at both ages originates with the same set of genes whose effects become amplified during development. In other words, even though genetic variance is relatively less important early in development than it is later, the little genetic variance that does exist in early childhood is substantially related to the genetic variance that affects the trait later in life.

The amplification model makes some strong and testable predictions. For example, it predicts that as the CAP children grow older, the genetic correlations from childhood to adulthood as estimated from parent–offspring correlations will continue to approach unity even though heritability increases. The model also predicts that longitudinal twin data will show a similar pattern of high age-to-age genetic correlations and increasing heritability from infancy to middle childhood. The data from the Louisville Twin Study could provide this information, although they have not as yet been analyzed in terms of age-to-age genetic correlations. It should be noted that the amplification model does not predict high phenotypic correlations from age to age, just high genetic age-to-age correlations. A related prediction from the amplification model is that increasing stability for IQ during childhood comes about because the high age-to-age genetic correlation begins to account for more of the phenotypic variance. That is, heritability increases and the high genetic correlation from age to age shows up in increasing phenotypic stability. This could explain the apparent relationship between heritability and stability in development.

Another prediction is that *some* phenotypic stability should exist from Bayley scores in infancy to adult IQ scores within individuals. This might seem to fly in the face of the zeitgeist that says there is no predictability from infancy to adulthood for IQ. However, a closer examination of the longitudinal data leaves this question open. The highest phenotypic correlations for mental ability between infancy and adulthood were reported by Bayley (1955): .25 from the first year to adulthood and .55 from the second year to adulthood. A review by McCall (1979) yielded a median correlation of .32 for three studies comparing test scores of 13- to 18-month-old infants to their IQ scores at 8 to 18 years of age. The amplification model as applied to the CAP data predicts that some phenotypic stability must exist between infancy and adulthood. How much? As described earlier (see also the path diagram in Fig. 3.1), genetic mediation of phenotypic stability is a multiplicative function of the square root of heritability in infancy, the square root of heritability in adulthood, and the genetic correlation between the ages. We have said that heritability in infancy is about .15 and that heritability in adulthood is about .50, and we estimated the genetic correlation between infancy and adulthood for IQ to be about .75. Thus, the genetic contribution to phenotypic stability from infancy to adulthood is about .20:

$$h_1 h_2 r_G = (\sqrt{.15})(\sqrt{.50})(.75) = .205$$

Actually, we did not need to calculate $h_1h_2r_G$ because this is equivalent to twice the correlation between the biological mothers and their adopted- away offspring ($.5h_Ch_Ar_G$). Thus, the amplification model's application to the CAP infancy data predicts that phenotypic correlations between infancy and adulthood should be at least .20. Environmental mediation of stability could add to this figure. This prediction is within the limits of stability found in previous studies, as indicated earlier.

It should be mentioned that the amplification model does not require that the processes underlying the measures be isomorphic in infancy and adulthood. For example, genetic continuity from infant Bayley MDI scores to adult IQ might be due to entirely different processes in infancy and adulthood. "Infancy genes" might affect rate of language acquisition, for example, whereas "adult genes" might affect symbolic reasoning. However, it is also possible that similar cognitive processes are involved at both ages, as has been argued in the case of infant novelty preference (Fagan, 1985).

The amplification model apparently is not limited to IQ: The model has been found to apply to physical characteristics as well (Plomin & DeFries, 1985).

Height and Weight. Data for height and weight are useful as "anchor" points for comparison to behavioral data. For these traits, a substantial genetic correlation from infancy to adulthood would not be as surprising as it is in the case of IQ because phenotypic stability is apparent for physical characteristics. For height, the correlation between infancy and adulthood is .67 at 12 months and .75 at 24 months (Tanner, 1978); for weight, the correlations are .42 and .48 (Tanner, Healy, Lockhart, Mackenzie, & Whitehouse, 1956). In the CAP, the correlation between biological mothers and their adopted-away offspring is .32 at both 12 and 24 months, similar to the correlations for nonadoptive parents and their offspring. For weight, the correlations are slightly lower, about .25. These significant correlations between biological mothers and their adopted-away offspring indicate genetic continuity from infancy to adulthood.

The amplification model predicts that as genes come to affect a character in infancy, they will continue to affect the character in adulthood. In other words, genetic covariance between infancy and adulthood accounts for nearly all of the genetic variance in infancy. For height and weight, unlike Bayley MDI scores, heritabilities are substantial in infancy: .70 and .68, respectively (Wilson, 1976). The heritability of height in adulthood is about .90 (Plomin & DeFries, 1981); the heritability of weight is about .80 (Stunkard, Foch, & Hrubec, 1985). Combined with the correlations for biological mothers and their adopted-away offspring, these data do, in fact, lead to estimates of substantial genetic correlations.

For height:

$$.32 = .5h_C h_A r_G$$
$$.32 = .5(\sqrt{.70})(\sqrt{.90})r_G$$
$$r_G = .81$$

For weight:

$$.25 = .5h_C h_A r_G$$
$$.25 = .5(\sqrt{.68})(\sqrt{.80})r_G$$
$$r_G = .68$$

The genetic correlations of about .80 and .70 for height and weight corroborate the amplification model: Although genetic variance accounts for somewhat less of the phenotypic variance in infancy than in adulthood, the genetic covariance between infancy and adulthood is substantial.

Other Domains.   Other domains of development are not nearly as well studied as are IQ and physical characteristics. Although the amplification model might not generalize to all domains of development, some support for the model was found in the CAP data on shyness, which appears to be one of the most heritable dimensions of temperament throughout the life span (Plomin & Daniels, in press). At 24 months of age, adoptees' shyness as rated by their adoptive parents correlated significantly with biological mothers' self-reports of sociability. Although the heritabilities of infant shyness or adult sociability are not known precisely, twin studies generally suggest at least moderate heritability in infancy and substantial heritability in adulthood (Buss & Plomin, 1984). Assuming a heritability of .30 for infants and .50 for adults, the genetic correlation between infancy and adulthood is .78; if the heritabilities in infancy and adulthood are both .30, the genetic correlation between infancy and adulthood is 1.0. In either case, substantial genetic continuity between infant shyness and adult sociability is predicted.

This example of genetic continuity between infant shyness and adult sociability raises a problem in terms of falsifying the amplification model. If we examine only traits selected because they show significant correlations between biological parents and their adopted-away offspring, we are loading the deck in favor of finding genetic continuity from infancy to adulthood: A significant correlation between biological parents and adopted-away offspring in itself indicates that some genetic continuity must be present. On the other hand, if we examine traits that are completely different in infancy and adulthood (even if they are given the same labels), no parent-offspring resemblance will be found because the genetic correlation from infancy to adulthood is zero. If these traits are found to be heritable in infancy and in adulthood, the results would appear to speak against the amplification model because, in this case, genetic variance in infancy is not found to covary highly with genetic variance in adulthood.

For example, next to shyness, the temperament that shows the best evidence for heritability in infancy from twin studies is emotionality (Buss & Plomin, 1984). However, the CAP parent-offspring data yield no evidence for genetic influence. Does this violate the amplification model? If we play the role of devil's advocate, it does. Yet the obvious differences between infant "emotionality" and adult "emotionality" leave some doubt: Measures of infant emotionality assess how often the baby cries and fusses, whereas adult emotionality involves fear and anger (Buss & Plomin, 1984).

As a safeguard against studying completely different traits in infancy and adulthood, disconfirmation of the amplification model should involve showing some, but only slight, genetic correlation from infancy to adulthood. Height presented a reasonable opportunity for disconfirming the model. If the correlation between biological parents and their adopted- away offspring had been .10 rather than .32, the genetic correlation from infancy to adulthood would have been .13 rather than .81. Because we already know that height correlates highly within individuals from infancy to adulthood, finding a genetic correlation of .13 between infancy and adulthood would strikingly disconfirm the model.

Even if the amplification model does not generalize to other domains, it is exciting that it does appear to apply to mental development and to height and weight. One implication with practical significance is that heritability of infant scores could be used as a criterion to maximize the prediction of adult scores from scores in infancy.

Summary

The concept of genetic change during development is the theme of this chapter. A cross-sectional look at genetic change involves age-to-age changes in heritability. Longitudinal behavioral genetic data can be used to estimate age-to-age genetic correlations, which index genetic change as well as genetic continuity. The amplification model suggests that as genes come to affect a trait in infancy, they increasingly affect the variance of the trait as their effects are amplified. Although genetic continuity is emphasized in the amplification model, the need for the model arises because of observed genetic change in heritabilities. The possibility that genetic effects become amplified as development proceeds seems the only way to explain high age-to-age genetic correlations coupled with increases in heritability from age to age.

Although the concept of genetic change is the most fundamental issue in developmental behavioral genetics, other important issues have emerged from the application of behavioral genetic concepts and methods to research in developmental psychology. However, these issues primarily involve nurture rather than nature, as described in the next five chapters.

II DEVELOPMENTAL BEHAVIORAL GENETICS AND THE ENVIRONMENT

4

Environmental Influences that Affect Development Are Not Shared by Members of a Family

Behavioral genetic research provides evidence—perhaps the best available evidence—for the importance of environmental influences on behavioral development. However, these same data indicate that environmental factors that affect behavioral development primarily operate in a manner that would go undetected by traditional environmental research. Attempts to identify environmental factors relevant to behavioral development have centered on the family environment, especially the environment provided by parents. This makes good sense: Parents are there first and most. The typical study assesses a characteristic of parental childrearing behavior—for example, their permissiveness—and relates this to some developmental outcome (e.g., psychological adjustment) in the children. Such environment-development correlations are calculated across families using covariance, the averaged cross-products of the parent's deviation from the parental mean and the child's deviation from the children's mean. The traditional approach to environmental research makes the reasonable assumption that the family is the unit by which environmental influence is doled out. If this is so, two children in the same family ought to experience roughly similar environments. However, the research reviewed in this chapter strongly indicate that, whatever they may be, environmental influences relevant to psychological development create differences rather than similarities among family members.

Observed similarities among family members may have beguiled investigators into thinking that shared family environmental experiences are responsible for familial resemblance. However, behavioral genetic research shows that most familial resemblance is due to heredity, not to shared family environment. At the same time, this research indicates that environmental influence is important. What is important are those environmental factors that are not shared by family members—that is, factors that make them different rather than similar. This finding of the importance of nonshared environmental influences is the topic of this chapter and may be the most important contribution that the field of behavioral genetics has made to the study of psychological development.

This chapter has three goals: 1) To describe behavioral genetic research that leads to the conclusion that nonshared environment is responsible for most environmental variation relevant to psychological development, 2) To discuss specific nonshared environmental influences that have been studied to date, and 3) To consider relationships between nonshared environmental influences and behavioral differences between children in the same family.

Methods for Assessing Nonshared Family Environment

The essence of quantitative genetics is the partitioning of phenotypic variation in a population into two components, a genetic component and the remainder of the variance, which we call *environmental*, but which is more properly thought of as nongenetic—that portion of the phenotypic variation that cannot be explained by genetic variance. In the same way, the environmental component of variance can be broken down further into two components: environmental variance shared by family members, making them similar to one another, and the remainder. The shared component has acquired several appellations: common, E_2, between-family, and family-similar. The rest of the environmental variance—environmental influence not shared by members of the same family—has been called nonshared, specific, E_1, within-family, and individual.

The reason for this somewhat arbitrary, but critically important, decomposition of environmental variance is that shared family environment contributes to familial resemblance. In nonadoptive families, familial resemblance for a trait could be due entirely to shared family environment, entirely to shared heredity, or to a combination of the two. For this reason, behavioral geneticists have long been interested in disentangling shared family environment from shared heredity. In studies of human behavior, one of the best ways to address this issue is to study resemblance in adoptive families to obtain direct estimates of the effects of shared family environment. That is, the correlation between pairs of unrelated children adopted at birth into the same adoptive homes represents the portion of phenotypic variance accounted for by shared family environment. For example, a correlation of .25 for a trait measured in pairs of adoptees reared in the same adoptive homes suggests that 25% of the phenotypic variation in the trait can be explained by shared family environment. A correlation of zero for pairs of adoptees, on the other hand, implies that shared family environment contributes nothing to phenotypic variance.

As mentioned earlier, total environmental variance is typically estimated as that portion of phenotypic variance not explained by genetic variance. Genetic variance can be estimated from adoption studies by examining correlations within pairs of genetically related individuals adopted apart—for example, the correlation between biological siblings adopted apart and reared in different homes. If this correlation for siblings reared apart were .25 for a particular trait, heritability would be estimated as 50%—the sibling correlation is doubled because it estimates only half of the genetic variance. Thus, the other half of the phenotypic variance would be attributable to environmental variance. Half of this environmental variance is due to shared family environment if the correlation for adoptee pairs reared together is .25. The rest of the environmental variance is due to nonshared family environment and error. The difference between the reliability coefficient (e.g., test-retest correlation) and 1.0 estimates the component of variance due to error of measurement.

In addition to the direct estimate of shared family environment based on the correlation for pairs of genetically unrelated individuals adopted into the same family, adoption studies can also provide an indirect assessment of the role of shared environment by comparing relatives adopted apart (as a direct estimate of genetic influence) and relatives reared together (a correlation that includes both heredity and shared family environment). If relatives reared together are no more similar than relatives adopted apart, we can conclude that growing up in the same family does not add to relatives' resemblance beyond the similarity induced by heredity. For example, if for a particular trait, identical twins reared together are no more similar than identical twins reared in uncorrelated environments, shared environment must be unimportant for that trait. On the other hand, if the correlation for identical twins reared together is .75 and the correlation for identical twins reared apart is .50, 25% of the phenotypic variance could be attributed to shared environment.

Shared and nonshared environmental variance can also be estimated from twin studies. Because identical twins are identical genetically, differences within pairs of identical twins estimate nonshared family environment and error. Thus, subtracting the identical twin correlation from 1.0 estimates the portion of phenotypic variance due to nonshared family environment and error. Twin studies estimate shared environmental variance as what is left of the phenotypic variance after genetic variance (estimated as twice the difference between the identical and fraternal twin correlations) and variance due to nonshared environment and error are removed. For example, if the correlations for identical and fraternal twins for a particular trait are .50 and .25, respectively, genetic variance is estimated as 50% (twice the difference between the identical and fraternal twin correlations). Environmental variance (including error) is also 50%, and all of the environmental variance is of the nonshared variety (1.0—identical twin correlation). In contrast, correlations of .75 and .50 for identical and fraternal twins, respectively, suggest 50% genetic variance, 25% nonshared environmental variance, and 25% shared environmental variance. The multiple regression approach to twin data, mentioned in chapter 1, is useful because it not only estimates the shared environment parameter but also provides a standard error of estimate (DeFries & Fulker, in press).

In summary, shared environment can be estimated in three ways: 1) from the correlation for genetically unrelated children reared together in the same adoptive families, 2) from the difference in correlations for relatives reared together and relatives adopted apart, and 3) from twin studies, as the remainder of phenotypic variance when genetic variance, variance due to nonshared environment, and error are removed. Environmental variance not due to shared environment is called nonshared environment. This component is usually estimated as the remainder of phenotypic variance once variance due to heredity, shared environment, and error of measurement is removed. Differences within pairs of identical twins reared together provides a direct estimate of nonshared environment as experienced by identical twins.

Shared environment cannot be assumed to be the same for twins and nontwin siblings. Twins are likely to experience more shared environment than is experienced by other relatives because twins are exactly the same age and thus are exposed to fluctuating environmental factors at the same time. Furthermore, it should be mentioned that the distinction between shared and nonshared environment is not limited to family relationships in which relatives are the same age such as twins or relatives who are nearly the same age such as siblings. We can also consider shared and nonshared environmental factors that affect the resemblance between parents and their offspring. In this case, shared environment refers to environmental influences that increase resemblance between parents and offspring. Shared environment does not assess all parental influences on offspring, only those that increase phenotypic similarity between parents and their offspring. A related issue is that shared environmental influences are not necessarily limited to events that occur within the home. The term *shared* refers to any environmental influences that increase the similarity of members of the same family regardless of the location of the experience. For example, attending the same schools and sharing the same friends might be sources of shared environment for siblings in addition to the more obvious sources such as sharing the same parents.

One final preliminary issue should be mentioned. What is the relevance of nonshared environment to the study of singletons? Because over 80% of U.S. families have more than one child, it is important to understand why children in a family are so different from one another even if nonshared environmental influences found in studies of siblings do not generalize to singletons. However, it is likely that the search for answers to the question why children in the same family are so different will also yield clues as to environmental factors important for singletons as well as siblings. The search for nonshared environmental influences will be aided by a methodological focus on differences between children in a family, a focus that could provide heightened sensitivity to subtle nuances of children's experience. The important point in the present context, however, is the obvious one that the study of singletons cannot isolate factors that make two children in the same family different from one another. Because this is the best clue that we have as to the source of environmental variance relevant to psychological development, it makes sense to focus on environmental sources of differences between children in the same family and then to explore generalizability of such findings.

Evidence of the Importance of Nonshared Environment

This section provides a brief review of behavioral genetic research in personality, psychopathology, and cognition and leads to the conclusion that the most important source of environmental variance in development is nonshared environment.

Personality

The importance of nonshared family environment was first highlighted by Loehlin and Nichols (1976) whose twin analyses of personality data led to the following conclusion:

> Thus, a consistent—though perplexing—pattern is emerging from the data (and it is not purely idiosyncratic to our study). Environment carries substantial weight in determining personality—it appears to account for at least half the variance—but that environment is one for which twin pairs are correlated close to zero. . . . In short, in the personality domain we seem to see environmental effects that operate almost randomly with respect to the sorts of variables that psychologists (and other people) have traditionally deemed important in personality development. (p. 92)

Loehlin and Nichols reached this conclusion because identical and fraternal twin correlations were consistently about .50 and .30, respectively, in this large study of high-school-aged twins that used self-report personality questionnaires. This pattern of correlations suggests 40% genetic variance and 60% environmental variance—over 80% of the latter is of the nonshared variety.

These results are not peculiar to Loehlin and Nichols' study of high-school twins. In a review of 10 recent twin studies of personality (Goldsmith, 1983), the average twin correlations were .47 (identical) and .23 (fraternal). This pattern of twin correlations suggests that heredity accounts for 50% of the variance and that nonshared environment explains the rest.

It might seem odd to report average correlations across a domain as diverse as personality. Nonetheless, the twin results are generally similar across the dozens of traits measured by self-report questionnaires. For example, consider the two "super-factors" in personality, extraversion and neuroticism, which are associated with Eysenck (e.g., 1965) but also emerge as major second-order factors from other personality questionnaires such as Cattell's Sixteen Personality Factor

Questionnaire (Cattell, Eber, & Tatsuoka, 1970). A study of over 12,000 adult twin pairs in Sweden (Floderus-Myrhed, Pedersen, & Rasmuson, 1980) revealed twin correlations of .51 (identical) and .21 (fraternal) for extraversion and .50 and .23 for neuroticism. Similar results emerge for less central dimensions of personality as well. Loehlin and Nichols' study employed the California Psychological Inventory that includes diverse scales such as Sense of Well-Being, Tolerance, and Good Impression. The identical and fraternal twin correlations, respectively, for these scales were: .50 and .30, .53 and .35, and .48 and .30. Another example involves twin results for a new personality questionnaire called the Differential Personality Questionnaire which assesses nontraditional dimensions of personality. A twin study of over 200 identical twin pairs and over 100 fraternal twin pairs yielded the following sampling of correlations for identical and fraternal twins, respectively: .50 and .36 for Danger Seeking; .61 and .37 for Authoritarianism; and .58 and .25 for Alienation (Lykken, Tellegen, & DeRubeis, 1978). The only personality trait that appears to show significant shared family environmental influence is masculinity-femininity, which one might argue falls more in the category of attitudes than personality (Loehlin, 1982).

These studies employed self-report questionnaires. Perhaps some artifact exists so that identical twins always rate themselves as 50% similar when asked about their personality. However, other assessment procedures yield generally similar results. For example, in recent years, several twin studies using parental ratings of children's personality have been reported (reviewed by Buss & Plomin, 1984). The average identical twin correlation is about .50, again suggesting that about half of the variance is due to nonshared environment. There is some evidence that, for both self-report and parental-rating data, molecular (narrow or specific) measures yield greater identical twin correlations than do molar (broad or general) measures (Plomin, 1981). The few studies that have employed objective observations of personality yield less evidence for nonshared environmental variance than do paper-and-pencil questionnaires (Plomin & Foch, 1980). Nonetheless, estimates of nonshared environmental influence from these studies are still substantial—usually greater than estimates of shared environmental variance—even when error variance is considered.

Studies of nontwin siblings and other family relationships confirm the hypothesis that shared environment accounts for a negligible amount of environmental variance relevant to personality development. For example, one of the earliest studies found an average sibling correlation of .12 (Crook, 1937). A recent large family study (Ahern, Johnson, Wilson, McClearn, & Vandenberg, 1982) yielded an average sibling correlation of .16 for three widely used personality questionnaires: Cattell's Sixteen Personality Factor Questionnaire (average sibling correlation = .10), the Comrey Personality Inventory (.19), and the Eysenck Personality Inventory (.14). The average parent/offspring correlation in the latter study was .12 for father/son, .10 for father/daughter, .13 for mother/son, and .14 for mother/daughter. Four recently reported adoption studies of personality indicate that this modest familial resemblance is not due to shared environment—the average adoptive sibling correlation is .04 and the average adoptive parent/adopted child correlation is .05 (Loehlin, 1985; Loehlin, Horn, & Willerman, 1981; Scarr, Weber, Weinberg, & Wittig, 1981; Scarr & Weinberg, 1981). Adoptive sibling correlations are also low in the first report of infant adoptive siblings, involving 61 pairs at 12 months and 50 pairs at 24 months as part of the Colorado Adoption Project (Daniels, 1985). Parental ratings of temperament yielded average adoptive sibling correlations of .11 at 12 months and .05 at 24 months; tester ratings on the Infant Behavior Record yielded average adoptive sibling correlations of -.14 at 12 months and .05 at 24 months.

Psychopathology

Behavioral genetic data on psychopathology are also consistent with the hypothesis that environmental variation is preponderantly of the nonshared variety. For example, a recent review of familial concordance rates for schizophrenia in a dozen studies found about 10% concordance for first-degree relatives (Gottesman & Shields, 1982). The concordance for fraternal twins is also about 10%; however, the concordance for identical twins is twice as high, about 20%. This suggests that most familial resemblance for schizophrenia is due to hereditary similarity. This hypothesis is confirmed by recent adoption studies in Denmark in which the same concordance of about 10% is found for individuals adopted away from a first-degree schizophrenic relative. This suggests that sharing the same family environment with a schizophrenic relative does not increase concordance. Manic-depressive psychosis yields similar results (Plomin, DeFries, & McClearn, 1980). Environmental influences on less severe forms of psychopathology such as neuroses and alcoholism also appear to be predominantly nonshared. Sibling concordances are generally less than 20% and, when twin and adoption studies have been conducted, most of this familial resemblance is found to be genetic in origin (Fuller & Thompson, 1978; Rosenthal, 1970). In other words, the most important influence by far in psychopathology lies in the category of nonshared environment.

Cognition

Until recently, environmental variance that affects individual differences in IQ was thought to fall primarily in the category of shared family environment. In 11 studies, the average IQ correlation for adoptive siblings is .30, suggesting that 30% of the variance in IQ scores is due to shared family environmental influences (Bouchard & McGue, 1981). Adoptive parent/adopted child IQ correlations are lower, about .20, but still suggest a substantial influence of shared family environment. Twin studies agree: The average IQ correlations in over 30 studies is .85 for identical twins and .58 for fraternal twins (Bouchard & McGue, 1981), which suggests again that about 30% of the variance of IQ scores can be accounted for by shared family environment.

Although these data appear to converge on the reasonable conclusion that shared family environment accounts for a substantial portion of environmental variance relevant to IQ, doubts have begun to arise. Twins share family environment to a greater extent than do nontwin siblings—the IQ correlation for fraternal twins is about .60 and the correlation for nontwin siblings is about .40—which means that the twin method substantially overestimates the importance of shared family environment in relation to nontwin families. The crucial piece of evidence in support of substantial shared environmental variance is the correlation of .30 for adoptive siblings reared together. However, with two exceptions, these studies have included adoptive siblings still living at home. The first exception was a study of postadolescent adoptee pairs by Scarr and Weinberg (1978, b) that found a correlation of -.03 for IQ. This suggests the important possibility that shared environment is important for IQ during childhood and then fades in importance after adolescence.

The results of another sibling adoption study suggests that the impact of shared environment on IQ declines even earlier, by the end of early adolescence (Kent, 1985). A battery of cognitive abilities, developed for administration over the telephone that correlated with face-to-face testing near the reliabilities of the tests, was administered to 52 pairs of adoptive siblings and 54 pairs of nonadoptive siblings with the average age of 13 years (ranging from 9 to 15 years). An unrotated first principal component, used as an index of IQ, yielded a reasonable correlation of .38 for nonadoptive siblings; however, the IQ correlation for adoptive siblings was -.16. A similar pattern of results emerged for specific cognitive abilities. The adoptive sibling correlations for verbal, spatial, perceptual speed, and memory abilities were -.06, -.07, -.10, and .16, respectively.

Because this estimate of shared environmental influence is estimated directly from the adoptive sibling correlation, reasonable confidence can be attached to these findings. For example, the sample of 52 pairs of adoptive siblings permits detection of a true correlation of .30 with 70% power; the standard error of the shared environment estimates were between .10 and .14 using the multiple regression model-fitting approach of DeFries and Fulker (in press), mentioned in chapter 1 (see also chapter 11).

Hierarchical multiple regression analyses, described in chapter 3, were conducted to determine whether shared environmental influence changes from 9 to 15 years. The interaction between co-sibling score and age in predicting sibling score was not significant, indicating that adoptive sibling resemblance does not differ as a function of age within this age group and for this relatively small sample. The results of this study extend those of Scarr and Weinberg by suggesting that the age during which shared environment declines in importance is early adolescence.

In summary, nonshared environmental influence is a major component of variance for personality, psychopathology, and IQ. Figure 4.1 is an approximate representation of the relative portions of variance accounted for by heredity, shared environment, and nonshared environment for these three domains. In the last half of this book, the relevant data are examined in considerable detail separately by developmental era. Figure 4.1 merely emphasizes the importance of nonshared environment.

Categories of Nonshared Environmental Influence

This brief review leads to the conclusion that nonshared environmental variance is the major category of environmental influence, a conclusion with far-reaching implications for the study of environmental influences on development. Previous studies have been conceptualized in terms of shared influences; nearly all previous research has studied only one child per family on the assumption that other children in the same family will experience a similar environment. The fact that children in the same family experience quite different environments points to the need for a reconceptualization of theories and measures of environmental influence. This reconceptualization need not be as drastic as it might first appear, however, because any environmental factor can be viewed in terms of its contribution to nonshared environmental variance rather than to shared environment. For example, parental affection can easily be construed as a source of differences among children in the same family, for most parents are more affectionate toward one child than another. Moreover, siblings might perceive differences in their parents' affection even when such differences do not exist. Divorce can serve as another example. Although divorce happens to the entire family and is usually considered to be a shared environmental factor, divorce probably differentially affects children in the same family.

If such factors are important within families, why are they not also important between families? That is, if it makes a difference that a parent loves one child more than another, why does it not make a difference that, across families, some parents love their children more than other parents love their children? In fact, there is no necessary relationship between the relative importance of shared and nonshared environment and whether relationships will be found between specific measures of the family environment and developmental outcomes of children. That is, environmental factors that create differences within families can act independently of factors that cause differences between families, even when the same factor is involved—parental love, for example. A child really knows only his own parents; the child does not know if his parents love him more or less than other parents love their children. However, a child is likely to be painfully aware

PERSONALITY

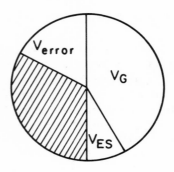

SCHIZOPHRENIA

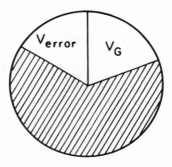

IQ (AFTER ADOLESCENCE)

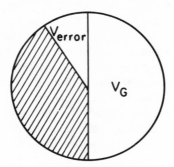

FIG. 4.1. The relative importance of nonshared environmental variance (shaded area) as compared to variance due to genetic influence (V_G), shared environmental influence (V_{ES}), and error (V_{error}).

TABLE 4.1
Categories of Nonshared Environmental Influence[a]

Categories	Examples
Error of measurement	Test-retest unreliability
Nonsystematic	Accidents, illnesses
Systematic	
Sibling interaction	Differential treatment; de-identification
Parental treatment	Differential treatment
Family structure	Birth order; sibling spacing
Extra-familial networks	Peer groups; teachers

[a]From Rowe and Plomin (1981).

that parental affection toward him is less than toward his sibling. Thus, nonshared experiences can be unrelated to shared experiences.

Categories of environmental factors that make children in the same family different from one another have been suggested by Rowe and Plomin (1981). Their scheme is presented in Table 4.1. As mentioned earlier, error of measurement is included in the variance assigned to within-family differences. Clearly, nonsystematic, serendipitous, or idiosyncratic events such as accidents, illnesses, and other trauma can have a marked effect on development, as biographies frequently attest. For example, in his autobiography, Darwin provides an example:

> The voyage of the *Beagle* has been by far the most important event in my life, and has determined my whole career; yet it depended on so small a circumstance as my uncle offering to drive me thirty miles to Shrewsbury, which few uncles would have done, and on such a trifle as the shape of my nose. (From F. Darwin, 1892, p. 28)

Darwin's comment about his nose refers to the quixotic captain of the *Beagle*, Captain Fitz-Roy, who nearly rejected Darwin for the trip because of the shape of his nose which indicated to Fitz-Roy that Darwin would not possess sufficient energy and determination for the voyage. Darwin wrote that, during the voyage, Fitz-Roy became convinced that "my nose had spoken falsely" (p. 27).

However, such capricious events are likely to prove a dead end for research. As reasonable as it seems to assume that nonshared environmental influences may be stochastic events that, when compounded over time, make children in the same family different from one another, systematic factors might also account for some nonshared environment.

Assessing Specific Nonshared Environmental Influences

In terms of systematic nonshared environmental influences, family structure variables such as birth order and spacing of siblings are most often studied. However, studies of differential environments provided by parents, peers, and siblings themselves are more promising.

Family Structure: Birth Order and Spacing

The only specific source of nonshared family environments to receive considerable attention is family structure—primarily birth order, spacing, and family size. For example, over 1,000 entries for "birth order" appear in Psychological Abstracts. Birth order is the prototype of nonshared environmental influences and cannot originate in genetic differences among siblings; paradoxically, however, most studies have analyzed its effect across families rather than within families. For example, studies describe the average IQ of children of different birth orders, family sizes, and spacing and find relationships for these aggregate data: Lower average IQs are found for children born later, with smaller spacing, and in larger families. However, the relationships are weak—for example, at each level of family size, IQ declines one to two points between birth ranks.

Zajonc and Markus (1975; Zajonc, 1983) developed a model called the *confluence model* to explain the within-family processes leading to lowered IQ in children born later, with smaller spacing, and in larger families. In brief, the model hypothesizes two influences: the overall intellectual level of the family environment and the presence of a younger sibling to teach. Although the confluence model is clearly a model of nonshared environmental influence, data aggregated across families have usually been used to test it. At the level of aggregate data, the model does well. For example, the model was originally developed to explain the aggregate IQ data for 368,114 nineteen-year-old men in the Netherlands (Belmont & Marolla, 1973), and it explains 97% of the variance of the aggregate data. The model is as successful in explaining aggregate data for a sample of 686,606 U.S. high school students (Breland, 1974). However, when individual IQ scores are considered rather than national averages for the various birth order groups, family size and birth order explain less than 2% of the variance in the Dutch data (Galbraith, 1982) and in the U.S. data (Svanum & Bringle, 1980).

Similarly, when the confluence model is applied to IQ scores of individual family members, little support for the model can be found (Galbraith, 1982; Grotevant, Scarr, & Weinberg, 1977; Pfouts, 1980; Rodgers, 1984). When SES is controlled, about 2% of the IQ variance can be explained by the model (Grotevant et al., 1977). Only one study (Berbaum & Moreland, 1980) concluded that the confluence model explains a substantial amount of variance of individual IQ scores; however, the fact that this study employed mental age rather than IQ greatly inflates the apparent variance explained by the confluence model (Galbraith, 1982). One interesting recent study (Rodgers & Rowe, 1985) used the Fels longitudinal IQ data for siblings and examined sibling IQ correlations as a function of the siblings' birth order. If birth order contributes to differences within sibling pairs, sibling correlations should be lower for pairs more distant in birth order. However, Rodgers and Rowe found that sibling IQ correlations did not differ as a function of the pairs' birth order.

Although most of the recent research on birth order and other family structure variables has focused on IQ, the picture remains unclear. It is also unclear for other domains. For example, for personality, birth order relationships are difficult to document (Schooler, 1972), although here, too, debate continues as to the importance of family structure variables (Ernst & Angst, 1983; Wagner, Schubert, & Schubert, 1979).

Family Structure: Deidentification

A specific theory involving birth order is the deidentification hypothesis (Schacter, Shore, Feldman-Rotman, Marquis, & Campbell, 1976; Schacter & Stone, 1985). This theory makes a prediction opposite to that of the confluence model, although deidentification is not thought to apply to IQ. Siblings with contiguous birth orders are hypothesized to be more jealous and to "deidentify"—that is, develop contrasting characteristics—to a greater extent than do "jump pairs." Similarly, same-sex pairs are hypothesized to deidentify more than opposite-sex pairs. Some support for the theory has been found, although it is not yet clear how much nonshared environmental variance can be explained by the deidentification process.

Other Attempts to Identify Specific Nonshared Environmental Influences

Few other attempts to identify sources of nonshared environment have been reported. In exploring possible nonshared influences, the first step is to ask whether siblings in a family have different experiences. If siblings do not differ in their experience for a particular measure of the environment, then the measure cannot be a source of developmental differences between siblings. For family structure variables, this first step is unnecessary because siblings obviously differ in birth order, spacing, and gender. Experiential differences, however, cannot be assumed to affect behavioral differences within pairs of siblings—demonstrating that nonshared experiences relate to differences in sibling behavior is the second step in research on specific nonshared environmental influences. The third step is to describe the direction of effects when associations are found between differential experience and differences in sibling behaviors. Do siblings' differences in experience affect or merely reflect differences in siblings' behavior?

One systematic approach to the topic is the construction of the Sibling Inventory of Differential Experience (SIDE; Daniels & Plomin, 1985). The 73-item SIDE asks each sibling to compare his or her experiences to those of a sibling in the domains of sibling interaction, parental treatment, peer characteristics, and events specific to the individual. For all items, siblings are asked to compare their relative experiences rather than to make absolute judgments about their experience. For example, rather than asking the extent to which "my sibling and I show understanding for each other," SIDE asks, "Who has shown more understanding for the other?" A 5-point scale is used for the siblings' ratings: 1 = My sibling has been much more this way than I have; 2 = My sibling has been a bit more this way than I have; 3 = My sibling and I have been the same in this way; 4 = I have been a bit more this way than my sibling; and 5 = I have been much more this way than my sibling. This provides relative scores indicating, for example, which sibling feels more loved by parents and how much more. Although somewhat unusual, these relative judgments have several advantages: They should be easier to make than absolute judgments; they do not require that a sibling difference be calculated in order to assess within-family environment; and they can be used when data are available from only one member of a sibling pair. The SIDE can also be coded to indicate the absolute rather than relative amount of differential sibling experience by disregarding the direction of the differential experience (i.e., 0 = no difference in sibling experiences; 1 = some difference; 2 = much difference).

The 11 scales of the SIDE (see Table 4.2) were devised using the results of factor analyses of data on a sample of 396 siblings ages 12 to 28 years and from the Denver metropolitan area. The word *differential* precedes the label for each scale because all items involve relative (differential) ratings. The 2-week, test-retest reliabilities are reasonable, with a mean of .84 and a range from .70 to .94. The scales are virtually independent of siblings' age, birth order, and sex. Also included in the table are sibling agreement correlations that indicate that siblings agree substantially as to differences in their interaction and in their peer groups. The sibling agreement correlations are .55, .73, and .60 concerning which sibling's peer group was more college oriented, delinquent, and popular, respectively. Siblings also agreed substantially as to which sibling was more jealous ($r = .56$) and to which sibling displayed more caretaking ($r = .56$). Siblings did not agree, however, on differences in parental treatment, especially concerning which sibling received more maternal affection ($r = .10$). Because the SIDE intentionally assesses siblings' perceptions of their differential experience, sibling agreement is not an important criterion for the usefulness of the measure as long as the measure is reliable. Other substantive data from the SIDE are interwoven throughout the following discussion.

Parental Treatment.   Traditional environmental research focuses on parental treatment because parents would seem to be the major environmental

TABLE 4.2
Scales of Nonshared Environmental Influence from the *Sibling Inventory of Differential Experience* (SIDE)[a]

Category	Scale	Test–Retest Reliability	Sibling Agreement
Sibling interaction	Differential Sibling Antagonism	.83	.34
	Differential Sibling Jealousy	.93	.56
	Differential Sibling Caretaking	.89	.56
	Differential Sibling Closeness	.70	.23
Parental treatment	Differential Maternal Affection	.82	.10
	Differential Maternal Control	.77	.25
	Differential Parental Affection	.77	.32
	Differential Paternal Control	.85	.49
Peers	Differential Peer College Orientation	.88	.55
	Differential Peer Delinquency	.94	.73
	Differential Peer Popularity	.84	.60

[a]From Daniels and Plomin (1985).

force in young children's lives. However, it has not been easy to document parental effects on children's development. A recent review of the relationship between parental treatment and children's development concludes that "in most cases, the relationships that have appeared are not large, if one thinks in terms of the amount of variance accounted for" (Maccoby & Martin, 1983, p. 82). Indeed, these findings led the authors to argue for the need to examine intrafamilial variation in the parent-child relationship. As mentioned earlier, there is no necessary connection between finding relationships between parental treatment and children's development across families and finding that nonshared environment accounts for most of the environmental variance. Nonetheless, if environment-development relationships are not found across families, it increases the reasonableness and usefulness of exploring differential parental treatment within families.

How similarly or differently do parents treat their several offspring? The SIDE data indicate that siblings perceive their parents to treat them quite similarly: Only 9% of the siblings report "much difference" in their parents' treatment on the average across nine parental treatment items. For the four SIDE scales that assess parental treatment, the mean absolute score is .50 (0 refers to no reported difference in sibling experiences, 1 indexes some difference, and 2 indicates much difference). Other categories of nonshared environmental influence show greater differentiation within sibling pairs and are thus more likely to be important sources of nonshared environmental influence. Nonetheless, it is possible that small differences in siblings' perceptions of their parents' treatment lead to large differences in the siblings' development.

Another study of adolescent siblings found similar results, not just for adolescents' reports of their parents' treatment, but also for the parents' reports of their treatment of their children (Daniels, Dunn, Furstenberg, & Plomin, 1985). The 1981 follow-up of the longitudinal National Survey of Children (Furstenberg, Winquist-Nord, Peterson, & Zill, 1983) included 348 families with two siblings 11 to 17 years of age (mean age = 13.7 years) from a nationally representative sample of 1077 families. In telephone interviews, each sibling and mother was interviewed individually concerning family cooperation, family stress, parental rule and chore expectations, closeness to mother and father, and child's say in decisions. In contrast to the SIDE study, the ratings of environment in this study are absolute in that parents and siblings were not asked to rate parental treatment as it differed between the siblings. Sibling intraclass correlations for the measures of parental treatment, as rated by parents and by the siblings themselves, are listed in Table 4.3. The sibling correlations indicate the extent to which parents and siblings themselves perceive that siblings share similar parental treatment. These data indicate that parents themselves perceive that they treat their two children quite similarly—the sibling correlations range from .38 to .65. Unlike the evidence for consistency of parental treatment from the SIDE study, the siblings themselves do not perceive their parents' treatment of them to be highly similar—the sibling correlations average about .20. However, reliability creates a ceiling for such correlations and, without information on reliability, it is difficult to compare correlations from different studies.

Two twin studies using "absolute" ratings of adolescents' perceptions of parental treatment (Rowe, 1981, 1983) found substantial correlations within twin pairs for parental treatment, although the correlations were lower than in the SIDE research, which employs "relative" or differential ratings. Different measures of parental affection and control were used in the two twin studies, and correlations of about .45 emerged. It makes sense that sibling correlations for absolute ratings of parental treatment are lower than those for relative ratings because the absolute rating procedure asks each sibling to rate his parents' treatment in relation to all other parents and differences within families are used to compute a correlation. The relative approach is more direct for assessing differences in siblings' experiences because it asks them about parental treatment specifically in comparison to their sibling.

Two analyses of sibling data in the Colorado Adoption Project include the first "objective" data concerning parental behavior. Sibling correlations were reported for the interview/observation measure, Home Observation for Measurement of the Environment (HOME; Caldwell & Bradley, 1978), for 133 sibling pairs in which both members of each pair were studied at 12 months of age and 103 sibling pairs studied at 24 months (Daniels, 1985). The average sibling spacing was nearly 3 years, nonetheless, the sibling correlations for the HOME were nearly as great as the stability of the HOME measure for all individuals

TABLE 4.3
Sibling Intraclass Correlations (N = 299–348 pairs) for
Environmental Measures in the National Survey of Children Sample[a]

Environmental Measure	Parental Ratings	Sibling Ratings
Parental rule expectations	—	.18*
Parental chore expectations	.49*	.21*
Maternal closeness	.38*	.19*
Paternal closeness	.49*	.26*
Child's say in decisions	.65*	.18*

[a]From Daniels, Dunn, Furstenberg, and Plomin (1985).
*$p < .05$.

from 12 to 24 months. When the siblings were studied at the age of 12 months, the sibling correlation for a general factor of the HOME was .42; the sibling correlation at 24 months was .43. Sibling correlations at 12 months for the Family Environment Scales (Moos & Moos, 1981) also approached the one-year stability of the measure.

The most impressive results suggesting that parents treat their children similarly within families come from a longitudinal study of 50 families in which mothers were videotaped while interacting with each of two siblings when each child was 12 months old (Dunn, Plomin, & Nettles, 1985). The children were nearly 3 years apart in age, which means that the observations of maternal behavior toward the two children were separated by nearly 3 years. Maternal behavior was reliably assessed, and factor analysis yielded three factors: affection, verbal attention, and control. The results indicate that the mothers were incredibly consistent in their behavior toward their two children at the same age: Corrected for unreliability, the average correlation for maternal behavior toward two siblings was .70. These data suggest that differential maternal treatment of their children in infancy does not appear to be a major source of the marked individual differences within pairs of siblings. Other longitudinal studies on this topic agree that mothers are quite consistent in their behavior toward their two children when studied at the same age (Abramovitch, Pepler, & Corter, 1982; Dunn & Kendrick, 1982; Jacobs & Moss, 1976).

However, siblings are different in age. Subsequent work by Dunn and her colleagues on 2-year-olds suggested that mothers were especially consistent in their affection and verbal responsiveness to their two children when they were 24 months old, but differed to a greater extent in their controlling behavior towards the two children. However, the results indicated that even though mothers treated their two children quite similarly when the children were the same age, longitudinal analyses from 12 to 24 months showed little stability for maternal behavior to the same child. The authors suggest that rank-ordering of the mothers on these dimensions changes from 12 to 24 months because different mothers respond differently to the new developmental advances of children:

Thus, differences between the mothers in their response to the delights and demands of 2-year-olds do not bear a close relation to the differences between the same mothers in their behavior toward 12-month-olds, although at both ages mothers are remarkably consistent in their affection and verbal responsiveness to their successive children. (Dunn, Plomin, & Daniels, in press)

The implication of these results is that, in a cross-sectional slice of time, one sibling is older and is treated quite differently, at least when direct observations are used and when the siblings are infants. However, the self-report data for adolescents suggest that adolescent siblings perceive that their parents treat them quite similarly. These differing results may be due to different methods— observation versus self-report questionnaire—or different ages—infancy versus adolescence.

Thus, questions remain concerning the first-level question of the extent of differential parental treatment. It is an important question because we would not expect parental treatment to be a major source of nonshared environmental influence if they treat their several children similarly. Nonetheless, as mentioned earlier, it is possible that small differences in parental treatment lead to large differences in development.

Sibling Interaction.   The possibility that siblings' interactions with each other are a source of nonshared environmental influences has not been studied as much as parental treatment. However, it is noteworthy that the results of intensive observational studies of mother-sibling-sibling triads emphasize the importance of sibling-sibling interactions (Dunn, 1983; Dunn & Kendrick, 1982). Twin data on sibling interaction have been reported for 88 pairs of high-school twins (Rowe & Plomin, 1981). For a Liking scale, the correlation for all 88 pairs of twins was .61, indicating that twins' liking and disliking of each other is mutual. However, twins generally like each other (the average response was 4.4 on a 5-point scale), which means that this result involves only a small amount of variance. Two other scales, Respect and Understanding, yielded more variance than the Liking scale and the twin correlations were .35 and .30, respectively, indicating considerable differences within pairs of twins. These twin correlations for twins' respect for and understanding of each other are lower than those found in Rowe's studies of twins' perceptions of their parents' treatment, thus suggesting that siblings provide more nonshared environment than do parents.

The SIDE explores sibling interaction extensively with scales that assess differential sibling antagonism, caretaking, jealousy, and closeness. As indicated earlier, only 9% of the siblings report "much difference" in their parents' treatment on the average and the mean absolute score is .50. In contrast, 19% of the siblings report "much difference" in their siblings' treatment of them and the mean absolute score is .80 (Daniels & Plomin, 1985).

Peer Characteristics. The only report of peers as a possible source of differential experience for siblings employed the SIDE (Daniels & Plomin, 1985). For the 26 peer characteristic items, 20% of the siblings report that their sibling's peer group is much different from their own. The mean absolute score is .83 for the three peer scales of the SIDE, which suggests that siblings experience peer differences as great as the differences they experience in their interaction with each other.

The Relationship Between Nonshared Factors and Sibling Differences in Behavior

The first question in studies of nonshared environmental factors is whether such factors exist. The answer is clearly affirmative: Siblings in the same family experience different environments, perhaps for parental treatment, and especially in their interaction with each other and in characteristics of their peer groups. The next question is whether these differences in experience are related to differences in behavioral development. Other than studies of family structure, the first study attempting to relate nonshared environmental influences to differences in sibling behavior compared twins' reports of their own interaction and self-reported personality (Rowe & Plomin, 1981). Even though, as mentioned earlier, the Liking scale showed considerable mutuality within twin pairs, differences in twins' liking for each other related strongly to personality differences, yielding correlations as high as .50. However, the results for the other scales of twin interaction, Respect and Understanding, were mixed.

The study of adolescent siblings from the National Survey of Children (Daniels et al., 1985) related differential parental treatment to differences in siblings' adjustment. As in all studies of personality and psychopathology, siblings are only moderately similar, with correlations of about .20, which means that the great majority of reliable variance is not shared by siblings. Table 4.4 lists multiple regression coefficients when sibling differences in environment (perceived by the parent or by the siblings themselves) are related to sibling differences in the various adjustment measures.

Most of the multiple regressions are significant, and adjusted R^2 values of about 10% on the average indicate that nonshared environmental influences are systematically related to differences in the siblings' adjustment. For example, the last row of Table 4 describes associations between nonshared environment and an aggregate measure of disobedience based on parent, sibling, and teacher ratings. The significant regressions indicate that, for both parental and sibling ratings of sibling experience, differential experiences of siblings are related to differences in disobedience. It is noteworthy that some significant relationships emerge when different individuals rate the siblings' adjustment and the siblings' environment. For example, parental perceptions of sibling differences in

TABLE 4.4
Multiple Regressions of Differences in Sibling Adjustment on
Differences in Sibling Environments (N = 149–226)[a]

	Multiple R's	
Adjustment Measure	Parental Ratings	Sibling Ratings
Parental perception of emotional distress	.38*	.25
Parental perception of delinquency	.37*	.25
Parental perception of disobedience	.37*	.26
Self-perception of emotional distress	.12	.28*
Self-perception of delinquency	.29*	.37*
Self-perception of dissatisfaction	—	.39*
Teacher perception of disobedience	—	.35*
Parent–teacher–sibling aggregate score of disobedience	.40*	.34*

[a]From Daniels, Dunn, Furstenberg, and Plomin (in press).
*p < .05.

environment are related to differences in the siblings' own perception of delinquency, and sibling perceptions of environmental differences are related to teacher ratings of disobedience. With regard to the specific environmental differences that relate to sibling differences in the adjustment measures, both the parent and sibling reports of the environment converge on the finding that the sibling who experiences more maternal closeness, more sibling friendliness, more say in family decision making, and more parental chore expectations, as compared to the other sibling, is more well adjusted psychologically.

Sibling differences on the SIDE have also been found to be related to differences in behavior. Daniels (in press) reported significant relationships between the SIDE scales and sibling differences on a self-report personality questionnaire. For example, differences in siblings' sociability yielded a multiple correlation of .43 when predicted by the four SIDE scales involving differential sibling interactions; the multiple correlation was .24 for sibling sociability differences as predicted by the three scales tapping differential parental treatment; and the multiple correlation was .60 for the four scales involving differential peer group characteristics. The SIDE scales also significantly predicted sibling differences in emotionality, but not in activity level. In general, differential sibling interaction and peer characteristics, but not differential parental treatment, were related to sibling personality differences.

A recent study of adoptive and nonadoptive infant siblings in the CAP did not have the advantage of using a measure such as the SIDE which was designed to assess differential sibling experiences (Daniels, 1985). However, it is noteworthy that standard measures of the environment—the HOME and FES—obtained separately when each sibling was 12 months of age, indicate little differential experience for the two siblings, as mentioned earlier. However, even these slight differential experiences of the siblings as assessed by the HOME and FES showed some association with behavioral differences between the infant siblings. Over 13% of the relationships between sibling differences on the HOME and FES and various sibling behavioral differences were statistically significant. For example, at 12 months, differences in the extent to which mothers consciously encouraged developmental advance (as measured by the HOME) correlated .31 with differences in the siblings' activity level (as assessed by the tester using the Infant Behavior Record).

Direction of Effects

Once relationships are identified between any environmental factor and children's development, one can address the issue of direction of effects: Does the environmental factor affect or merely reflect differences among children (Bell, 1968)? The direction of effects issue is just as relevant to the study of nonshared environmental influences as it is to traditional studies of shared environment. For example, differential parental affection might be related to differences in siblings' sociability because pre-existing differences in the siblings' sociability elicit differences in their parents' affection toward them. Similarly, in the example just mentioned, mothers might encourage developmental advance to a greater extent for the more active sibling because the child is more active.

Behavioral genetic designs can be profitably applied to this issue because one possible explanation for child-to-environment direction of effects is genetic differences between the siblings. As discussed in chapter 7, environmental measures can be influenced genetically, and this includes measures of nonshared environmental factors. That is, siblings might report differences in treatment that occur as a result of genetic differences between them. In order to explore this possibility, SIDE data from 222 adoptive sibling pairs were compared to data from 174 biological sibling pairs in the study by Daniels and Plomin (1985). If the SIDE reflects genetic differences, mean SIDE differences should be greater for adoptive than for biological pairs because adoptive siblings are 100% different from each other genetically for segregating genes in the absence of selective placement, whereas biological siblings are 50% different genetically. Samples of this size have 80% power to detect mean differences in experience that account for as little as 2% of the variance. In general, the SIDE measures of differential experience were similar for the adoptive and nonadoptive siblings: correlations of .69 for adoptive siblings and .76 for biological siblings. Thus, the SIDE scales do not suggest much genetic influence, which implies that the origins of perceived differential experience are indeed environmental. However, 4 of the 11 SIDE scales yielded significantly greater differences within adoptive pairs than within biological pairs; these results are discussed in chapter 7.

The Dunn et al. (1985) observational study of mothers' behavior toward each of two siblings when each child was 12 months old indicated that mothers were quite consistent in their behavior toward the two children. However, this study of 50 families included both adoptive and nonadoptive families, and it was revealed that mothers were more different in their affection toward adoptive siblings than toward nonadoptive siblings. This finding suggests genetic influence on mothers' differential affection toward their children. Other scales of maternal behavior did not suggest genetic influence, and a follow-up study when the siblings were 24 months of age replicated these findings (Dunn, Plomin, & Daniels, in press). The possible genetic influence on parental differences in affection toward siblings suggests caution in assuming that nonshared influences are truly environmental in origin.

Dissertation research of Daniels (1985) suggested possible genetic influence on differential parental treatment of siblings as assessed by the HOME. The sibling correlations for nonadoptive and adoptive siblings, respectively, are .49 and .34 at 12 months and .46 and .40 at 24 months for the HOME general factor. For the HOME toys factor, the respective correlations are .44 and .29 at 12 months and .53 and .32 at 24 months.

Even more important is the issue of genetic mediation of relationships between nonshared environmental influences and differences in siblings' development. If an environmental measure shows no genetic influence, it is unlikely that its relationship to children's development is mediated genetically; however, there are ways to take into account the possibility of genetic mediation of relationships between environment and development, as discussed in chapter 8.

One approach is to study experiential differences within pairs of identical twins as they relate to behavioral differences within the twin pairs. Because identical twins share exactly the same heredity, differences within pairs cannot be explained by genetic differences. Twin studies also offer the option of assessing possible genetic influences on these within-family relationships by comparing the relationship between experiential and behavioral differences within identical twin pairs to the relationship within fraternal twin pairs. If heredity affects these relationships, the correlations will be greater for fraternal twins than for identical twins because differences within pairs of fraternal twins are due to genetic differences as well as nonshared environmental influences.

Although this approach has not been employed systematically, the study by Rowe and Plomin (1981) mentioned earlier examined the relationship between differences in interpersonal treatment of the twins and differences in self-reported personality. The authors noted that the relationships between twin differences in the measures of nonshared environment and twin differences in the measures of personality were generally weak for both identical and fraternal twins. The fact that the fraternal twin correlations were no greater than the identical twin correlations suggests that what little relationship exists between nonshared environment (as measured in this study in terms of the twin interpersonal relationship) and personality does not appear to be mediated by heredity. Even if it can be shown that nonshared environmental influences are not merely reflecting genetic differences within pairs of siblings, this does not prove that the measured nonshared environmental influence causes behavioral differences within pairs. It is possible, for example, that behavioral differences within pairs of siblings originate from prior environmental influences and are merely indexed by the measure of nonshared environment.

As mentioned earlier, twins probably share more environmental influences than do nontwin siblings. For this reason, the use of the identical twin method might be lacking in power to identify relationships between nonshared environmental influences and twin behavioral differences that are independent of hereditary differences between nontwin siblings. Another method that is less direct but might prove to be more generalizable to the nontwin situation is to compare correlations between nonshared environmental influences and behavioral differences for pairs of adoptive and nonadoptive siblings. Behavioral differences within pairs of nonadoptive siblings could be either genetic or environmental in origin because siblings are 50% different genetically for segregating genes. However, in the absence of selective placement, adoptive sibling pairs are 100% different genetically. Thus, if nonshared environmental measures reflect genetic differences within pairs of siblings, we would expect correlations for sibling differences in environment and in behavior to be greater for adoptive siblings than for nonadoptive siblings. The original SIDE study did not include a sufficient number of sibling pairs in which both members of the pair completed a personality questionaire to permit the study of personality differences within sibling pairs separately for adoptive and nonadoptive siblings. Dissertation research on this topic found little evidence for genetic mediation of relationships between nonshared environmental indices and behavioral differences using adoptive and nonadoptive infant siblings (Daniels, 1985).

Conclusion

It was less than a decade ago that the importance of nonshared family environment was brought to the attention of developmentalists. In this short time, the following conclusions have become warranted, at least as hypotheses for future research:

Behavioral genetic studies consistently point to nonshared environmental influences as the most important source of environmental variance for personality and psychopathology and IQ after adolescence.

When more than one child is studied per family, it is apparent that siblings in the same family experience considerably different environments, in terms of their treatment of each other and their peer interactions, and perhaps in terms of parental treatment. Family structure variables such as birth order and spacing appear to account for only a small portion of the variance of sibling differences in development.

Differences in siblings' experiences relate significantly to siblings' differences in behavior, implying that nonshared environmental influences are at least in part systematic.

Measures of nonshared environment do not primarily reflect genetic differences between children in the same family.

5 Genotype-Environment Interaction

Stimulating environments foster development of gifted children and overwhelm slow learners. Life's slings and arrows are more stressful for emotionally reactive children. Traditional, highly structured classrooms create behavioral problems for active children. These are hypothetical examples of interaction, and—to the extent that heredity is involved in learning ability, emotionality, and activity—they are also examples of possible genotype-environment interaction. Genotype-environment interaction denotes an interaction in the statistical, analysis-of-variance sense of a conditional relationship: The effect of environmental factors depends on genotype.

It is reasonable to expect that genotype-environment interactions are important in development. Indeed, it seems odd that so much environmental research has been devoted to finding "main effects," environmental influences that affect all children on the average. In this chapter, the concept of genotype-environment interaction, methods to assess it, and results of research on the topic are discussed.

Genotype-Environment Interaction vs. Interactionism

In the developmental literature, it is not uncommon to read that the separate effects of genotype cannot be analyzed because "they interact," a view that has been called *interactionism* (Plomin, DeFries, & Loehlin, 1977). Usually, interactionism merely connotes the truism that behavior cannot occur unless there is both an organism (nature) and an environment (nurture)—as indicated in the frequently cited quotation, "the organism is a product of its genes and its past environment" (Anastasi, 1958, p. 197). It is certainly true that for an individual there can be no behavior without both environment and genes. However, as discussed in chapter 1, behavioral genetics does not address the causes of behavior of a single individual but rather the causes of differences among individuals in a population. Environmental differences can occur when genetic differences do not exist (for example, individual differences observed within pairs of identical twins). Also, genetic differences can be expressed in the absence of environmental differences (for example, differences among animals of a genetically heterogeneous population reared in the same controlled laboratory environment).

If interactionism were to be believed in the realm of individual differences, it would imply that "main effects" cannot be found because everything interacts with everything else. If this view is taken seriously, it implies that one cannot study environmental influences just as much as it implies that one cannot study genetic influences, although I have never seen the issue of interactionism raised in the context of environmental studies. For example, parental contingent responsiveness could not be found to relate to children's cognitive development if nature and nurture interacted completely because each environmental factor would affect each child differently. Similarly, genetic "main effects" could not be found. For example, adopted-away children of bright biological parents would have the same average IQ as adopted-away children of less bright parents if nature and nurture interacted completely. To the contrary, main effects have been isolated, especially substantial genetic main effects.

A legitimate concern underlying interactionism and organismic theories in general is an emphasis on the child's active, seeking out or even creating environments. This concern is addressed by genotype-environment correlation, discussed in the next chapter.

In behavioral genetics, *interaction* refers to the usual meaning of the word: "The phenomenon is well named. Interaction variations are those attributable not to either of two influences acting alone but to joint effects of the two acting together" (Guilford & Fruchter, 1973, p. 249). Interactions represent conditional relationships; that is, the relationship between X and Y depends upon another variable. In other words, if asked about the relationship between X and Y, one could only respond, "It depends."

Some hypothetical examples of genotype-environment interaction are illustrated in Fig. 5.1. Main effects and interactions are independent: Main effects can occur with no interaction as in the top example in Fig. 5.1, and interactions can occur without main effects as in the bottom example—although such reversed effects are likely to be rare. The most likely type of interaction is described in the middle example: An environmental factor has an effect only for certain children. For example, emotional and unemotional children might not differ in adjustment when reared in a stable environment (E_1); however, in an unstable environment (E_2), behavioral problems might erupt for emotional children, but not for those who are unemotional.

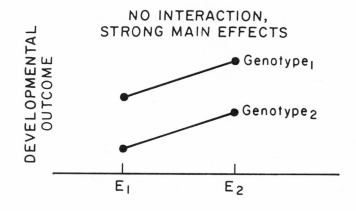

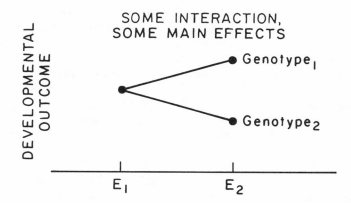

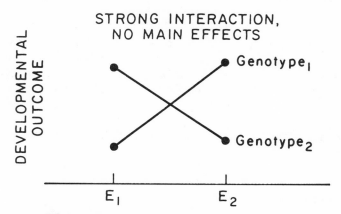

FIG. 5.1.Hypothetical genotype-environment interactions.

TABLE 5.1
Hypothetical Genetic and Environmental Deviations from the Mean
for Five Individuals When There is Interaction Between Genotype
and Environment[a]

Individual	G	+	E	+	G×E	=	P
1	−2		+1		−2		−3
2	−1		−2		+2		−1
3	0		0		0		0
4	1		+2		+2		+5
5	2		−1		−2		−1
	$V_G = 2.0$		$V_E = 2.0$		$V_{G \times E} = 3.2$		$V_P = 2.0 + 2.0$ + 3.2 = 7.2

[a]Adapted from Plomin, DeFries, and Loehlin (1977).

A hypothetical numerical example of this type of interaction is contained in Table 5.1. The example assumes that genetic deviations, environmental deviations, and deviations due to genotype-environment interaction are known. To keep the example simple, the five individuals in the example are considered as constituting a population rather than a sample, thus ignoring problems of sampling and computing variances by dividing the summed squared deviations by N rather than $N - 1$. Genetic deviations and environmental deviations in this example are uncorrelated—an example involving genotype-environment correlation is described in the next chapter. Genotype-environment interaction refers to nonadditive effects of genotype and environment on the phenotype; in this example, the genotype-environment interaction term is literally the product of the genetic and environmental deviations. Each individual's phenotypic deviation from the mean is the sum of his genetic deviation, environmental deviation, and deviation due to genotype-environment interaction. If these phenotypic deviations were plotted as a function of genotype and environment, it would be seen that genotype- environment interaction occurs because genotype has a large effect in positive environments and little effect in negative environments. Phenotypic variance is the sum of genetic variance, environmental variance, and variance due to genotype-environment interaction. If genotype-environment interaction of the type indicated in the example had no effect on phenotypic deviations, the phenotypic variance would be reduced from 7.2 to 4.0.

Genotype-Environment Interaction, "Reaction Range," and Canalization

Reaction range is a popular concept related to genotype-environment interaction. Reaction range refers to the possible range of phenotypic expressions of a genotype in different environmental circumstances. Although this can be construed to be genotype-environment interaction, the reaction range concept has many connotations. A frequently used example of reaction range is that substantial differences in height can occur for a particular genotype in restricted and enriched environments. Although this range of heights is referred to as this genotype's range of reaction, it is really a straightforward environmental effect. Other genotypes might show the same increase from restricted to enriched environments, and we could say that they have similarly large reaction ranges, but the environment in fact is operating as a simple main effect—increasing heights of all the genotypes in the enriched environment. Thus, if reaction ranges are similar for all genotypes, no genotype-environment interaction occurs regardless of the magnitude of the "range of action."

If reaction ranges differ across genotypes, then genotypes are responding differently to environmental treatments. This is precisely the meaning of genotype-environment interaction and no other term is needed to describe it, especially a term such as reaction range that has many vague connotations. Indeed, the connotations of the phrase may be responsible for its popularity: Reaction range suggests the notion that, regardless of genotype, an individual can grow up to be a pauper or a prince depending upon environmental circumstances. Although such plots make good fairy tales, all we can assess is environmental variance, genetic variance, and variance due to genotype-environment interaction. The term *reaction range* adds nothing to these concepts.

Another popular metaphor is Waddington's (1957) epigenetic landscape representing embryological development. The fertilized egg is depicted as a ball rolling down a terrain molded by the genotype. Environmental forces act to displace the ball; depending upon the steepness of the valley walls (canalization), the ball will return to its normal trajectory. This normative model of development can be generalized to consider differences among individuals—perhaps individuals differ in their genetically determined terrain (Scarr, 1976). However, it may not be wise to push a metaphor too far. Waddington cautioned that the model is not to be interpreted literally but rather as a "rough and ready picture of the developing embryo . . . it has certain merits for those who, like myself, find it comforting to have some mental picture, however vague, for what they are trying to think about" (Waddington, 1957, p. 30).

One problem with the canalization metaphor is that it considers the genotype as a preformed, unchanging landscape. Few geneticists would agree that the genetic contribution to development is so static. In this sense, the model is formally similar to the reaction range concept, although the canalization model gives more weight to genetic hardwiring, whereas reaction range emphasizes the power of the environment. Both models imply that genotype is fixed and that the environment creates variation. In the canalization model, the environment is responsible for deviations from the genetically determined developmental trajectory; in the reaction range model, genotype determines a range of reaction to the environment but the environment determines where development will end up. One could turn both models on their head: The environment is the landscape through which the organism develops and genetic factors create deviations from this developmental trajectory. As formalized in quantitative genetic theory, both genetic deviations and environmental deviations can contribute to phenotypic deviations observed in a population and this is just as true in development.

Assessing Genotype-Environment Interaction

Although a hypothetical numerical example is useful for clarifying the concept of genotype-environment interaction, genetic deviations and environmental deviations cannot be measured directly. Quantitative genetics proceeds indirectly, estimating genetic and environmental components of variance from relationships that differ in genetic or environmental similarity. The methods of quantitative genetics are useful for demonstrating the existence of genotype-environment interaction, although they are not so good at determining the overall contribution of genotype-environment interaction to phenotypic variance.

Contribution of Genotype-Environment Interaction to Phenotypic Variance

It has been said that genotype-environment interaction is included in environmental variance in behavioral genetic studies, but that is not always true. Genotype-environment interactions affecting one member of a family may be similar to those experienced by other family members because they share heredity and react to a similar environment. In twin studies, we compare resemblances of identical and fraternal twins. If genotype-environment interaction contributed equally to the similarity of both types of twins, estimates of genetic influence based on the difference between the correlations for identical and fraternal twins would not be affected. In this case, variance due to genotype-environment interaction would be included in estimates of environmental variance. However, because identical twins are twice as similar genetically as fraternal twins, it is more reasonable to suppose that genotype-environment interaction contributes more to the similarity of identical twins than of fraternal twins, in which case some variance due to genotype-environment interaction would be included in estimates of genetic variance. At the same time, environmental influence would also be overestimated because only part of the increase in phenotypic variance caused by genotype-environment interaction is interpreted as genetic variance. Thus, it is difficult if not impossible to use the twin design to estimate the overall contribution of genotype-environment interaction to phenotypic variance.

Jinks and Fulker (1970) proposed a test of the overall magnitude of a certain type of genotype-environment interaction in which twin data are analyzed to investigate correlations between identical twin intrapair differences and pair sums. A positive correlation indicates, for example, that the environment differentiates between members of high-scoring twin pairs. However, intrapair differences only assess nonshared environment (see chapter 4) and the pair sums confound purely environmental effects with genotype-environment interaction because pair sums for identical twins reared together reflect both genetic and shared family environmental influences. Nonetheless, few interactions of this type were found for cognitive or personality traits. Although the correlation between pair sums and differences for identical twins reared apart is a true test of genotype-environment interaction in the absence of selective placement, this method is limited by the rarity of identical twins reared apart.

Adoption designs are less affected by genotype-environment interaction: It does not contribute to the resemblance between genetically related individuals in uncorrelated environments nor does it contribute to the resemblance between genetically unrelated individuals in the same adoptive family. By comparing estimates of genetic and environmental influences in adoptive families to those in nonadoptive families, it may be possible to obtain a rough estimate of the magnitude of phenotypic variance contributed by genotype-environment interaction. However, the comparison between estimates from adoptive families and estimates in nonadoptive families includes genotype-environment correlation as well as genotype-environment interaction. The method is discussed in greater detail in the next chapter whose focus is genotype-environment correlation.

Isolating Specific Genotype-Environment Interactions

Although it is difficult to estimate the overall contribution of genotype-environment interaction to phenotypic variance, quantitative genetic methods are particularly valuable for isolating specific genotype-environment interactions. Most of this research has been conducted with nonhuman animals, although human data from adoption studies have recently been reported.

Nonhuman Animal Research.   Studies of genotype-environment interaction are facilitated by the availability of inbred strains of mice that differ genetically among strains, but are nearly identical genetically within each strain. Rearing various inbred strains in various environments permits direct tests of genetic effects, environmental effects, and genotype-environment interaction.

The best known study of genotype-environment interaction (Cooper and Zubek, 1958) used selectively bred lines of rats rather than inbred strains. The rats had been selectively bred to run through a maze with few errors ("maze bright") or with many errors ("maze dull"). Rats from these two lines were reared under one of two conditions from weaning at 25 days of age to 65 days

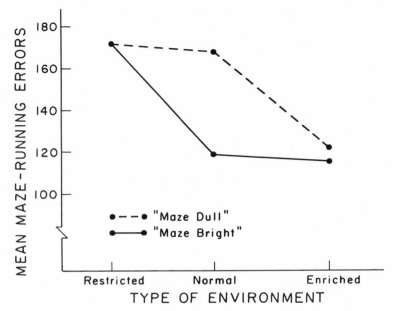

FIG. 5.2.   Genotype-environment interaction: Maze-running errors for maze-bright and maze-dull rats reared in restricted, normal, and enriched environments. (Adapted from Cooper & Zubek, 1958.)

of age. One condition was "enriched" in that the cages were brightly colored and contained many movable toys. For the "restricted" condition, gray cages without movable objects were used. Animals reared under these conditions were compared to maze-bright and maze-dull animals reared in a normal laboratory environment (data from another study).

Figure 5.2 shows the maze-running errors for these rats. In the normal environment in which the lines were selectively bred, there is a large difference between the two lines. The results suggest genotype-environment interaction because the effect of restricted and enriched environments depends on the genotype of the animal. The enriched condition had no effect on the maze-bright animals, but it substantially improved the performance of the maze-dull rats. On the other hand, an impoverished environment was extremely detrimental to the maze-bright rats, but had little effect on the maze-dull ones. Although it is worrisome that "ceiling " and "floor" artifacts of measure could produce the same results, this study with its connotations for human cognitive development stimulated interest in the concept of genotype-environment interaction.

In a series of studies involving thousands of mice, Henderson (1967, 1970, 1972) systematically explored genotype-environment interaction. For example, in one study (Henderson, 1972), mice from six inbred strains and their hybrid crosses were reared in impoverished or enriched conditions for the first 6 weeks of life. Instead of traditional learning tasks, mice were tested in two life-threatening, escape-learning situations (escape from water and escape from shock) that provided uniformly high motivation and minimized curiosity. As in other studies, learning proved to be substantially influenced by genetic factors as evidenced by large strain differences. However, rearing environment and genotype-environment interaction had little effect. Henderson argued that in previous studies strain differences in temperament characteristics, curiosity, and motivation may have led to apparent genotype-environment interactions.

Henderson's earlier work and dozens of other studies occasionally report significant genotype-environment interactions. However, the significant interactions are not consistent within studies nor are they replicated across studies. Moreover, these interactions, although significant given the large samples used in these studies, account for miniscule portions of variance. For example, a study of 12 Drosophila strains reared under 20 different environmental conditions (Taylor & Condra, 1978) found several significant genotype-environment interactions, but, as noted by DeFries (1979), the largest effect only accounted for 2% of the total variance.

In a review of animal studies of genotype-environment interaction, Fuller and Thompson (1978), conclude:

> All the studies in this section support the idea that genotypes react differently to treatments as diverse as handling, rearing in an enriched environment, electric shock, and water immersion. However, variability in procedure, experimental design, and outcome is so great that we have not yet determined the rules of the game that produce or do not produce statistical interactions. Henderson's (1967) experiment involving sixteen genotypes and three levels of stimulation illustrates the need for parametric studies which employ a wide range of genotypes, not simply two strains that happen to differ on a point of interest. Even this experiment raises more questions than it answers. (p. 173)

Human Research.   In research with human beings, it is not possible to select genotypes as different as inbred strains of mice, nor is it possible to subject them to environments as extreme as the deprived and enriched environments used in laboratory research on nonhuman animals. Human behavioral genetic research is subject to the mixed blessing of working with naturally occurring genetic and environmental variation: The cost is a loss of experimental control, and the benefit is the increased likelihood that the results of the research will generalize to the world outside the laboratory.

Plomin, DeFries, and Loehlin (1977) proposed a method for isolating specific genotype-environment interactions using the adoption design. The test is analogous to the method used in the strain-by-treatment mouse studies described earlier. An illustrative design is depicted in Table 5.2. This is a 2 × 2 factorial arrangement in which one variable is the genotype and the other is the

TABLE 5.2
Illustrative Design for Testing Genotype-Environment Interaction

	Environment	
Genotype	Low	High
Low	Cell 1	Cell 2
High	Cell 3	Cell 4

TABLE 5.3
2 × 2 Analysis of Variance of Genetic, Environmental, and
Genotype-Environment Interaction Factors in Skodak and Skeels'
(1949) Study (re-analyzed by Plomin, DeFries, & Loehlin, 1977)

Source	df	MS	F
Genotypes (A)	1	2401.4	11.8*
Environments (B)	1	145.7	<1
Genotype-Environment Interaction (AB)	1	74.24	<1
Error	55	204.26	

*$p < .01$.

environment. For any dependent variable, the design can be used to investigate the effect of genotype independent of the environment, the effect of environment independent of genotype, and genotype-environment interaction. Adoption studies permit the use of this design for human data. The genotype of adopted children can be estimated from the scores of their biological parents. The environment of adopted children can be estimated using any measure of the adoptive home environment or characteristic of the adoptive parents. For example, Cell 1 would contain scores on a dependent variable for individuals who, like the maze-dull rats reared in restricted environments, receive both genotypes and environments likely to lead to low scores on the dependent variable.

This approach was applied in a re-analysis of data from the classic study by Skodak and Skeels (1949) using educational levels of the biological and adoptive parents as measures of genotype and environment, respectively, and IQ of the adopted children as the dependent variable. Figure 5.3 summarizes the average IQs of adopted children born to biological parents above or below the educational level (9.9 years) and reared by adoptive parents above or below the mean (12.1 years). The illustration suggests that adopted children's IQs are not affected by their environment as indexed by the educational level of their adoptive parents. Genetic influence, indexed by the educational level of biological parents, is considerable. A 2 × 2 analysis of variance bears this out, as indicated in Table 5.3. The genetic main effect is highly significant; the environmental main effect and the genotype-environment interaction are not statistically significant. A more

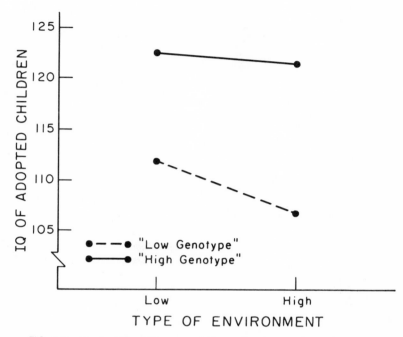

FIG. 5.3. Stanford-Binet IQ scores of 59 13-year-old adopted children in the study by Skodak and Skeels (1949). (Re-analyzed by Plomin, DeFries, & Loehlin, 1977.)

powerful use of the data entails analysis of the same variables in a continuous rather than dichotomous manner using hierarchical multiple regression (Cohen & Cohen, 1975), which removes main effects of genotype and environment and then assesses their interaction. The interaction term is a "dummy" variable created by the product of the main variables of "genotype" and "environment," although other models of interaction such as threshold effects could also be employed. The results of a hierarchical multiple regression analysis of the Skodak and Skeels data are quite consistent with those of the 2 × 2 analysis of variance, as indicated in Table 5.4.

The use of adoptive parents' education provides a limited vision of the environment, just as biological parents' education is a weak index of genotype. Plomin et al. (1977) concluded:

> We feel that the use of adoption data to screen for genotype-environment interaction is an unusually promising tool for the more refined analysis of environmental effects in psychology . . . We reiterate the need for detailed studies of the biological and adoptive parents, the adopted children, *and* extensive environmental assessments. This would permit an interesting variety of analyses. For

TABLE 5.4

Hierarchical Multiple Regression Analysis of Genetic,
Environmental, and Genotype-Environment Interaction Factors in
Skodak and Skeels' (1949) Study (re-analyzed by Plomin,
DeFries, & Loehlin, 1977)

Source	df	MS	F
Genotypes (A)	1	2031.9	11.0*
SSy $(R^2_{A,B} - R^2_B)$			
Environments (B)	1	108.8	<1
SSy $(R^2_{A,B} - R^2_A)$			
Genotype-Environment Interaction (AB)	1	7.9	<1
SSy $(R^2_{A,B,AB} - R^2_{A,B})$			
Residual			
SSy $(1 - R^2_{A,B,AB})$	55	184	

*$p < .01$.

example, one could analyze the effects of adopted children's genotypes, childrearing practices of adoptive parents, and the interaction between the two, using some relevant aspect of the adopted children's behavior as a dependent variable. Any aspect of the genotype and of the environment can in this way be screened for genotype-environment interaction with respect to any trait in the children, provided only that all three are measurable. (p. 317)

Genotype-Environment Interaction Analyses

Providing these recommended data is one of the goals of the Colorado Adoption Project (CAP), a longitudinal study of children adopted away from their biological parents at birth and matched nonadopted children (Plomin & DeFries, 1985). The parents—biological and adoptive parents of the adopted children and the parents of the nonadopted children—are tested on a 3-hour battery of psychological measures, and the children and their home environments are studied in their homes yearly from 1 to 4 years of age. The CAP measures are diverse, including mental development, temperament, and behavioral problems for the children and similar domains of assessment for the parents. Measures of the home environment include Caldwell and Bradley's (1978) Home Observation for Measurement of the Environment (HOME) and Moos and Moos' (1981) Family Environment Scales (FES).

Hierarchical multiple regression analyses of the type described earlier were applied to the CAP infancy data at 12 and 24 months in order to assess genotype-environment interaction. For mental development, 15 analyses of genotype-environment interaction were conducted using biological mothers' IQ as an estimate of genotype and several indices of environmental influence in the adoptive homes: adoptive mothers' and fathers' IQ, HOME general factor, and two second-order factors (Personal Growth and Traditional Organization) from the FES. The dependent measures were 12-month Bayley Mental Development Index (MDI; Bayley, 1969) scores, 24-month MDI, and the average of 12- and 24-month MDI scores. None of the interactions was significant. Thus, systematic, nonlinear effects of genetic and environmental influences on infant mental development are not apparent in the CAP.

The same conclusion was drawn from analyses of genotype-environment interaction in other domains of infant development (Plomin & DeFries, 1985). For behavioral problems, 30 genotype-environment analyses produced only four significant interactions. In the domain of infant temperament, 80 genotype-environment interaction analyses were conducted and only two significant interactions were found, fewer than expected on the basis of chance alone when $p < .05$. Given the novelty of this approach, however, the significant interactions are worth mentioning. Moreover, they do not seem to be chance associations because they both involve activity of the infants and activity level of the biological mothers. In one case, the environmental measure was a HOME factor, Restriction/Punishment, and it interacted significantly with biological mothers' activity to predict 12-month-old activity (R^2 change $= .027, p < .05$). As indicated in Fig. 5.4, even though there was no main effect of biological mothers' activity level on their adopted-away infants' activity, activity scores of adoptees were high when their biological mothers' were highly active and they were reared in restrictive adoptive homes. One possible interpretation of this interaction is that parents are likely to be particularly restrictive when a child is genetically predisposed towards high activity.

The other significant interaction is especially interesting. Adopted infants' activity at 24 months of age was significantly predicted by the interaction between biological mothers' activity and FES Traditional Organization (R^2 change $= .031, p < .05$). As indicated in Fig. 5.5, genetic differences in activity are revealed in families low on the FES Traditional Organization factor. This suggests the possibility that genetic differences among children emerge more clearly in less constrained environments—a hypothesis that has been proposed on the basis of genotype-environment interaction research with mice (Henderson, 1970).

Two other genotype-environment interaction analyses of the CAP data support this hypothesis, even though the interactions attained probability values of only .10. The two interactions appear to be other than chance phenomena for four reasons: First, they both involve infants' emotionality as predicted by biological and adoptive mothers' emotionality-anger. Secondly, the interaction in both cases explains more than the usual amount of variance at both 12 and 24 months. Thirdly, the interactions are similar at 12 and 24 months. Finally, the interactions at both 12 and 24 months support the hypothesis that genetic differences among children emerge more clearly in less constrained environ-

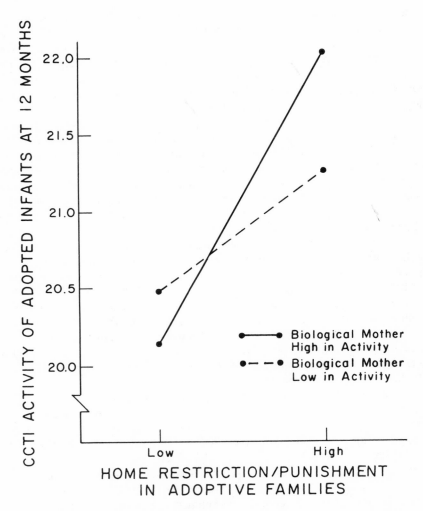

FIG. 5.4. Rating of adopted infants' activity at 12 months of age as a function of biological mothers' activity and adoptive families' HOME Restriction/Punishment. (From Plomin & DeFries, 1985. Reprinted by permission.)

ments: Genetic differences in emotionality appear only when adoptive mothers are low in emotionality. When adoptive mothers are above average in emotionality, adopted infants are emotional regardless of their genetic predisposition. These interactions between mothers' emotionality-anger and infants' emotionality at 12 and 24 months are depicted in Fig. 5.6 and Fig. 5.7.

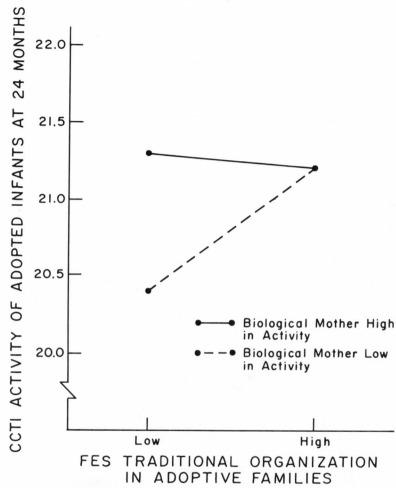

FIG. 5.5   Rating of adopted infants' activity at 24 months of age as a function of biological mothers' activity and adoptive families' FES Traditional Organization. (From Plomin & DeFries, 1985. Reprinted by permission.)

It is noteworthy that these first analyses of genotype-environment interaction found so few significant interactions. Nonetheless, the hypothesis that genetic differences appear more clearly in more permissive environments may be important heuristically. Limitations of these CAP analyses should also be considered. For example, the analyses focus on infancy—it is possible that genotype-environment interactions will be more apparent later in childhood. Also, large samples are needed to detect interactions. Cohen and Cohen (1975) indicate that the probability of detecting significant interactions will increase as

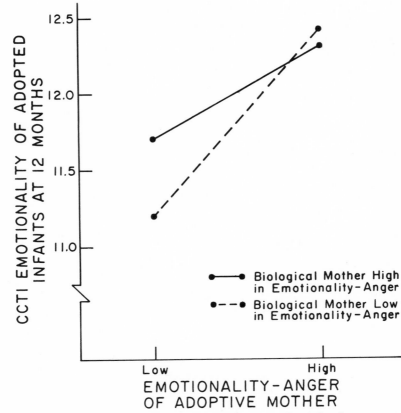

FIG. 5.6.   Rating of adopted infants' emotionality at 12 months of age as a
function of biological mothers' and adoptive mothers' emotionality. (From Plomin
& DeFries, 1985. Reprinted by permission.)

the amount of variance explained by the interaction effect increases in relation to
the total variance explained by the multiple regression, as the number of subjects
increases, and as the number of variables decreases. Given its sample size and
total variance explained of 10% to 20%, these CAP analyses had approximately
80% power to detect interactions that account for 5% of the total variance.
However, if interaction effects account for as little as 1% of the variance, one
would need a sample size of over 600 to detect a significant interaction with 80%
power given an R^2 of 10% to 20%.

It is also possible that other combinations of parental measures, environmental
measures, and measures of children's development would yield more evidence
for genotype-environment interaction. However, the CAP analyses lead to the
conclusion that genotype-environment interactions in infancy, if they exist at all,

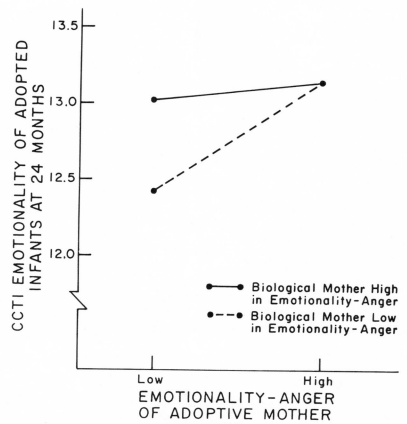

FIG. 5.7.   Rating of adopted infants' emotionality at 24 months of age as a function of biological mothers' and adoptive mothers' emotionality. (From Plomin & DeFries, 1985. Reprinted by permission.)

do not account for much variance. For this reason, Plomin and DeFries (1985) proposed the following principle concerning the development of individual differences in infancy: "Genetic and environmental influences on infant development coact in an additive manner" (p. 341).

Conclusions

It has been a major disappointment to me that specific genotype-environment interactions have been so difficult to find because I believed that such interactions would provide unequivocal evidence for the usefulness of behavioral genetic studies of development: "Environmental factor X shows no main effect overall on children's behavior Y; however, for children with a genetic propensity toward Z, factor X makes a huge difference in the development of behavior Y.'' Also, I used to think that nonhuman animal research found ubiquitous evidence of genotype-environment interaction, which buoyed my confidence that similar interactions could be found in human data; however, I now see that the animal research is quite ambiguous concerning the importance of genotype-environment interaction.

Perhaps my less-than-optimistic feeling about genotype-environment interaction is premature, because it is primarily based on CAP analyses of data in infancy. As mentioned, other combinations of measures of parents, environments, and children might yield more evidence for genotype-environment interaction. At the 1985 meeting of the Society for Research in Child Development, a symposium on organism-environment interaction convened researchers from diverse fields in child development to discuss problems they had all experienced in finding interactions. Several suggestions were offered. For example, the wrong types of environmental assessments may have been employed (Urie Bronfenbrenner and Ted Wachs), and analyses of extreme groups might yield greater evidence for interactions (Craig Ramey).

It is possible, of course, that additive "main effects" account for most of the systematic variance that can be explained. Educational researchers have put the most effort into finding interactions, specifically interactions involving aptitude and treatment. However, after two decades of research, Cronbach and Snow (1975), in their definitive review on the topic of aptitude-by-treatment interactions, conclude:

> We have reviewed findings on the hunches of a decade or more ago. No Aptitude × Treatment interactions are so well confirmed that they can be used directly as guides to instruction. . . . While results in Aptitude × Treatment interaction studies have often been negative, this does not deny the hypotheses. Most studies used samples so small that a predominance of "chance results" was rendered inevitable. What the results deny is the hope that a few years of research on a limited scale will produce both a solid theory and a set of practically useful generalizations about instruction. Learner × Treatment interaction is an essentially new scientific problem, and reaching consolidated understanding in such matters often requires decades. (pp. 492-494)

Behavioral genetic research on human genotype-environment interaction began much more recently than did the study of aptitude-by-treatment interactions, and Cronbach and Snow's rather gloomy conclusion might still be shown to be inapplicable to such research. However, so far, it has certainly been easier to talk about genotype-environment interactions than it has been to find them. Although much less attention has been paid to genotype-environment correlation than to genotype-environment interaction, the results look more promising in that area, which is the topic of the next chapter.

6 Genotype-Environment Correlation

Genotype-environment correlation is what developmentalists frequently mean when they say genotype-environment "interaction." *Genotype-environment correlation* literally refers to a correlation between genetic deviations and environmental deviations as they affect a particular trait. In other words, genotype-environment correlation describes the extent to which children are exposed to environments on the basis of their genetic propensities. For example, if musical ability is inherited (and the behavioral genetic research has not yet been done to investigate whether it is), then musically gifted children will have musically gifted parents on the average who provide them with a musical environment as well as a musical heritage. The children might be picked out as gifted and given special opportunities at school even if the parents did not do anything about it. Even if no one does anything about the child's talent, the child will gravitate toward musical environments that might mean musically inclined peers, radios, records, or just humming and whistling. As Galton said, "ability will out."

The purpose of this chapter is to describe the concept of genotype-environment correlation and the bits of data that indicate its importance in developmental psychology. Genotype-environment correlation has been of interest to behavioral geneticists because it represents variance that is neither solely genetic nor solely environmental, but both. It is an important concept in developmental psychology because it can represent a detectable form of the child-to-parent direction of effects: Parents respond to gene-based characteristics of their child. Causality cannot otherwise be assumed on the basis of correlations between environmental measures and infant development because variations in environmental measures might reflect rather than cause differences in the children's development. This is the issue of direction of effects (Bell, 1968). For example, a relationship between parental punitiveness and children's aggression could be brought about by parental reactions to children's inherent aggressiveness. Developmentalists have attempted to use cross-lagged panel analysis (Kenny, 1979) of longitudinal data to untangle cause and effect; however, this method has been subjected to severe criticism because of the assumptions it requires (Rogosa, 1979). As discussed later, a method has been proposed to assess specific genotype-environment correlations that involve one form of the child-to-parent direction of effects.

Genotype-environment correlation is also important for developmentalists because the concept suggests new ways of thinking about developmental transactions between nature and nurture. A general theory of development based on genotype-environment correlation is discussed at length later in this chapter.

Three Types of Genotype-Environment Correlation

The three examples mentioned earlier of how musically gifted children may be exposed to musical environments are examples of three categories of genotype-environment correlation: passive, reactive, and active (Plomin, DeFries, & Loehlin, 1977). Passive genotype-environment correlation is most frequently described: By virtue of sharing genes as well as family environment with their parents, children can passively inherit environments correlated with their genetic predispositions. For example, to the extent that sociability is inherited, sociable parents have children who are more sociable than average, and they also provide a "sociable environment" filled with friends, social activities, and the parents' own interactions with the child. The passive form of genotype-environment correlation can be considered in quantitative genetic analyses just by adding double-headed arrows in path diagrams between G's and E's; thus, it has been studied quite often by behavioral geneticists, as described later in this chapter. However, this interesting and reasonable form of double-barreled influence of parents on children has not been considered by developmentalists.

Much less frequently studied, but probably even more important, are reactive and active forms of genotype-environment correlation. Reactive or evocative genotype-environment correlation refers to experiences of the child that derive from reactions of other people to the child's genetic propensities. Athletic ability is something that can be seen on the school playground. Parents, playmates, and teachers notice children who are talented athletically and encourage them in athletic pursuits. It also works the other way: Klutzy kids get sufficient negative reinforcement from their teammates so that even the pushiest parents are worn down in their efforts to produce a new Olympic star. If athletic ability is inherited (and, once again, this research has not been done), this is an example of reactive genotype-environment correlation because children evoke environments correlated with their genetic endowment.

Active genotype-environment correlation describes the situation in which children actively select or even create their own environments that are correlated with their genetic propensities. It has been called niche-building or niche-picking (Scarr & McCartney, 1983) and is likely to be a crucial process by which genotype plays out its role in development. Budding socialites will create a social environment that meets their social needs even if it takes imaginary playmates to do it. Worriers will find things to worry about no matter how smoothly things seem to be going. Active children will turn the most placid situations into jungle gyms.

Passive genotype-environment correlation requires interactions between genetically related individuals. Reactive genotype-environment can be induced by anyone who reacts to children on the basis of their inherent proclivities. Active genotype-environment correlation can be brought about by anything or anybody. Table 6.1 summarizes these three types of genotype-environment correlation. It should be mentioned that genotype-environment correlation can be negative, even though examples of positive correlations come to mind more readily. For example, slow learners may be given special attention to boost their performance. Cattell (1973) suggested that negative genotype-environment correlation may be common for personality. For example, using dominance as an example, "society likes to 'cut down' individuals naturally too dominant and to help the humble inherit the earth" (p. 145). Cattell refers to such examples of negative reactive genotype-environment correlation as "coercion to the biosocial norm." Passive and active genotype-environment correlations can also be negative. Emotionally labile parents who are easily angered may have children with a proclivity to be quick-tempered, and yet the parents are likely to assail expressions of anger in their children, creating a negative passive genotype-environment correlation. Negative active genotype-environment correlation sounds almost pathological because we would not expect individuals to seek environments that rub against the grain of their predispositions. However, it seems reasonable to suppose, for example, that emotionally unstable children might seek calm environments and stable friends to steady their psyches, thus producing negative genotype-environment correlations. Cattell (1982) has described other ways in which negative genotype-environment correlation might emerge.

Scarr and McCartney's Theory

A general theory of development proposed by Scarr and McCartney (1983) uses these categories of genotype-environment correlation to describe processes involved in the developmental interface between nature and nurture. They refer

TABLE 6.1
Three Types of Genotype-Environment Correlation

Type	Description	Pertinent Source of Environmental Influence
Passive	Children receive genotypes correlated with their family environment	Parents and siblings
Reactive	Children are reacted to on the basis of their genetic proclivities	Anybody
Active	Children seek or create environments conducive to the development of their genetic propensities	Anybody or anything

to their theory as genotype/environment effects rather than genotype-environment correlation because they believe that:

> Genetic differences prompt differences in which environments are experienced and what effects they may have. In this view, the genotype, in both its species specificity and its individual variability, largely determines environmental effects on development, because the genotype determines the organism's response to environmental opportunities. . . . We propose that development is indeed the result of nature *and* nurture but that genes drive experience. (pp. 424-425)

Their theory has three parts. The first part of the theory elevates the three categories of genotype-environment correlation to a role as major processes of development:

> The process by which children develop is best described by three kinds of genotype/environment effects: a *passive* kind, whereby the genetically related parents provide a rearing environment that is correlated with the genotype of the child (sometimes positively and sometimes negatively); an *evocative* kind, whereby the child receives responses from others that are influenced by his genotype; and an *active* kind that represents the child's selective attention to and learning from aspects of his environment that are influenced by his genotype and indirectly correlated with those of his biological relatives. (p. 427)

The crux of the theory lies in two novel propositions:

> The relative importance of the three kinds of genotype/environment effects changes with development. The influence of the passive kind declines from infancy to adolescence, and the importance of the active kind increases over the same period. . . . The degree to which experience is influenced by individual genotypes increases with development and with the shift from passive to active genotype-environment effects, as individuals select their own experiences. (p. 427)

Scarr and McCartney suggest that passive genotype/environment effects predominate in infancy because much of the environment that reaches the child is provided by parents who are genetically related to the child. Older children, however, extend their experiences beyond the family and create their own environment to a greater extent. Concerning reactive genotype-environment correlations, they suggest that these "persist throughout life, as we elicit responses from others based on many personal, genotype-related characteristics from appearance to personality and intellect" (p. 428).

These processes are thought to be responsible for familial resemblance and are used to address some questions from previous behavioral genetic research. For example, why do IQ correlations for fraternal twins and adoptive sibling pairs tend to decline from infancy to adolescence, whereas IQ correlations for separated identical twins do not? It is odd that family members become less similar the longer they live together. Scarr and McCartney suggest that passive genotype-environment correlation is shared to a great extent by fraternal twins in infancy and early childhood and then declines in importance as the children take a more active role in selecting their environments, thus increasingly differentiating members of fraternal twin pairs. Adoptive siblings may have received similar early environments from their adoptive parents; however, "because their genotypes are hardly correlated at all, neither are their chosen environmental niches" (p. 431). Consideration of the possible importance of active genotype-environment correlation makes it less surprising that identical twins reared apart from birth are so similar: Their identical genotypes lead them to seek similar environments.

> Finally, the theory makes some explicit, testable predictions: If parent treatment of their children is not related to children's talents, interests, and personalities, the theory is wrong. . . . If others do not respond differentially to individual characteristics for which there is genetic variability, then the theory is wrong. . . . Our theory predicts that children select and build niches that are correlated with their talents, interests, and personality characteristics. If not, the theory is wrong. . . . If adopted children are as similar to their adoptive parents and each other in late adolescence as they were in early childhood, that aspect of the theory is wrong. (p.433)

Scarr and McCartney's theory represents an important step towards using behavioral genetic concepts to go beyond components of variance to consider underlying developmental processes. If these processes are important in children's development, their effect should be detectable in terms of components of variance. For example, if passive genotype/environment effects commonly occur in infancy and early childhood, they should lead to passive genotype-environment correlation in the components-of-variance sense. The remainder of this chapter examines the genotype-environment correlation component of variance as well as some recent attempts to isolate specific genotype-environment correlations.

TABLE 6.2

Hypothetical Genetic and Environmental Deviations from the Mean
for Five Individuals When There is a Perfect Correlation Between
Genotype and Environment[a]

Individual	G	+	E	=	P
1	−2		−2		−4
2	−1		−1		−1
3	0		0		0
4	1		1		1
5	2		2		4

$$V_G = 2.0$$
$$V_E = 2.0$$
$$2Cov(G)(E) = 4.0$$
$$V_P = 2.0 + 2.0 + 4.0 = 8.0$$

[a]Adapted from Plomin, DeFries, and Loehlin (1977).

Assessing Variance Due to Genotype-Environment Correlation

In the previous chapter, a hypothetical numerical example was used to illustrate the contribution of genotype-environment interaction to phenotypic variance (see Table 5.1). In that example, there was no correlation between individuals' genetic deviations and environmental deviations: Genetic variance was 2.0, environment variance was 2.0, and genotype-environment interaction variance was 3.2. Thus, the phenotypic variance was 7.2. Table 6.2 illustrates what happens when genetic deviations and environmental deviations are perfectly correlated. Unlike genotype-environment interaction, no separate term is added to represent phenotypic variance due to genotype- environment correlation. This follows from the quantitative genetic model in which phenotypic deviations are decomposed into a component that consists of genetic deviations and a component that includes all other deviations: $P = G + E$. Because G and E are expressed as deviations, they are merely squared in order to express them as variances:

$$V_P = (G + E)(G + E)$$
$$= V_G \times V_E \times 2Cov(G)(E)$$

In other words, when genotype and environment are correlated, twice the covariance between genotype and environment is added to the phenotypic variance. This added variance is neither genetic nor environmental—it is both. In Table 6.2, the covariance between genotype and environment is 2.0; because genotypes and environment are perfectly correlated, the phenotypic variance is 8.0 rather than 4.0.

Note that genetic and environmental variances remain unchanged even when genotypes and environments are perfectly correlated. In fact, correlations between genotype and environment will contribute substantially to phenotypic variance only when both genetic variance and environmental variance are substantial. Moreover, variance due to genotype-environment correlation cannot exceed the sum of genetic and environmental variances (Jensen, 1976), as seen in our hypothetical numerical example. One implication is that if evidence is found for genotype-environment correlation, both genetic variance and environmental variance must be substantial. The example in Table 6.2 shows a positive correlation between genotypes and environments. If genotype-environment correlation is negative, it will decrease rather than increase phenotypic variance.

Just as it is sometimes said that variance due to genotype-environment interaction is included solely in the environmental component of variance, which is not the case, genotype-environment correlation is mistakenly thought to be included entirely in estimates of genetic variance. However, the effects of genotype-environment correlation and genotype-environment interaction are the same: If they contribute more to phenotypic resemblance for identical twins than for fraternal twins, then the classical twin design will overestimate both genetic and environmental variance. Similarly, adoption estimates of genetic influence derived from comparisons between correlations in adoptive and nonadoptive families can include variance due to genotype-environment correlation in both genetic and environmental estimates of variance:

> Adopted children may respond to their adoptive parents' genetic dispositions, and conversely, adoptive parents may react to their adoptive children's propensities. If an adoptive parent responds to a child's gene-influenced behavior in such a way as to change the child to be more like the parent, a genotype-environment correlation component in the phenotypic parent-child covariance could result. (Plomin et al., 1977, p. 319)

If the adoptive parent-adopted child correlation contains some genotype-environment correlation, then the difference between nonadoptive parent-offspring correlations and adoptive parent-adopted child correlations includes only part of the genotype-environment correlation; the rest is included with the estimate of environmental variance.

In the case of genetically related individuals adopted apart, reactive and active genotype-environment correlations can contribute to their similarity and will be included in estimates of genetic variance. For example, biological mothers and their adopted-away children might be responded to similarly on the basis of physical appearance, talents, and personality or they might seek environments compatible with their genetic predispositions. However, passive genotype-environment is not a factor in parent-offspring similarity because the biological mother does not rear the child. These facts can be used to estimate the importance of the three types of genotype-environment correlation.

Passive Genotype-Environment Correlation

In the case of interaction between genotypes and environment, the previous chapter noted that the methods of quantitative genetics are not so good at determining the overall contribution of genotype-environment interaction to phenotypic variance. In contrast, considerable attention has been given to the issue of estimating the contribution of passive genotype-environment correlation to phenotypic variance. Two major methods have been used: comparing variances of adopted and nonadopted individuals, and using path models of parent-offspring resemblance which explicitly incorporate passive genotype-environment correlation.

The first method for assessing the contribution of passive genotype-environment correlation to phenotypic variance follows from the previous discussion. Passive genotype-environment correlation does not occur for adopted children because their adoptive parents do not contribute both genes and environment to their development. This means that phenotypic variance of adopted children has one less component than that of nonadopted children, which suggests a test of the importance of passive genotype-environment correlation: If passive positive genotype-environment correlation is important, the phenotypic variance of adopted children will be less than that of nonadopted children raised by their parents who contribute both genes and environment to the children's development. One might argue that lower variance of adopted children could be caused by factors other than reduced passive genotype-environment correlation—most obviously, restriction of range for biological parents or adoptive parents. However, if the variances for adoptive and biological parents are known, this becomes an empirical question.

Loehlin and DeFries (submitted) have recently reviewed analyses of this type for IQ and compared them to analyses based on parent-offspring path models. Although the comparison of variances of adopted and nonadopted children is straightforward, large samples are required because the standard error of a difference in standard deviations is large. For example, with 150 adopted and 150 nonadopted children, the standard error of a difference in IQ standard deviations is about 1.2 IQ points which, as Loehlin and DeFries show, makes a sizable difference in estimates of passive genotype-environment correlation. Their review of IQ data from five adoption studies indicates that the range of IQ standard deviation differences between adopted and nonadopted children is 0 to 3 IQ points. Estimates of passive genotype-environment correlation in each study were obtained from the proportion of variance in nonadoptive families accounted for by the variance differences in adoptive and nonadoptive families. Even though the range of IQ standard deviation differences was only 0 to 3 IQ points, the estimates of passive genotype-environment correlation fluctuate widely, from -.04 to .69. The median estimate is .20.

Loehlin and DeFries suggest that path models of parent-offspring similarity in

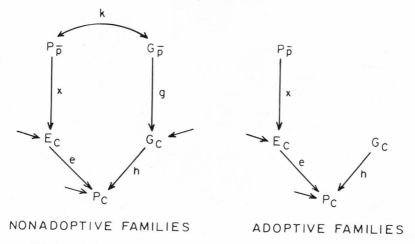

FIG. 6.1. Path model of passive genotype-environment correlation in nonadoptive and adoptive families. G_p, P_p = average parental genotype and phenotype for a trait; the other symbols are defined in the text. (From Loehlin & DeFries, submitted.)

adoptive and nonadoptive families yield more reliable estimates of passive genotype-environment correlation than do comparisons of variances in adopted and nonadopted children. They use the simple path diagram shown in Fig. 6.1 to express similarity between midparent (average score of the two parents) and offspring measures in nonadoptive families and adoptive families. Passive genotype-environment correlation is literally the correlation between G_c (genetic deviations that affect the child's phenotype, P_c) and E_c (environmental deviations), which is xkg in nonadoptive families, where x is the path of influence of parental phenotype on children's environment, g is the path of influence of parental genotype on children's genotype, and k is the correlation between parental phenotype and genotype. There is no passive genotype-environment correlation in adoptive families. Loehlin and DeFries show that xkg, passive genotype-environment correlation, can be estimated from the difference between parent-offspring correlations in nonadoptive and adoptive families. In nonadoptive families, parent-offspring correlation involves paths xe plus paths kgh; in adoptive families, the expectation for parent-offspring correlation is simply xe. The difference in correlations is thus kgh, genetic influence from parent to offspring. Multiplying this difference in correlations by xe (adoptive parent-adopted child correlation) yields $xekgh$, which contains the genetic relationships xkg and the products of e and h, the square roots of environmentality and heritability. If reasonable values of environmentality and heritability are substituted, the passive genotype-environment correlation, xkg, can be estimated. For example, in the adoption study by Burks (1928), parent-offspring correlations for

IQ are .52 and .20 in nonadoptive and adoptive families, respectively. Thus, xe is .20, kgh is .32, and $xekgh$ is .064. If we take the heritability of IQ to be .50, then the passive genotype-environment correlation is .13. Furthermore, Loehlin and DeFries note that the product eh does not vary much over a considerable range of e and h values. Using Burks' data, the product eh varies from .325 to .436 for ratios of environmentality and heritability as extreme as 5 to 1 in either direction and, thus, the passive genotype-environment correlation (xkg) is estimated by Loehlin and DeFries to be about .15.

In a review of five adoption studies, Loehlin and DeFries show that parent-offspring correlations in adoptive and nonadoptive families yield a range of estimates of passive genotype-environment correlation from .06 to .24, with an average estimate of about .15. Taking measurement error into account raises the average estimate to about .20. Selective placement, assumed to be negligible in the model, in fact has little effect on this estimate of passive genotype-environment correlation.

Thus, the evidence points to the possibility that passive genotype-environment correlation has a substantial influence, at least for IQ, the only trait for which sufficient data exist to make these estimates. Scarr and McCartney's theory predicts that the effects of passive genotype-environment correlation diminish in importance during childhood. Although Loehlin and DeFries' analysis did not address this issue, their review provides support for the theory: Studies with the youngest children show the most passive genotype-environment correlation. In the studies by Burks (1928) and Leahy (1935), children were from 5 to 14 years old; Loehlin and DeFries' estimates of passive genotype-environment correlation center around .18 and .21, respectively. In an adoption study of children from 16 to 22 years of age, passive genotype-environment correlation was estimated to be .12. These three studies employed the matched-group approach by comparing adoptive families and matched nonadoptive families and yield results consistent with Scarr and McCartney's theory.

The two studies of adoptive and nonadoptive relationships within the same families (Horn, Loehlin, & Willerman, 1979; Scarr & Weinberg, 1977) yielded mixed results; however, the children varied widely in age—from 3 to 26 years and from 4 to 16 years, respectively. Moreover, the nonadopted children were substantially older than the adopted children. These conditions do not provide a good test of Scarr and McCartney's hypothesis because their hypothesis predicts that passive genotype-environment correlation will be observed only for nonadopted children and that it will occur primarily in infancy and early childhood. However, data from the three studies with relevant data support Scarr and McCartney's theory in that passive genotype-environment correlation accounts for substantial variance and in that passive genotype-environment correlation diminishes in importance during adolescence.

Reactive and Active Genotype-Environment Correlations

No test has been proposed to assess the overall contribution of reactive and active genotype-environment correlations to phenotypic variance. If passive genotype-environment correlation accounts for such a substantial amount of variance, it seems reasonable to suppose that reactive and active genotype-environment correlations also are important, and perhaps increasingly important throughout development as predicted by Scarr and McCartney's theory.

It is tempting to think that active genotype-environment correlation might account for all phenotypic variance in the sense that genes drive experience as Scarr and McCartney suggest. However, as noted earlier, variance due to genotype-environment correlation cannot exceed variance due to genes and environment, and it is actually greatest when genetic and environmental variances are equal. Consider individual differences in weight, which are highly heritable (Stunkard, Foch, & Hrubec, 1985). No one gains weight without eating. If a measure of caloric intake were developed, it would surely correlate with genetic differences among children in their propensity to gain weight. If caloric intake were employed as a measure of environment, this example could be viewed in terms of genotype-environment correlation as illustrated in the hypothetical numerical example in Table 6.2. Even if the correlation between genetic propensities toward weight and caloric intake were 1.0, genetic variation and environmental variation must remain substantial as long as one accepts the basic quantitative genetic model. If phenotypic differences in weight were solely caused by differences in caloric intake, there would be no genetic variance for weight independent of caloric intake and thus caloric intake would be a pure environmental effect with no genetic variance or variance due to genotype-environment correlation. Of course, one might argue about the appropriateness of using caloric intake as a measure of environment. Although such arguments would have merit, the issue of genotype-environment correlation can be discussed only after one defines what is meant by the term *environment*.

Loehlin and DeFries (submitted) have suggested that, in their model, reactive genotype-environment correlation is not likely to account for much variance. If a measure of the environment is substituted for the parental phenotype (P_p) in Fig. 6.1, a path can be added from the children's phenotype (P_c) to the environmental index to depict genotype-environment correlation of the reactive type. This path could also represent active genotype-environment correlation if an environmental measure were used that assesses the child's niche-building or niche-seeking. This path would be added for the adoptive families as well as the nonadoptive families—parents and others respond to adopted children's hereditary differences just as they do to such differences among nonadopted children. Thus, for both adopted and nonadopted children, reactive genotype-environment correlation adds to the correlation between measures of the children's environment and measures of their development. Loehlin and DeFries note that reactive genotype-environment correlation can be no greater than the environment-development correlation in adoptive families which, in the Colorado Adoption Project (Plomin & DeFries, 1985), tends to be quite low. Thus, they conclude that reactive genotype-environment correlation does not appear to account for much variance. However, it should be noted that this conclusion is limited to specific measures of the environment in infancy and does not refer to the overall contribution of reactive and active genotype-environment correlations to phenotypic variance.

One way to assess the overall effect of reactive and active genotype-environment correlation follows from the earlier discussion of its effect in behavioral genetic analyses. Some methods, such as the twin method and comparisons between adoptive and nonadoptive families, include part of the variance due to genotype-environment correlation in their estimates of genetic influence and include the rest in environmental estimates. In contrast, estimates of genetic influence based on the correlation between adopted-apart biological relatives include all reactive and active genotype-environment correlations. Thus, just considering reactive and active genotype-environment correlations, genetic estimates from studies of adopted-apart relatives should be greater than those from other twin and adoption studies if reactive and active genotype-environment correlations are important. However, the fact that passive genotype-environment correlation is not included in genetic estimates based on adopted-apart relatives makes it more difficult to find evidence for reactive and active genotype-environment correlations because it reduces the differences between genetic estimates from adopted-apart comparisons and other behavioral genetic designs. Thus, passive genotype-environment correlation provides a conservative bias against finding evidence for the other types of genotype-environment correlation; moreover, as described above, the contribution of passive genotype-environment correlation to phenotypic variance can be estimated and taken into account in these calculations. However, as mentioned in the previous chapter, some variance due to genotype-environment interaction could also be included in the difference betweeen genetic estimates from adopted-apart comparisons and other behavioral genetic designs.

Extant data for IQ suggest the possibility of substantial reactive and active genotype-environment correlations. The most direct estimate of genetic influence comes from adopted-apart identical twins. Their IQ correlation is .75 (Plomin & DeFries, 1980), which suggests a heritability of 75%. The classical twin design yields correlations of about .85 for identical twins and .62 for fraternal twins, suggesting a heritability of .48. Some of the genetic variance estimated by the classical twin design is due to passive genotype-environment correlation, which, as discussed earlier, may account for 20% of the variance in IQ. Even taking into account selective placement and other complications such as nonadditive genetic variance, the substantially greater estimate of genetic influence from adopted-apart identical twins than from the classical twin design supports the hypothesis that genotype-environment correlations of the reactive and active varieties may be influential.

The analogous comparisons using nontwin siblings lead to the same conclusion. The IQ correlation for nontwin siblings reared together is .34, and the correlation for unrelated children reared together is .25. Doubling the difference between these two correlations suggests a heritability of .18, which includes variance due to passive genotype-environment correlation. In contrast, the correlation of siblings reared apart is .24, which suggests a heritability of .48. Again, even when complicating factors such as selective placement are considered, these large differences in heritability estimates are consistent with the possibility of substantial reactive and active genotype-environment correlations.

Finally, IQ data for parents and offspring are also consistent with this hypothesis. The IQ correlation for nonadoptive parents and offspring is .35, and the correlation for adoptive parents and their adopted children is .15. Doubling the difference between these two correlations suggests a heritability of .40. However, the correlation between biological parents and their adopted-away offspring is .31, which suggests a heritability of .62.

Thus, the available data suggest that reactive and active genotype-environment correlations may account for substantial variance. In all cases, heritability estimates based on correlations for adopted-apart relatives are about .20 greater than heritability estimates derived from comparisons of genetically related or genetically unrelated individuals living together. This suggests that 20% of the variance of IQ may be due to reactive and active genotype-environment correlations. These studies primarily involve older individuals, thus providing indirect support for Scarr and McCartney's theory that predicts substantial reactive and active genotype-environment correlations after childhood. Attempts to identify genotype-environment correlations using specific measures of the environment are discussed in the next section.

Isolating Specific Genotype-Environment Correlations

For genotype-environment interaction, numerous nonhuman animal studies have been conducted because environmental treatments can be imposed upon animals of different inbred strains to assess differential responding of various genotypes to an environmental treatment. However, genotype-environment correlation cannot be studied by imposing environmental treatments, so there have been few studies of genotype-environment correlation in nonhuman animals. Nonetheless, animal studies could provide powerful tests of correlations between genotypes and environments by studying the types of environments to which animals of different strains are exposed in their family (passive genotype-environment correlation) and in their social environment (reactive genotype-environment correlation). Animal studies may be most useful for exploring active genotype-environment correlation by studying environments selected by animals of different genotypes.

A method for isolating specific genotype-environnment correlations in human development has been proposed using the adoption design (Plomin, DeFries, & Loehlin, 1977). Similar to the adoption method used to isolate genotype-environment interaction, the genotype of adopted children can be estimated from the scores of their biological parents and the environment of adopted children can be estimated using any measure of the adoptive home environment or characteristics of the adoptive parents. If adoptive parents react to their adopted children on the basis of genetic differences among the children, correlations between the scores of the biological parents and the environmental measure should be observed. For example, if parents' responsiveness to their children depends upon genetic differences in their children's sociability, a measure of adoptive parents' responsiveness would be expected to correlate with the sociability of the adopted children's biological mothers (which is a "genotypic" estimate of the adoptees' sociability). In the absence of selective placement, this test will detect genotype-environment correlation when there is a heritable relationship between the phenotypes of the biological mother and the adopted child and when there is a relationship between the environmental measure and the adopted child's phenotype. Although these appear to be quite restrictive limitations, they really define genotype-environment correlation: Genetic differences among children are correlated with differences among their environments.

Previous adoption studies do not permit the use of this test because no study obtained data on biological parents and adoptive home environments. For example, Skodak and Skeels (1949) only obtained information on the educational and socioeconomic status levels of adoptive parents, and these measures cannot be expected to change in reaction to (reactive genotype-environment correlation) or be changed by (active genotype-environment correlation) the genetic predispositions of adopted children. As in the case of genotype-enviroment interaction, Plomin, DeFries, and Loehlin (1977) concluded that "What is needed is an adoption study with behavioral data on biological parents, adoptive parents, adopted children, and extensive measures of the adopted children's environment" (p. 320).

As indicated in the previous chapter, the Colorado Adoption Project (CAP; Plomin & DeFries, 1985) meets these needs. The environmental measures in the CAP—Caldwell and Bradley's (1978) Home Observation for Measurement of the Environment (HOME) and Moos and Moos' (1981) Family Environment Scales (FES)—can be used to explore the extent to which parents respond to genetic differences among their children, an example of reactive genotype-environment correlation. Even though the genotypic estimate for the adopted children in the CAP is limited to biological mothers' scores—for a completely heritable trait, biological mothers' scores will correlate only .50 with scores of

TABLE 6.3
Significant Genotype-Environment Correlation in the Colorado
Adoption Project: Correlations Between Environmental Measures
in Adoptive Homes and Biological Mothers' Personality[a]

Biological Mothers' Characteristic[b]	Adoptive Home Environmental Measure	Correlation
16 PF Neuroticism	FES Personal Growth	− .20
EASI Emotionality-Fear	FES Personal Growth	− .18
EASI Emotionality-Fear	FES Traditional Organization	− .15
EASI Activity	HOME General Factor (12 months)	− .17
EASI Activity	HOME General Factor (24 months)	− .16
EASI Sociability	FES Traditional Organization	.15
EASI Impulsivity	FES Personal Growth	.15

[a]From Plomin and DeFries (1985).

[b]16 PF is Cattell's Sixteen Personality Factor Questionnaire (Cattell, Eber, & Tatsuoka, 1970) and EASI refers to a self-report measure of temperament (Buss & Plomin, 1975). The environmental measures are described in the text.

their adopted-away children—the analyses disclosed some evidence of reactive genotype-environment correlation. For temperament, 7 of 28 genotype-environment correlations attained significance. Seven major factors of biological mothers' personality were compared with two second-order factors from the FES administered when the infants were 12 months old. The second-order factors are *Personal Growth* (high scores indicate parents are intellectual, active, permissive, and expressive) and *Traditional Organization* (high scores indicate parents are high in moral-religious emphasis, organization, and control). The seven personality factors were also compared with a HOME general factor. The general factor is an unrotated first principal component score derived from a quantitative scoring scheme for the HOME items which captures variability in middle class homes to a greater extent than does the qualitative scoring of the original HOME. The HOME was administered during home visits when the infants were 12 and 24 months old.

The seven significant correlations that resulted from these 28 comparisons are listed in Table 6.3. In general, the genotype-environment correlations are reasonable. For example, biological mothers' activity level is negatively correlated with the HOME general factor at both 12 and 24 months, which suggests the reasonable hypothesis that parents are less responsive when their infants are genetically predisposed towards high activity. The FES Personal Growth factor relates negatively to biological mothers' emotionality as assessed by 16 PF Neuroticism and by EASI Emotionality-Fear. This suggests that parents rate the social climate of their family as less conducive to personal growth (intellectual, active, permissive, and expressive) when their infants are predisposed to be emotional. The FES Traditional Organization factor yields two significant correlations that suggest more organization or control when the infants' biological background provides a propensity towards less fearfulness and greater sociability. Importantly, all of these could be viewed as examples of *negative* genotype-environment correlation, which Cattell (1973) predicted are common in the realm of personality.

It is noteworthy that the CAP analyses did not reveal reactive genotype-environment correlation for mental development in infancy. For example, the correlations between biological mothers' IQ and the HOME general factor in the adoptive famlies were -.06 and -.02 at 12 and 24 months, respectively (Plomin & DeFries, 1985). The only significant genotype-environment correlation from 18 comparisons was a positive correlation between FES Personal Growth and biological mothers' IQ. Although this could well be a chance result, it is possible that parents rate the social climate of their family as more conducive to personal growth when their children are predisposed to be bright. Behavioral problems of biological mothers—depression, hysteria, and sociopathy—also showed few significant correlations with environmental measures in adoptive homes.

Although no reactive genotype-environment correlation was detected in the CAP infancy data for mental development, preliminary results in early childhood indicate the presence of reactive genotype-environment correlation, as predicted by Scarr and McCartney's theory. The correlations between biological mothers' IQ and HOME scores in the adoptive families were .12 and .10, respectively, when the adopted-away children were 3 and 4 years of age.

It should be mentioned that the CAP infancy data described by Plomin and DeFries (1985) revealed no evidence of passive genotype-environment correlation as assessed by the comparison of variances for adopted and nonadopted infants. However, as discussed earlier, this is a weak test of passive genotype-environment correlation. The more powerful parent-offspring approach suggested by Loehlin and DeFries (submitted) is not appropriate for the CAP infancy data because the parent and infant measures cannot be assumed to be isomorphic. However, by substituting an environmental measure for the parental phenotype P_p in Fig. 6.1, it is possible to use the same approach to assess specific passive genotype-environment correlations. With this model, Loehlin and DeFries (submitted) estimated passive genotype-environment correlation to be .07 in the case of infants' difficult temperament and FES Personal Growth.

Conclusion

Several breakthroughs combine to make the study of genotype-environment correlation a promising field for developmental research. The previous chapter indicated that the amount of variance accounted for by genotype-environment interaction is uncertain and that attempts to isolate specific interactions have so far failed. In contrast, genotype-environment correlation accounts for substantial variance, at least for IQ. It seems reasonable to suppose that genotype-environment correlation will also be found to be important in other domains of development such as temperament. In addition, analyses of the CAP infancy data have been successful in isolating several examples of specific reactive genotype-environment correlations for temperament, all of which could be interpreted as negative.

The possibility of negative genotype-environment correlation in personality development as predicted by Cattell (1973) is one direction for developmental research. So far, negative genotype-environment correlation is at most mentioned in passing in discussions of genotype-environment correlation, and it deserves more serious treatment. Negative genotype-environment correlation might be important for cognitive development, as well as personality, in that more attention might be given to fostering the cognitive development of slower children.

The most important spur for research in this field is Scarr and McCartney's theory based on the three types of genotype-environment correlation that suggests processes by which genotypes transact with environments during development. Some support was found for their theory in that passive genotype-environment correlation appears to diminish in importance from childhood to adolescence for IQ, and reactive and active genotype-environment correlations appear to account for substantial variance after childhood. In addition to its heuristic predictions, the value of the theory lies in its attempt to bridge the gap between quantitative genetic components of variance and developmental processes.

The following chapters continue this discussion of the developmental interface between genes and environment, turning to specific measures of the environment and considering the possibility that genetic factors account for some of the variability observed for environmental measures.

7 Genes Affect Measures of the Environment

To say that the environment is affected by genes sounds like something from *Alice in Wonderland* where things become "curiouser and curiouser." In this case, however, much of the curiousness is definitional, as it was in Alice's adventures with Humpty-Dumpty in *Through the Looking-Glass*. The obsolete nature-nurture dichotomy put genes on one side of the battle line and environment on the other. It is only this odd definition that makes it sound curious to say that genes affect measures of the environment.

The apparent paradox disappears with the realization that measures of the environment are often measures of behavior. In developmental psychology, environmental measures are measures of parental behavior. If parental behavior underlies measures of the environment, it is only a short leap to imagine that heredity can affect parental behavior and thereby indirectly affect measures of the environment.

Environmental Measures Depend Upon Parental Behavior

Parental behavior is clearly involved in the two major "superfactors" of childrearing—parental love and control. Some parents hug and kiss their children whenever they are within reach; others rarely display physical affection. Parental behavior also is ultimately responsible for measures of physical aspects of the home environment. For example, the most widely used environmental measure in studies of mental development is the number of books in the home. But books do not magically appear on the shelves—parents put them there.

Once said, it seems obvious that environmental measures involve parental behavior. However, because this issue is fundamental to the recognition of genetic effects on environmental measures, a few additional examples are in order. The two most common measures of the family environment are Caldwell and Bradley's (1978) Home Observation for Measurement of the Environment (HOME) and the Family Environment Scales (FES) of Moos and Moos (1981). The HOME uses observations and interviews to assess environmental factors relevant to cognitive development. Each of the 45 items clearly involves parental behavior; for example, the first item is "Mother spontaneously vocalizes to child at least twice during visit." The six scales of the HOME also reflect the influence of parental behavior: Emotional and verbal responsivity of the mother, avoidance of restriction and punishment, organization of the physical and temporal environment, provision of appropriate play materials, maternal involvement with child, and opportunities for variety in daily stimulation.

The FES, a 90-item self-report questionnaire, "focuses on the measurement and description of the interpersonal relationships among family members, on the directions of personal growth which are emphasized in the family, and on the basic organizational structure of the family" (Moos, 1974, p. 3). Because it is a self-report instrument, the FES assesses perceptions of the environment rather than objective features. Nonetheless, perceptions of the environment are just as interesting as objective measures. If discrepancies exist between subjective perceptions of one's environment and objective measures of the environment (little is known about the magnitude of this relationship), both types of assessment could be useful in description, prediction, and intervention. The input of feelings, attitudes, and personality is apparent in an individual's perceptions of the family's cohesion, expressiveness, conflict, independence, achievement orientation, intellectual-cultural orientation, active-recreational orientation, moral-religious emphasis, organization, and control. For parents of infants, scores on the FES primarily involve parental behavior; for families with older children, behaviors of the children as well as the parents are likely to affect FES reports.

Assessing Genetic Influence on Environmental Measures

Behavioral Genetic Studies of Parents

If measures of the home environment are viewed as indirectly assessing parental behavior, the measures can be used in behavioral genetic studies in the same way as any other phenotypic measure such as tests of cognitive abilities and personality questionnaires. For example, adult identical and fraternal twins who are parents with their own families could be observed and interviewed using the HOME instrument. Although it is certainly reasonable to hypothesize that the way in which one rears one's children is influenced by one's own rearing as a child, it is also possible that heredity affects individual differences in parenting. If heredity is important, identical twins will be more similar in their childrearing than will fraternal twins. That is, when the HOME scores obtained in each twin's home are correlated within pairs of identical twins and fraternal twins, a genetic hypothesis predicts that correlations for identical twins will be greater than those for fraternal twins.

The effect of shared family environment can also be assessed using methods discussed in chapter 4; in this case, shared family environment means that growing up in the same family makes siblings similar to one another in the home environments that they provide for their offspring. It obviously would be difficult to observe a large sample of adult twins interacting with their offspring; self-report questionnaires such as the FES that can be administered by mail would make the task easier. Despite the importance of understanding the etiology of individual differences in parenting styles, no research of this type has as yet been reported.

Behavioral genetic designs other than the twin method could also be used to study genetic and environmental effects on parenting. For example, family designs that compare pairs of individuals who share both heredity and family environment (e.g., parents and offspring, siblings), can provide evidence for the hallmark of heredity: family resemblance. If family members show no resemblance for environmental measures, heredity cannot be an important factor. However, familial resemblance does not prove the case for genetic influence because resemblance can be mediated by environment as well as heredity. Nonetheless, family studies of environmental influence are important because normal families are the population to which we wish to generalize. Family studies are likely to use siblings because they, in contrast to parent-offspring comparisons, provide contemporaneous comparisons. However, parent-offspring studies are possible if parental assessments made at least two decades ago can be compared to data collected on the offspring as they become parents. An easier method is to compare parents' childrearing with their perceptions of their parents' childrearing, although interpretation would be made difficult by possible biases inherent in retrospective recollections of parental behavior.

In addition to twin and family studies, data from adoption designs would be useful because they can provide direct estimates of genetic influence by comparing pairs of genetically related individuals reared apart in uncorrelated environments rather than subtracting one correlation from another as in the twin method. The most persuasive data for demonstrating genetic influence on environmental measures would come from a study of adult identical twins who had been reared apart. If genetics affects environmental measures such as the HOME, the environments identical twins provide for their offspring will be similar even though the twins were reared in different families. The power of estimates of genetic influence would be enhanced by including separated fraternal twins as well as matched pairs of identical and fraternal twins reared in the same families. Just such a study is in progress in Sweden using the FES for over 200 pairs of middle-aged twins reared in different homes and a comparable number of matched twins reared together (Pedersen, Friberg, Floderus-Myrhed, McClearn, & Plomin, 1983), although no results are as yet available from this study. Analogous to genetic estimates using the adoption design, a direct estimate of the impact of family upbringing on one's own childrearing could be derived from environmental assessments in the homes of genetically unrelated pairs of individuals who had been reared together.

Behavioral Genetic Studies of the Environments of Children

The discussion so far has focused on behavioral genetic studies of adults rearing their own families. Although no data have as yet been reported using this approach, such studies could provide a direct answer to the question of genetic influence on measures of the home environment. What have been reported are behavioral genetic studies of children's environments, especially studies of adolescent twins and their perceptions of their environments. Conceptually, these approaches are quite different: A study of adult twins rearing their own separate families considers the home environment that twins provide for their children, whereas a study of twin children in the same family focuses on the home environment provided by the twins' parents.

For this reason, the two approaches could yield dissimilar estimates of genetic influence on environmental measures. A study of twin parents will implicate genetic influence to the extent that any parental characteristics—personality, psychopathology, cognitive abilities—are genetically related to environmental measures. In addition, genetic influence will emerge to the extent that the twin parents respond to genetic differences among their children, a reactive genotype-environment correlation as discussed in chapter 6. For example, identical twins will respond more similarly to their children than will fraternal twins because the children of identical twins are, from a genetic point of view, half-siblings whereas the children of fraternal twins are cousins. In contrast, a study of twin children's environment is limited to genetic influence that accrues because parents respond to genetic characteristics of the children. A special case involves the use of children's perceptions of their environment: If these perceptions are nonveridical, genetic effects must be due entirely to genetically influenced characteristics of the children.

A complete picture of genetic influence on environmental measures will require studies that focus on the origins of parental childrearing behavior. However, research to date has exclusively involved behavioral genetic studies of children's environments. This research is the topic of the following sections on twin and adoption research.

Twin Research

Only four twin studies have been reported with data relevant to the topic of genetic influence on environmental measures. Two of these studies incidentally included measures of twins' environments; the only systematic research on the topic has been conducted by David Rowe (1981, 1983).

Rowe's Research

Rather than observing parental behavior or asking parents to complete questionnaires, Rowe's pioneering research employed adolescent twins' ratings of their parents' treatment:

> A novel approach to the study of the home environment is to model environmental treatments using behavioral genetic methods. The "environment" that is experienced by a child is certainly not a phenotypic characteristic of the child in the traditional sense of a measurable trait. The type of environment a child experiences is the result of a long history of parent-child interaction that involves both characteristics of the parent and of the child. However, when the environment is measured independently for each child in a family, behavioral genetic approaches are applicable to it. The environment of sibling A can be correlated with the environment of sibling B. (Rowe, 1983, p. 416)

In his first study, Rowe (1981) focused on three dimensions of perceived parenting—a love dimension which he called *acceptance-rejection* and two control dimensions labelled *control-autonomy* and *firm-lax control*—using an abbreviated version of Schaefer's Children's Reports of Parental Behavior Inventory. The study included 89 adolescent twin pairs and each twin rated his or her mother's and father's parenting separately. The twin results suggested substantial genetic influence on the love dimension: The identical and fraternal twin correlations were .74 and .21, respectively, when the adolescents described their fathers' acceptance-rejection and .54 and .17 when the twins rated their mothers. The identical and fraternal twin correlations did not differ significantly for the two control dimensions.

Similar results were obtained in a second study using a different environmental measure (Rowe, 1983). The FES was completed by 90 pairs of adolescent twins and 118 pairs of nontwin siblings. Two second-order factors were derived which appear to be related to the love and control dimensions typically found in studies of parental behavior. As in the first study, the twin correlations suggested genetic influence for the love dimension and no genetic influence for the control dimension. The identical and fraternal twin correlations for the love dimension were .63 and .21, respectively; for the control dimension, the correlations were .44 and .54. One might wonder whether twins are hypersensitive to perceived differences in their parents' treatment of them and their same-aged cotwins;

however, the nontwin siblings in Rowe's (1983) study were as similar as fraternal twins for both the love and control dimensions. As indicated earlier, it is an open question whether adolescents' perceptions of their parents' affection reflect actual differences in parental treatment. However, regardless of the answer to this question, subjective perceptions may be as important as objective observations in predicting the course of adolescent development.

In summary, Rowe's research suggests that differences in adolescents' perceptions of their parents' affection are substantially mediated by genetic factors. That is, genetics plays a role in what could be called the "Smothers' Brothers" effect: One of the folk-singer twins explained away all of his problems with his twin partner by saying, "Mother always loved you best."

Other Twin Research

No research other than Rowe's has systematically explored the possibility of genetic influence on environmental measures. However, two twin studies provide data that are relevant. In a report on 850 pairs of high-school twins (Loehlin & Nichols, 1976), an appendix contains twin resemblance data for over a thousand items. Several items relate to twins' perceptions of their parents' treatment. Intraclass correlations for these quantitative ratings are listed in Table 7.1. Each item shows greater similarity for identical twins than for fraternal twins, thus supporting the hypothesis that heredity influences environmental measures based on adolescents' perceptions of their parents' treatment. The average twin correlations are .54 and .36 for identical and fraternal twins, respectively.

These data also support the hypothesis that genes influence perceptions of parental love more than perceptions of parental control. The only control-related item for the adolescents' self-report was "Swore in presence of your parents;" it yielded identical and fraternal twin correlations of .58 and .48, respectively, one of the smallest difference between identical and fraternal twin correlations in the table. Another item that yielded a small difference in identical and fraternal twin correlations was "Had a quarrel with your father" and this item, too, might be related to control. In contrast, two items most related to parental love (items 835 and 836, which ask how well each twin gets along with mother and father) show the greatest difference between identical and fraternal twin correlations.

The Loehlin and Nichols' data set also includes parental ratings of their treatment of their twin children. To the extent that genetic effects on childrearing are mediated by genetic differences among children rather than genetic differences among parents, parents' reports of their treatment of their children should correlate more highly for identical twins than for fraternal twins. Table 7.2 lists discordance percentages for 10 qualitative ratings by parents concerning their treatment of their twin children. The data consistently show greater differential treatment of fraternal twins as compared to identical twins which, implicates

TABLE 7.1
Twin Correlations for Adolescents' Perceptions of Their Environment
(Loehlin & Nichols, 1976)

	Twin Correlations	
	Identical	Fraternal
Environmental Measure	505 pairs	329 pairs
Objective Behavior Inventory[a]		
207. Swore in the presence of your parents	.58	.48
233. Discussed sexual matters with your mother	.44	.21
255. Had a quarrel with your mother	.42	.17
256. Had a quarrel with your father	.55	.47
286. Kissed your mother	.65	.51
287. Kissed your father	.67	.55
Interpersonal Relations Scale[b]		
During the past year, how well did you get along with the following people?		
835. Your mother	.50	.26
836. Your father	.50	.20

[a]The Objective Behavior Inventory consists of 324 items rated as occurring frequently, occasionally, or not at all during the past year.

[b]On these items, each twin used a 5-point scale: very well, fairly well, just "so-so," fairly poor, very poorly.

TABLE 7.2
Twins' Percent Discordance for Parents' Reports of Their Treatment
of Adolescent Twins (Loehlin & Nichols, 1976)[a]

	Twin Discordance	
	Identical	Fraternal
Environmental Measure	505 pairs	329 pairs
121. Frequently disagreed openly with parents	.05	.14
122. Often talked over personal problems with parents	.03	.08
238. Received more attention from the mother	.10	.19
239. Received more attention from the father	.08	.15
243. Was closer to the mother	.19	.31
244. Was closer to the father	.16	.25
246. Had stricter discipline as a child	.08	.12
247. Had stricter discipline as an adolescent	.08	.13
264. Was spanked more often as a child	.11	.31
265. Was rocked and held more often as a child	.10	.24

[a]The parents of the twins answered 198 questions about their twins. The following items listed in the appendix of Loehlin and Nichols' book involve environmental questions that showed no differentiation within the pairs of twins: 20, 21, 28, 32, 46, 50, 57, 80, 103, 119, 128, 130, 132, 150, 151, 153, 155. For items 121 and 122, parents indicated whether the statement was true of one or the other twin, both twins, or neither twin. The remaining items in the table were concerned with differences between the twins, and parents responded whether an item was most appropriate for one of the twins or for neither.

genetic influence. The average percent discordance for the 10 items is 9% for identical twins and 19% for fraternal twins. Thus, parents of fraternal twins are twice as likely as parents of identical twins to report that they treat their children differently.

The parental report data provide some support for the hypothesis that genetic influences play a larger role in parental love than in parental control, although the results for item 264, "Was spanked more often as a child," are problematic for this hypothesis. This item yielded the greatest difference between identical and fraternal twin discordances. Although one might argue that the item relates to parental love, a more straightforward interpretation considers the item as parental control. If the item taps control, its substantial genetic influence speaks against the hypothesis that heredity influences parental love more than parental control. However, the other items in Table 7.2 tend to support the hypothesis. After item 264, the two items with the largest differences between identical and fraternal twins are item 265 ("Was rocked and held more often as a child") and item 243 ("Was closer to the mother"). Two clear control items ("Had stricter discipline as a child;" "Had stricter discipline as an adolescent") showed the smallest differential treatment of identical and fraternal twins. The ambiguous nature of item 264, the supporting data from the other items, and the heuristic value of the hypothesis argue for retention of the hypothesis that genetic differences affect parental love more than parental control.

Although these parental report data implicate genetic influence on measures of the environment, it should be noted that parents do not often report treating their children differently, perhaps because this goes against social conventions. The greatest twin discordance in Table 7.2 is 31% and, as explained in the footnote to the table, parents reported virtually no difference in treatment for an additional 16 items listed in the appendix of Loehlin and Nichols' book. Because these items show negligible variability, they cannot be analyzed using the twin method.

This point is underlined in the only other relevant twin study (Cohen, Dibble, & Grawe, 1977). In a study of young twins from 1 to 6 years of age, parents rated their treatment of each of their twin children separately using a questionnaire developed as an amalgamation of other parenting questionnaires. Correlations for both identical and fraternal twin pairs exceeded .90 for both love and control dimensions. The high rate of professed similarity of treatment leads to minimal differences between identical and fraternal twin correlations. Thus, if the data are taken at face value, they suggest that parents do not respond to genetic differences between their children. Although parents of adolescent twins in Loehlin and Nichols' study also reported treating their twins quite similarly, the degree of similarity of treatment was not nearly as high as in the study by Cohen et al. and evidence for genetic influence was found in that identical twins were treated more similarly than fraternal twins. Although methodological and measurement artifacts could be responsible for these differing results, the more interesting possibility is that there may be a developmental trend towards greater differentiation of parental treatment from early childhood to adolescence with a concomitant increase in genetic mediation of this differentiation.

Conclusions from Twin Research

The data from these studies of Rowe, Loehlin and Nichols, and Cohen et al. are limited in three ways. Most importantly, the data are limited to paper-and-pencil questionnaires. Observations and interview data are needed, although these self-report data would be interesting even if they turned out to be unrelated to objective observations. Secondly, with the exception of the study by Cohen et al., the data are limited to adolescence; it is hazardous to generalize too far from the tumultuous world of adolescence for genetic as well as environmental reasons. Third, with the exception of Rowe's (1983) inclusion of data on a nontwin sibling sample, the studies are limited to twins, whose unusual condition of having a sibling of exactly the same age might make them hypersensitive to perceived differences in their parents' treatment. Recently, data have been collected that begin to fill in some of these gaps—this is the topic of the next section.

Despite these limitations, the twin data suggest three exciting hypotheses:

1. Genetic variation affects variation in adolescents' perceptions of their parents' love.

2. Genetic variation does not affect variation in adolescents' perceptions of their parents' control.

3. Parents' own reports of parenting indicate that they treat twin partners quite similarly. When differential treatment of adolescent twins is found, genetic factors are implicated.

Adoption Research

Studies of genetically related family members separated by adoption and genetically unrelated individuals brought together in adoptive homes can also be used to assess the extent of genetic involvement in measures of the home environment. As mentioned earlier, studies of separated identical twin parents would provide the most persuasive evidence for genetic influence; similarly, resemblance for environmental measures for separated twins or nontwin siblings reared in different families would also implicate genetic influence. However, most adoption studies employ a parent-offspring design that is inefficient for addressing this issue because of the difficulty of assessing comparable environments for parents and their offspring.

Another type of adoption design relies on comparisons of correlations for two types of family relationships as in the twin method. Instead of comparing the similarity of pairs of identical and fraternal twins who are similar genetically 100% and 50%, respectively, comparisons can be made between pairs of biological siblings and pairs of genetically unrelated individuals reared together who are similar genetically 50% and 0%, respectively. If genetic factors are important in the etiology of environmental differences, correlations for biological siblings will exceed those for genetically unrelated pairs reared together. Selective placement, the matching of biological and adoptive parents, attenuates the clean separation of genetic and environmental influences in an adoption study. In this case, however, the bias is a conservative one: If selective placement exists, it serves to make adoptive siblings genetically similar to one another and decreases the difference in correlations between biological and adoptive siblings, thus lowering estimates of genetic influence.

Adolescents and the SIDE.   A recent study has used this approach in an attempt to study nonshared family environmental influence as discussed in chapter 4. The Sibling Inventory of Differential Experience (SIDE) was developed to assess nonshared experiences of siblings in relation to parents, peers, and each other (Daniels & Plomin, 1985). Siblings rate their experiences relative to their sibling rather than in an absolute sense. For example, one of the parental treatment items of the SIDE is, "Mother has been sensitive to what we think and feel." Each sibling answers on a 5-point scale: 1 = toward sibling much more, 2 = toward sibling a bit more, 3 = same toward my sibling and me, 4 = toward me a bit more, and 5 = toward me much more. The relative scoring of the SIDE can be transformed so that perceived differences in experience can be assessed regardless of which twin was favored. Specifically, scores of 1 ("sibling much more") and 5 ("me much more") are made equal to 2; scores of 2 and 4 are set to 1; and scores of 3 are changed to 0. Thus, for each item, scores for siblings' experiences can range from 0 (no difference) to 2 (much difference).

Although the SIDE assesses within-family environment that may be unrelated to the usual measures of between-family environment, comparisons of adoptive and nonadoptive sibling pairs provide some support for genetic influence on adolescents' perceptions of their differential experiences. Table 7.3 presents mean differences reported by genetically unrelated and genetically related pairs. If genes affect the SIDE measures of within-family environment, the means for adoptive pairs will exceed those for nonadoptive pairs because the adoptive pairs differ genetically to a greater extent than do biological sibling pairs. This greater genetic difference within adoptive pairs will lead to greater differences in the adoptees' perceptions of their environment.

Overall, the 11 SIDE scales yield a mean difference of .76 for adoptive pairs and .69 for nonadoptive pairs. Four scales showed significantly greater differential experience for adoptive than for adoptive siblings. One of these scales is Differential Sibling Closeness. This result is interesting because the Sibling Closeness scale is a love-related dimension and thus this finding supports the

TABLE 7.3
Adoptive and Nonadoptive Sibling Mean Differences on the Sibling
Inventory of Differential Experience (Daniels & Plomin, 1985)[a]

SIDE Scales	Adoptive Siblings		Nonadoptive Siblings	
	Mean Difference	Standard Deviation	Mean Difference	Standard Deviation
Differential Sibling Antagonism	.83	.37	.75	.38
Differential Sibling Caretaking	.85	.35	.79	.32
Differential Sibling Jealousy	.89	.43	.83	.45
Differential Sibling Closeness	.78*	.46	.62	.46
Differential Maternal Affection	.49	.44	.49	.45
Differential Maternal Control	.62	.48	.64	.51
Differential Paternal Affection	.50	.45	.54	.48
Differential Paternal Control	.64	.50	.69	.54
Differential Peer Orientation	.84*	.38	.72	.36
Differential Peer Delinquency	.96*	.50	.80	.48
Differential Peer Popularity	.97*	.45	.73	.45

*Mean of adoptive siblings significantly (p < .05) greater than mean of nonadoptive siblings.
[a]The sample sizes vary from 175 to 205 for adoptive siblings and from 149 to 179 for nonadoptive siblings with the exception of the three peer scales with samples of 157, 106, and 166, respectively, for the adoptive siblings and 136, 115, and 149 for the nonadoptive siblings.

hypothesis that affection scales involve genetic influence. On the other hand, the parental affection scales do not show genetic influence, a result that conflicts with the twin results mentioned earlier and with adoptive and nonadoptive sibling data in infancy described later. However, the SIDE parental affection scales include the following items: proud, enjoy being with, sensitive to feelings, show interest in, and favoritism—these items convey a flavor of the parent wanting to be with the sibling which is only one component of affection.

The other three SIDE scales displaying significant genetic influence involve peer characteristics. Adoptive siblings perceived greater differences than did biological siblings in the extent to which one sibling is more likely than the other to be in a college-oriented peer group, a delinquent peer group, or a popular peer group. It is possible that personality characteristics or cognitive abilities that are genetically influenced might lead each sibling to seek out peers with matching characteristics:

For example, differences in intelligence, delinquency, and sociability—characteristics that appear to be influenced genetically—could lead an individual to join peer groups that are more or less college oriented, delinquent, or popular in nature. However, after different peer groups have been chosen, differing characteristics of the groups could accentuate behavioral differences between siblings (Daniels & Plomin, 1985, p.759)

Infants and Observations of Maternal Behavior. The research by Dunn and her colleagues described in chapter 4 adds two new dimensions to this area: observational data and infants. These researchers rated videotapes of mothers interacting with each of two siblings when each child was 12 months old (Dunn, Plomin, & Nettles, 1985) and when each child was 24 months old (Dunn, Plomin, & Daniels, in press). The major finding from these studies is the discovery that mothers treat their two successive children quite consistently at 12 months and at 24 months even though three years separate the two children on average. However, because the siblings were participants in the Colorado Adoption Project, some were adoptive siblings. Given the substantial similarity in mothers' responding to their two children, it seemed unlikely that the mothers' behavior would be influenced by genetic differences between the siblings. Nonetheless, as a preliminary check on this possibility, correlations for mothers' behavior toward biological siblings (32 pairs) were compared with correlations for mothers' behavior towards adoptive siblings (14 pairs) at 12 months. For two scales, maternal verbal responsiveness and maternal control, correlations for adoptive siblings and biological siblings were nearly identical. However, mothers' affection yielded a correlation of .37 for adoptive siblings and .70 for biological siblings at 12 months (Dunn et al., 1985). Although the difference in correlations is not statistically significant, the finding is interesting because it is in the direction expected if mothers' behavior is influenced by genetic differences between their children and because it corresponds with Rowe's (1983) finding that measures of parental affection show genetic influence, whereas measures of parental control do not.

The finding assumes more significance because the same result was found in analyses of 24-month-olds: The correlation for the mothers' affection towards her two children is .31 for adoptive siblings and .60 for biological siblings. The item loading most highly on this scale of mothers' affection was maternal supportive presence, and the correlation for this item is -.04 for mothers' behavior toward adoptive siblings and .58 for mothers of nonadoptive siblings. Even with the small sample size, this latter difference in correlations is statistically significant. Thus, taken together, these observational results suggest that maternal affection, even though quite similar toward successive children, is affected by genetic differences between the children.

The CAP sibling data in infancy were also examined in a similar way for two standard measures of home environment, Home Observation for Measurement of the Environment (HOME; Caldwell & Bradley, 1978) and the Family Environment Scales (FES; Moos & Moos, 1981), assessed separately for each child in 72 nonadoptive and 61 adoptive sibling pairs at 12 months and for 53 nonadoptive and 50 adoptive pairs at 24 months (Daniels, 1985). As mentioned in chapter 4, sibling correlations were in general quite substantial for these environmental measures. Nonetheless, some evidence for genetic influence emerged. For example, for the HOME general factor at 12 months, the correlations were .49 for nonadoptive siblings and .34 for adoptive siblings; at 24 months, the correlations were .46 and .40, respectively. For two second-order factors of the FES at 12 months, the nonadoptive and adoptive sibling correlations were, respectively, .67 and .54 for "personal growth" and .86 and .71 for "traditional organization."

Thus, the adoption data add to the growing support for genetic influence on measures of the environment. They extend the twin studies in four ways:

1. Genetic effects on environmental measures can be found using the adoption design as well as the twin method. Although both methods involve potential problems, the problems are different for the two methods and strong support is provided for the hypothesis that genes influence environmental measures because both methods converge on this conclusion.

2. Genes influence measures of nonshared family environment as well as traditional measures of shared family environment. That is, genes not only affect adolescents' perceptions of their experiences, they also affect siblings' perceptions of *differences* in their experiences.

3. Genes affect sibling interactions as well as parent-child interactions. Differential sibling closeness, a love-related dimension, shows significant genetic influence.

4. Genes affect experiences beyond family interactions. Sibling differences in peer group characteristics are nonshared environmental factors affected by genetic characteristics of adolescents.

These hypotheses are rife with implications for developmentalists. At a conceptual level, they suggest a reconceptualization of environmental influences that recognizes the possibility of genetic influence. Empirically, research is needed to discover which aspects of the family environment are influenced most by heredity and which parental characteristics are responsible for genetic influence on environmental measures. These issues are discussed in the following section.

Implications

Once one recognizes that environmental measures indirectly assess behavior, it no longer seems paradoxical to assert that genetic factors account for some of the variability in measures of the environment. Twin and adoption data generally support this hypothesis and suggest that perceptions of affection might be influenced by genetic factors to a greater extent than perceptions of control. Also, genetic effects emerge more clearly for adolescents' perceptions of treatment by their parents than for parents' reports of their treatment of their children. Finally, in addition to influencing traditional environmental measures of shared family environment, heredity also seems to affect nonshared environmental measures, perhaps to a lesser extent. For nonshared environment, genetic effects are seen more often for sibling interaction variables than for parental treatment variables. Genetic effects on nonshared environment also extend beyond the family to peer groups.

It should be noted that the studies described in this chapter assessed only a limited portion of possible genetic effects on environmental measures. A twin study of adult twins rearing their own families could assess in a straightforward manner the extent of genetic involvement in measures of the home environment. However, existing data are limited to behavioral genetic studies of children rather than parents. Because of this, the studies primarily address genetic influences brought about by parental responses to genetic differences among their children and the results thus support the existence of reactive genotype-environment correlation as described in chapter 6. To the extent that parents do not respond to genetic differences among children, this approach will not find evidence for genetic influence on measures of the home environment even though a study of adult twins might find substantial genetic influence on the same environmental measures. This is the case for twin studies of children using parental reports of the home environment as well as children's perceptions of their environment, assuming that the children's perceptions accurately reflect their parents' behavior. If children's perceptions of their home environment are completely subjective, twin studies using children's perceptions will reveal genetic influences mediated by personality and cognitive characteristics of the children. Genetic influences of this type are likely to differ from those found in a study of the home environments provided by adult twins rearing their own children.

One major implication of these findings is that labelling a measure *environmental* does not make it an environmental measure. Heredity can play a role in such measures via genetically influenced characteristics of parents and children. One direction for research is to identify environmental measures most and least influenced genetically. For example, will research continue to support the hypothesis that love-related aspects of parental and sibling interaction are influenced by heredity to a greater extent than are control-related aspects of family interaction? Moreover, extant environmental measures are crude and the data reported so far primarily utilize self-report questionnaires. There is a need for fine-grained research on family interactions, especially research involving naturalistic observations of parent-child interactions. Knowledge about the most and least genetically influenced environmental measures would undoubtedly advance our understanding of the nature of environmental influences in the family and it might also help in planning interventions.

A second implication and direction for research is to identify parental and child characteristics that mediate genetic influence on environmental measures. A start in this direction is the examination of phenotypic correlations between environmental measures and parental characteristics. It is only a beginning

TABLE 7.4
Correlations between HOME and FES Environmental Measures
and Parental Characteristics in the Colorado Adoption Project
(Plomin & DeFries, 1985)[a]

Parental Characteristic	HOME General Factor	FES Personal Growth
IQ		
Mother	.11	.13
Father	.14*	.15*
Emotionality-fear		
Mother	−.07	−.20*
Father	−.07	−.15*
Emotionality-anger		
Mother	.01	−.16*
Father	.03	.03
Activity		
Mother	.11	.16*
Father	.06	.21*
Sociability		
Mother	.24*	.24*
Father	.12*	.19*
16PF Extraversion		
Mother	.21*	.23*
Father	.13*	.18*
16PF Neuroticism		
Mother	−.19*	−.36*
Father	−.10	−.18*

*$p < .05$.

[a]The environmental measures and measures of parental characteristics are described elsewhere (Plomin & DeFries, 1985). The environmental measures were administered when the parents' children were about 1 year old. The FES scores are midparent ratings (i.e., the average of the mother's and father's ratings in each family). Sample sizes vary from 271 to 331 for mothers and 272 to 324 for fathers.

because such phenotypic correlations could be mediated environmentally rather than genetically. Multivariate genetic-environmental analysis is needed to disentangle genetic and environmental sources of covariance between environmental measures and parental characteristics (Plomin & DeFries, 1979). Nonetheless, the first step is to identify phenotypic relationships between environmental measures and parental and child characteristics.

For example, does parental personality affect parental affection? One study found a strong relationship between parental sociability and parental love (Zuckerman & Oltean, 1958). However, this question has not been systematically explored. For this reason, in Table 7.4, correlations between HOME and FES environmental measures and parental personality and IQ are reported for

TABLE 7.5
Correlations Between College Students' Ratings of Family
Environment and Their Self-Reported Personality[a]

	Personality Measure				
Environmental Measure	Emotionality (Anger)	Emotionality (Fear)	Activity	Sociability	Shyness
Sibling antagonism	.19*	.06	.02	.09	.04
Sibling jealousy	.00	.20*	.17	.05	.13
Sibling caretaking	−.22*	.09	.05	.07	.18*
Sibling closeness	−.18*	.04	.09	−.05	−.05
Maternal affection	.04	−.11	.04	.22	−.21*
Maternal control	−.13	.05	.14	.14	.06
Paternal affection	−.06	−.07	−.10	−.07	.03
Paternal control	.01	−.10	.12	.14	−.14
Peer delinquency	.13	−.11	−.09	.18*	−.11
Peer college orientation	−.08	−.25*	.15	.05	−.17
Peer popularity	−.05	−.32*	.36*	.32*	−.18*

*p < .05.

[a]The environmental measure is an "absolute" version of the relatively-scored SIDE questionnaire described elsewhere (Daniels & Plomin, 1985). The personality questionnaire is a modified version of the EAS (Buss & Plomin, 1984). The sample includes 90 college students.

mothers and fathers in 182 adoptive and 165 nonadoptive families in the Colorado Adoption Project (Plomin & DeFries, 1985). The HOME correlates modestly with parental IQ and with parental extraversion and sociability, two of the most highly heritable aspects of personality (Loehlin, 1982). The FES Personal Growth second-order factor correlates positively with parental IQ, activity, sociability, and extraversion and negatively with parental emotionality and neuroticism. Although these relationships are modest, they could add up to produce substantial genetic influence on these measures of the home environment.

Table 7.5 shows similar results for young adults' perceptions of their home environment. These data, previously unpublished, were collected as part of the study by Daniels and Plomin (1985). In Table 7.5, self-report personality data are related to college students' perceptions of their family environment using an "absolute" version of the relatively-scored SIDE questionnaire, described earlier in this chapter and in chapter 4. Instead of asking participants to indicate how they are treated relative to their sibling as in the SIDE questionnaire, college students were asked to rate their family experiences in an absolute sense. Ratings of their experiences were related to a modified version of the EAS (Buss & Plomin, 1984) personality questionnaire.

The correlations between environmental perceptions and personality are somewhat lower for these young adults than for parents (see Table 7.4 for comparison). The greatest correlations with personality occur for peer popularity, which correlates negatively with fearfulness and shyness and positively with activity and sociability. Similar results were obtained when the relatively scored version of the SIDE was used: Siblings who reported that they were, compared to their sibling, less fearful and shy and more active and sociable also reported that their peer groups were more popular than their siblings' peer groups. Because peer group popularity is one of the SIDE scales which displayed genetic influence, sibling personality might account for some of the genetic influence on this dimension of experience. However, children's personality as assessed by the EAS questionnaire is not likely to be a major explanation for the SIDE Differential Sibling Closeness scale which showed the greatest evidence for genetic involvement. Although sibling closeness correlates negatively with emotionality-anger, its other personality correlates are negligible. In general, fearfulness and shyness show the most correlations with the SIDE scales, correlating positively with sibling jealousy and caretaking and negatively with maternal affection and peer group popularity and college orientation.

In summary, some environmental measures are related to measures of personality and IQ, and these relationships might at least in part account for genetic influence on environmental measures. However, it is likely that traditional measures of personality and cognition do not entirely capture the genetically-influenced concomitants of environmental measures in the intense, emotion-laden context of parent-child and sibling relationships. Research on this topic is thus likely not only to extend our knowledge of environmental processes, but also will lead to new ways of thinking about behavior of parents and children in the context of the family.

As interesting as it is to consider genetic influence on environmental measures, the real importance of this issue lies in the possibility that genetic influences on environmental measures are translated into genetic effects on the relationship between environmental measures and children's development. This is the topic of the next chapter.

8

Genes Mediate Relationships Between Environment and Development

For developmentalists, what is important about the environment is its impact on children. The previous chapter focused on environmental measures per se without concern about their relationship to children's development. This chapter addresses the etiology of relationships between environmental measures such as the HOME and measures of development such as Bayley's Mental Development Index. The consistent finding that heredity influences variability in environmental measures increases the plausibility of the hypothesis that relationships between environmental measures and measures of development can be mediated genetically. In fact, unless environmental measures show genetic influence, genes cannot be involved in the relationship between environment and development. On the other hand, one cannot assume that environment-development relationships are mediated genetically just because environmental measures and developmental measures are influenced genetically. For example, variance among parents on the HOME could be substantially genetic, as could variance among children in IQ, yet the covariance between the HOME and children's IQ could be due solely to the nongenetic portions of HOME variance and IQ variance. This issue gets at the heart of the nature-nurture interface in development and is likely to be the meeting place of environmentalists and behavioral geneticists. For example, a well-known environmentalist has written about the need to integrate environmental research and behavioral genetic research and alludes to the theme of this chapter:

> One major factor blocking this sorely needed integration of disciplines is a continued reliance on outmoded conceptions about the nature of each discipline. Thus, most environmentalists are more or less ignorant of current theories, concepts, and results in the area of behavior genetics. As a consequence,

environmentalists all too often ingore the possibility of genetic influences in their research (Plomin et al., 1980). Thus, correlations between parental behaviors and child development are commonly viewed as due solely to the contributions of the environment; rarely do we find consideration of the possibility that these correlations may reflect the contribution of shared genes that influence both the parents' behavior and the child's development. . . . In contrast, in behavioral genetic studies the environment is either estimated but not measured or is only measured indirectly. . . . Eventually, an understanding of the nature of human development will require the joint input of environmentalists and behavior geneticists. (Wachs, 1983, pp. 396-397)

The present chapter examines the possibility that heredity can mediate relationships between measures of the home environment and measures of child development. Data from older adoption studies and from the Colorado Adoption Project are then presented along with a path model that permits estimates of the genetic portion of environment-development relationships. Finally, implications of these findings are discussed.

Assessing Genetic Influence on Environment-Development Relationships

Twin Studies

How can genetic influence be detected, not for environmental or developmental measures, but for the covariance between them? For measures of perceived environment used in most of the research discussed in the previous chapter, multivariate genetic-environmental analysis (chapter 3) is relevant if the environmental measures are viewed as phenotypes of the individual. Multivariate genetic-environmental analysis estimates the genetic contribution to covariance between two phenotypic measures in a way analogous to the estimates provided by the traditional univariate quantitative genetic analysis of the variance of a single character (Plomin & DeFries, 1979).

For example, Rowe's studies, discussed in the previous chapter, suggest that parental affection as perceived by adolescent twins is genetically influenced. If measures of development—adjustment, for example—had been included in the same studies, twin cross-correlations could be used to determine the extent to which a relationship between perceived parental affection and adolescent adjustment is mediated genetically. If this particular environment-development relationship is mediated genetically, the cross- correlations between one twin's perceptions of parental affection and the other twin's adjustment should be greater for identical twins than for fraternal twins. As discussed in Chapter 3, finding greater cross-correlations for identical twins than for fraternal twins would suggest that the gene systems that affect perceptions of parental affection also affect adolescent adjustment. If the twin cross-correlations did not differ for identical and fraternal twins and if the cross-correlations were similar to the phenotypic correlation for all individuals between perceptions of parental affection and adolescent adjustment, the results would suggest that the environment-development relationship is mediated by shared environmental factors.

This use of the twin method assumes that measures of perceived environment are phenotypes of the twins themselves, which is the case if perceptions of the environment are completely subjective. However, to the extent that these measures are veridical or when more objective measures of the environment are used, multivariate genetic-environmental analysis of this type is not applicable because the environmental measure cannot be viewed as a phenotype of the twin. More complicated path models are needed; however, the crucial comparison for such models remains the cross-correlation between environmental measures and developmental measures for identical and fraternal twins. For example, if twin cross-correlations between the HOME and children's IQ are greater for identical twins than for fraternal twins, the relationship between the HOME and children's IQ must be influenced genetically. As discussed in the previous chapter, the genetic effects may be brought about by parents' responsiveness to IQ-related genetic differences among their children.

Adoption Studies

A more powerful approach to the analysis of environment-development relationships is the adoption design. Although the parent-offspring adoption design is not ideal for studying genetic effects on environmental measures, it provides a straightforward method for assessing genetic contributions to the relationship between environmental measures and measures of children's development. In nonadoptive homes, in which parents share heredity as well as family environment with their children, relationships between environmental measures and measures of children's development could be mediated genetically via parental characteristics. However, in adoptive homes, adoptive parents share only family environment with their adopted children; for this reason, correlations between measures of environment and children's development in adoptive homes cannot be mediated genetically. Thus, if genes underlie relationships between measures of the home environment and children's development, environment-development correlations in nonadoptive homes will be greater than in adoptive homes. The greater the difference between the correlations in the nonadoptive and adoptive homes, the greater the extent to which the environment-development correlation is mediated genetically.

Genetic effects on environment-development correlations in nonadoptive homes are caused in part by passive genotype-environment correlation which, as explained in chapter 6, refers to a correlation between a child's genotype and environment. This genotype-environment correlation arises passively in the sense that the child receives both genes and family environment conducive to the development of a particular character. For example, if it is found that the relationship between the HOME and children's IQ is influenced genetically, this implies that children receive a family environment indexed by the HOME that is correlated with parental characteristics that have a genetic influence on children's IQ, thus passively creating a correlation between the child's environment and genotype.

Reactive and active genotype-environment correlations could also contribute to correlations between environmental measures and children's development. For example, parents might respond to genetic differences among their children, which would lead to reactive genotype-environment correlation. Active genotype-environment correlation would emerge if children actively sought an environment correlated with their genotype—for example, if bright children elicited more stimulating conversation from their parents. However, both reactive and active genotype-environment correlations mean that a correlation between an environmental measure and children's development in adoptive homes would no longer be purely environmental. It would contain a genetic component. Thus, the difference between environment-development correlations in nonadoptive and adoptive homes would be reduced and genetic influence on environment-development relationships would be underestimated.

As discussed in chapter 6, Scarr and McCartney's genotype/environment theory suggests that passive genotype-environment correlation declines in importance during childhood, whereas reactive and active types of genotype-environment correlation becomes more influential. Finding genetic mediation of relationships between measures of environment and development depends upon passive genotype-environment; reactive and active genotype-environment correlation decreases the difference between environment-development correlations in nonadoptive and adoptive families. Putting these two notions together leads to the prediction that genetic mediation of environment-development relationships should be most easily found in infancy, an hypothesis to which we return later.

Selective placement also biases the method against finding genetic mediation of environmental influences. If adoptive parents are matched to biological parents of the adoptees, adoptive parents and adoptees will resemble each other genetically; environment-development relationships in adoptive homes will be mediated genetically to some extent. Thus, genetic influence on environment-development relationships will be underestimated in the presence of reactive and active genotype-environment correlations and selective placement.

Less variance in adoptive families than in nonadoptive families could lead to overestimates of the genetic component of environment-development relationships. Reduced variance in environmental measures in adoptive homes could lower environment-development correlations in adoptive homes and thus increase the difference between correlations in adoptive and nonadoptive homes that is used to estimate the genetic component of environmental influence. However, reduced variance in a measure of adoptees' development is to be expected when passive genotype-environment correlation affects the measure in nonadoptive homes, as indeed it should if genes mediate environmental influences. Variance is expected to be slightly lower for adoptees because they do not experience one source of variability, the component of variance brought about by passive genotype-environment correlation (see chapter 6). Thus, reduced variance in adoptive families would need to be lower than expected on the basis of passive genotype-environment correlation and sufficiently low to attenuate environment-development correlations.

These issues concerning possible biases in the comparison of environment-development relationships between adoptive families and nonadoptive families are discussed more fully in an article that first presented this approach to understanding genetic mediation of relationships between environment and development (Plomin, Loehlin, & DeFries, 1985). The bottom line is that the comparison of environment-development relationships in adoptive and nonadoptive homes provides a remarkably straightforward method to investigate genetic mediation of environmental influences. Selective placement can be assessed; moreover, its effects introduce a conservative bias in terms of finding evidence for genetic influence. Genotype-environment correlations of the reactive and active varieties are difficult to assess; however, they too create conservative biases in that they reduce the difference between correlations in adoptive and nonadoptive homes and thus cause underestimation of genetic influence on environment-development relationships. Variance differences in measures of adoptive and nonadoptive home environments are easily measured. Thus, if environment-development correlations are greater in nonadoptive homes than in adoptive homes, it can reasonably be concluded that genes mediate relationships between environment and development to some extent. The greater the difference between the correlations in the nonadoptive and adoptive homes, the greater the extent of genetic mediation.

Previous Relevant Studies

No twin studies of the type described have been reported; however, relevant adoption data do exist. What is needed is a study in which a correlation between an environmental measure and a measure of children's development is obtained in both adoptive and nonadoptive families, in the absence of marked selective placement or reduced variance in the adoptive families. Although most existing adoption studies have used distal indices of the home environment such as parental education and occupation, seven studies have included proximal environmental assessments. Of these, four included only adoptive families and thus do not permit comparisons between environment-development relationships in adoptive and nonadoptive homes (Beckwith, 1971; Duyme, 1981; Hoopes, 1982; Yarrow, Goodwin, Manheimer, & Milowe, 1973).

Three studies are relevant: Burks (1928); Freeman, Holzinger, and Mitchell (1928); and Leahy (1935). All three studies focused on IQ of children and used composite measures of the quality of the home environment thought to be related to children's IQ. Each study will be described in turn.

Burks

In 1928, Barbara Burks reported a study of approximately 200 adoptive families and 100 nonadoptive families. Home environments were assessed using the Whittier Scale for Home Grading that includes ratings on five items: ''necessities'' (essentially socioeconomic status), neatness, size of house, ''parental conditions'' (parents' level of functioning), and parental supervision. These five ratings were summed to create the Whittier Scale. Also included was a ''culture scale'' that summed five ratings: parents' ''speech'' (vocabulary), parental education, intellectual interests of parents, ''home library'' (number of books), and artistic taste.

Adoptive and nonadoptive homes did not differ in means or standard deviations for the two environmental scales or their constituent ratings. Selective placement was also slight—as mentioned earlier, the effect of selective placement is to reduce the difference between environment-development relationships in nonadoptive and adoptive homes; thus, selective placement makes it less likely that evidence for genetic influences will be discovered. Similarly, if environment-development relationships arise because of reactive genotype-environment correlation (that is, parents' behavior reflects rather than affects children's development), the chances of finding evidence for genetic effects are attenuated.

The correlations of the Whittier Scale and the culture scale with children's IQ in the adoptive and nonadoptive families are listed in Table 8.1. The correlation between the Whittier Scale and children's IQ in nonadoptive homes is .42, which is similar to the results of other studies relating environmental measures to children's IQ. However, the correlation in adoptive homes is significantly lower, exactly half the size of the correlation in the nonadoptive homes. This result supports the hypothesis that relationships between environmental assessments and children's IQ typically found in nonadoptive homes may be mediated substantially by heredity. The environment-development correlation for the culture scale is also substantially, albeit not significantly, greater in nonadoptive than in adoptive homes.

Burks (1928) noticed this difference in environment-IQ correlations in the adoptive and nonadoptive homes and made the following observation:

> These correlations can be taken as actual measures of the effect of environment in the Foster Group, and as measures of the combined effects of heredity and environ-

TABLE 8.1
Correlations of Environmental Indices with Children's IQ in Adoptive
and Nonadoptive Homes (Burks, 1928)

Environmental Index	Adoptive		Nonadoptive Homes	
	Correlation	N	Correlation	N
Whittier Scale	.21	206	.42[a]	104
Culture Scale	.25	186	.44	101

[a]Correlation in nonadoptive homes significantly greater than in adoptive homes ($p < .05$, one-tailed).

ment in the Control Group. The point is emphasized in this section . . . that *the differences between corresponding correlation coefficients in the Foster Group and Control Group are striking and consistent.* (p. 282)

However, Burks did not emphasize the obvious conclusion from these results: The relationship between these environmental indices and children's IQ is substantially mediated by genetic factors.

Freeman, Holzinger, and Mitchell

The adoption study by Freeman, Holzinger, and Mitchell (1928) included over 200 adoptive families. Although no nonadoptive families were studied, the adoptive families contained 40 nonadopted children. The mean age of the children was 10 years, although they ranged in age from 2 to 22 years. A composite home index was obtained by summing the following ratings: "material environment" ("including the neighborhood, building and grounds, furnishings, care and upkeep"), "evidence of culture" (number and quality of books, magazines, newspapers, pictures, and music), social activity (a rating "made on the basis of information given concerning social activity and use of leisure time" such as church activities, offices held, and leisure activities including interests and hobbies).

Unfortunately, it would be difficult to detect genetic influence on environment-development relationships in this study because substantial selective placement occurred: The home index correlated .34 with the children's IQ *at the time of placement* of the child into the adoptive home. Nonetheless, some evidence for genetic mediation of the correlation between the home index and children's IQ emerged. For 36 nonadopted children, the correlation between the home index and IQ was .47; however, for 185 adopted children, the correlation was only .32, which is nearly the same as the selective placement correlation at the time the children were placed in their adoptive home.

Leahy

Leahy's (1935) study of nearly 200 adoptive families and 200 nonadoptive families was similar to Burks' in design. Leahy was not specific concerning her measure of the home environment, saying only that it involved "88 questions relative to the cultural, economic and social status of the adoptive home" (p. 265). Later in the article, Leahy indicates that "environmental status score is a combined expression of occupational status, education of parents, economic status, degree of social participation, cultural materials and child training facilities in the home" (pp. 279-280). Because Leahy's study was designed to resolve differences between the studies by Burks and Freeman et al., it is likely that her environmental indices were similar to the assessments of the home environment employed in the other studies.

As in Burks' study, the adoptive and nonadoptive homes did not differ in variance for the environmental measures. However, some selective placement occurred in Leahy's study, probably more than in Burks' study and less than in the study by Freeman et al. Again, it is important to recognize that the presence of selective placement makes it more difficult to discover genetic influence in environment-development relationships.

Correlations between the environmental indices and two measures of children's development in the adoptive and nonadoptive families are listed in Table 8.2. For a subset of 72 adoptive families and 77 nonadoptive families, ratings of emotional stability were obtained. The cultural index and child training index correlated only slightly with children's emotional stability; nonetheless, on the average, the correlations in the nonadoptive homes are about twice as large as those in the adoptive homes.

The correlations between the four environmental indices and children's IQ for the full sample yielded results similar to those in the study by Burks, with even greater differences between correlations in the adoptive and nonadoptive homes. The average correlation between the environmental indices and IQ in the nonadoptive homes is .46; in the adoptive homes, the average correlation is .16. Leahy asks why the correlations differ in the adoptive and nonadoptive homes, but leaves the question unanswered (p. 291).

Conclusions

The evidence from these studies is impressive in suggesting substantial genetic influence on the relationship between environmental measures and children's IQ, evidence that has previously gone unnoticed. Across the three studies, the average correlation between environmental measures and children's IQ is .45 in nonadoptive homes and .18 in adoptive homes.

However, the environmental measures employed in these studies are imbued with socioeconomic status and parental education and thus mix such distal

TABLE 8.2
Correlations of Environmental Indices with Children's IQ and Personality in Adoptive and Nonadoptive Homes (Leahy, 1935)

| | Developmental Measure | | | |
| | Emotional Stability[a] | | IQ | |
Environmental Index	Adoptive	Nonadoptive	Adoptive	Nonadoptive
Cultural index	.06	.13	.21	.51[b]
Child training index	.11	.18	.18	.52[b]
Economic index of home	—	—	.12	.37[b]
Sociality index	—	—	.11	.42[b]
N	72	77	194	194

[a]Correlations between the ratings of emotional stability and the economic and sociality indices were not reported.

[b]Correlation in nonadoptive homes significantly greater than in adoptive homes ($p < .05$, one-tailed).

measures with more proximal measures of the home environment. Given that socioeconomic status and IQ are substantially correlated, it is not surprising that, in Burks' study, the Whittier Scale correlates .60 with parental IQ and the culture scale correlates .70 with IQ of the parents. In fact, in multiple correlation analyses, Burks showed that the relationship between the environmental measures and children's IQ disappears when parental IQ is taken into account. This suggests that the environmental measures indirectly assess parental IQ. This takes some of the lustre off the discovery of genetic influence because we already know that the relationship between parental IQ and children's IQ is strongly influenced by heredity.

Nonetheless, the data presage caution in assuming that an environmental measure is in fact a measure of the environment because it is called environmental. A recent controversy in developmental psychology is related to this issue, even though genetic effects have not explicitly been considered. As in Burks' data, it has been argued that relationships between measures of home environment and children's IQ disappear when the effects of parental IQ are removed:

> The most important single conclusion we would draw from our findings is that studies that report only zero-order correlations between home environment and child IQ vastly overestimate the true relationship between these variables. When maternal IQ covariance is removed, the relationship is considerably attenuated—in the present study, to nonsignificance. Maternal IQ, on the other hand, continues to share significant variance with child IQ when home environment and parental education variance are both removed. (Longstreth, et al., 1981, p. 532)

However, not all measures of the home environment simply reflect parental IQ. Several studies have shown that some home environmental measures contribute to children's mental development independently of parental IQ (Gottfried & Gottfried, 1984; Yeates, MacPhee, Campbell, & Ramey, 1983). It is important that adoption studies include such measures of the environment. Environmentalists have argued against the use of "demographic indices such as social class or educational level" and have prescribed the use of more specific measures of the environment:

> More recently, another methodological criterion has been added, namely, the importance of coding or manipulating specific *parameters* of the environment rather than using global interventions or collapsing specific environmental codes into a general environmental index (Wachs & Gruen, 1982). The major reason for this shift appears to be a growing realization that use of global intervention or global summary scores may conceal more than is revealed. . . . A number of instruments are currently available that fit the . . . criteria delineated above. Perhaps the most popular is the Caldwell HOME Inventory. (Wachs, 1983, p. 398)

Thus, what is needed is an adoption study that includes newer measures of the home environment such as the HOME Inventory rather than distal measures such as parental occupation and education. However, with the exception of the Colorado Adoption Project, recent adoption studies have not obtained such data on home environments.

The Colorado Adoption Project

The Colorado Adoption Project (CAP) is a prospective, longitudinal, adoption study of behavioral development that has included measures of the environment (Plomin & DeFries, 1985). The 185 adoptees from whom data are included in the present analyses were placed in their adoptive homes in the first month of life and had no contact with their biological parents after placement. The infants were tested in their adoptive homes at 12 and 24 months of age; data were obtained concerning mental development, language development, temperament, and behavioral problems. In addition, 162 nonadoptive families matched to the adoptive families were studied in the same manner. Biological, adoptive, and nonadoptive parents were tested using a 3-hour battery of behavioral measures. Details of the CAP design and its preliminary results can be found elsewhere (DeFries, Plomin, Vandenberg, & Kuse, 1981; Plomin & DeFries, 1983, 1985).

Environmental Measures

Two major environmental measures are employed in the CAP: Caldwell and Bradley's (1978) Home Observation for Measurement of the Environment (HOME) at 12 and 24 months, and the Family Environment Scale (FES; Moos

& Moos, 1981) at 12 months. The total score and 6 scales of the HOME and the 10 scales of the FES yield an unwieldy number of correlations with the various infant measures at 12 and 24 months of age. In order to reduce the number of environment-infant correlations to a manageable number, composites of the environmental measures were derived using factor analysis. As explained elsewhere (Plomin & DeFries, 1985), an unrotated first principal component score was used to represent a general HOME factor and four rotated factors were used to summarize major dimensions within the HOME. Quantitative scoring of the HOME items rather than the traditional dichotomous scoring was also used in order to increase the variance of the items in middle-class homes. Two second-order factors were used to summarize the 10 scales of the FES.

Infant Measures

Composite measures were also obtained for infant behavioral problems, temperament, mental development, and language acquisition. Behavioral problems were assessed using midparent ratings for factors derived to measure difficult temperament, sleep problems, eating problems, and soothability. Temperament was assessed using midparent ratings on four scales of the Colorado Childhood Temperament Inventory (Rowe & Plomin, 1977): Emotionality, Activity, Sociability, and Attention Span. The Mental Development Index (MDI) from the Bayley Scales of Infant Development (Bayley, 1969) was used as a measure of infant mental development, and the Sequenced Inventory of Communicative Development (SICD; Hedrick, Prather, & Tobin, 1975) was used as a measure of language development.

Assumptions

A prerequisite for these analyses is that environmental measures show relationships to measures of development. Without an environment-development relationship, it makes no sense to assess the genetic contribution to the environment-development relationship. Furthermore, precise estimation of genetic components of relationships between environmental measures and measures of development require similarity of means and, especially, variances for adoptive and nonadoptive families; minimal selective placement; and no reactive or active genotype-environment correlation. In the CAP, adoptive and nonadoptive families were matched for sex of the proband; number of other children in the family; and paternal age, education, and occupational status. As expected from the matching procedure, the adoptive and nonadoptive families showed no significant mean or variance differences for educational attainment or occupational status. No mean or variance differences emerged from the HOME measures. For the two FES factors, adoptive families showed higher mean scores than nonadoptive families, although the variances did not differ significantly.

Concerning the second assumption, selective placement is negligible in the CAP for educational and occupational status, cognition, and personality. The median selective placement correlations between biological parents and adoptive parents are .02 for educational and occupational status, .01 for IQ, and .02 for personality.

With regard to the third assumption, we can certainly not rule out the possibility that the child's behavior has some influence on the HOME and FES measures. However, the data presented indicate that the correlations in the adoptive families between these scales and the children's development are quite low for many of the measures, which restricts the possible magnitude of such influences. Nevertheless, some possible instances of reactive and active genotype-environment correlations were observed. As indicated earlier, this will result in underestimates of the genetic component of environmental influences. It should also be noted that the children in the CAP analyses are infants who, according to the theory of Scarr and McCartney, should be subjected to more passive genotype-environment correlation and to less reactive and active genotype-environment correlation than older children.

Results

Even though the number of infant and environmental measures has been greatly condensed, 113 environment-infant correlations in nonadoptive families and 113 correlations in adoptive families constitute the basic data. Because we cannot assess genetic components of environment-development relationships if no relationship exists between a particular environmental measure and a measure of infant development, 34 relationships were selected in which the correlation reached a nominal .05 level of statistical significance in either adoptive or nonadoptive families. In order to summarize these correlations in a meaningful way, they were reflected so that "good" environments are scored in the same direction as "good" developmental outcomes. For example, the FES second-order factor, Personal Growth, involves familial cohesiveness and expressiveness. This scale relates negatively to difficult temperament; the correlation was changed to show a positive sign.

Of the 34 environment-development correlations that were significant in either the adoptive or nonadoptive families, 28 yielded greater correlations in the nonadoptive families than in the adoptive families. Furthermore, the correlations in adoptive and nonadoptive families are significantly different in 12 comparisons; for all 12, the correlations in the nonadoptive families are greater than those in the adoptive families. This consistent pattern of greater correlations in the nonadoptive homes as compared to the adoptive homes suggests genetic involvement in relationships between environmental measures and major domains of infant development. For all 34 correlations, the mean correlation for adoptive families is .09; for nonadoptive families, the mean correlation is .24.

TABLE 8.3
Mean Environment-Infant Correlations in the Colorado Adoption
Project for Adoptive and Nonadoptive Families (Plomin,
Loehlin, & DeFries, 1985)[a]

Infant Domain	Number of Correlations	Mean Environment-Infant Correlations	
		Adoptive	Nonadoptive
Behavioral problems	10	.07	.23
Temperament	14	.06	.20
Mental development	6	.21	.27
Language development	4	.25	.36

[a]Sample size varies from 139 to 180 for adoptive families and 130 to 165 for nonadoptive families.

Of the 113 environment-development correlations, the 34 that were significant in either adoptive or nonadoptive families were distributed as follows in the four domains of infant development: 10 of 48 for behavioral problems, 14 of 48 for temperament, 6 of 12 for mental development, and 4 of 5 for language development. Table 8.3 summarizes the average environment-development correlations for these four domains. All four domains show the trend towards greater environment-development correlations in nonadoptive families as compared to adoptive families. Although genetic influence appears from the table to be greater for behavioral problems and temperament than for mental and language development, these summary data obscure some important trends that are discussed in the following sections.

Mental Development.   Table 8.4 presents environment-infant correlations for infant mental development for the six relationships that yielded significant correlations in either adoptive or nonadoptive homes. The general factor score on the HOME, the most widely used measure of the home environment, correlates .44 in nonadoptive families with the Bayley MDI score at 24 months of age, a result similar to correlations found in other studies of nonadoptive families (Gottfried, 1984). The correlation in adoptive families is .29. The HOME general factor is not significantly correlated with Bayley MDI scores at 12 months of age in nonadoptive families (or in adoptive families), which is also consistent with other studies.

The reason why the mean correlations for mental development suggest only modest genetic influence despite evidence for substantial genetic influence on the HOME general factor is that two rotated factors of the HOME show little or no evidence of genetic influence for mental development. These rotated HOME factors are Variety of Experience (essentially a toys factor) and Maternal Involvement (maternal emotional involvement such as praising the child's

TABLE 8.4

Significant Environment-Infant Correlations for Mental Development
in the Colorado Adoption Project (Plomin et al., 1985)[a]

| Environmental Measure | Environment-Bayley MDI Correlations | | | |
| | 12 Months | | 24 Months | |
	Adoptive	Nonadoptive	Adoptive	Nonadoptive
FES Traditional Organization	−.16	−.09	—	—
HOME General Factor			.29	.44
HOME Variety of Experience	.12	.19	.22	.16
HOME Maternal Involvement			.23	.25
HOME Encouraging Advance			.22	.44[b]

[a]Measures were obtained at both 12 and 24 months with the exception of the FES which was administered only at 12 months.

[b]Correlation in nonadoptive families significantly greater than in adoptive families ($p < .05$, one-tailed).

qualities and conveying positive feeling when speaking of the child). At 24 months, the Variety of Experience factor yields correlations of .22 and .16 for the Bayley MDI in adoptive and nonadoptive families, respectively; correlations for the Maternal Involvement factor are .23 and .25. Thus, the pattern of correlations for these two HOME scales do not suggest genetic influence. Of the other two rotated HOME factors, one (Restriction/Punishment) yielded no significant correlations with mental development. The other rotated factor, Encouraging Advance (including items such as "mother consciously encourages developmental advance"), like the results for the HOME general factor, suggests substantial genetic influence. The correlation with the Bayley MDI at 24 months is .44 in nonadoptive families, significantly greater than the correlation of .22 in adoptive families. In general, these results suggest some specificity of genetic mediation of environment-development relationships.

Language Development.   The results for language acquisition as assessed by the SICD at 24 months are quite similar to those for the Bayley MDI, as indicated by the correlations presented results in Table 8.5. The HOME general factor and one of the rotated factors, Encouraging Advance, indicate genetic influence—in both cases, the correlation in the nonadoptive homes is significantly greater than in the adoptive homes. The other two rotated HOME factors show little or no genetic influence. Also similar to the results for the Bayley MDI is the fact that the significant correlations in the adoptive homes show, for the first time, environmental influences unbiased by heredity.

Temperament and Behavioral Problems.   The results for temperament (Table 8.6) and behavioral problems (Table 8.7) are similar and will be

TABLE 8.5
Significant Environment-Infant Correlations for Language
Development in the Colorado Adoption Project (Plomin et al., 1985)

Environmental Measure	Environment-SICD Correlations at 24 Months	
	Adoptive	Nonadoptive
HOME General Factor	.32	.50[a]
HOME Variety of Experience	.22	.08
HOME Maternal Involvement	.20	.31
HOME Encouraging Advance	.27	.50[a]

[a]Correlations in nonadoptive families significantly greater than in adoptive families ($p < .05$, one-tailed).

discussed together. Genetic influences are not limited to any particular temperament or behavioral problem nor are they limited to a particular environmental measure. However, 4 of the 12 significant differences between the nonadoptive and adoptive correlations involve the second-order FES Personal Growth factor. At 12 months of age, this environmental index correlates -.39 with emotionality in the nonadoptive families and -.10 in the adoptive families; it correlates .34 with sociability in nonadoptive families and .16 in adoptive families; .41 with soothability in nonadoptive and .06 in adoptive families; and -.32 with difficult temperament in nonadoptive and -.07 in adoptive families. These measures of infant temperament intercorrelate in the range .32 to .58, and an equally weighted composite of the four measures correlates with FES Personal Growth .49 in the nonadoptive homes and .13 in the adoptive homes.

One other point should be made in relation to Tables 8.6 and 8.7. Of the six comparisons in which correlations are greater in the adoptive families than in the nonadoptive familes, three involve the HOME Restriction/Punishment factor. Since the adoptive home correlations are not significantly greater than the nonadoptive home correlations, they presumably represent chance departures from no difference. Although these correlations could represent purely environmental effects, the possibility of a negative reactive genotype-environment correlation should also be considered. The Restriction/Punishment factor relates positively to difficult temperament at 24 months and to activity at both 12 and 24 months, suggesting the possibility of negative feedback-based relationships involving the child's genetic propensities.

Preliminary Results in Early Childhood

The suggestion of strong genetic mediation of environment-development relationships in infancy led us to conduct preliminary analyses of the CAP data in early childhood (Pelton & Plomin, 1985). We expected that environment-

TABLE 8.6
Significant Environment-Infant Correlations for Temperament in the
Colorado Adoption Project (Plomin et al., 1985)

Infant Measure	Environmental Measure	Environment-Temperament Correlations 12 Months		24 Months	
		Adoptive	Nonadoptive	Adoptive	Nonadoptive
Emotionality	FES Personal Growth	−.10	−.39[a]	—	—
Activity	FES Personal Growth	.06	.18	—	—
Sociability	FES Personal Growth	.16	.34[a]	—	—
Attention	FES Personal Growth	.10	.19	—	—
Emotionality	HOME Restriction			.05	.17
Activity	HOME General Factor			.02	−.18[a]
Activity	HOME Encouraging Advance			−.01	−.20[a]
Activity	HOME Restriction	.24	.18	.22	.12
Sociability	HOME General Factor	.16	.17		
Attention	HOME General Factor			.16	−.12[a]
Attention	HOME Variety	−.03	−.16		
Attention	HOME Encouraging Advance	−.07	−.21	.08	−.18[a]

[a]Correlations in nonadoptive families significantly greater than in adoptive families ($p < .05$, one-tailed).

TABLE 8.7
Significant Environment-Infant Correlations for Behavioral Problems
in the Colorado Adoption Project (Plomin et al., 1985)

Infant Measure	Environmental Measure	Environment-Problem Correlations 12 Months		24 Months	
		Adoptive	Nonadoptive	Adoptive	Nonadoptive
Soothability	FES Personal Growth	.06	.41[a]	—	—
Difficult temperament	FES Personal Growth	−.07	−.32[a]	—	—
Sleep problems	FES Traditional Organization	−.11	−.19	—	—
Eating problems	FES Traditional Organization	−.12	−.21	—	—
Soothability	HOME Variety			.03	−.27[a]
Soothability	HOME Encouraging			.03	.20
Difficult temperament	HOME Involvement			−.07	−.20
Difficult temperament	HOME Restriction			.17	.14
Eating problems	HOME Encouraging			−.01	.17
Eating problems	HOME Restriction			.08	.17

[a]Correlations in nonadoptive families significantly greater than in adoptive families ($p < .05$, one-tailed).

development relationships would be stronger in early childhood than in infancy which would give the analyses a better chance to assess genetic mediation of environment-development relationships. To the contrary, preliminary analyses indicate that the HOME and FES in early childhood relate *less* strongly to developmental outcomes in early childhood than they do in infancy. This increases the difficulty of decomposing environment-development relationships into their genetic and environmental components. Nonetheless, the results in early childhood replicate the infancy results, although the magnitude of the correlations are lower and the difference between the nonadoptive and adoptive homes are smaller. Consider the significant differences between nonadoptive and adoptive family correlations in Tables 8-4 to 8-7. For nonadoptive and adoptive families, respectively, the HOME-IQ correlations were .50 and .32; at 3 the correlations were .24 and .16. HOME-SICD correlations in infancy were .50 and .32; at 3 years, they were .21 and .13. FES Personal Growth yielded four significant correlational differences in nonadoptive and adoptive families: Soothability, Difficult Temperament, Emotionality, and Sociability. The nonadoptive and adoptive correlations, respectively, in infancy for these four comparisons were .41 and .06, .32 and .07, .39 and .10, and .34 and .16. At 3 years, the correlations are .33 and .15, .29 and .16, .32 and .14, and .23 and .21. These results suggest less genetic mediation of environment-development relationships in early childhood than in infancy. As noted earlier, genetic mediation depends on passive genotype-environment correlation and is made less likely by the presence of reactive and active genotype-environment correlation. Scarr and McCartney's genotype/environment theory, discussed in chapter 6, suggests that the impact of passive genotype-environment correlation decreases during development, whereas reactive and active genotype-environment correlation assume increasingly important roles. Thus, their theory predicts that less genetic mediation of environment-development relationships will be found in early childhood than in infancy. Although the CAP analyses in early childhood are preliminary, they support this prediction: On average, environment-development correlations in nonadoptive families are no larger than those in adoptive families. Caution is in order, however, because none of the environment-development correlations in early childhood are as large as they were in infancy which might indicate the need for better environmental measures in early childhood.

Path Model of Environment-Development Relationships

A simple path model that depicts relationships between environmental measures and children's development in nonadoptive and adoptive homes is illustrated in Fig. 8.1 (from Plomin et al., 1985). I is a environmental index, and P_c refers to a measure of children's development. The path diagram reiterates the point

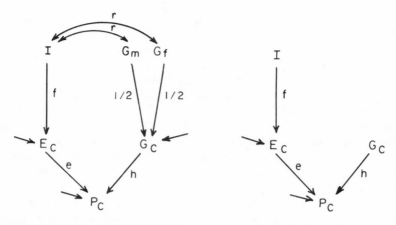

NONADOPTIVE FAMILIES   ADOPTIVE FAMILIES

FIG. 8.1.   Path diagram illustrating the relationship between a measure of the environment (I) and a measure of children's development (P_c) in nonadoptive and adoptive families. See text for explanation. (From Plomin, Loehlin, & DeFries, 1985. Reprinted by permission.)

emphasized in the preceding sections: In nonadoptive families, correlations between environmental measures and measures of children's development can be mediated genetically as well as environmentally; in adoptive families, the correlation arises only for environmental reasons. More precisely in terms of the path diagram, the child's phenotype is assumed to be causally determined by its genotype, G_c, and its environment, E_c, via genetic and environmental paths h and e; the residual arrow impinging on P_c allows for measurement error. The environmental variable I is assumed to act via path f on the immediate environment that affects the trait in question. The environmental measure I is assumed to be correlated to an extent, r, with the parents' (unmeasured) genotypes. For simplicity, r is assumed to be equal for mother and father, but this is not critical—if the correlations differ, the average can be used.

On the left side of Fig. 8.1, it can be seen that the correlation between the measured environmental variable and the child's behavioral phenotype can occur in two ways in nonadoptive families: either environmentally via the path fe or genetically via the parents' and child's genotypes, with a value of $.5rh$ for the path through each parent, i.e., a combined value of rh for the genetic paths.

For adoptive families, described on the right side of Fig. 8.1, the environmental variable I has only an environmental connection to the child's phenotype if selective placement for the trait in question is negligible. Under these circumstances, the genotypes of the absent biological parents will not contribute in any way to the correlation between the environmental measure and the phenotype of the child. This correlation then simply takes on the value fe.

Thus, in nonadoptive homes, the correlation between an environmental measure and a measure of children's development can be represented as:

$$\text{Nonadoptive } r_{\text{IPc}} = fe \times rh$$

In adoptive homes, the environment-development relationship is:

$$\text{Adoptive } r_{\text{IPc}} = fe$$

It follows that the difference between the correlation r_{IPc} in the nonadoptive and the adoptive families yields an estimate of rh, the genetic component of the correlation. The correlation in the adoptive families itself provides an estimate of fe, the environmental component of the correlation. Thus, given suitable data from adoptive families and comparable nonadoptive families, one can decompose the correlation between an environmental characteristic and a child's trait into additive components: one environmental and one genetic. The correlation in the adoptive families directly estimates the environmental component, and the difference between the correlations in the nonadoptive families and adoptive families estimates the genetic component.

Applying this model to the results described earlier in this chapter suggests that fully half of environment-development relationships may be mediated genetically. The average environment-IQ correlations in the Burks and Leahy studies were .45 in nonadoptive families and .18 in adoptive families, which suggests that 40% (i.e., $.18 \div .45$) of the environment-IQ correlation in nonadoptive homes is due to environmental influences and 60% (i.e., $.27 \div .45$) is due to heredity. However, as mentioned earlier, these studies employed measures of the environment imbued with IQ-related characteristics such as socioeconomic status. The CAP data, with its better measures of the proximal environment in infancy, lead to the same conclusion, however. For the 34 environment-development relationships that yielded significant correlations in either the adoptive or nonadoptive families, the mean correlation for adoptive families was .09; for nonadoptive families, the mean correlation was .24. These data again suggest that 60% (i.e., $.15 \div .24$) of the environment-development relationship in nonadoptive families is mediated genetically.

A multivariate model-fitting extension of this approach using three cognitive scores confirmed the appropriateness of the model and substantiated the finding of significant and substantial genetic mediation of environment-development relationships for the HOME and mental and language development at 24 months (Thompson, Fulker, & DeFries, submitted). As indicated earlier, if selective placement or reactive and active genotype-environment correlations are important, the role of genetic mediation has been underestimated. However, preliminary analyses of CAP environment-development relationships in early childhood indicate that environment-development relationships are generally weaker in early childhood than in infancy and that environment-development relationships in adoptive and nonadoptive homes are of similar magnitude, a finding that is to be expected if the influence of passive genotype-environment correlation decreases and reactive and active genotype-environment correlation increases during development.

Implications

Not only does heredity account for some of the variance of ostensibly environmental measures as discussed in the previous chapter, heredity also mediates the covariance between environmental measures and measures of children's development. The most obvious implication of this conclusion is that, in nonadoptive families, relationships between environmental measures and measures of development cannot be assumed to be environmental in origin. Labeling a measure *environmental* does not free its relationship to developmental measures from genetic influence. The data reviewed in this chapter suggest that it is safer to assume that fully half of the environment-development relationship in nonadoptive homes is mediated genetically. For example, the greatest environment-development relationships in Tables 8.4 to 8.7 consistently suggest substantial genetic mediation. The four greatest environment-development relationships in nonadoptive homes involve correlations of the HOME general factor and HOME Encouraging Advance with the Bayley MDI and the SICD measure of language development; the two correlations for the Bayley MDI are .44 and the two correlations for the SICD are .50. The correlations for these relationships in adoptive homes are .29, .22, .32, and .27.

The conclusion that environment-development relationships in nonadoptive families are often substantially greater than in adoptive homes is novel and important in its suggestion of genetic influence on relationships between environmental measures and measures of development. At the same time, however, these same data sometimes show significant environment-development relationships in adoptive homes—as in the examples just mentioned for the Bayley MDI and SICD—thus adducing evidence for pure environmental influence, unless reactive genotype-environment correlation is involved. The general point is that correlations between environmental measures and measures of development in nonadoptive families can be useful in suggesting environment-development relationships that *might be* environmental; however, other methods are needed to demonstrate that such relationships are indeed environmental in origin.

Genetic mediation of environment-development relationships does not imply that such relationships are immutable. These results, as in all behavioral genetic research, are descriptive in the sense that they describe existing covariation between environmental variables and developmental variables given all the existing causes of variation in these measures. In this case, behavioral genetic studies ascribe a substantial portion of this observed environment-development covariation to genetic factors. For example, the relationship between FES Personal Growth and infant soothability appears to be largely mediated genetically; however, this does not imply that parental expressiveness, infant soothability, or the relationship between them is unalterable. Other things equal, it does mean that persuading parents to act in a more expressive and supportive way toward their infants would not be expected to increase noticeably the soothability of the infants. Had the correlations been equal in adoptive and nonadoptive families, one would expect that it would. This is one reason why it is important to know the extent to which specific environment-development relationships are mediated genetically: Implications for application differ depending on the answer to the question of genetic mediation.

It should be mentioned that the possibility of genetic mediation of environment-development relationships is not removed in longitudinal studies of nonadoptive families. For example, the HOME at 1 year of age predicts 3-year-old IQ better than it predicts 1-year-old IQ (Elardo & Bradley, 1981). However, this longitudinal environment-development relationship does not necessarily imply that early environmental influences affect later IQ because genetic influence on IQ increases from 1 to 3 years of age (e.g., Plomin, 1985). Thus, the greater correlation between the HOME at 1 year and 3-year-old IQ (as compared to the correlation between 1-year-old HOME and 1-year-old IQ) could be mediated genetically. That is, parental characteristics indexed by the HOME might relate genetically to infant development at 3 years to a greater extent than they relate to infant development at 1 year. As mentioned later, however, longitudinal extensions of behavioral genetic designs are needed to explore developmental processes that result in genetic mediation of environment-development relationships.

Environmental research requires designs that can disentangle genetic and environmental influences. Studies of adoptive and nonadoptive families represent one powerful strategy for accomplishing that goal. Adoptive families are not as difficult to study as it might at first seem. A wave of adoptions in the 1960s and early 1970s led to about 1% of all children born in the United States during that period being adopted by families who are not biologically related to the adoptee (Mech, 1973). Thus, many adoptive families are available whose children are now adolescents or young adults. Importantly, data on birth parents of adoptees are not needed in order to study genetic and environmental components of environment-development relationships. Other behavioral genetic designs are applicable to the study of environment-development relationships. For example, the families-of-twins design (e.g., Nance, 1976) could provide interesting data on this topic. A simple twin study comparing twin correlations for identical and fraternal twins rearing their own families could provide much-needed information about genetic influences on childrearing behavior as discussed in the previous chapter. Comparing environment-development relationships between Twin A and his children and relationships between Twin A and his twin partner's children could elucidate the etiology of these relationships. In the case of identical twins, Twin A is as genetically related to his nephews/nieces as he is to his own children. Thus, if heredity mediates environment-development relationships, these relationships will be just as great across identical twins' families as they are within an identical twin's family. For fraternal twin families, however, relationships will be greater within a twin family than they are across twin families.

Step-families are completely unexploited as a resource for behavioral genetic analysis. The high divorce rate produces many families in which one parent is genetically unrelated to the children in the family. An unexplored potential of step-parent families is the opportunity to compare, within the same family, environmental measures assessed separately for the two parents, only one of whom is genetically related to the child. The several environmental factors that might affect environment-development correlations in step-families (such as the age at which the child is exposed to the step-parent, the child's perception of the divorce and remarriage, and the continued influence of the out-of-home parent) can potentially be assessed and the impact of these factors on environment-development correlations can thus be evaluated. Moreover, these are interesting environmental data in themselves.

In addition to increased use of methods such as adoption, families-of twins, and step-family designs, Plomin et al. (1985) suggest three substantive directions for research in this area: (a) Pursue the possibility that genetic mediation of environment-development relationships is greater for some measures of the environment than for others; (b) explore possible parental mediators of the genetic component of environment-development relationships; and (c) study the developmental processes by which genetic factors permeate relationships between environmental measures and measures of development.

Specificity of Genetic Mediation

The results for the HOME are promising in suggesting that specific environment-development relationships are differentially affected by heredity. The relationships of the HOME general factor and HOME Encouraging Advance with infant mental and language development appear to be substantially mediated by genetic factors. In contrast, relationships of two other HOME factors, Variety of Experience and Maternal Involvement, with infant mental and language development are little if at all influenced genetically. Ordering environmental measures along a continuum of genetic mediation of their effects on development might elucidate possible environmental and genetic processes underlying environment-development relationships.

Parental Mediators

Characteristics of the parents must be the conduit for genetic mediation of environment-development relationships. What is it in the parents that serves this purpose? All we know so far is that the answer is not obvious. For example, it has been assumed that the relationship between the HOME and infant Bayley scores in nonadoptive families is freed from genetic influence when parental IQ is partialed from the correlation between the HOME and Bayley scores (e.g., Gottfried & Gottfried, 1984; Yeates, MacPhee, Campbell, & Ramey, 1983). As in these other studies, the CAP data also indicate that partialing out parental IQ has little effect on the relationship between the HOME general factor and Bayley scores in nonadoptive homes (Plomin & DeFries, 1985). However, this lack of effect of parental IQ is observed in adoptive as well as in nonadoptive homes, which means that the correlations between the HOME and Bayley scores continue to be greater in nonadoptive homes than in adoptive homes even after the effects of parental IQ have been removed statistically. Thus, we are left with the intriguing notion that the parental characteristics responsible for genetic mediation of the HOME-Bayley relationship must be largely independent of IQ in the parents. Similar results are found for other domains of infant development in the CAP: Partialing out apparently equivalent parental behaviors has little effect on environment-development relationships. Thus, genetic mediation of environment-development correlations remains greater for nonadoptive than for adoptive families.

This suggests that another important direction for research in this area is to identify the characteristics of parents that underlie genetic mediation of environment-development relationships. Research in this vein certainly would be useful for understanding environmental processes as they transact with genetic influence and possibly would contribute to understanding of parenting behavior. The CAP results yield evidence for greater genetic influence on environment-development relationships than on relationships between traditional measures of parental behaviors, such as IQ and personality, and measures of infant development. What could account for this paradoxical set of results? One possibility is that the environmental measures provide a more vivid picture of parental behavior than do the typical direct measures, perhaps because the environmental measures assess parental behavior in a context of great significance, family life and childrearing.

Developmental Processes

Another direction for research is to identify the developmental processes by which environmental measures come to relate both to infants' development and to heredity. The approach to understanding the etiology of environment-development relationships described in this chapter is merely a first step; it is a static approach which considers outcomes of developmental processes that occur prior to the time that environment and development are assessed. Identification of the developmental processes leading to genetic mediation of environment-development relationships requires longitudinal extensions of the adoption, families-of-twins, and step-families designs described earlier. Such research might profitably include variables that are more process-oriented than the global environmental and developmental outcome measures that have been employed in the research described in this chapter.

 DEVELOPMENTAL
BEHAVIORAL GENETICS
THROUGHOUT THE
LIFE SPAN

9

Infancy

This chapter begins a new section that consists of a review of research in human behavioral genetics as it relates to the major developmental epochs of infancy, childhood, adolescence, adulthood, and late adulthood. A final chapter attempts to pull these diverse data together in a life-span perspective.

The first 2 years of life have been a focus of behavioral genetics research only since the 1970s. Behavioral geneticists' interest in infancy was aroused in part by the intense research effort in the 1960s among developmentalists interested in the first year of life. Another major factor has been increasing interest in genetic change, the hallmark of developmental behavioral genetics. Otherwise, why study infants? Infants certainly are more difficult to study than adolescents and adults—for one thing, they cannot complete the paper-and-pencil tests and questionnaires that produce the bulk of behavioral genetic data. However, from the perspective of developmental behavioral genetics, the rapid and dramatic changes in every sphere of development during infancy make it a fascinating period for research.

The purpose of this chapter is to review behavioral genetic research on infancy. Perhaps because of the newness of the topic, only one review focused on infancy has appeared (Plomin, in press, b); this chapter leans heavily on that review.

As always, behavioral geneticists consider differences among individuals in a population rather than group differences or species-typical approaches that focus on average developmental trends in our species. However, it should be noted that infancy is a mammalian theme that is exaggerated in primates. Infant sensorimotor development appears to be highly canalized in the sense that developmental differences among primate species, including Homo sapiens, are scant in infancy, and differences among human infants are small compared to differences later in development (Scarr, 1976). As McCall (1979) has argued, developmentalists should eventually attempt to explain both species-typical developmental patterns (e.g., why the human species begins to walk and talk in infancy) and individual variations on these themes. Important questions related to the issue of individual variations include why some infants are slow to walk or talk, the extent to which genetic and environmental variation accounts for the observed differences in infants' development, and whether a relatively slow developmental rate in infancy portends difficulties later in life.

Despite the importance of individual diferences, the majority of developmental theory and research on infancy is normative. For example, nearly 70% of the *Handbook of Infant Development* (Osofsky, 1979) is based on normative data (Plomin, in press, b). However, an encouraging sign is that experimental psychologists—who have developed ingenious techniques for measuring infant behavior, although always from a normative perspective—have become interested in individual differences (e.g., Fagan, 1985). The conceptual leap to be made is from a normative to an individual differences perspective; once that leap is accomplished, it is a small step to recognition of the usefulness of quantitative genetic theory and methods.

Two large-scale longitudinal behavioral genetic studies of infancy have been mentioned previously. The first is the Louisville Twin Study (LTS) that was initiated more than 25 years ago. Approximately 25-35 pairs of twins have been recruited each year since 1963, resulting in a sample of about 500 pairs of twins now participating in the longitudinal research program in which the children are studied from the age of 3 months to 15 years (Wilson, 1983). The twins are tested at 3, 6, 9, 12, 18, 24, 30, and 36 months and annually thereafter to 9 years of age. A final test session is administered when they are 15 years old. Until recently, the focus of the LTS was IQ and physical growth, although some data relevant to temperament were collected by means of maternal interviews concerning behavioral differences within twin pairs and the Infant Behavior Record, a 30-item rating scale that is completed by the examiner following administration of the Bayley Scales of Infant Development (Bayley, 1969). Beginning in 1976, however, the focus has turned to the study of temperament in infant twins using a structured laboratory assessment sequence that is videotaped and rated later using a modification of the Infant Behavior Record (Wilson & Matheny, 1986).

In the Colorado Adoption Project (CAP), adopted children and matched nonadopted children and their home environments are assessed yearly when the children are 1 to 4 years of age during visits to the adoptive and nonadoptive homes (Plomin & DeFries, 1985). The biological and adoptive parents of the adopted children and the parents of the nonadopted children are tested on a 3-hour battery of diverse measures including assessments of cognitive abilities, personality, and interests and talents. Testing of biological parents began in 1975 and was completed in 1983; the foundation sample consists of 250 adoptive and 250 matched nonadoptive families. Testing of younger siblings of the adopted and nonadopted children in the same manner is beginning to yield the important additional comparison of adoptive (biologically unrelated) and nonadoptive (biological) siblings (Daniels, 1985).

CAP parent-offspring results have been analyzed to examine the diverse data obtained at 12 and 24 months for 182 adopted infants and 165 nonadopted infants who were tested at both ages. These results have been brought together in a book, *Origins of Individual Differences in Infancy: The Colorado Adoption Project* (Plomin & DeFries, 1985), from which the data reported in this chapter are taken. Importantly, the CAP sample is quite representative of metropolitan populations in the United States. For socioeconomic status, the sample is representative of the entire United States population with respect to variance, although its mean is about one standard deviation above the national average. Even more importantly, selective placement—the matching of adoptive parents to biological parents—appears to be negligible for a variety of domains including cognitive abilities, personality, and demographic characteristics such as education and socioeconomic status.

Data from these studies and other behavioral genetic research on infancy will be reviewed in this chapter, beginning with a brief section on physical development and then turning to mental development (including language acquisition), temperament, and other characteristics of infancy.

Physical Development

Data for height and weight are useful as "anchor" points for comparison to behavioral data. In infancy, from 12 to 24 months, infants increase in height by 15% and in weight by 25% on the average. However, these dramatic average changes in height and weight are accompanied by considerable stability of individual differences, with correlations of about .70 from 12 to 24 months. This is a concrete example of the independence of normative (means) and individual differences (variances and covariances) data.

Data for about 400 pairs of twins from the Louisville Twin Study (Wilson, 1976, 1979) yield identical and fraternal twin correlations for height of about .86 and .66, respectively, at 12 months. The twin correlations at 24 months are .89 and .54, suggesting an increase in heritability from about .40 to about .70 during infancy. For weight, the twin correlations are .88 and .55 at 12 months and .88 and .53 at 24 months. These twin correlations suggest heritabilities of about .70 for weight at both ages, although heritability of weight at birth is negligible and increases linearly during the first year.

As described in chapter 3, weight and, especially height, in infancy correlate substantially with adult measures. Heritabilities of height and weight are even greater in adulthood, about .80 for height and for weight. Results from the Colorado Adoption Project that suggested substantial genetic continuity from infancy to adulthood were also reviewed in chapter 3. These data and those for mental development led to the amplification model of developmental genetics that hypothesizes that as genes come to affect a character in infancy, they continue to affect the character throughout the life span.

Mental Development

Twin Data on IQ

Although IQ has been the prime target for human behavioral genetic research, the Louisville Twin Study (LTS) is the only major longitudinal twin study of infant mental development. The Bayley Scales of Infant Development (Bayley, 1969) are administered through 24 months of age, and the Stanford-Binet (Terman & Merrill, 1973) is administered at 30 and 36 months. Figure 9.1 summarizes 2 decades of research.

On the whole, these data suggest little genetic influence in infancy, especially as compared to IQ data on adolescent and adult twins. After the first 6 months, during which there is no difference between identical and fraternal twin correlations, identical twin correlations are about .10 greater than those for fraternal twins. The average twin correlations from 3 to 36 months are .77 for identical twins and .67 for fraternal twins. Although the identical-fraternal differences are small, they are consistent in suggesting genetic influence. Taken at face value, these correlations suggest that 20% of the total variance in Bayley scores in infancy can be explained by genetic variance. (See chapter 1 for issues related to calculating heritability from twin studies.) Explaining 20% of the variance of anything in infancy is a remarkable accomplishment.

Notice that the magnitude of the twin correlations exceeds the age-to-age correlations. In other words, twin partners resemble each other at a given age at least as much as they resemble themselves a few months later. Because this occurs for fraternal as well as for identical twins, it suggests that powerful environmental factors operate to make infant twins similar. The hypothesis is supported by another finding shown in Fig. 9.1 and in Table 9.1: Fraternal twins are twice as similar as nontwin siblings during the first year of life. What is responsible for this large environmental effect? One possibility is artifact. Twins are tested on the same day, whereas the younger siblings are tested at least a year later. However, the fact that the twins are tested by different examiners in different rooms makes it less likely that artifacts of this type could be responsible.

A more likely hypothesis is that twins have substantially more perinatal problems than do singletons and that they share these environmental factors to a

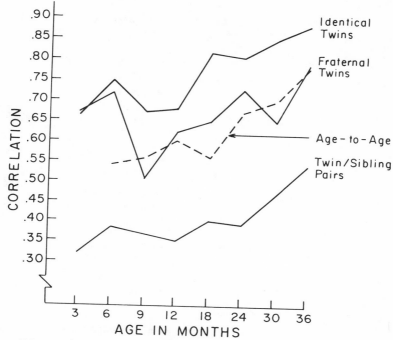

FIG. 9.1. Louisville Twin Study results for infant mental development (data from Wilson, 1983). The sample sizes include approximately 80 identical twin pairs, 100 fraternal pairs, 35 twin/sibling pairs, and 300 to 400 individuals for the age-to-age correlations.

much greater extent than do nontwin siblings. For singletons, the correlation between birth weight and 8-month Bayley scores is about .20 (Broman, Nichols, & Kennedy, 1975). In twins, however, the correlations are .50, .48, and .30 at 3 months, 6 months, and 12 months, respectively, and they continue to decline to .14 at 24 months and to .11 at 3 years (Wilson, 1977). Although twin correlations corrected for birth weight have not been presented, it is likely that twin correlations during the first year are substantially inflated by shared perinatal influences. In fact, if the twin correlations at 3 and 6 months in Fig. 9.1 were lowered by about .20, the twin data would be much more in line with the pattern of increasing correlations shown elsewhere in the figure.

The LTS results suggesting little genetic variance in Bayley scores in the first year of life (Wilson, 1983) are confirmed by a report on twin data from the Collaborative Perinatal Project (Nichols & Broman, 1974). The Bayley test was administered to over 300 pairs of 8-month-old twins. The identical and fraternal twin correlations were .84 and .55, respectively; however, removing data on the 8% of the twins who had Bayley scores less than 57 from the analyses yielded

TABLE 9.1
Familial Correlations for Infant General Mental Development

Reference	Sample	(N/Pairs)	Results
	A. Twin and Nontwin Sibling Studies		
Nichols & Broman (1974)	8 months	identical twins (110)	.55
		fraternal twins (205)	.55
		siblings (4,347)	.22
Wilson (1983)	3 + 6 + 9 months	identical twins (80)	.69
		fraternal twins (100)	.63
		siblings (35)	.35
	12 + 18 + 24 months	identical twins (80)	.77
		fraternal twins (100)	.67
		siblings (35)	.40
McCall (1972)	6 + 12 months	siblings (142)	.24
	6 + 12 + 18 + 24 months	siblings (142)	.40
Daniels (1985)	12 months	adoptive siblings (72)	.03
		nonadoptive siblings (61)	.42
	24 months	adoptive siblings (53)	.24
		nonadoptive siblings (50)	.46
	B. Parent-Offspring Studies		
Skodak & Skeels (1949)	12–24 months	biological mothers (39)	− .01
Snygg (1938)	12–24 months	biological mothers (227)	.08
Eichorn (1969)[a]	6 + 12 months	nonadoptive parents	− .14 (− .01)
	18 + 24 months	nonadoptive parents	.16 (.04)
Casler (1976)	9 + 15 months	biological mothers (145)	.09[b]
	21 + 27 months	biological mothers (145)	.11[b]
Plomin & DeFries (1985)	12 months	nonadoptive mothers (157)	.04[c]
		nonadoptive fathers (157)	.09[c]
		nonadoptive mothers (122)	.00[d]
		nonadoptive fathers (123)	.09[d]
		biological mothers (176)	.12[c]
		biological fathers (41)	.29[c]
		biological mothers (144)	.16[d]
		biological fathers (36)	.23[d]
		adoptive mothers (177)	.12[c]
		adoptive fathers (169)	.00[c]
		adoptive mothers (143)	− .04[d]
		adoptive fathers (138)	.01[d]
	24 months	nonadoptive mothers (157)	.22[c]
		nonadoptive fathers (157)	.21[c]
		biological mothers (176)	.06[c]
		biological fathers (41)	.38[c]
		adoptive mothers (177)	.10[c]
		adoptive fathers (169)	.08[c]

[a]The first correlation is for the parents tested at the same age as the infant in the Berkeley Growth Study; the correlation in parentheses refers to parents' scores at age 17. Sample size not reported.
[b]Average of correlations for Gesell language and adaptive subtests.
[c]Parental first principal component score and infant Bayley Mental Development Index.
[d]Parental first principal component score and infant score on the Uzgiris-Hunt Ordinal Scales of Psychological Development.

twin correlations of .55 for both identical and fraternal twins. As shown in Fig. 9.1, the LTS data show no genetic influence at 8 months of age and only slight genetic influence at 9 months. The LTS included few retarded infants, and the twin correlations were essentially unchanged when data on these children were removed from the analyses (Wilson & Matheny, 1976). Both studies suggest substantial shared environmental variance because the twin correlations are so large—about .60 on average—and because there is little difference between correlations for identical and fraternal twins (see Table 9.1).

The Collaborative Perinatal Project, like the Louisville Twin Study, found a sibling correlation much lower than the fraternal twin correlation. For 8-month Bayley scores for 4,347 pairs of nontwin siblings, the sibling correlation is .22, substantially lower than the fraternal twin correlation of .55. Similarly, as shown in Table 9.1, McCall (1972) reported a correlation of .24 for 142 pairs of nontwin siblings in the first year of life. It is also noteworthy that the LTS yields correlations for identical twins, fraternal twins, and nontwin siblings that are about .10 higher than other studies; this is also the case for age-to-age correlations. One possible explanation is that infant assessment, a delicate matter, is more reliable in the LTS.

Table 9.1 also reports preliminary adoptive and nonadoptive sibling correlations for the Bayley MDI at 12 and 24 months from the Colorado Adoption Project (Daniels, 1985). The adoptive sibling correlation is negligible at 12 months, suggesting that shared family environment is of no importance at 12 months of age—in stark contrast to the results of twin studies. The nonadoptive sibling correlation is significantly greater than the adoptive sibling correlation, suggesting significant and substantial genetic influence at 12 months. Although the nonadoptive sibling correlation is somewhat higher than in other studies, taken at face value, these results suggest a heritability of .78 for Bayley MDI scores at 12 months.

At 24 months, the adoptive sibling correlation is .24 which is similar to adoptive sibling correlations for IQ found in studies later in childhood; this suggests significant influence of shared family environment. The nonadoptive sibling correlation is greater than the adoptive sibling correlation, although not significantly so. At 24 months, the sibling correlations suggest a heritability of 28%. At 24 months and especially at 12 months, these results from the first sibling adoption design indicate greater heritability than do twin studies. The difference in results may be due to the considerable impact of perinatal factors on infant twin performance, although the large standard error in these heritability estimates needs to be considered—the standard error of the heritability estimate at 12 months is .33. Nonetheless, these preliminary sibling correlations from the CAP raise questions concerning the heritability of Bayley MDI scores during infancy.

In the 1970s, several tests of infant mental development were constructed within the framework of Piagetian theory. In the LTS (Matheny, 1975), 20

Bayley test items administered at 3, 6, 9, and 12 months were identified that are equivalent to items used in Piagetian scales such as the Uzgiris-Hunt Ordinal Scales of Psychological Development (Uzgiris & Hunt, 1975). A scale constructed by summing these 20 items suggests somewhat greater genetic influence in the first year: The twin correlations were .80 for 88 pairs of identical twins and .61 for 44 pairs of fraternal twins summed across the four ages. Caution must be exercised in interpreting these correlations because the results are not significantly different from those based on the total Bayley score and other research suggests that Piagetian measures of cognitive development correlate at or near their reliability with the Bayley test (Gottfried & Brody, 1975). Nonetheless, these results suggest the possibility that certain components of the Bayley test might show more genetic influence than others, a topic discussed later.

Age-to-Age Patterns of Development

Because the LTS is one of the few longitudinal behavioral genetic studies, its longitudinal analyses are particularly noteworthy from the perspective of developmental behavioral genetics. One of the most remarkable findings of the study is the high degree of familial patterning of spurts and lags in mental development. Twins' scores frequently change during infancy, as would be expected from stabilities of about .50 and .60 for 3-month periods during the first and second year, respectively. However, both identical and fraternal twins appear to change in dramatically similar patterns, whether their scores are increasing, decreasing, or going up and down.

Twin trend correlations based on profiles of tests at 3, 6, 9, and 12 months and profiles based on scores at 12, 18, 24, and 36 months are very similar to the cross-sectional twin correlations. The trend correlations for identical and fraternal twins are .69 and .63 for the first year and .80 and .72 for the second year. As do the cross-sectional results, these findings suggest substantial familial resemblance but show little evidence of genetic influence on age-to-age profiles of Bayley scores in infancy. Also similar to the cross-sectional results is the finding of substantially lower trend correlations for twin/sibling pairs than for fraternal twins, a result also reported by others (McCall, 1972).

The similarity of the results of analyses of profiles to those of the cross-sectional analyses of twin scores is not coincidental. Trend correlations include twin similarity both for overall level—that is, twin scores at each age—and for age-to-age changes in twin scores. We have already seen that overall level shows strong familial resemblance and relatively little genetic influence in infancy. The LTS trend correlations are always very similar to the twin correlations for overall level, suggesting either remarkable coincidence or the possibility that trend correlations primarily reflect overall level and are not much affected by age-to-age changes.

Trend correlations are complex functions of heritabilities at each age and genetic and phenotypic correlations among the ages. It would be interesting to explore age-to-age genetic correlations, the extent to which genes affecting Bayley scores at 12 months overlap with those genes that affect Bayley scores at 24 months, as described in chapter 3. The amplification model of developmental genetics predicts that genetic correlations from age to age will be high even though heritability is low.

Adoption Data on IQ

How well do adoption data fit with the conclusion from twin data that genetic influence on general mental development in infancy is slight? Although over 20 adoption studies involving IQ have been reported, only the Colorado Adoption Project (CAP) has focused on infancy (Plomin & DeFries, 1985).

One of the most frequently cited articles in developmental psychology is Skodak and Skeels' (1949) report of a longitudinal adoption study of IQ. IQ scores of 100 adopted children tested four times between early childhood and adolescence were compared to the educational level and occupational status of their adoptive parents, to education and occupation of their biological parents, and to IQ scores of 63 of the biological mothers. Although the average age of the children at the first test was 2 years and 3 months, their ages varied from 6 months to 6 years. Thus, the frequently cited correlation of .00 between biological mothers' IQ and the adoptees' scores for their first testing on the Kuhlman Revision of the Binet test could be misleading as an index of genetic resemblance in infancy. However, when the raw data provided by Skodak and Skeels were analyzed by Plomin and DeFries (1985), the biological mother-child correlation for 39 infants tested between 12 and 24 months was found to be -.01. (See Table 9.1.)

Less well known is an adoption study of IQ reported by Snygg (1938), who studied 227 infants from 1 to 2 years of age. The Kuhlman test was administered to the infants, and the biological mothers were tested on the Stanford-Binet. Unfortunately, there is no doubt that the biological mothers were a biased sample because "girls who had passed high school entrance examinations were seldom asked to take psychological tests" (Snygg, p. 403); their average IQ was only 78 and the range was probably restricted, although no information concerning variance was reported. The correlation between infants and their biological mothers was .08.

Casler (1976) reported a third adoption study of IQ in which 150 biological mother-child pairs were studied when the infants were 2, 9, 15, 21, and 27 months. The mean correlation was .09 between the biological mothers' Stanford-Binet scores and their adopted-away infants' scores on the Gesell.

Most surprisingly, there has been only one small IQ study of nonadoptive parents and their infant offspring (Eichorn, 1969). Not a single study has compared IQ scores of adoptive parents and their adopted infants.

Data from the CAP (Plomin & DeFries, 1985) add substantially to this literature because the CAP includes a large sample of adopted and nonadopted infants tested at both 12 and 24 months and because general and specific cognitive ability data are available for the biological and adoptive parents of adoptees and for the parents of nonadopted children.

During visits to the homes of the adopted and nonadopted infants at 12 and 24 months of age, the Bayley Scales of Infant Development (Bayley, 1969) are administered. In the CAP, the test-retest reliability of the Bayley Mental Development Index (MDI) is .80. At 12 months, four of the seven scales of the Ordinal Scales of Psychological Development (OSPD; Uzgiris & Hunt, 1975) are also administered; test-retest reliability for the total OSPD score in the CAP is only .52. For the biological, adoptive, and nonadoptive parents, an unrotated first principal component score based on 16 cognitive tests is used as a measure of general cognitive ability, or IQ (DeFries, Plomin, Vandenberg, & Kuse, 1981).

The CAP design includes "genetic" parents, "environmental" parents, and "genetic-plus-environmental" parents. As explained in chapter 3, this parent–offspring design is restricted in terms of finding genetic variance in infancy because it is limited to revealing genetic variance that is shared by infants and their adult parents. However, this limitation adds to the excitement of finding genetic relationships between biological parents and their adopted- away infant offspring because it implicates genetically mediated continuity between infancy and adulthood. Environmentally, the parent–offspring design is limited to the parental phenotype as a measure of the environment. However, as described in chapter 8, adoptive families provide an opportunity to isolate specific environmental influences unconfounded by genetic bias, regardless of their relationship to the parental phenotype, when environmental assessments are included in an adoption study.

The CAP parent–offspring correlations are listed in Table 9.1 following a summary of the twin and nontwin sibling data and the data from previous adoption studies. At 24 months, the results are suggestive of both genetic and environmental influences: The "heredity" correlation (weighted average correlation for biological mothers and fathers) is about .10; the "environmental" correlation (adoptive parents-adoptees) is about .10; and the "heredity-plus-environment" correlation (nonadoptive parents-nonadopted infants) is about .20. At 12 months, however, the results are less straightforward. The weighted average biological parent-adoptee correlation is .17, suggesting genetic influence; the average adoptive parent-adoptee correlation is .06, suggesting slight family environmental influences; but the average nonadoptive parent-offspring correlation is only .07. Similar results are seen for the Bayley MDI and the OSPD. Nonetheless, the hypothesis of genetic influence at 12 months is supported by maximum-likelihood, model-fitting analyses (Fulker & DeFries, 1983) which have considerably more power to detect relationships as weak as these. At 24 months, the pattern of correlations clearly is consistent with the hypothesis of hereditary influence and some effect of family environment on infant mental development. Taken at face value, these results suggest that about 20% of the variance of MDI scores in infancy is due to genetic variance and that about 10% is due to family environmental factors shared by parents and their offspring. The majority of the variance is left unexplained.

Adoption Data on Specific Components of Mental Development

Much work remains to be done even for global measures of infant mental development. However, an important direction for future research is to explore the differentiation of specific cognitive abilities in infancy and in the transition to early childhood. For the adults in the CAP, tests are administered that tap four specific cognitive abilities: verbal, spatial, perceptual speed, and memory. Although the state of the art in infant assessment limits the CAP in addressing the issue of differentiation of specific cognitive abilities in infancy, pertinent analyses have been conducted at the level of the Bayley total score, Bayley factor scores, and Bayley items as they relate to parental general cognitive ability and specific cognitive abilities (Plomin & DeFries, 1985).

Are Bayley scores in infancy related to specific cognitive abilities of parents? No. Even though parental factor scores for specific cognitive abilities are as reliable as IQ, infant Bayley scores correlate only with parental IQ, not with parental specific cognitive abilities. This suggests that infant mental development as measured by the Bayley primarily relates to adult g.

Are certain clusters of Bayley items related to specific cognitive abilities of parents? No. Two types of analyses have been conducted. The first type involves verbal and nonverbal Bayley items. In a bivariate model-fitting analysis that compared infant verbal and nonverbal scores to parental verbal and nonverbal scores, parent-offspring correlations suggested a pattern of results similar to those found for the Bayley MDI score (Baker, 1983). Moreover, correlations between parental verbal and infant nonverbal scores and parental nonverbal scores and infant verbal scores were nearly the same as the isomorphic correlations between parental and infant verbal scores and between parental and infant nonverbal scores for all three sets of parents. This suggests that infant verbal and nonverbal abilities are not differentiated genetically or environmentally in terms of their prediction of adult cognitive abilities.

The second type of analysis employed spatial, verbal, and memory scales derived from factor analyses of Bayley items (Lewis, 1983). The relationship between these Bayley scales and parental general and specific cognitive abilities has been investigated in the CAP (Thompson, Plomin, & DeFries, 1985). Parent-offspring correlations between 12-month Bayley scale scores and parental cognitive abilities suggest only minimal relationships for both parental *g* and specific abilities. At 24 months, more parent-offspring resemblance is found; however, Bayley scales that appear to be related to parental cognition are related to parental *g*, not to specific abilities.

Finally, analyses of Bayley items and of scales constructed to eliminate item dependencies on the Bayley test support the emerging conclusion that the nature of infant mental development as it relates to adult cognition is global rather than differentiated (Plomin & DeFries, 1985). Bayley items and scales that correlated significantly with parental cognitive abilities in nonadoptive families were selected for analysis. Replication of significant nonadoptive family correlations by correlations between biological mothers and their adopted-away offspring would suggest genetic links between infancy and adulthood and would attenuate the possibility of capitalizing on chance in such analyses. As in the other analyses, insofar as infant items predict adult cognition, they predict IQ, not specific cognitive abilities. Interestingly, at 12 months, Bayley items and scales yield three significant correlations with IQ scores of nonadoptive parents, and all three of these significant correlations were replicated by correlations between biological mothers and their adopted-away infants. This finding suggests genetic mediation between scores on these Bayley measures and adult IQ. The three Bayley measures are the Tower of Cubes scale, the Pinkboard scale, and an item (115) that involves closing the lid on a round container. These items hint of spatial processes, and it is noteworthy that they do not include language items.

In summary, all of these analyses lead to the conclusion that infant mental development, insofar as it predicts adult cognitive abilities, predicts adult general cognitive ability, not specific cognitive abilities. This suggests that infant mental development is itself general and undifferentiated. An alternative possibility is that the items on the Bayley test lack sufficient diversity to assess adequately the structure of specific cognitive abilities in infancy. Fortunately, the CAP data set includes other, quite different, measures of two domains of infant mental development: language/communication and preference for novel stimuli.

At 24 months, the Expressive and Receptive scales of the Sequenced Inventory of Communication Development (SICD; Hedrick, Prather, & Tobin, 1975) are administered to provide measures of language production and comprehension. Furthermore, for a subsample of the CAP infants, videotaped communication measures at 12 months of age have been analyzed. The parent-offspring results for the SICD are similar to those reported above for the Bayley MDI, which is not surprising because the SICD correlates .66 with the Bayley MDI in the CAP. However, partialing out the Bayley MDI score from the parent-offspring correlations for parental IQ and infant SICD scores indicates that the SICD does not contribute to parent–offspring correlations independently of the Bayley MDI. This fits with the hypothesis that infant mental development as it relates to adult cognitive abilities is general in nature.

Videotaped data on communicative responses of 50 adopted and 50 nonadopted 12-month-olds in the CAP are in accord with this pattern of results

(Hardy-Brown, 1981, 1982; Hardy-Brown & Plomin, 1985; Hardy-Brown, Plomin, & DeFries, 1981). An unrotated first principal component called *communicative competence* included maternal reports of a word diary and vocal imitation and a scale of Bayley language items, as well as videotaped observations of the use of phonetically consistent forms, vocalization context, vocal signals, true words, use of request prosody, and syllable structure. When 12-month communicative competence scores were related to parental cognitive abilities, they correlated significantly only with parental IQ, not with parental specific cognitive abilities. These parent-offspring results strongly suggest genetic influence in that IQ scores of nonadoptive parents and of biological parents of the adoptees were found to correlate significantly and substantially with infant communicative competence. Because infant communicative competence predicts adult IQ, not adult specific cognitive abilities such as verbal ability, these results confirm those described above. When Bayley MDI scores were partialed from the parent-offspring correlations for parental IQ and infant communicative competence, the correlations were lowered only slightly. This suggests that communicative competence involves genetic precursors of adult IQ at 12 months of age that are independent of the processes assessed by the Bayley items.

Finally, Fagan's (1985) measure of preference for novel stimuli has been administered to CAP infants at 5 and 7 months of age since 1982. Twelve follow-up studies assessing preference for novel stimuli yielded a mean correlation of .44 between scores on this measure at 3 to 7 months and IQ scores at 2 to 7 years of age. Because no other measure has been shown to predict school-age IQ from the first year of life, Fagan's measure appeared to be a good candidate for parent-offspring analysis. Preliminary analyses of CAP data on nonadoptive families indicate some relationship with parental IQ; as we have seen repeatedly, the measure correlates only with parental IQ, not with parental specific cognitive abilities (Thompson & Fagan, 1983).

In summary, the CAP data lead to the conclusion that the prediction of adult cognitive ability from measures of infant mental development involves *g*. That is, any measure in infancy that predicts adult cognitive abilities predicts only adult *g*, not specific abilities. These data suggest that infant mental development is undifferentiated. Greater differentiation can be expected following the transition from infancy to early childhood. An important implication is that long-term predictiveness of infant mental tests would be likely to be improved by focusing on *g*.

Temperament

The term *personality* covers an incredible variety of behavior; dozens of personality traits have been suggested, each of which could turn out to be as complex as intelligence. A theory of temperament that focuses on genetic influence as one possible criterion to winnow the mind-boggling complexity of personality has been proposed (Buss & Plomin, 1975, 1984). This approach to personality considers genetically influenced, early-developing personality traits, which are referred to as *temperament*, and suggests that three broad traits meet these criteria: emotionality, activity, and sociability—known collectively by the acronym EAS. Emotionality refers to distress, the tendency to become upset easily and intensely; it is assumed to differentiate into fear and anger during the first year of life. It is the foundation of adult neuroticism, with its anxiety component not yet developed. Sociability refers to gregariousness or the preference to be with other people; it is the key component of extraversion in infancy, when the impulsivity facet of adult extraversion is not very important. Shyness, responses to interactions with strangers, tends to be assessed in infancy rather than sociability. In adulthood, extraversion and neuroticism are the most heritable dimensions of personality (Loehlin, 1982). Activity, which includes both tempo and vigor, is simply not included in many personality questionnaires for adults, although it is nearly always included in rating instruments for children, perhaps because of the conspicuousness of this dimension in childhood.

In this section, behavioral genetic studies of the EAS traits in infancy are reviewed. Because the EAS traits are central to most personality approaches, this selective review covers most behavioral genetic studies of personality during infancy while providing some focus to this sprawling field. An overview of these studies is presented in Table 9.2.

Emotionality

Dimensions similar to EAS emotionality are paramount in nearly every other approach to temperament (Plomin & Dunn, 1986). For example, Intensity of Reaction, Threshold of Responsiveness, and Quality of Mood are included in the New York Longitudinal Study (Thomas & Chess, 1977); temperament-as-affect is the focus of Goldsmith and Campos' approach (1982a, b); reactivity and self-regulation are emphasized by Rothbart and Derryberry (1981); and Kagan and his colleagues have concentrated on behavioral inhibition (Garcia-Coll, Kagan, & Reznick, 1984; Kagan, 1982).

Four twin studies related to emotionality are summarized in Table 9.2. The studies employed diverse types of measures including parental interviews (Matheny Dolan, & Krantz, 1981), parental questionnaire ratings (Goldsmith & Campos, 1982a, b), tester ratings on Bayley's (1969) Infant Behavior Record (Matheny, Dolan, & Wilson, 1976), and observational ratings in a playroom setting after the mother leaves the room (Matheny & Dolan, 1975). The twin data consistently support the hypothesis that individual differences in emotionality in infancy are affected by genetic factors.

Preliminary data from the CAP sibling adoption design, however, yield low

TABLE 9.2
Behavioral Genetic Studies of EAS Temperaments in Infancy

Reference	Sample	Measure	Results[a]	
		A. Twin Studies		
Matheny & Dolan (1975)	9–30 months; 25–57 MZ, 19–34 DZ	Observer ratings emotionality	.66 vs.	.30
Matheny et al. (1976)	3–12 months; 18–30 months; 47–55 MZ, 27 DZ	Tester ratings: IBR fearfulness item		
		first year	.74 vs.	.54
		second year	.65 vs.	.22
		IBR activity item		
		first year	.34 vs.	−.06
		second year	.52 vs.	.08
		IBR energy item		
		first year	.44 vs.	.26
		second year	.81 vs.	.22
		IBR persons item		
		first year	.63 vs.	.34
		second year	.44 vs.	.45
Matheny (1980)	6, 12, 18, 24 months; 72–91 MZ, 35–50 DZ	Tester ratings: IBR activity factor		
		6 months	.55 vs.	.10
		12 months	.43 vs.	.07
		18 months	.49 vs.	.37
		24 months	.53 vs.	.03
		IBR extraversion factor		
		6 months	.24 vs.	.11
		12 months	.33 vs.	.28
		18 months	.43 vs.	.14
		24 months	.58 vs.	.14
Matheny et al. (1981)[b]	6, 24, 36 months 68–78 MZ, 38–48 DZ	Parental interviews hurt feelings		
		24 months	37 vs. 13	
		36 months	40 vs. 14	
		temper: frequency		
		6 months	39 vs. 26	
		24 months	41 vs. 15	
		36 months	40 vs. 34	
		irritability		
		6 months	45 vs. 29	
		24 months	46 vs. 28	
		36 months	45 vs. 21	
		crying		
		6 months	62 vs. 51	
		24 months	59 vs. 39	
		36 months	50 vs. 21	
		activity		
		6 months	32 vs. 13	
		24 months	45 vs. 19	
		36 months	47 vs. 28	

(Continued)

TABLE 9.2
(Continued)

Reference	Sample	Measure	Results[a]		
		cuddling			
		6 months	53 vs. 13		
		24 months	41 vs. 11		
		36 months	37 vs. 33		
		accepting people			
		6 months	72 vs. 55		
		24 months	55 vs. 17		
		36 months	40 vs. 9		
Cohen et al.	1–5 years;	Parental ratings:			
(1977)	181 MZ,	zestfulness (energy)	.78 vs. .54		
	84 DZ	shyness	.69 vs. .29		
Torgerson &	2 and 9 months	Parental interview:			
Kringlen	34 MZ,	approach to	MZ more similar		
(1978)	16 DZ	stranger	than DZ at 9 months[c]		
Plomin & Rowe	22 months mean;	Time-sampled observations			
(1979)	21 MZ,	during interactions			
	25 DZ	with stranger:			
		approach	.50 vs. − .05		
		proximity	.40 vs. − .03		
		positive vocalizations	.58 vs. .34		
		smiling	.08 vs. .25		
		looking	.65 vs. .08		
Goldsmith &	8 months;	Tester ratings:			
Gottesman	115 MZ	activity	.57 vs. .35		
(1981)	209 DZ	interest in persons	.28 vs. .20		
Goldsmith &	9 months;	Parental ratings:			
Campos	39 MZ,	fear	.66 vs. .46		
(1982, a,b)	61 DZ	distress to limitations	.77 vs. .35		
		soothability	.71 vs. .69		
		activity	.75 vs. .57		
B. Sibling Adoption Study					
Colorado Adoption	12 months;		*12 months*		*24 months*
Project	72 nonadoptive,	CCTI emotionality	.15 vs. .08	− .21 vs. .18	
(Daniels, 1985)	61 adoptive	CCTI activity	.21 vs. .07	− .06 vs. − .16	
	24 months;	CCTI sociability	.10 vs. .24	.11 vs. − .05	
	53 nonadoptive,	IBR activity	.24 vs. − .27	.22 vs. − .01	
	50 adoptive	IBR extraversion	.07 vs. − .25	.40 vs. .04	
C. Parent-Offspring Adoption Study					
Colorado Adoption	12 and 24	Midparent ratings of	*12 months*	*24 months*	
Project	months;	infants' emotionality			
(Plomin &	182 adoptive,	Nonadoptive mothers			
DeFries, 1985)	164 nonadoptive	EAS emotionality-fear	− .02	.01	
		16 PF neuroticism	.25	.10	

(Continued)

TABLE 9.2
(Continued)

Reference	Sample	Measure	Results[a]	
			12 months	24 months
	Nonadoptive fathers			
		EAS emotionality-fear	.17	.21
		16 PF neuroticism	.07	.14
	Biological mothers			
		EAS emotionality	.00	.04
		16 PF neuroticism	.07	.20
	Adoptive mothers			
		EAS emotionality	.16	.15
		16 PF neuroticism	.16	.07
	Adoptive fathers			
		EAS emotionality	.14	.00
		16 PF neuroticism	.09	.03
	Midparent ratings of infants' activity			
	Nonadoptive mothers			
		EAS activity	.02	−.03
	Nonadoptive fathers			
		EAS activity	.21	.19
	Biological mothers			
		EAS activity	.06	.05
	Adoptive mothers			
		EAS activity	−.10	.02
	Adoptive fathers			
		EAS activity	.01	.01
	Midparent ratings of infants' shyness			
	Nonadoptive mothers			
		EAS sociability	−.23	−.22
		16 PF shyness	.17	.16
	Nonadoptive fathers			
		EAS sociability	−.09	−.13
		16 PF shyness	−.02	.18
	Biological mothers			
		EAS sociability	−.02	−.15
		16 PF shyness	.08	.10
	Adoptive mothers			
		EAS sociability	−.19	−.24
		16 PF shyness	.11	.04
	Adoptive fathers			
		EAS sociability	−.15	−.25
		16 PF shyness	.07	.19

[a]Results are presented as twin correlations or concordances in Part A—identical (MZ) vs. fraternal (DZ)—and as parent-offspring correlations in Part B.

[b]Parents were interviewed concerning twin differences and the results were presented as twin concordances, i.e., the percentage of twins whose parents indicated that the twins were not different.

[c]Twin correlations were not reported.

correlations for both nonadoptive and adoptive siblings and little evidence of genetic influence for parental ratings of emotionality (Daniels, 1985). The higher twin than sibling correlations and the higher twin as compared to sibling adoption design estimates of heritability could be explained in several ways. As is the case for mental development, twins, who are exactly the same age, might experience more shared family environment than nontwin siblings who, although tested at the same ages in CAP, are in fact nearly 3 years apart in age. The difference in age spacing between twins and siblings could also inflate twin correlations as compared to sibling correlations when parental ratings are employed. A more interesting possibility is that nonadditive genetic variance is important (Lykken, 1982). As explained in chapter 1, the coefficient of relationships for first-degree relatives is .50. However, this refers only to additive genetic variance (genetic influences that sum linearly in their effect on the phenotype and thus breed true). First-degree relatives scarcely share any genetic variance due to nonadditive effects. Identical twins, however, share all genetic effects whether additive or nonadditive. The twin results for emotionality are somewhat supportive of the hypothesis that nonadditive genetic variance is important: Of 16 twin comparisons related to emotionality in Table 9.2, fully half involve identical twin correlations that are more than twice as large as the fraternal twin correlations.

Studies employing parental ratings and interviews dominate temperament research just as self-report questionnaires supply nearly all personality data on adolescents and adults, as described in chapters 11 and 12. For this reason, studies using observational ratings of infants in structured settings are particularly noteworthy (Plomin, 1983). The most widely used instrument is Bayley's Infant Behavior Record (IBR), used by testers to rate an infant's behavior during administration of the Bayley test. It offers the important advantages of assessing infants' reactions to a standard, mildly stressful, situation and of providing comparable data across studies. The LTS data suggest increasing heritability during infancy for the IBR fearfulness item (Matheny et al., 1976). IBR-like ratings of emotionality in a playroom setting following mother's departure also show significant heritability during infancy (Matheny & Dolan, 1975). A recent report based on laboratory ratings of emotional tone for a sample of about 30 pairs of each type of twin suggests little genetic influence in the first year of life but substantial genetic influence in the second year (Wilson & Matheny, 1986).

The study by Goldsmith and Campos (1982a, b) included a laboratory-based assessment of emotionality. Preliminary results indicate genetic influence on the high-arousal emotion of fear in such situations as approach of strangers and the visual cliff at 9 months. The less arousing positive emotions indicated by smiling and laughing show no genetic influence (Goldsmith, 1983). A similar lack of genetic influence on individual differences in smiling and laughing was found in studies involving parental reports (Goldsmith & Campos, 1982a, b; Wilson, Brown, & Matheny, 1971).

In general, more behavioral genetic data exist for twins than for nontwin family members such as siblings or parents and offspring. Table 9.2 presents some of the results from the parent-offspring design of the CAP. As discussed earlier, the parent-offspring design is limited in terms of finding genetic influence in infancy because it requires genetic continuity from infancy to adulthood. Nonetheless, the data provide a hint of genetic influence in that a significant correlation emerges between biological mothers' 16 PF neuroticism and the midparent rating of their adopted-away infants' emotionality.

Activity

Measures of activity level have been included in six twin studies and in the CAP, as summarized in Table 9.2. Two twin studies that employed parental ratings yielded similar patterns of correlations for identical and fraternal twins: .75 and .57, respectively, for 9-month-olds (Goldsmith & Campos, 1982a), and .78 and .54 for children from 1 to 5 years of age (Cohen, Dibble, & Grawe, 1977). An LTS analysis based on parental interviews concerning differences within pairs of infant twins showed large differences in concordances for activity for identical and fraternal twins (Matheny et al., 1981).

More twin studies of activity in infancy have used tester ratings than parental ratings. The LTS IBR factors (Matheny, 1980) include activity. During the first 2 years of life, the IBR activity factor yielded average correlations of .40 for identical twins and .17 for fraternal twins (Matheny, 1980). Twin correlations for the IBR items were reported by Matheny et al. (1976), and the results for the activity and energy items are included in the table. In both the first and second years, these items yield identical twin correlations that are substantially greater than the fraternal twin correlations, although the fraternal twin correlations are too low to fit a simple genetic model. Similar results are emerging from LTS laboratory observations of activity (Wilson & Matheny, 1986). Another twin study using a tester rating instrument similar to the IBR has been reported for 8-month-old twins in the national Collaborative Perinatal Project (Goldsmith & Gottesman, 1981). The ratings for activity yielded twin correlations quite similar to those reported for the IBR activity factor in the LTS. Matheny (1983) analyzed trend correlations for twins during infancy for the IBR activity factor. For 66 identical and 40 fraternal LTS twin pairs at 12, 18, and 24 months of age, the trend correlations were significantly higher for identical twins (.52) than for fraternal twins (.18).

Similar to the results for emotionality, activity yields some evidence for nonadditive genetic variance: 8 of the 14 twin comparisons show identical twin correlations that are more than twice as large as the fraternal twin correlations. Nonetheless, the CAP sibling adoption data suggest genetic variance for parent-rated activity level at 12 months; the sibling correlations at 24 months are negative for both nonadoptive and adoptive siblings—perhaps due to contrast effects—although the nonadoptive sibling correlation is less negative than the adoptive sibling correlation. The IBR activity factor yields consistent evidence for genetic influence at 12 and 24 months. Results from the CAP parent-offspring adoption design suggest at most slight genetic continuity from infancy to adulthood: Parent-offspring correlations in nonadoptive families average .10, and the biological mother-adopted infant correlation is only .06.

In summary, although the CAP parent-offspring data suggest only slight genetic continuity from infancy to adulthood, the twin data without exception point to substantial genetic influence on individual differences among infants in their activity level as assessed by parental report or tester ratings.

Sociability and Shyness

As mentioned earlier, studies of temperament in infancy tend to assess shyness (social responding to strangers) rather than sociability (gregariousness). Seven twin studies and the CAP have obtained data on sociability or shyness in infancy (see Table 9.2).

Parental interviews were used in two studies (Matheny et al., 1981, which is an update of an earlier report by Wilson et al., 1971; Torgerson, 1982; Torgerson & Kringlen, 1978) and both yield evidence for genetic influence on sociability and shyness in infancy. Tester ratings were employed in three twin studies. LTS analyses of the IBR yielded a Test Affect/Extraversion factor that has been shown to correlate significantly with parental ratings of sociability and shyness (Buss & Plomin, 1984), even though the factor also includes items related to cooperativeness, endurance, and happiness (Matheny, 1980). The LTS results for this factor, shown in Table 9.2, yield average twin correlations during the first 2 years of .50 for identical twins and .14 for fraternal twins. In an earlier LTS analysis (Matheny et al., 1976), scores on the IBR item, Responsiveness to Persons, yielded mixed results. For the first year, the identical twin correlation was significantly greater than the fraternal twin correlation (.63 vs. .34); however, in the second year, no difference was found between the identical and fraternal twin correlations. Moreover, another twin study of 8-month-olds found little evidence of genetic influence on a tester rating of responsiveness to persons (Goldsmith & Gottesman, 1981). A possible reason for this discrepancy is that this IBR item, Responsiveness to Persons, involves rating social responding of infants who have already had time to become familiar with the tester prior to the administration of the Bayley tests. Given the strong evidence for genetic influence on shyness, it is likely that this item would show genetic influence if infants were rated in terms of their initial interactions with the tester before the administration of the Bayley test.

As described earlier, Matheny (1983) applied the repeated-measures analysis of variance to assess trend correlations during infancy. For 66 identical and 40 fraternal twin pairs at 12, 18, and 24 months of age, the trend correlations for the IBR Test Affect/Extraversion factor were .37 for identical twins and .21 for fraternal twins, suggesting significant genetic influence on age-to-age profiles of change and continuity.

An ethological observational study of specific social behaviors assessed in the homes of infant twins has been reported (Plomin & Rowe, 1979). Members of 21 identical twin pairs and 25 same-sex fraternal twin pairs with an average age of 22 months were observed in their homes using time-sampled observations of specific behaviors in seven situations. Each twin partner was rated by a different observer who took an unobtrusive position in the home, kept a neutral facial expression, and did not return overtures for attention from the children. An important feature of the study was that social responding to the stranger and to the mother was recorded in alternating 15-second intervals. The first situation, *warm-up*, included measures of the infants' social responding to the mother and to the stranger while they were discussing the research and attempting to avoid interaction with the children. The measures included infants' approaches, proximity, touches, positive vocalizations, smiles, and looks. In the second episode, *stranger approach*, the stranger enticed the children to play with him using a standardized protocol. The third situation involved play with the stranger using an interactive toy. The other situations were play with the mother, cuddling with the stranger and mother, and separation from the mother. In the first three situations (when the stranger was strangest), social responding toward the stranger suggested genetic influence. The same social responses directed toward the mother showed no genetic influence. This is one of the few observational studies in behavioral genetics, and it buoys confidence in the assertion that individual differences in shyness, even in infancy, show genetic influence.

The CAP appears to be the only behavioral genetic study of infant sociability and shyness that has used a design other than the twin method. Because the twin data for sociability and shyness suggest some nonadditive genetic variance (11 of 19 comparisons involve identical twin correlations more than twice as large as the fraternal twin correlations), designs based on first-degree relatives may fail to detect genetic variance. However, the CAP sibling adoption design shows some genetic influence for the IBR extraversion factor, although parental ratings yield no evidence of genetic influence. The parent-offspring design provides some evidence for genetic influence. Midparent ratings of the infants on the Colorado Childhood Temperament Inventory (Rowe & Plomin, 1977) shyness scale were compared with parents' personality as measured by a sociability scale from the EAS Temperament Survey of Buss and Plomin (1975) and a "shyness" factor (Factor H) from Cattell's Sixteen Personality Factor (16 PF) Questionnaire (Cattell, Eber, & Tatsuoka, 1970). As shown in Table 9.2, the correlations for the nonadoptive families suggest that infant shyness is negatively related to parental sociability and positively related to parental shyness. In nonadoptive families, parent-offspring relationships can be mediated either genetically or environmentally. However, the correlations between the biological mothers and their adopted-away offspring at 24 months suggest the influence of heredity. The significant negative correlation between biological mothers' sociability and infant shyness is particularly noteworthy because this correlation involves the biological mothers' self-report of sociability and the adoptive parents' midparent rating of the adoptees' shyness more than 2 years later. As discussed in chapter 3, this finding implies the existence of some genetic continuity for shyness from infancy to adulthood.

The correlations between adoptive parents and their adopted infants suggest a major role for family environmental influences as indexed by parents' personality. Adoptive parents' shyness and sociability are related to shyness of the adopted infants. Thus, this first adoption study of shyness suggests parent-offspring similarity even in infancy. This resemblance possibly involves heredity and certainly involves family environmental influences.

Summary

The studies described in this section usually assessed other personality traits in addition to emotionality, activity, and sociability; these other traits do not show the consistent pattern of genetic influence shown by the EAS traits. A few studies were not mentioned because their sample sizes are so small that their data are likely to be unreliable (Freedman, 1974; Reppucci, 1968; Van den Daele, 1971). One important twin study in infancy included no measures relevant to the EAS traits, but deserves mention because of its novelty. Lytton, Martin, and Eaves (1977) assessed social interaction between mothers and their infants at home and in the laboratory. Measures of attachment (defined behaviorally as a combination of seeking attention, help, and proximity) and compliance revealed no genetic influence and no influence of shared family environment. Observational ratings of specific behaviors in unstructured settings also showed no evidence of genetic influence, but shared family environment appeared to be more important for these measures. This latter result might be due to procedural artifacts in that a single rater rated both twins. Finally, one ongoing study should be mentioned. The LTS has been extended to include structured laboratory episodes designed to elicit emotionality, activity, and sociability (Matheny & Wilson, 1981). These data will be obtained primarily by use of IBR-like ratings, although some specific behavioral observations are also planned. Because of its EAS formulation, the results of this study will be particularly useful for systematically replicating the EAS results from previous twin studies (Wilson & Matheny, 1986).

In summary, the EAS traits show genetic influence in infancy. Buss and Plomin (1984) summarize their theory of temperament as follows:

> A major distinction between our theory and other approaches to temperament is that we specify a genetic origin, whereas other theorists tend to be vague about the origins of temperament. We have been impressed during the past decade with the extent to which behavioral genetic data—often obtained by researchers with perspectives quite different from ours—support our major contention that emotion-

ality, activity, and sociability are among the most heritable aspects of personality in early childhood. . . . Another major distinction is that we take a personality perspective, regarding temperaments as a class of personality traits. . . .

In describing our theory, we have tried to be specific and to outline ways of testing it. We propose that emotionality, activity, and sociability are the major dimensions of personality in infancy and early childhood; if not, the theory is wrong. We propose that these three traits are heritable; if not, the theory is wrong. If other early-appearing personality traits are shown to be heritable and not derivable from our three temperaments, the theory must be amended. If there are better ways to slice the personality pie early in life, the theory may have to be discarded. (pp. 155-157)

Other Characteristics in Infancy

Certainly there is more to infants' development than is captured in measures of mental development and temperament. Psychopathology and less severe behavioral problems in infancy have scarcely been considered by behavioral geneticists. Little is known, for example, about infantile autism (Hanson & Gottesman, 1976; Stabenau, 1975). The incidence of infantile psychosis is only 1 in 10,000—in contrast, the incidence of adult schizophrenia is 1 in 100—which makes it difficult to study such disorders (Gottesman & Shields, 1982). For example, aside from single-case studies, the only systematic study of psychoses before the age of 5 attempted to find all autistic twins in Great Britain (Folstein & Rutter, 1977). Only 11 identical and 10 fraternal pairs were found with at least one member diagnosed as autistic; four identical twin pairs were concordant and none of the fraternal pairs were concordant. Although this finding is consistent with a genetic hypothesis, the sample is much too small to form any conclusions.

What is the genetic relationship between childhood psychoses and adult schizophrenia? For 936 parents of autistic infants and young children, about 2% were hospitalized for schizophrenia as compared to the population risk of 1% (Gottesman & Shields, 1982). For 743 siblings of autistic children, 1.7% were psychotic. Because psychotic individuals seldom reproduce, no data are available for their offspring. In contrast to these risk figures, a study of late-onset childhood schizophrenia (7 to 11 years) found that 8.9% of 204 parents of these children were themselves hospitalized for schizophrenia and 7.7% of 234 siblings were psychotic (Kallman & Roth, 1956), results similar to those found in family studies of adult schizophrenia. Data such as these lead to the tentative conclusion that infantile psychosis is genetically distinct from schizophrenia, although later-onset childhood psychoses, which actually emerge most of the time in adolescence, are related to adult schizophrenia.

Because behavioral problems in infancy, such as sleeping and eating disturbances, are so common and because infants outgrow such difficulties, the etiology of these problems has seldom been studied. Nonetheless, these problems can cause considerable distress for parents (Dunn, 1981). A longitudinal study of behavioral problems in London infants found that 8% of the parents of 1-year-olds and 11% of the parents of 2-year-olds worried about their infants' behavioral problems, especially those related to sleeping and eating (Jenkins, Owen, Bax, & Hart, 1984). Receiving more attention during the 1970s was the global construct *difficult temperament*, a construct developed by the New York Longitudinal Study (NYLS) research group (Thomas & Chess, 1977). Difficult temperament refers to a constellation of temperament dimensions—low rhythmicity, negative mood, low approach, low adaptability, and high intensity. Much of the initial interest in difficult temperament was aroused by its possible predictiveness of later behavioral problems; however, difficult temperament in infancy has been found not to be related to later adjustment difficulties (Thomas & Chess, 1982). Nonetheless, infants who cry and fuss and who are fearful of and not adaptable to new situations clearly present problems for their parents. Although behavioral problems in infancy have scarcely been studied as to etiology, it is often assumed that these problems are brought about by faulty management on the part of parents.

These behavioral problems of infancy were explored in the CAP by relating their occurrence to characteristics of the parents and home environments. The CAP parent-offspring data on biological parents' personality and psychopathology revealed little evidence of genetic influence. Similarly, preliminary results using the CAP sibling adoption design also found little evidence for genetic influence, although these data suggest substantial shared environmental influence. More interesting were the results for environmental measures. First, the results did not support the hypothesis that faulty management on the part of parents is responsible for behavioral problems in infancy: Correlations between infant behavioral problems and environmental measures, including parenting styles, were negligible in adoptive families. Second, such correlations were often substantially greater in nonadoptive homes than in adoptive homes, suggesting that ostensibly environmental relationships in the sphere of infant behavioral problems are in fact mediated genetically, as discussed in chapter 8.

The CAP also has explored other neglected areas of infant development such as illness, motor development, handedness, and interests (Plomin & DeFries, 1985). For common illnesses in infancy, the CAP results suggest no genetic influence but some influence of shared family environment. For motor development, genetic as well as family environmental influence is indicated by correlations between infants' motor development as assessed by the Bayley (1969) test and parents' athletic ability. The emergence of hand preference in infancy and infant interests show neither genetic nor family environmental influence.

Conclusions

Because the amount of developmental behavioral genetic research on infancy is miniscule, at least as compared to other fields of infancy research, most of the potential of developmental behavioral genetics for the description and explanation of individual differences in infancy is as yet unrealized. Nonetheless, some exciting conclusions are beginning to emerge:

1. Twin studies suggest that heredity explains about 15% of the variance on Bayley Mental Development Index scores. Most impressive is the extent to which genetic influence in infancy is less than genetic influence on IQ scores later in life, when estimates of genetic influence are closer to 50%.

2. Individual differences in language acquisition at 12 and 24 months are influenced by heredity.

3. When such measures of infant mental development as Bayley scores or language acquisition scores are related to parental cognitive ability, they are related to general cognitive ability, not to specific abilities of parents. This suggests that infant mental development is general and undifferentiated, especially as it predicts adult cognitive ability.

4. The temperament traits of emotionality, activity, and sociability/shyness show significant and possibly substantial genetic influence in infancy.

5. Whenever the relative magnitude of genetic variance changes during development, its impact increases rather than decreases. This is contrary to the commonly held view that genetic influences are most important early in development.

6. Although genetic influence is generally less in infancy than later in childhood, what little genetic variance exists in infancy covaries highly with genetic variance in adulthood. This suggests an amplification model of developmental genetics: Genes make only a small contribution to phenotypic variance in infancy, but these genetic effects are amplified as development proceeds. The amplification model is discussed in chapter 3.

7. Relationships between widely used measures of the home environment and major domains of infant development are mediated genetically to a substantial extent. Genetic components of "environmental" relationships with infant development are discussed in chapter 8.

10 Childhood

So much happens developmentally from 3 to 9 years of age that it seems woefully inadequate to consider all of this development as occurring during a single period, *childhood*. However, so few behavioral genetic studies have been conducted on children in this age group that finer distinctions are not yet possible. Perhaps authors of future books on developmental behavioral genetics will be privy to enough data to be able to include chapters on the transition from infancy to early childhood (2-3 years), early childhood (3-5 years), early school years (6-7 years), and middle childhood (7-9 years). (Late childhood has been lost, a victim to the steady downward push of early adolescence that is now viewed as 9-12 years.)

Moreover, behavioral genetic data that are available do not address developmental issues of specific relevance to childhood such as children's increasing ability to adopt the perspectives of others, expanding conceptions of self, and increasing self-control. No behavioral genetic studies have focused on developmental changes wrought by one of the most significant events in life, the transition to formal schooling. Most of the data that we have are in the domains of cognition and personality, partly because these domains have been assumed to be "development-free" in the sense that developmental changes are thought to be relatively unimportant in comparison to continuity. It should be kept in mind that results in these domains, with their emphasis on continuity rather than change, may not be representative of what we eventually learn about developmental behavioral genetics in childhood. In addition to cognition and personality, this chapter also briefly considers scholastic achievement. It begins with physical development.

Physical Development

The brain has reached 90% of its adult size by 2 years of age; however, functional brain changes such as changes in neurotransmission and neuromodulation continue during childhood. Although developmental neurobiology is an extremely fertile field for the application of developmental behavioral genetics, the only available data in the realm of physical development involve the relatively static variables of height and weight. The rate of growth in height and weight continues at a steady pace during childhood until early adolescence—both increase at the rate of about one standard deviation per year. As shown in Table 10.1, twin data from the Louisville Twin Study suggest that genes are largely responsible for individual differences in height and weight despite substantial average year-to-year increases. For height, identical twin correlations remain unchanged from 3 to 8 years, whereas fraternal twin correlations decline slightly; for this reason, heritability estimates increase from about 74% to about 90% from 3 to 8 years. A similar pattern is observed for weight, although the change in heritability is slight (from 72% to 78%). Parent-offspring correlations for height and weight, also included in Table 10.1, decline slightly from 3 to 8 years (Tiisala & Kantero, 1971). When the children are 8 years old, parent-offspring correlations are .36 for height and .28 for weight. These correlations are consistently lower than the correlations for fraternal twins. Even if the parent-offspring correlations were entirely genetic in origin, they would suggest heritabilities of 72% for height and 56% for weight; these lower heritability estimates as compared to twin estimates could be due to the presence of nonadditive genetic variance or genetic discontinuities from childhood to adulthood.

TABLE 10.1
Familial Correlations for Height and Weight for Twins in the Louisville
Twin Study (Wilson, 1976, 1979)[a] and for Parents and Offspring
(Tiisala & Kantero, 1971)[b]

Measure	Age	Twin Correlations		Parent-Offspring Correlation
		Identical	*Fraternal*	
Height	3 years	.93	.56	.40
	5 years	.94	.51	.42
	8 years	.94	.49	.36
Weight	3 years	.88	.52	.33
	5 years	.85	.48	.35
	8 years	.88	.49	.28

[a]Twin correlations include approximately 150 pairs of each type on average.
[b]Parent-offspring correlations averaged for mothers and fathers in 177 families.

IQ

There is a striking developmental change in individual differences in mental development from infancy to early childhood: Long-term predictiveness increases dramatically. There is some question whether infant mental development scores predict later IQ at all; if there is any prediction from infancy to adulthood, the relationship is weak. Correlations with adult IQ increase from perhaps .10 in infancy to about .40 in early childhood and to about .70 by the early school years (Plomin & DeFries, 1981). As we shall see, heritability mirrors these increases in predictiveness. It is possible, however, that these developmental changes are due to the instruments used to assess intelligence rather than intelligence itself—there are striking differences in the types of items included from age to age, especially from infancy to early childhood.

Twin Studies

Twin data from the longitudinal Louisville Twin Study are presented in Fig. 10.1 (Wilson, 1983). Twins are tested yearly during childhood from 3 to 9 years of age using age-appropriate IQ tests—the Stanford-Binet at 3; the Wechsler Preschool and Primary Scale of Intelligence at 4, 5, and 6; and the Wechsler Intelligence Scale for Children at 7, 8, and 9. The results show that identical twins are as similar to each other as individuals are similar to themselves year to year. That is, the average identical twin correlation is .85 and the average year-to-year correlation for individuals is .84. Identical twin correlations do not change during childhood, whereas fraternal twin correlations decline from .79 at 3 to .59 at 6 and 7 years. For this reason, the twin results show progressively increasing heritability up to middle childhood: The heritability estimates at each year from 3 to 7 years are .18, .24, .38, .54, and .50. As discussed in later chapters, the heritability of IQ is about .50 in late adolescence and adulthood. Thus, by the early school years, the heritability of IQ is similar to estimates during adolescence and adulthood. However, we cannot conclude that ''adult genes'' affect IQ by middle childhood—these data merely indicate that the relative contributions of genetic and environmental influences are in the same proportion as later in life. The data in Fig. 10.1 suggest that heritability is lower, about .35, at 8 and 9 years, which might signal changes of early adolescence, as discussed in the next chapter. Analyses of twin developmental profiles during childhood yield profile correlations similar to the single-age correlations: The identical and fraternal twin profile correlations for IQ across ages 3, 4, 5, and 6 years are .87 and .65, respectively; at 6, 7, and 8 years, the twin profile correlations are .81 and .66.

Only a handful of other childhood twin studies have been reported. A study of 35 identical pairs and 36 fraternal pairs from 5 to 8 years of age found twin correlations of .79 for identical twins and .45 for fraternal twins for IQ scores on

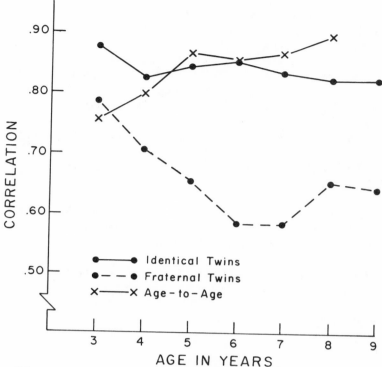

FIG. 10.1.   Summary of twin and age-to-age IQ correlations from the longitudinal Louisville Twin Study. Data from Wilson (1983) for over 100 pairs each of identical and fraternal twins. Age-to-age correlations involve from 242 to 424 individuals and represent yearly intervals; the age-to-age correlation shown for 3 years is the correlation from 3 to 4 years, that shown for 4 years if the correlation from 4 to 5 years, and so on.

the Primary Mental Abilities test (Koch, 1966). Two studies yielded much lower estimates of heritability for Raven's Coloured Progressive Matrices for Children. In a study of 4- to 7-year-old twins, age-corrected correlations for Raven scores were .57 and .48, respectively, for 137 pairs of identical twins and 72 pairs of fraternal twins (Garfinkle & Vandenberg, 1981), suggesting little genetic influence. A similar result was obtained for the Raven in a study of 51 pairs of identical twins and 33 pairs of fraternal twins with an average age of 7.6 years, most of whom were 6 to 9 years old (Foch & Plomin, 1980). In this study, the fraternal twin correlation (.44) was actually greater than the identical twin correlation (.26), although not significantly so. It is likely that these odd results for Raven's Matrices are due to low reliability. For age-corrected scores, consistency is only .53 and 2-month, test-retest reliability is only .26. This contrasts sharply with the internal consistency of .90 and 3-month, test-retest reliability of .90 reported by Raven (1965). Raven's sample consisted of 25 school children whose ages ranged from 6 to 12 years. Although Raven's discussion of the procedure used for calculating test-retest reliability is not clear, it appears that he used raw scores rather than age-adjusted scores (Raven, 1965). Because the correlation between Raven scores and age in childhood is greater than .60, age adjustment is critical, not just for twin correlations (because twins are identical for age) but also for computing reliability. Low reliability for the Raven's Coloured Matrices has been reported in another study as well (Knaack, 1978). Thus, at least for children in this age range, the reliability of the Raven test is in doubt.

The closest replication of the Louisville Twin Study is a study in which the Wechsler Intelligence Scale for Children was administered to 69 identical twin pairs and 35 fraternal twin pairs from 5 to 13 years of age, with an average age of 8 years (Segal, 1985). The twin IQ correlations for identical and fraternal twins were .85 and .42, respectively, suggesting substantial heritability, more than twice as great as the heritability found in the Louisville Twin Study at 8 years of age.

In summary, twin results for IQ in childhood based on studies other than those using the Raven test suggest substantial heritability. However, as indicated in the following section, recent adoption data on IQ in childhood yield much less consistent evidence for genetic influence.

Adoption Studies

The classic adoption study by Skodak and Skeels (1949) found little IQ resemblance between biological mothers and their adopted-away infants. When the adoptees were tested at an average age of 4 years on the Stanford-Binet, the correlation of their scores with IQ of their biological mothers was .28. At an average age of 7 years, the correlation was .35. Selective placement inflated these correlations somewhat—number of years of education of the biological parents was correlated about .25 with education of the adoptive parents. Nonetheless, the results of this longitudinal adoption study correspond well with those of the longitudinal Louisville Twin Study in pointing to a sharp increase in genetic influence during the transition from infancy to childhood. No IQ data were obtained for adoptive parents in this study.

Seldom reported is a study, mentioned in the previous chapter, in which IQ scores were obtained for 312 children placed in adoptive homes before 4 years of age (Snygg, 1938). Although the test protocol is not specified in detail, each child was tested about three times at ages varying from under 1 year to 5 years or more. For 513 IQ scores of about 300 children, the average weighted correlation between scores of biological mothers and their adopted-away children 3 years and older was .11. As discussed in the previous chapter, the biological mothers in this study were clearly a biased sample and restriction of range is likely to curtail its mother-child IQ correlation.

Other early adoption studies did not include IQ information on biological parents, were not longitudinal, and included children of a wide age range. Rather than assessing the impact of heredity directly from the resemblance between biological parents and their adopted-away offspring, genetic influence was estimated by comparing correlations in adoptive families in which parents share only family environment with their adopted children and correlations in nonadoptive families in which parents share heredity as well as family environment with their children.

Burks (1928) conducted the first adoption study of this type, a study that included about 200 adoptive families and 100 nonadoptive families in which the children were between the ages of 5 and 14 (average age of 9 years). Selective placement was negligible in that the occupational status of the biological fathers and the adoptive fathers yielded a correlation of .02. The adoptees were placed in their adoptive homes at 3 months of age on average; all children were placed before they were 12 months old. The correlation for nonadoptive parents and their children (.46) was significantly greater than the correlation for adoptive parents and their adopted children (.13). Thus, these results agree with the studies described earlier in suggesting substantial genetic influence on IQ during childhood; however, the results were not reported as a function of the children's age so that they cannot be used to pinpoint the age at which genetic influence reaches asymptote or to reveal whether genetic influence shows a decline after the early school years.

Conflicting results emerged in another study of this type (Freeman, Holzinger, & Mitchell, 1928). The offspring were from 2 to 22 years of age, with an average age of 11 years. The obtained IQ correlation for adoptive parents and their adopted children was .32 in 255 families; this correlation is slightly greater than the correlation of .27 reported for adoptive parents and their nonadopted children in 40 families in which the adoptive parents had their own biological children in addition to adopted children. However, the children in this study were adopted late, about 4 years of age on the average, and they were known to the adoption agency workers for almost a year on the average before they were placed in an adoptive home. As these circumstances suggest, selective placement was considerable—the correlation between the IQ of the adopted children at the time of their placement in the adoptive homes and the social status of the adoptive home was .34. Thus, it seems likely that at least part of the observed resemblance between the adopted children and their adoptive parents may be attributed to selective placement. Similar problems affect the interpretation of the correlation of .25 reported for 112 pairs of unrelated children living in the same adoptive family. The study also found a correlation of .25 for 125 pairs of siblings reared apart for 7 years on average. However, the fact that their average age at separation was 5 years makes it difficult to interpret this correlation as well. (A similar problem exists for two other studies of siblings reared apart; Elderton, 1922; Hildreth, 1925.) For these reasons, the summary evaluation of the Freeman et al. (1928) study in a review of adoption studies of IQ concluded that "all in all, it is a most inconclusive study" (Munsinger, 1975, p. 635).

The disparity between the results of these two studies prompted a third study by Leahy (1935). The design of this study was like that of the study by Burks, and it included 194 adoptive families and 194 nonadoptive families. Adopted children were placed in adoptive homes prior to 6 months of age and were between 5 and 14 years old (9 years on the average) when tested. Although some selective placement occurred—correlations between biological and adoptive parents ranged from .09 to .20 for occupational status and from .20 to .25 for education, the results clearly confirm those of Burks' study. The parent-offspring correlations were .46 in nonadoptive families and .14 in adoptive families. Thus, the adoption studies by Burks and Leahy suggest substantial genetic mediation of parent-child IQ correlations. The correlations of .13 and .14 in the adoptive families indicate some influence of shared family environment. For 35 pairs of unrelated children reared together, the IQ correlation was .08, which suggests that the effect of shared family environment is no greater for siblings than it is for parents and their offspring.

Two studies of this type in the 1970s confirm the earlier findings of significant genetic influence and some influence of shared family environment. Most relevant to childhood is a longitudinal study of 94 adoptive families and 50 nonadoptive families in which children were tested at 4 and 7 years of age. Mother-child IQ correlations at 4 years were .07 in adoptive homes and .35 in nonadoptive homes; at 7 years, the correlations are .08 and .26 (Fisch, Bilek, Deinard, & Change, 1976). These results, in contrast to the results of the Louisville Twin Study and the longitudinal adoption study by Skodak and Skeels, suggest no change in genetic influence from 4 to 7 years of age. However, somewhat more weight needs to be given to the Skodak and Skeels' results because genetic influence was estimated directly from the correlation between biological mothers and their adopted-away children, whereas the design of the study by Fisch et al. estimates genetic influence from the difference between parent-offspring correlations in nonadoptive and adoptive families.

Another study is a transracial study in which children most of whom had one black biological parent were adopted into Caucasian homes during the first year of life (Scarr & Weinberg, 1977). Correlations between adoptive parents and their adopted children ($N = 111$) were compared to correlations between these parents and their biological children ($N = 142$). The children were from 4 to more than 16 years of age when tested; the average age of the children was 7 for the adoptees and 10 for the biological offspring. The correlation between adoptive parents and their adopted children was .19; the correlation between these same parents and their biological children was .37. These results suggest genetic influence in childhood and adolescence; however, parent-offspring correlations were not analyzed as a function of the children's age. Substantial genetic influence is also suggested by a correlation of .32 between education of 94 biological mothers and IQ of their adopted-away children.

Scarr and Weinberg's study also included 187 pairs of unrelated children reared together and 107 pairs of genetically related siblings. Unlike Leahy's finding of a correlation of .08, this study yielded a correlation of .33 for adoptive siblings, suggesting that shared family environment plays a major role in the IQ similarity of siblings. The IQ correlation for nonadoptive siblings was .42, only slightly greater than that for adoptive siblings. Thus, these sibling data suggest little genetic influence on IQ. Although some selective placement occurred in this study—the correlation between biological parents and adoptive parents for education was .22, it cannot explain much of the high adoptive sibling correlation.

From a developmental genetic viewpoint, these results are puzzling. *More* genetic influence seen in sibling analyses than in parent-offspring analyses would make sense if genetic changes occur during development. Also, siblings share some nonadditive genetic variance due to dominance, whereas parents and their offspring share only additive genetic variance; this would also serve to make sibling estimates of genetic influence greater than parent-offspring estimates. However, the finding of *less* genetic influence for siblings than for parents and their offspring makes no genetic sense. Furthermore, this finding for siblings conflicts with the twin data, as well as with Leahy's (1935) findings, and could be discounted as a chance result were it not for the fact that another modern study yielded somewhat similar results.

In the Texas Adoption Project, the only adoption study other than the Colorado Adoption Project to obtain IQ scores for biological as well as adoptive parents, adopted and nonadopted children were reared in the same families and were of a wide age range—from 3 to 26 years, with an average age of 8 for the adopted children and 10 for the nonadopted children (Horn, Loehlin, & Willerman, 1979). In one report (Horn, 1983), the results based on Beta IQ of the parents and the children's Wechsler Performance IQ are broken down by age of the children. For adopted children from 5 to 7 years of age, the IQ correlation between 169 biological mothers and their adopted-away children was .36, suggesting substantial genetic influence. However, this correlation is substantially larger than the correlation of .20 between adoptive parents and their 66 nonadopted children (from 5 to 9 years of age), which suggests a problem because these parents share heredity with their children to the same extent as do biological parents and their adopted-away children. Furthermore, the correlation between adoptive parents and their adopted children was .15 for 188 pairs, which suggests that shared family environment should add to the hereditary similarity between parents and their nonadopted children. Thus, although the correlation for biological mothers and their adopted-away children suggests substantial genetic effects, the difference between the adoptive and nonadoptive parent-child correlations suggests only slight genetic influence.

As in the study by Scarr and Weinberg (1977), the correlation between biological siblings reported by Horn et al. (1979) is only slightly greater than the correlation between genetically unrelated children reared together. Unfortunately, the sibling correlations are presented only for the total sample of children from 3 to 26 years. For 40 families that included biological siblings, the correlation was .35; for 236 families in which pairs of genetically unrelated children were reared together, the correlation was .26. This pattern of sibling results is similar to Scarr and Weinberg's findings and suggests little genetic influence on IQ in childhood.

Thus, these two recent adoption studies cloud the picture of substantial genetic influence on IQ during childhood that is seen in the earlier adoption studies and by most twin studies. The power of the adoption design in general, and the size and carefulness of these two adoption studies in particular, counterbalance the weight of the other studies and leave open the question of genetic influence on IQ in childhood. However, a definite weakness of these studies from a developmental behavioral genetic perspective is the wide age range of the children. It is noteworthy that the only direct estimate of genetic effects—the correlation between biological mothers and their adopted-away children in the Texas Adoption Project—suggests substantial genetic influence. The contradiction arises from estimates of genetic influence based on the difference in correlations between pairs of adoptive and pairs of nonadoptive relatives.

Preliminary analyses of data on IQ in early childhood from the longitudinal Colorado Adoption Project (CAP) yield similar results (Plomin & DeFries, in press). The Stanford-Binet IQ test was administered to 186 adopted children and 151 nonadopted children at 3 years of age and to 162 adopted and 138 nonadopted children when they were 4 years old. Parental IQ was measured by an unrotated first principal component scores of 13 cognitive tests for biological, adoptive, and nonadoptive parents. Biological mothers' IQ scores correlated significantly with their adopted-away children's IQ scores at 3 years ($r = .18$) and at 4 years ($r = .22$), suggesting significant genetic mediation of correlations between parents and their offspring in early childhood. Adoptive parent-adoptee correlations (.15 at 3 years and .15 at 4 years) also were significant. However, as in the other recent studies, correlations in nonadoptive families were lower than expected on the basis of these direct estimates of genetic and environmental influence: The nonadoptive parent-offspring correlations at 3 and 4 years were .14 and .15, respectively. Thus, if one were estimating genetic influence on the basis of the difference in parent-offspring correlations between adoptive and nonadoptive families, no genetic influence would be found. However, the direct estimate of genetic influence derived from scores of biological parents and their adopted-away children suggests significant genetic involvement. Moreover, similar to the results of the Skodak and Skeels study and the Louisville Twin Study, the CAP data suggest increasing heritability from infancy to childhood in model-fitting analyses (LaBuda, DeFries, Fulker, & Plomin, in press).

What could account for the lower-than-expected correlations in nonadoptive families? Selective placement could inflate parent-child correlations for both biological and adoptive parents, but that would make these correlations too high rather than making the nonadoptive family correlations too low. In any event, selective placement is negligible in the CAP.

The possibility that reactive and active genotype-environment correlation accounts for results such as these was discussed in chapter 6. Reactive genotype-environment correlation can occur in adoptive as well as nonadoptive families if parents react to their children's propensities or if children respond to their parents' dispositions in such a way as to increase parent-child resemblance. If parent-child correlations in adoptive and nonadoptive families contain some genotype-environment correlation of these types, the difference between nonadoptive and adoptive parent-child correlations does not include this component of variance. In contrast, reactive and active genotype-environment correlation can contribute to the resemblance between biological mothers and their adopted-away offspring. For example, biological mothers and their adopted-away children might be responded to similarly or they might actively seek environments compatible with their genetic propensities.

There are two other possibilities as well. Perhaps adoptive parents have more environmental impact on their children than do nonadoptive parents; however, comparisons of parenting in adoptive and nonadoptive families in the CAP yield few differences (Plomin & DeFries, 1985). The lower-than-expected correlations in nonadoptive families could also be due to chance—this is the explanation favored by model-fitting approaches to the CAP data, which have found an adequate fit between adoption models and the data when all of the data are analyzed simultaneously. Resolution of this issue will require additional research.

The significant IQ correlations between biological mothers and their adopted-away children at 3 and 4 years suggest some genetic continuity between early childhood and adulthood for IQ. How much genetic continuity? Using the approach described in chapter 3, the genetic correlations from 3 years to adulthood and from 4 years to adulthood are 1.0 based on the biological mother-adopted children correlations of .18 at 3 years and .22 at 4 years and using the Louisville Twin Study estimates of heritability of about .20 at 3 years and .25 at 4 years. In other words, even though less of the IQ variance in childhood is due to genetic variance than in adulthood, the genetic variance that affects childhood IQ covaries completely with IQ-relevant genetic variance in adulthood. Thus, these IQ results support the amplification model discussed in chapter 3 that posits that any genetic variance that exists early in development continues to affect traits later in development.

An implication of the CAP results for IQ in early childhood is that, by itself, genetic continuity from childhood to adulthood should lead to IQ stability correlations of about .35 and .45, respectively, between measures at 3 and 4 years and in adulthood (about twice the correlation between the biological mothers and their adopted-away children). The Berkeley Growth and Guidance Studies (Bayley, 1954; Honzik, MacFarlane, & Allen, 1948) yield IQ stability correlations from childhood to adulthood of about .40 from 3 years of age and .50 from 4 years of age. This suggests that most of the phenotypic stability observed for IQ from childhood to adulthood is mediated genetically.

Another analysis of the CAP parent-offspring data at 3 and 4 years is relevant: Children's IQ scores have been compared to their parents' specific cognitive abilities in order to elucidate the long-term predictive nature of childhood IQ. Are IQ scores of children equally related to all four cognitive abilities of parents, or is the prediction from childhood to adulthood limited to one or two adult cognitive abilities? The answer appears to lie between these alternatives: Childhood IQ is genetically related to parental verbal, perceptual speed, and memory abilities, but not to parental spatial ability. Parent-offspring correlations between adoptees' IQ at 3 and 4 years, respectively, and biological mothers' specific cognitive abilities are .19 and .16 for biological mothers verbal ability, .14 and .14 for perceptual speed, and .10 and .20 for memory. However, the correlations between biological mothers' spatial ability and adoptees' IQ at 3 and 4 years are only .00 and .04. Similarly, nonadopted children's IQ scores at 3 and 4 yield significant correlations with their parents' verbal ability—.16 and .24 for mothers and .19 and .23 for fathers. No significant correlations emerged for nonadoptive parents' spatial ability: The parent-offspring correlations at the two ages were .11 and .06 for mothers and .04 and .08 for fathers. Thus, it appears that childhood IQ is related genetically to several cognitive abilities in adulthood, but not to spatial ability. This finding might simply reflect inadequate assessment of spatial ability by the Stanford-Binet test in childhood; nonetheless, it is noteworthy that childhood IQ does not predict adult spatial ability.

In conclusion, the data from the Colorado Adoption Project are consistent with data from the study by Skodak and Skeels and the Texas Adoption Project in suggesting substantial genetic influence when direct estimates of heredity are obtained from correlations between biological mothers and their adopted-away children. Estimates based on comparisons between correlations in nonadoptive and adoptive families are much less consistent; however, twin studies, which are based on comparisons between correlations for identical twins and fraternal twins, offer a fairly consistent picture of genetic influence on IQ in childhood.

Specific Cognitive Abilities

Despite the tendency of behavioral geneticists to move away from the study of IQ towards consideration of specific cognitive abilities, few studies of specific abilities during childhood have been reported. Nearly all of the studies have examined twin correlations for subtest scores on IQ tests such as the Wechsler Intelligence Scale for Children rather than systematically studying specific cognitive abilities.

Mittler (1969) reported twin correlations for the performance of 4-year-olds on subtests of the Illinois Test of Psycholinguistic Abilities (ITPA) that assess channels of communication, levels of organization, and processes such as decoding, encoding, and association. Twin correlations for the nine subtests for a sample of 28 identical pairs and 64 fraternal pairs are listed in Table 10.2. The twin correlations for the total ITPA—.90 for identical twins and .68 for fraternal twins—suggest both substantial genetic influence and substantial shared environment.

The subtests display a wide variation in heritability that does not appear to be due to differential subtest reliability. For example, heritability is essentially zero for auditory decoding, which assesses the ability to understand spoken words, and for the visual-motor sequential subtest, which involves the ability to

TABLE 10.2
Twin Correlations for 4-Year-Olds on the Illinois Test
of Psycholinguistic Abilities (Mittler, 1971)

| Subtest | Twin Correlations | |
	Identical (28 pairs)	Fraternal (64 pairs)
Representational Level		
Decoding		
1. Auditory	.52	.72
2. Visual	.74	.24
Association		
3. Auditory	.81	.68
4. Visual motor	.78	.15
Encoding		
5. Vocal	.63	.43
6. Motor	.66	.35
Automatic-Sequential		
Automatic		
7. Auditory vocal	.82	.55
Sequential		
8. Auditory vocal	.56	.49
9. Visual-motor	.46	.49
Total	.90	.68

reproduce a series of visual stimuli from memory. Mittler suggests that visual and motor channels show greater genetic influence than do auditory or vocal channels. Although channels of communication might well make a difference in behavioral genetic studies of specific cognitive abilities, it should be noted that, aside from this distinction, most of the ITPA tests—such as a verbal analogies test ("auditory association") and digit span ("auditory-vocal sequential")—are quite similar to standard tests of specific cognitive abilities. Examined in this light, five verbal ITPA subtests (auditory and visual reception, auditory and visual association, and verbal expression) yield an average identical twin correlation of .70 and an average fraternal twin correlation of .44; two memory ITPA subtests (auditory and visual sequences) yield average twin correlations of .41 for identical twins and .49 for fraternal twins. Thus, these results could be interpreted as indicating that verbal ability shows substantial genetic influence in childhood, whereas memory shows little if any genetic influence.

One twin study (Munsinger & Douglass, 1976) focused on syntactic abilities in twins and siblings whose average age was 9 years—although the age range was exceptionally large, from 3 to 17. An age-corrected composite language score based on two tests, the Assessment of Children's Language Comprehension and the Northwestern Syntax Screening Test, yielded an identical twin correlation of .83 (37 pairs), a fraternal twin correlation of .44 (37 pairs), and a nontwin sibling correlation of .50 (29 pairs). Notably, these results are independent of nonverbal IQ in that the language scores were corrected for scores on the WISC Picture Completion test. Thus, this study, in which most subjects were in middle childhood, and the study by Mittler of early childhood suggest substantial genetic influence on verbal/language measures in childhood.

Several twin studies have reported twin correlations for subtests of IQ measures. For example, the results of a reanalysis of Primary Mental Abilities subtest scores obtained by Koch (1966) for 5- to 7-year-old twins are reported in Table 10.3 (Plomin & Vandenberg, 1980). Other than for the perceptual subtest, these results suggest substantial genetic influence on specific cognitive abilities in childhood. A multivariate analysis suggested that verbal and spatial abilities, both substantially influenced by heredity, are genetically independent. In other words, the genes that influence verbal ability are not the same as those that influence spatial ability.

Two studies have reported childhood twin results for subtests of Wechsler scales. Twin correlations for subtests of the Wechsler Primary and Preschool Scale of Intelligence (WPPSI; Wilson, 1975) and the Wechsler Intelligence Scale for Children-Revised (WISC-R; Segal, 1985) are presented in Table 10.4. For the verbal tests (the first five subtests), the two studies show remarkably similar results that suggest substantial genetic influence. However, the fraternal twin correlations are greater in the Wilson study of 5- and 6-year-olds than in the Segal study, in which children were 8 years old on average. This implies that shared environment decreases in importance following school entry, a reasonable

TABLE 10.3
Twin Correlations for Primary Mental Abilities (Koch, 1966; from
Plomin & Vandenberg, 1980)

	Twin Correlations	
PMA Subtests	Identical (34 pairs)	Fraternal (32 pairs)
Verbal	.62	.30
Perceptual	.49	.36
Quantitative	.73	.49
Spatial	.65	.23

TABLE 10.4
Twin Correlations for Wechsler Subtests in Childhood

	WPPSI Twin Correlations Wilson (1975)[a]		WISC-R Twin Correlations Segal (1985)[b]	
Subtest	Identical (50 pairs)	Fraternal (34 pairs)	Identical (69 pairs)	Fraternal (35 pairs)
Information	.81	.51	.79	.38
Similarities	.73	.58	.76	.29
Arithmetic	.65	.52	.68	.28
Vocabulary	.71	.50	.78	.42
Comprehension	.80	.62	.65	.43
Picture Completion	.69	.26	.32	.42
Block Design	.68	.43	.61	.19
Picture Arrangement	—	—	.33	.25
Object Assembly	—	—	.54	.20
Coding	—	—	.68	.40
Animal House	.82	.40	—	—
Mazes	.61	.45	—	—
Geometric Design	.72	.25	—	—

[a]In this report from the Louisville Twin Study, the twins were 5 and 6 years old.
[b]The twins varied in age from 5 to 13 years, with an average of 8 years.

hypothesis that must be tempered by the fact that somewhat different tests were used for the two age groups. The results for the performance subtests are less clear. Picture Completion yields completely different results in the two studies, although the results for Block Design suggest substantial genetic influence at both ages. The three subtests unique to the WPPSI show genetic influence; of the three subtests unique to the WISC-R, one test (Picture Arrangement) suggests little effect of heredity. On the whole, however, these two studies suggest genetic influence, especially for verbal and possibly for spatial tests.

Both studies also reported twin correlations for verbal and performance IQs.

The Louisville results were reported separately at 4, 5, and 6 for about 60 pairs each of identical and fraternal twins (Wilson, 1975). For performance IQ, the twin results were similar at each age: Identical and fraternal twin correlations, respectively, were .76 and .53 at 4 years, .79 and .49 at 5 years, and .82 and .51 at 6 years. The twin results for verbal IQ suggest an interesting developmental pattern of increasing genetic influence: .76 and .73 at 4 years, .77 and .65 at 5 years, and .82 and .56 at 6 years. The low heritability of verbal scores at 4 years conflicts with Mittler's (1969) results described earlier. However, the finding of substantial genetic influence on both verbal and performance IQ in middle childhood is confirmed by the Segal study—identical and fraternal twin correlations were .87 and .45, respectively, for verbal IQ and .71 and .34 for performance IQ.

In addition, in both studies, twin subtest profiles were analyzed using trend correlations across all 10 Wechsler subtests. The twin trend correlations for identical and fraternal twins, respectively, in the Louisville study were .38 and .19 at 4 years, .42 and .26 at 5 years, and .43 and .24 at 6 years; in the Segal study, in which the children were 8 years of age on average, the profile correlations were .45 and .24. These results thus suggest genetic influence on patterns of cognitive strengths and weaknesses in childhood.

One twin study of children who were 7.5 years old on average (Foch & Plomin, 1980) focused on specific cognitive abilities rather than subtests of IQ tests, and it yielded somewhat different results (see Table 10.5). The verbal tests of reading recognition and vocabulary show some genetic influence, as does the WISC-R Mazes spatial test. However, the overriding conclusion from Table 10.5 is that genetic influence counts for little, especially for memory and perceptual speed tests. It should be noted that the only previous study that included measures of memory (Mittler, 1969) found no genetic influence on memory tests, and the perceptual speed measure showed the lowest heritability in the Plomin and Vandenberg (1980) reanalysis of Koch's data. At any rate, the Foch and Plomin results are not likely to be due to a sampling problem because reasonable twin correlations were found for the anchor variables of height (identical and fraternal twin correlations of .95 and .50, respectively) and weight (.89 and .46). A cross-sectional analysis of these data using hierarchical multiple regression found no evidence for age-dependent changes in the relative influence of heredity and environment (Ho, Foch, & Plomin, 1980).

The results of this study received some support from a larger study (137 identical and 72 fraternal pairs) of children 4 to 7 years of age (Garfinkle & Vandenberg, 1981). The identical and fraternal twin correlations were .69 and .52, respectively, for a picture vocabulary test and .17 and -.08 for picture memory. Thus, as in the study by Foch and Plomin (1980), some genetic influence is suggested for vocabulary and little, if any, for memory. No perceptual speed or memory measures were included in this study, however. A novel aspect of the study should be mentioned: For a battery of 15 tasks

TABLE 10.5
Twin Correlations for Tests of Specific Cognitive Abilities
(Foch & Plomin, 1980)[a]

Measure	Twin Correlations	
	Identical (51 pairs)	Fraternal (33 pairs)
McCarthy and WISC-R Vocabulary	.81	.68
PIAT Reading Recognition	.74	.46
PIAT Mathematics	.55	.64
WISC-R Mazes	.60	.44
WISC-R Block Design	.25	.40
ETS Identical Pictures	.31	.52
Colorado Perceptual Speed	.51	.42
GFW Auditory Recognition Memory	.28	−.06
Picture Memory, Immediate	.43	.40
Picture Memory, Delayed	.24	.15

[a]The twins varied in age from 5 to 12 years, with an average of 7.5 years.

representing Piagetian mathematical concepts such as conservation, classification, and seriation, identical and fraternal twin correlations of .73 and .56, respectively, suggested some genetic influence on these traditional Piagetian measures in childhood.

Nearly all of these studies indicate that verbal skills are influenced by genetic factors. The studies also agree that perceptual speed and memory tests tend to show little genetic influence. However, there is some discrepancy concerning spatial measures. Overall, specific cognitive abilities do not seem as much influenced by heredity in childhood as they are later in life, as discussed in subsequent chapters. If heritability of specific cognitive abilities does not change during childhood, as suggested by the analyses reported by Ho et al. (1980), increasing genetic influence must be predicted for adolescence.

Much needed are adoption data on specific cognitive abilities in childhood. We have seen that recent adoption data on IQ suggest the possibility that heredity may not be as influential as twin studies imply. The only adoption study of specific cognitive abilities in childhood is the longitudinal Colorado Adoption Project (CAP), which, as described earlier, has obtained cognitive data on biological, adoptive, and nonadoptive parents and their adopted and nonadopted children—186 adopted children and 151 nonadopted children at 3 years of age, and 162 adopted and 138 nonadopted children at 4 years. The parents were tested on a battery of 13 cognitive tests that yield four rotated factors: Verbal, Spatial, Perceptual Speed, and Memory (DeFries, Plomin, Vandenberg, & Kuse, 1981). Two tests were constructed to tap each factor for the CAP children at 3 years (Singer, Corley, Guiffrida, & Plomin, 1984) and at 4 years (Rice, Corley,

Fulker, & Plomin, 1985); psychometric properties, including test-retest reliability and factor structure, are reasonable for the two batteries.

As described in the previous chapter, CAP analyses of infant data led to the conclusion that insofar as components of infant mental development predict adult cognitive abilities, the infant measures primarily predict adult general cognitive ability, not specific abilities. This conclusion implies that genetic factors that affect infant cognitive functioning also affect adult IQ, but not adult specific cognitive abilities. In other words, the results suggest that infant mental development is undifferentiated in the sense that components of infant mental functioning relate more to adult IQ than to specific cognitive abilities in adulthood.

Despite the evidence mentioned earlier concerning significant genetic and family environmental influence on IQ at 3 and 4 years of age, little evidence emerged for either genetic or environmental influence on specific cognitive abilities. Table 10.6 presents isomorphic parent-offspring correlations (for example, parents' verbal ability correlated with children's verbal ability). Although several parent-offspring correlations are significant in nonadoptive families, the results for biological parents and for adoptive parents are not nearly as consistent as the parent-offspring results for IQ. However, for verbal ability at 3 and 4, the positive correlations for biological mothers and for adoptive parents suggest a trace of genetic and family environmental influence, although both are weaker than for IQ.

If specific cognitive abilities in early childhood are not differentiated in terms of their prediction of specific cognitive abilities in adulthood, we would expect to find that a certain ability, say memory, correlates as highly with other specific cognitive abilities in adulthood as it does with adult memory. This issue was addressed by comparing the isomorphic parent-offspring correlations in Table 10.6 with parent-offspring "cross correlations"—for example, the average correlation of children's verbal scores with their parents' spatial, perceptual speed, and memory scores. For children's spatial, perceptual speed, and memory abilities, the average parent-offspring cross correlations are as high as or higher than the isomorphic parent-offspring correlations listed in Table 10.6. However, the cross correlations for children's verbal ability at both 3 and 4 years are somewhat lower than the isomorphic parent-offspring correlations for biological mothers and for nonadoptive parents. This suggests the possiblity that verbal ability in early childhood is to some extent genetically distinct in terms of its predictiveness of adult verbal ability.

In summary, isomorphic comparisons between specific cognitive abilities in parents and their offspring suggest that specific cognitive abilities at 3 and 4 years of age, with the possible exception of verbal ability, show less influence of family environment and of heredity than does IQ. From the environmental perspective, this implies that aspects of the family environment relevant to cognitive development in early childhood are general in the sense that family

TABLE 10.6
Parent-Offspring Correlations for Specific Cognitive Abilities in
the Colorado Adoption Project (Plomin & DeFries, 1985b)

	Biological		Adoptive		Nonadoptive	
	Mother	Father	Mother	Father	Mother	Father
3-Year-Olds						
Verbal	.12	.02	.07	.09	.16*	.21*
Spatial	.11	.12	−.05	.15*	.14	.15*
Perceptual Speed	.00	−.09	.05	.12	.14*	.08
Memory	.10	.27*	.07	−.07	.11	−.06
4-Year-Olds						
Verbal	.08	.07	.11	.16*	.22*	.04
Spatial	.09	−.24	−.01	.06	.08	.21*
Perceptual Speed	−.04	.14	.06	.04	.15*	.06
Memory	−.01	−.16	.10	−.05	.00	−.11
N for 3-year-olds	177−	42−	174−	174−	142−	144−
	180	43	180	177	144	145
N for 4-year-olds	155−	35−	154−	152−	131−	133−
	159	36	158	155	134	135

*$p < .05$.

environment reflects parental general intelligence, but not parental specific cognitive abilities. For example, parents with good memory skills do not transmit those skills to their children environmentally even though parental IQ is related environmentally to children's IQ. From the genetic perspective, these results suggest less genetic continuity from childhood to adulthood for specific cognitive abilities than for IQ. Because we know that specific cognitive abilities are relatively independent genetically later in life (DeFries, Vandenberg, & McClearn, 1976), these results imply that differentiation of specific abilities occurs later in development.

Scholastic Abilities

Although the most important life event of childhood is entering the school system, behavioral genetic studies have scarcely begun to consider school-related behavior. This section describes the few studies of scholastic abilities and disabilities.

One of the earliest sibling studies of IQ also included analyses of data on school achievement (Hildreth, 1925). The rationale of the analysis was that if training is more important for school achievement than for IQ, siblings should be more similar for achievement measures than for measures of IQ. In fact, it was found that sibling correlations for IQ and school achievement were quite comparable: In one sample of 105 sibling pairs from 5 to 13 years of age, the sibling correlations were .65 for IQ and .58 for school achievement scores; in another sample of 83 pairs, the correlations were .31 and .42, respectively.

There appears to be not a single twin study of achievement in the early elementary school years. What is needed is a longitudinal behavioral genetic study that includes measures of general and specific cognitive abilities and measures of school achievement in order to study the etiology of ability and achievement domains and their interrelationship.

One of the most widespread scholastic problems for children is reading disability, with typical prevalence estimates in the range of 5% to 10%. Several family studies (reviewed by Finucci, 1978) have been conducted. One of the first family studies in which objective test data were obtained for probands and their relatives strongly suggests that reading disability runs in families (Finucci, Guthrie, Childs, Abbey, & Childs, 1976). Thirty-four of the 75 first-degree relatives of the probands were classified as being reading disabled. In 16 families in which both parents were tested, 81% of the probands had at least one affected parent.

The Colorado Family Reading Study (FRS) is a large-scale, longitudinal study of reading disability in probands, their parents, and their siblings (DeFries, Vogler, & LaBuda, 1985). Probands were known to have normal IQ (90 or above) and reading scores one half of grade level expectancy or lower (e.g., a fourth-grader reading at or below second-grade levels); the probands were between 7.5 and 12 years of age. A 3-hour battery of tests was administered to 1044 individuals in 125 families with a reading-disabled proband and in 125 matched control families. The results demonstrate familial resemblance for reading disability in that the siblings and parents of probands performed significantly worse on reading tests than did siblings and parents of control children. The FRS also indicates that family data can be used to improve the accuracy of prognosis for reading-disabled children. Five years after the original testing, 69 matched pairs of reading-disabled and control children were retested. The persistent nature of reading disability is indicated by reading differences between the probands and controls that were just as great 5 years later. However, individual stability in reading across the 5 years was less for probands than for controls, suggesting that the performance of some reading-disabled children improves whereas that of others worsens. FRS analyses indicate that incorporating parental data into a prediction equation significantly improves the prediction of later reading performance of reading-disabled children.

Case studies of identical and fraternal twins suggest that familial resemblance for reading disability is substantially heritable in origin (Zerdin-Rudin, 1967). A study of 97 twins reported as reading disabled showed 84% concordance for identical twins and 29% for fraternal twins (Bakwin, 1973).

Personality

As explained in the previous chapter, Buss and Plomin (1984) proposed that the EAS traits of emotionality, activity, and sociability are the most heritable aspects of personality in childhood. We shall focus on these three traits in an attempt to pare down the complexity of childhood personality. For adolescents and adults, the question has been raised whether any personality traits show greater genetic influence than others (Loehlin, 1978a), a topic discussed at length in the next chapter. The difficulty of finding personality traits that are not influenced by heredity seems to occur because of the pervasiveness of the highly heritable superfactors of extraversion and neuroticism throughout personality question-naires (Loehlin, 1982). Evidence of genetic influence is widespread in studies of childhood personality; however, nonheritable traits are also found, especially in newer studies that involve observations of specific behaviors and other nonrating measures of temperament for which genetic influence is by no means ubiquitous (Plomin, 1983). Nonetheless, Loehlin's hypothesis that the heritable traits of extraversion and neuroticism pervade measures of personality may apply to childhood personality as well: Emotionality and sociability may be childhood analogs of neuroticism and extraversion. In childhood, extraversion-like items emphasize gregariousness and shyness rather than the complexities of adult behaviors such as liking lively parties. Neuroticism-like items in childhood emphasize emotional arousal and reactivity without the anxiety aspect typical of adult neuroticism items. The third EAS trait, activity, is not included in adult self-report questionnaires for reasons of historical happenstance, although it is usually included in measures of childhood personality.

In this section, behavioral genetic studies of the EAS traits in childhood will be reviewed separately for twin studies using parental ratings and those using other measurement techniques; data from two recent adoption studies are also reviewed. These methods are considered separately because the results they yield differ somewhat.

Parental Ratings Using EAS Questionnaires

The results of several early childhood twin studies that used parental ratings on EAS questionnaires have been summarized by Buss and Plomin (1984; see Table 10.7). Although the samples are not large, they are of respectable size and the findings are consistent. The average correlations across these studies for identical twins and fraternal twins, respectively, are as follows: for emotionality, .63 and .12; for activity, .62 and -.13; and for sociability, .53 and -.03. The differences between the identical and fraternal twin correlations are highly significant, but they are too large to be accommodated by the classical twin model. Fraternal twins, like other first-degree relatives, share half their heredity and should thus

TABLE 10.7
Twin Studies Using EAS Questionnaires (Buss & Plomin, 1984)

Reference	Sample	EAS scale	Twin Correlations	
			Identical	Fraternal
Buss & Plomin	81 identical	Emotionality	.64	.03
(1975)	57 fraternal	Activity	.62	.09
	mean age:	Sociability	.62	.13
	55 months			
Plomin (1974)	60 identical	(midparent ratings)		
	51 fraternal	Emotionality: distress	.47	.10
	mean age:	Emotionality: fear	.70	.38
	54 months	Emotionality: anger	.57	−.12
		Activity: tempo	.41	−.41
		Activity: vigor	.57	−.14
		Sociability	.47	−.12
Plomin & Rowe	36 identical	Emotionality	.70	.06
(1979)	31 fraternal	Activity	.65	−.38
	mean age:	Sociability	.48	−.16
	43 months			
Plomin, unpub-	51 identical	Emotionality	.60	.27
lished (see	33 fraternal	Activity	.73	.05
(Plomin &	mean age:	Sociability	.56	.05
Foch, 1980)	7.6 years			

be approximately half as similar as identical twins. However, for all three EAS traits, the fraternal twin correlations are not significantly greater than zero. This problem is particularly obvious for activity. Buss and Plomin (1984) suggest that contrast effects might be responsible:

> One explanation for lower-than-expected fraternal twin correlations may be nonadditive genetic variance, but nonadditive genetic variance cannot produce negative correlations. A post hoc speculation is *contrast*. Parents might contrast their fraternal twins, labeling one as active and the other as inactive. The twins might contrast themselves and become more differentiated behaviorally. One twin partner, who might be slightly more active than the other, converts this slight edge into a consistent advantage in initiating activities, and the other twin relinquishes the initiative to this partner. Why does this not also happen for identical twins? Presumably, identical twins are so alike behaviorally that contrast is difficult. (1984, p. 119)

Buss and Plomin discuss studies relevant to the issue of contrast effects such as analyses in which each parent rated both twins, yielding an average or midparent rating, and analyses in which each parent rated only one twin (one member of a twin pair was rated by the mother and the other was rated by the father) and

TABLE 10.8
Parent–Offspring Correlations for EAS Measures for 137 Families
(from Plomin, 1974)

	Correlation between midparent ratings of children's EAS and:			
	Mothers' self-rating	Fathers' self-rating	Fathers' ratings of mothers	Mothers' ratings of fathers
Emotionality: distress	.34	.00	.25	− .03
Emotionality: fear	.38	.19	.41	.23
Emotionality: anger	.25	.18	.16	.18
Activity: tempo	.06	.12	.08	.04
Activity: vigor	.14	.12	.10	.10
Sociability	.26	.11	.23	.16

cross-rating correlations were obtained. They conclude that "if there is a bias in parental rating data, it is not limited to one parent rating both twins" (p. 122) and they suggest that contrast effects might lie in the behavior of the children rather than in the eye of the beholder.

The problem of the contrast effect makes it important to collect familial data from relatives other than twins. In a study of 137 families, each parent rated both twins, themselves, and their spouse (Plomin, 1974). Parent-offspring correlations for the EAS scales are listed in Table 10.8. Although the correlations are low, they are higher than the fraternal twin correlations, especially for maternal emotionality and sociability. Parent-offspring correlations include only additive genetic variance, and they do not reflect any genetic differences that occur between early childhood and adulthood; they also are affected by methodological differences between adult self-reports and parental ratings of children's temperament. Nonetheless, if these parent-offspring correlations were due solely to genetic similarity between parents and offspring, they would suggest heritabilities of .20 to .40 on the average.

Of course, parent-offspring correlations could be due to shared family environment rather than shared heredity. One aspect of the data strongly suggests a role for family environment: Mother-offspring correlations are twice as large as father-offspring correlations on the average. Evidence for a maternal effect is consistent for parents' self-reports as well as for ratings by the spouse. Anger and activity do not show a clear maternal effect, however. An adoption study is needed to distinguish between genetic and environmental influences in such familial correlations. Unfortunately, parent-offspring correlations in the Colorado Adoption Project, which includes EAS measures of parents and children, are as yet available only for infancy data (see chapter 9). Other adoption studies of childhood are described in the next section.

Other Parental Rating Studies of Twins

In addition to studies using EAS questionnaires, there are five childhood twin studies that have used measures with at least one scale relevant to EAS. These studies are summarized in Table 10.9. Scarr (1969) used Gough's Adjective Checklist to obtain maternal ratings of twin girls in middle childhood. The twin results suggest that two EAS-like scales, Need for Affiliation (sociability) and Counseling Readiness (emotionality), were among those that showed the most heritability. Other Adjective Checklist scales such as Dominance, Succorance, and Nurturance showed no genetic influence.

Willerman (1973) measured activity in twins from 3 to 12 years of age with a questionnaire that assesses specific behaviors (such as "gets up and down") in specific situations (such as "during meals" and "television"). As typically occurs in rating studies of specific behaviors, the twin correlations are high, but the difference between the identical and fraternal twin correlations is nonetheless substantial.

A study of twins from 1 to 5 years of age (Cohen, Dibble, & Grawe, 1977) used the Childhood Personality Scale, a parental rating instrument that yields five scores. One factor, Sociability-Shyness, is similar to EAS sociability and another factor, Zestfulness, is related to EAS activity. Both scales show significant genetic influence.

Yet another parental rating approach was reported by Matheny and Dolan (1980) for 7- to 10-year-old twins. Mothers rated their children on 23 bipolar rating scales that comprised six factors, two of which were labeled Emotionality and Sociability. An Activity-Distractibility factor consisted of just two items, "overly active" and "inattentive," which, though showing genetic influence, are not the same as EAS activity. Both the emotionality and sociability factors show significant genetic influence. One of the other scales, Tough-minded, showed no significant genetic influence. Matheny and Dolan (1980) concluded:

> According to method, behaviors, and the age of the twins, previous efforts by Buss and Plomin (1975) were most comparable to the present study. Buss and Plomin isolated emotionality, activity, sociability, and, to a lesser extent impulsivity, as the primary factors of a temperament theory of personality development, and presented evidence for highly homogeneous scales that there was a pronounced genetic influence on these four temperaments. The first three of their factors were identified in the present study, and both lines of investigation indicate that emotionality, sociability, and activity are isolable, and genetically influenced, aspects of children's behavior. (pp. 232-233)

One parental rating twin study focused on specific behavioral problems in children who average 7.6 years of age (O'Connor, Foch, Sherry, & Plomin, 1980). The children were rated by their mothers on the Parent Symptom Rating (PSR) questionnaire which yields 12 scales, two of which appear to be relevant to the EAS traits. An Emotionality factor correlated .58 with EAS emotionality

TABLE 10.9
Twin Studies Using Other Parental Rating Measures
(from Buss & Plomin, 1984)

References	Sample	Measure	Twin Correlations	
			Identical	Fraternal
Scarr (1969)	24 identical 28 fraternal 6–10 years	Counseling Readiness (emotionality) Need for Affiliation (sociability)	.56 .83	.03 .56

Wilson et al.
(1971)
	95 identical
	73 fraternal
	longitudinal
	3 to 72 months
		Parental ratings of specific
		behavioral differences:
		temperament (emotionality)
		  temper intensity
		  irritability
		  crying
		  `emper frequency
		sociability
		  seeking affection
		  accepting people
		  smiling
			Mean Twin
			Concordance
			
			49%
			52%
			57%
			25%
			
			37%
			44%
			43%
				
				32%
				36%
				35%
				17%
				
				26%
				30%
				31%

Matheny et al.
(1981)
	70 identical
	44 fraternal
	3 to 72 months
		Parental ratings of
		behavioral differences
		temperament (emotionality)
		  irritability
		  crying
		  temper frequency
		activity
		sociability
		  accepting people
		  smiling
		  cuddling
			Mean Twin
			Concordance
			
			42%
			53%
			40%
			42%
			
			50%
			52%
			43%
				
				22%
				35%
				23%
				22%
				
				24%
				37%
				23%

Willerman (1973)	54 identical 39 fraternal 3–12 years	activity	.88	.59
Cohen et al. (1977)	181 identical 84 fraternal 1–5 years	zestfulness (activity) sociability	.78 .69	.54 .24
Matheny & Dolan (1980)	68 identical 37 fraternal 7–10 years	emotionality sociability	.45 .56	−.11 .06
O'Connor et al. (1980)	54 identical 33 fraternal 7.6 years	emotional shy	.71 .69	.31 .27
Goldsmith & Campos (1982)	29 identical 31 fraternal 9 months	activity level distress to limitations fear	.75 .77 .66	.57 .35 .46

and a Shyness scale correlated -.69 with EAS sociability. Both measures yield estimates of significant and substantial genetic influence.

In summary, behavioral genetic studies of childhood that have used parental ratings other than the EAS measures have found genetic influence for emotionality, activity, and sociability. This conclusion is strengthened by the diversity of measures, including an adjective checklist, interviews, direct ratings of differences within twin pairs, a situationally specific measure of activity, bipolar scales, and ratings of behavioral problems. These studies also provide some evidence for differential heritability; that is, the EAS traits appear to be more heritable than other personality traits.

Twin Studies Employing Measures Other Than Parental Ratings

Few childhoood twin studies have used measures other than parental ratings; these are summarized in Table 10.10. For example, only two studies have employed tester ratings. In one study (Goldsmith & Gottesman, 1981), 4- and 7-year-old twins were rated by testers as part of the Collaborative Perinatal Project. Although the items differed at 4 and 7 years, an Irritability factor emerged at 4 years and a Fearfulness factor was found at 7 years. Twin correlations for these two factors, components of EAS emotionality, suggest substantial genetic influence, whereas other factors showed more modest genetic influence. In a later report, longitudinal analyses of these data were conducted (Goldsmith, 1984). For a composite measure called reactivity—composed of emotional reactivity, activity level, impulsivity, and verbal spontaneity—twin correlations and cross-correlations (one twin's score at 4 years and the cotwin's score at 7 years) were examined. The twin correlations suggest genetic influence at each age. Although longitudinal stability is only .17 from 4 to 7 years, the twin

TABLE 10.10
Twin Studies Using Measures Other Than Parental Ratings

Reference	Sample	Measure	Twin Correlations	
			Identical	Fraternal
Scarr (1969)	24 identical	Tester ratings:	.88	.28
	28 fraternal	Social Apprehension (shyness)		
	6–10 years	Friendliness (sociability)	.86	.28
Goldsmith & Gottesman (1981)	107 identical	Tester ratings:		
	82 fraternal	Irritability (4 years)	.57	.19
	4 & 7 years	Fearfulness (7 years)	.39	.12
Plomin & Foch (1980)	54 identical	Pedometer assessment of activity		
	33 fraternal		.99	.94
	7.6 years mean			

cross-correlations indicate that what little stability exists is largely genetic in origin. Nonetheless, most of the genetic variance is specific to each age. These conclusions were confirmed in longitudinal model-fitting analyses.

A twin study of girls from 6 to 10 years of age (Scarr, 1969) used the Fels Behavior Scales (Richards & Simons, 1941), which include two scales related to EAS sociability: Social Apprehension and Friendliness. Both scales suggest substantial genetic influence.

Only two twin studies involving children have used measures other than ratings. Most studies employing objective assessments have been conducted in infancy and consist of observations of infants in structured settings. One childhood study that used objective measures (Scarr, 1966) included measures only tangentially related to the EAS temperaments such as preferred inspection time. The other study (Plomin & Foch, 1980) assessed diverse behaviors by means of videotaped observations in free-play and standardized situations, objective tests, and mechanical measures in a study of 87 pairs of twins with the average age of 7.6 years. The twins were studied individually in a large playroom equipped with a one-way mirror through which time-sampled video-taped observations were made. The most EAS-relevant measure was activity as measured by a week-long assessment using pedometers. Other measures included fidgeting as rated from videotapes of the children after they were told to lie still in a beanbag chair for 9 minutes; selective attention assessed by the Goldman-Fristoe-Woodcock test in which a child listens to a recording through headphones in order to identify a signal word from background noise that increases in intensity during the test; and aggression as measured by play with a large, inflated "Bobo" clown. Test-retest reliability was obtained for all measures; details of the procedure and measures can be found in Plomin and Foch (1980).

Although rater reliability was high for all measures derived from the videotapes, test-retest reliability was nonsignificant for some of them—most notably, the free-play observational measures—so these were deleted from subsequent analyses. Age-corrected twin correlations yielded results quite different from those based on parental rating data. Although the twin correlations yielded the usual finding of substantial genetic influence for height and weight, they provided little evidence of genetic influence upon objectively assessed and reliable measures of personality. The only significant genetic effect was detected for the week-long pedometer assessment of activity. The pattern of twin correlations for this measure was very unusual, however—the correlations for identical and fraternal twins were .99 and .94, respectively. The high level of the correlations is responsible for detecting significant but slight genetic influence and suggests very substantial effects of shared environment, perhaps because children's activity may be more a function of the family's activities than of each child's own activity level. Although samples of this magnitude can detect only substantial genetic effects, the pattern of twin correlations was not even suggestive of genetic influence for the selective attention and the aggression measures. The fraternal twin correlations for these measures were as great or greater than the identical twin correlations. It should be noted that these measures are not EAS traits.

The most interesting aspect of these results is that the objective measures yielded a diverse pattern of results, from high twin correlations for activity level to correlations of about .40 for the various selective attention and aggressiveness measures to correlations of about zero for other measures such as vigilance. The apparent differences between these results and results of parental rating studies suggest that this might be a profitable area for further research.

In summary, twin studies employing parental ratings and tester ratings consistently provide strong evidence that the EAS traits are heritable in childhood. However, data from designs other than the twin method are needed to substantiate this conclusion.

Adoption Studies

Extant EAS data from adoption studies is quite limited, although this situation will be improved when the Colorado Adoption Project reports its results for childhood. However, some relevant data have been reported from the Minnesota transracial adoption study (Scarr, Webber, Weinberg, & Wittig, 1981; Scarr & Weinberg, 1977) and the Texas Adoption Project (Loehlin, Horn, & Willerman, 1981; Loehlin, Willerman, & Horn, 1982, 1985). Both studies included a wide age range—from 4 to 16 in the Minnesota study and from 3 to 26 in the Texas study; nonetheless, the average age in both studies is about 7 for adoptees and about 10 for nonadopted children. The Minnesota study used the Junior Eysenck Personality Inventory (Eysenck, 1965) for the children and the adult version of the Eysenck Personality Inventory for parents. Both sibling and parent-offspring designs were used: Adoptive sibling and nonadoptive sibling correlations were compared, as were correlations between adoptive parents and their adopted and nonadopted children. Unfortunately, the results are reported only in terms of the mean of the three Eysenck scales of Extraversion, Neuroticism, and Psychoticism (Scarr, Webber, Weinberg, & Wittig, 1981); the first two of these scales are relevant to the EAS dimensions of sociability and emotionality, respectively. For 64 pairs of adoptive siblings, the correlation was .01; for 40 pairs of nonadoptive siblings, it was .19. These sibling results suggest genetic influence, on the order of 36% heritability. However, the parent-offspring results suggest no genetic influence: Correlations for adoptive parents and their adopted children (92 pairs) and for adoptive parents and their nonadopted children (162 pairs) both were near zero. These results suggest the possibility that contemporaneous genetic influences in childhood do not continue to affect personality in adulthood.

The Texas study included MMPI data for biological mothers (Loehlin et al.

1982); however, it is not possible to relate the MMPI to EAS dimensions in children. Although children under 8 were rated by their parents, older children were given an age-appropriate Cattell test; parents completed the adult version of the Cattell questionnaire. The design, like that of the Minnesota study, included adoptive and nonadoptive sibling pairs as well as adoptive parents and their adopted and nonadopted children. For 122 pairs of adoptive siblings, the mean correlations were .02 for three extraversion scales and .11 for neuroticism. Thus, the Texas data agree with the Minnesota data in suggesting only a miniscule role for shared environment in the etiology of personality. Because the Texas study included only 24 pairs of nonadoptive siblings, it cannot provide a useful confirmation of the Minnesota finding of genetic influence—that is, greater correlations for nonadoptive siblings than for adoptive siblings. For extraversion, the results were in this direction—the nonadoptive sibling correlation was .12; however, the nonadoptive sibling correlation for neuroticism was -.03. The parent-offspring results are similar to the Minnesota results in suggesting negligible genetic influence when adoptive parents are compared to their adopted offspring (409 families) and to their nonadopted offspring (179 families) in childhood: For adoptive and nonadoptive parent-offspring comparisons, respectively, the correlations were .06 and .05 for extraversion and .08 and .15 for neuroticism.

In an important subsidiary analysis, Loehlin et al. (1981) considered parent-offspring correlations for a quarter of the sample who were ''well-measured'' in the sense that the children's self-reports were consistent with the parental ratings. This approach yielded evidence of greater family environmental influence and greater genetic influence as compared to the results for the total sample: For extraversion, the adoptive parent-adopted child correlation was .11 (115 families) and the adoptive parent-nonadopted child correlation was .36 (37 families). For neuroticism, the comparable correlations were .15 and .21. This approach can be viewed in the context of contemporary personality theory as an attempt to address the possibility that individuals differ in the consistency of their personality; individual differences in consistency can be considered as a moderator variable.

In summary, the story told by the adoption data is not as simple as the twin story. Nonetheless, the sibling results of the Minnesota study suggest substantial genetic influence. The role of heredity in parent-offspring personality relationships remains an open question, especially given the evidence for genetic influence from the ''well-measured'' sample in the Texas study.

Psychopathology

Childhood psychopathology is likely to become a major area of interest for behavioral geneticists as more is learned about depression, aggression, and attention disorders in childhood. So far, however, behavioral genetic studies have been limited primarily to attention deficit disorders, formerly known as hyperactivity and generally thought to be the most common behavioral problem in childhood, particularly for boys (Cantwell, 1975).

Attention Deficit Disorders

Two studies have been reported in which familial resemblance for hyperactivity was compared in adoptive and nonadoptive families (Cantwell, 1975; Morrison & Stewart, 1973). The two studies included 109 hyperactive children reared by their natural parents, 74 hyperactive children reared by adoptive parents, and a control group of 91 nonhyperactive children reared by their natural parents. Parents were interviewed concerning their own hyperactivity as children. The fact that significantly more childhood hyperactivity was reported by the natural parents of hyperactive children (10%) than by the adoptive parents (2%) supports a genetic hypothesis. No more hyperactivity was reported by the adoptive parents of hyperactive children than by the natural parents of nonhyperactive children (3%), suggesting that rearing environment may not be important in the development of hyperactivity.

The retrospective reports of parental hyperactivity in these studies make their interpretation somewhat tenuous. The contemporaneous relationships of twins and siblings are more useful for studying such developmental disorders. However, only one small study of 19 siblings and 22 maternal half-siblings of 14 hyperactive children has been reported (Safer, 1973). On the basis of social workers' records of visits to the adoptive homes, 9 of the 19 siblings and 5 of the 22 half-siblings were diagnosed as hyperactive, results suggestive of strong familial resemblance.

Other Common Behavioral Problems

One twin study mentioned earlier focused on common behavioral problems as assessed by parents on the Parent Symptom Rating questionnaire (O'Connor et al., 1980). The sample consisted of 54 pairs of identical twins and 33 pairs of fraternal twins (average age of 7.6 years) that were not selected for problem behavior. Although the normal distribution of individual differences for behavioral problems could yield results quite different from those based on studies of the extremes of problem behavior, such studies are relevant to childhood psychopathology, especially for such commonly occurring problems as bullying, restlessness, shyness, tenseness, feelings easily hurt, and stealing. The results of the O'Connor et al. (1980) study suggested significant and substantial genetic influence for each of these scales of behavioral problems.

Another study based on the same sample focused on children's videotaped interaction with a Bobo clown as an index of aggressiveness originally developed to study imitation of aggression (Plomin, Foch, & Rowe, 1981). This measure correlates .76 with peer ratings and .57 with teacher ratings of aggression (Johnston, DeLuca, Murtaugh, & Diener, 1977). For the number of times the children hit the Bobo clown, the identical and fraternal twin correlations both were .42. For intensity of hits, the identical and fraternal twin correlations were .39 and .47, respectively. The 2-month, test-retest reliabilities of these two measures were .44 and .75, respectively, suggesting that most of the reliable variance is due to shared family environment. Thus, the results of this first objective study of aggressive behavior in children revealed no genetic influence, but strong evidence for the influence of shared family environment.

Risk Research

Also relevant are "at risk" studies in which children whose parents had been diagnosed as schizophrenic, depressed, or alcoholic are studied longitudinally. The aim of these studies is to find developmental genetic correlates of adult psychopathology, although it is quite possible that the genes that affect adult disorders have no effect in childhood.

Fifteen long-term studies of children at risk for schizophrenia have cooperated in the Risk Research Consortium which includes 1200 probands and 1400 normal control subjects (Watt, Anthony, Wynne, & Rolf, 1984). Some differences between children with schizophrenic parents and control samples have been found such as attention deficits (Erlenmeyer-Kimling et al., 1984). However, differences between risk and control children are by no means dramatic in early childhood and it has been suggested that the few differences observed could be a function of perinatal complications that are experienced more often by children of schizophrenic mothers than by control children (Watt, 1984). By the middle childhood years, more differences have been found. Moreover, the oldest children in these studies are just now entering the age of onset for schizophrenia so that in the next few years it will be possible to determine which of the at-risk probands in fact are schizophrenic—only 10% of the probands are expected to become affected.

Over a dozen studies of children of patients with affective disorders, primarily depression, are also in progress (Orvaschel, 1983) and preliminary reports also indicate some differences between children reared by depressed parents and children in control groups (e.g., Cytryn et al., 1984). Indeed, studies comparing children at risk for schizophrenia and children at risk for affective psychosis indicate similar findings, leading to the following conclusion:

> This set of findings is consistent with the view that a general vulnerability to psychosis is genetically transmitted but that the specific form is a function of environmental factors. . . . Until proven otherwise, such an interpretation of the studies. . . . would seem to be the most parsimonious. (Watt, 1984, p. 547)

Summary and Conclusions

Much more is unknown than is known about developmental behavioral genetics in childhood. For physical characteristics and for IQ, there appears to be a continuation of the trend seen in infancy toward increasing genetic influence. The two major longitudinal studies of IQ, one an adoption study (Skodak & Skeels, 1949) and the other a twin study (Wilson, 1983), suggest increasing heritability from early to middle childhood. However, even this basic issue is unresolved because two recent cross-sectional adoption studies provide mixed results concerning the heritability of IQ in childhood. Thus, even for IQ, the best-studied trait in human behavioral genetics, no firm conclusion can be reached concerning heritability in childhood. I would put my money on longitudinal studies because cross-sectional studies average effects across the years and involve different children at each age.

Specific cognitive abilities can be studied, at least in middle childhood. Twin studies tend to show some genetic influence for verbal and possibly for spatial tests; perceptual speed and memory tests tend to show little genetic influence, a finding that emerges from studies of adolescents as well (see chapter 11). No study of scholastic abilities in the elementary school years have been reported. Reading disability shows familial resemblance that is mediated at least in part by heredity.

The EAS personality traits show consistent evidence of genetic influence in childhood, just as they do in infancy in twin studies, although results from recent adoption studies are less clear. Changes in heritability from infancy to childhood or during childhood are not apparent for these three personality traits. Very little behavioral genetic research has been reported for childhood psychopathology, although the relevant bits of extant data suggest that genetic influences are likely to be quite important.

Studying developmental changes in the relative contributions of nature and nurture is merely a first step in developmental behavioral genetics. In childhood, we are still mid-stride even for this first step. Nonetheless, most of the questions of developmental behavioral genetics will remain after this first step has finally been taken. Does genetic change occur during the transition from infancy to childhood or during childhood? Does the amplification model of developmental genetics hold up in childhood? What are the relative contributions of shared and nonshared environmental variance? Do their relative contributions shift during childhood as children begin to spend significant amounts of time outside their homes? Do children of different genotypes react differently to environmental stressors such as entering school? Does genotype-environment correlation shift from passive to reactive and active forms during childhood, as predicted by Scarr and McCartney's theory (see chapter 6)? In the home, school, and playground, does heredity affect measures of the environment? Is heredity involved in relationships between environmental measures and measures of children's development?

The answers to these questions are likely to differ for different domains of behavioral development, for different phases of childhood, for different populations, and for different cohorts within these populations. Although there is much to do, developmental behavioral genetics provides the conceptual and methodological tools needed to provide definitive answers to these questions.

11 Adolescence

Other than infancy, adolescence is the fastest-changing period of development, and that makes it especially interesting from the perspective of developmental behavioral genetics. G. Stanley Hall (1904), in his field-defining two-volume work, described adolescence as a period of "storm and stress." Although a handful of behavioral genetic studies have used adolescent subjects, few have focused *on* adolescence—that is, considered the storms and stresses of adolescence, the transitions from childhood to adulthood, or phenomena relevant specifically to adolescent development. Another problem is that behavioral genetic research on adolescence primarily has used high-school subjects in late adolescence who can complete adult versions of tests, whereas adolescence researchers are now primarily interested in early adolescence—about 10 to 13 years of age—when the physical changes of adolescence begin to occur (Hill, 1982).

One special contribution of behavioral genetic research on adolescence has been the study of nonshared, within-family environmental influence, as discussed in chapter 4. This chapter begins with a discussion of behavioral genetic research on physical characteristics and then considers cognitive abilities and personality. Some of the material in this chapter is based on a recent review of behavioral genetics and adolescence (Plomin & Fulker, in press).

Physical Characteristics

As in infancy, height and weight change dramatically during adolescence and yet heritability remains high. Figure 11.1 illustrates the height and weight results

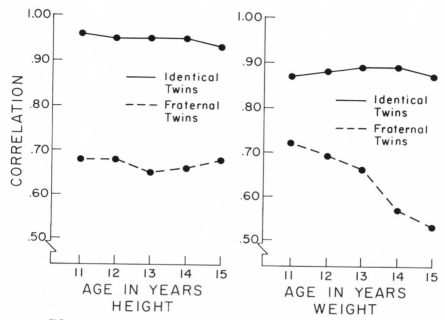

FIG. 11.1.   Twin correlations for height and weight in a longitudinal study of adolescent Swedish twins. (Adapted from Fischbein, 1977a.)

from a longitudinal study of Swedish twins from 11 to 15 years when the sample size is largest (84 pairs of identical twins and 125 pairs of fraternal twins on average; Fischbein, 1977b). For height, genetic influence is substantial and remarkably stable; the average correlations for identical and fraternal twins are .95 and .67, respectively. The fact that the fraternal twin correlations are considerably greater than half the identical twin correlations suggests that shared environment also is important. For weight, the correlations for identical twins are also stable throughout adolescence; however, fraternal twin correlations steadily decline, which suggests increasing genetic influence on weight. The average correlations for identical and fraternal twin correlations for weight are .88 and .63.

As indicated in Table 11.1, age at peak height velocity and peak weight velocity also shows substantial genetic influence. Variance in height due to differences in age at peak growth is included in the variance of height; thus, it is not too surprising that age at peak height velocity shows genetic influence. Nonetheless, the fact that the magnitude of heritability is just as great for age at peak height velocity as it is for height itself implies that developmental timing in puberty may be influenced genetically. Analyses of age-to-age profiles also suggest genetic influence on spurts and lags in the development of height during adolescence (Fischbein & Nordqvist, 1978).

TABLE 11.1
Twin Correlations for Physical Characteristics in Adolescence
(from Fischbein, 1977a)

Characteristic	Twin Correlations			
	Identical		Fraternal	
	r	N/pairs	r	N/pairs
Height[a]	.95	84	.67	125
Weight[a]	.88	84	.57	125
Age at Peak Height Velocity	.82	82	.41	120
Age at Peak Weight Velocity	.76	81	.44	117
Age at Menarche	.93	28	.62	48
Development of Secondary Sex Characteristics[a]	.93	82	.65	120

[a]Average correlations from 11 to 15 when samples are largest.

The Swedish study also included yearly assessments of the development of secondary sex characteristics and age at menarche. As shown in Table 11.1, these traits show twin correlations similar to those for height, suggesting substantial genetic influence. Again, the differences between identical and fraternal twin correlations are quite stable even from 11 to 15 years of age, a period of maximal development. Tanner (1978) also reports that sister-sister and mother-daughter correlations are high, about .40, for age at menarche.

IQ

Even for IQ, the most frequently studied trait in behavioral genetics, few behavioral genetic studies have specifically considered adolescence. The following sections review what is known about IQ in adolescence with an emphasis on newer studies. Before beginning this review, however, an interesting issue specific to adolescence should be mentioned. Bayley (1949) observed that for both mental age and the ratio between mental age and chronological age, variances increase at 9, 10, and 11 years:

> More significant than the means, it seems to me, is the trend of the standard deviations of mental ages from birth through 17 years. . . . It is plain that the SD's do not increase at the constant rate which is necessary if IQ's are to remain constant during growth. The SD's are too small during most of the first year and too large after seven years, and especially at 9, 10, and 11 years. These variations cannot be attributed to inequalities in the sampling of cases, as they are based on essentially the same cases throughout. (pp. 172-173)

The following review supports the hypothesis that increased genetic variance might be responsible for increased phenotypic variance for IQ during early adolescence.

Twin Studies

The first adequate twin study of IQ was reported in 1924 by Merriman. The subjects were 105 pairs of twins from 5 to 18 years of age who were tested on the Stanford-Binet test. As in earlier studies by Galton (1875) and Thorndike (1905), twin IQ correlations for children and adolescents were compared. These authors concluded that twin resemblance does not change from childhood to adolescence; however, there was a consistent downward trend in the twin correlations. In Merriman's study, the twin correlation for children from 5 to 9 years was .81 and the correlation for adolescents from 10 to 18 years was .76. Although this decrease is not statistically significant, virtually the same difference was observed in a later study (Stocks, 1933): The correlation for children under 10 was .84 and the correlation for adolescents 10 and older was .73. However, neither of these studies presented twin correlations separately for identical and fraternal twins as a function of age. If the slight decrease in twin correlations from childhood to adolescence was primarily brought about by a decrease in fraternal twin correlations whereas identical twin correlations remain unchanged, an increase in heritability from childhood to adolescence would be implied.

This possibility is suggested by the results of the major longitudinal twin study of IQ, the Louisville Twin Study (Wilson, 1983). Twin IQ correlations for identical and fraternal twins are .83 and .65, respectively, at 9 years and .88 and .54 at 15 years, suggesting an increase in heritability from .36 to .68 from childhood to adolescence. This finding is exciting, although it clearly needs to be replicated before it can bear much weight; other twin studies in adolescence have used high-school samples so that it is not possible to check this result even in a cross-sectional analysis.

In addition to providing evidence suggesting an increase in IQ heritability during adolescence, the Louisville Twin Study has also provided an opportunity to explore the etiology of changes in IQ from 8 to 15 years of age using developmental trend correlations. (Trend correlations were described in chapters 3 and 9.) The twin trend correlations are .82 and .50 for identical and fraternal twins, respectively, suggesting substantial genetic influence on profiles of scores from 8 to 15 (Wilson, 1983). As discussed in chapter 9, analyses of trend correlations involve both overall level and age-to-age changes and are complex functions of heritability at each age and genetic correlations between the ages. Nonetheless, these data are consistent with the hypothesis that genetic factors affect individual differences in age-to-age changes.

Other twin studies suggest that heredity significantly affects IQ scores in adolescence. An early study of 45 identical and 31 fraternal twins from 8 to 15 years old found correlations of .91 for identical twins and .70 for fraternal twins for scores on the Stanford-Binet IQ test (Wingfield, 1928). A study of adult twins who had been reared apart included comparison groups of twins reared together, 50 pairs of identical twins and 50 pairs of fraternal twins whose average age was 13 (Newman, Freeman, & Holzinger, 1937). For Stanford-Binet IQ, the identical and fraternal twin correlations were .91 and .64, respectively; for Otis IQ, the correlations were .92 and .62. Somewhat lower twin correlations—but similar heritability estimates—were obtained from another twin study using the Otis test (Herrman & Hogben, 1932–1933). For 65 identical and 96 fraternal pairs whose age was 11, identical and fraternal twin correlations were .84 and .47, respectively. A Swedish twin study included 128 identical twin pairs and 141 fraternal twin pairs from 9 to 15 years of age and found identical and fraternal twin correlations of .85 and .70 for one IQ test and .91 and .73 for another, suggesting heritabilities of about 30% (Wictorin, 1952).

One twin study is noteworthy because it involved the administration of the Wechsler Adult Intelligence Scale (WAIS) to 120 pairs of twins 13 to 18 years of age (Block, 1968). Unfortunately, twin correlations were not reported for this study; nonetheless, a heritability estimate based on variance within identical and fraternal twin pairs was 71% for the total WAIS IQ score. An analysis comparing 13- to 15-year-old twins with 16- to 18-year-old twins showed little effect of age.

Although twin studies suggest the possibility that heritability of IQ scores increases during adolescence, they agree that genetic influence is substantial throughout adolescence. Only one small twin study departs from this general conclusion (Adams, Ghodsian, & Richardson, 1976). However, in this study of 41 identical and 55 fraternal pairs tested on a verbal and a nonverbal reasoning test, zygosity was determined merely by asking the parents if the twins were "identical" or "non-identical." Results for opposite-sex fraternal twins who could not be misdiagnosed, yielded a correlation of .48, similar to the results of other studies. However, the identical twin correlations were lower (.73) and the fraternal twin correlations were higher (.63) than in other studies, exactly what would be expected if zygosity had been misdiagnosed.

These twin studies also appear to suggest substantial—about 25% of the total IQ variance—influence of shared environment. However, twin studies exaggerate the importance of shared environment because fraternal twins are more similar for IQ than are nontwin siblings. For example, a sibling correlation of .45 was found in the 1947 Scottish Mental Survey (Maxwell & Pilliner, 1960) for 1,036 siblings for the Stanford-Binet IQ test administered when the children were 11 years old. In another sibling study involving 5,054 pairs of English 11-year-olds, two verbal reasoning tests yielded a sibling correlation of .55. Thus, fraternal twin correlations are about .10 to .20 higher than correlations for nontwin siblings, which implies that twin estimates of shared environmental influence may be twice as great as they should be.

Adoption Studies

The well-known longitudinal adoption study of Skodak and Skeels (1949) assessed IQ of adopted children at the average age of 13 years on the 1916 and 1937 versions of the Stanford-Binet. For 63 adopted children whose biological mothers had been tested on the Stanford-Binet, the mother-offspring correlations were .38 and .44, respectively, for the 1916 and 1937 versions of the children's Stanford-Binet. These correlations are slightly greater than the correlations of .28 and .35 observed at 4 and 7 years of age, which is consistent with the hypothesis of increasing genetic influence on IQ from childhood to adolescence. The magnitude of the IQ correlation between biological mothers and their adopted-away offspring as adolescents suggests very substantial genetic influence on IQ scores; however, this correlation is inflated by selective placement as well as by assortative mating (DeFries & Plomin, 1978).

Cross-sectional analyses of data from the recent Texas Adoption Project (Horn, 1983), unlike the longitudinal Louisville Twin Study results and the data from the longitudinal adoption study of Skodak and Skeels, suggest less genetic influence on IQ scores in adolescence than in childhood. Dividing the sample of 297 adoptees at their median age, a correlation of .36 was observed for biological mothers and their adopted-away offspring between the ages of 5 and 7. The biological mother-offspring correlation for adoptees from 8 to 14 years was .16. However, in the same study, data for nonadoptive parents and their children revealed slightly increasing parent-offspring correlations: .20 for the younger group and .28 for the older group.

The Texas study, unlike Skodak and Skeels' study, also obtained IQ data from the adoptive parents. The younger and older adoptee groups yielded adoptive parent-adopted child correlations of .15 and .13, respectively, suggesting little change in the impact of shared environment relevant to IQ from childhood to early adolescence.

Other adoption studies have not obtained IQ data from biological parents and thus cannot provide direct estimates of genetic influence. These studies estimate genetic influence by comparing parent-offspring IQ resemblance in adoptive and nonadoptive families (Burks, 1928; Freeman, Holzinger, & Mitchell, 1928; Leahy, 1935; Scarr & Weinberg, 1977). Although some of the adoptees in these studies were adolescents at the time of testing, the results were not presented separately by age of the offspring and most of the offspring were 10 years or younger. For this reason, these studies were described in the previous chapter.

A recent dissertation study employed the sibling adoption design in adolescence (Kent, 1985). Twelve cognitive tests were administered to 52 adoptive sibling pairs and to 54 nonadoptive sibling pairs from 9 to 15 years of age with an average age of 12.8. A novel feature of the study was that the tests were administered entirely over the telephone; analyses comparing telephone testing and face-to-face testing showed that scores obtained from the two procedures correlate near the reliability of the tests. An unrotated first principal component was used as an index of g or IQ; sibling correlations for this measure were .38 for biological siblings and -.16 for adoptive siblings, suggesting significant and substantial genetic influence. Most striking, however, is the low adoptive sibling correlation which, as discussed in chapter 4, indicates that growing up in the same family has negligible influence after early adolescence. Hierarchical multiple regression analysis, discussed in chapter 3, was employed to explore changes in sibling resemblance from 9 to 15 years. Adoptive sibling IQ was regressed on co-sibling IQ, age, and the two-way interaction of co-sibling IQ and age. A significant regression coefficient for the interaction term would indicate that adoptive sibling resemblance changes with age; however, the interaction was nonsignificant and accounted for less than .1% of the total variance.

Developmental changes in genetic influence were explored by the three-way interaction of co-sibling IQ, age, and adoptive status (i.e., adoptive = .00; nonadoptive = .50). A significant regression coefficient for the three-way interaction indicates whether differential resemblance of adoptive siblings and nonadoptive siblings (i.e., genetic influence) differs as a function of age. No evidence for change in heritability was found for this age group. As indicated in the previous section, the two major longitudinal studies in childhood and adolescence—the Louisville Twin Study and Skodak and Skeels' adoption study—both suggest that genetic influence on IQ increases from childhood to adolescence. The results of this new study that employs the sibling adoption design finds substantial genetic influence on IQ for a sample whose average age is about 13. These results are consistent with the hypothesis that genetic influence on IQ is substantial after early adolescence.

Specific Cognitive Abilities

Similar to the IQ results reviewed in the previous section, there is some suggestion in the twin literature that genetic influence increases during adolescence for specific cognitive abilities (Foch & Plomin, 1980; Ho, Foch, & Plomin, 1980). For example, longitudinal study of twins in adolescence and early adulthood supports this hypothesis (Fischbein, 1981). A test of verbal ability and a test of inductive reasoning were administered to 44 identical and 66 fraternal twin pairs at 12 years of age, and the tests were administered again at 18 years of age to 39 of the identical twin pairs and 56 of the fraternal twin pairs. At 12, the verbal test yielded an identical twin correlation of .70 and a fraternal twin correlation of .60; at 18, the twin correlations were .78 and .50, respectively. These patterns of correlations suggest heritabilities of .20 at 12 and .56 at 18. A similar pattern of increasing genetic influence from 12 to 18 emerged for the inductive reasoning test. The twin correlations were .59 and .46 at age 12 and .78 and .56 at age 18, suggesting a rise in heritability from .26 to .44.

Preliminary results from the LaTrobe Twin Study (Hay & O'Brien, 1983) also support this hypothesis. Twin correlations for vocabulary and block design scores were compared for a small sample (N not specified) of 10-year-olds and 14-year-olds (Hay, 1984). At 10 years, the identical and fraternal twin correlations for vocabulary were .61 and .40, respectively; at 14, the correlations were .75 and .41. This pattern of correlations suggests that heritability is 38% at 10 years and 68% at 14 years. Evidence for increasing heritability also emerged for the block design test: At 10, the twin correlations were .50 and .28 and at 14 the correlations were .72 and .33, suggesting heritabilities of 44% at 10 years and 78% at 14 years. Although the small samples imply that the precise estimates of heritability should not be taken too seriously, the consistency of the finding of increasing heritability during adolescence is noteworthy.

Most exciting for future developmental behavioral genetic analysis is that the LaTrobe study is a mixed-longitudinal design—twins from 3 to 15 years of age are accepted into the project and studied repeatedly. A longitudinal analysis of the block design data using twin cross-correlations between 10 and 14 years has been reported (Hay, 1984). The age-to-age cross-correlation for identical twins is .63 and for fraternal twins the cross-correlation is .31. This result suggests that genetic factors play a major role in continuity of block design scores during early adolescence, even though heritability is apparently increasing.

The results of another Swedish twin study support the hypothesis that heredity significantly affects specific cognitive abilities in adolescence (Wictorin, 1952), although it does not speak to the issue of increasing heritability from childhood to adolescence. Twelve cognitive tests were administered to 128 pairs of identical twins and 141 pairs of fraternal twins from 9 to 15 years of age. Table 11.2 lists the twin correlations for the 12 tests grouped according to their probable factor identification. The magnitude of heritability is comparable to the heritability found for 12-year-olds (the mean age of the Wictorin sample) in the previously described longitudinal study. For the verbal, spatial, and perceptual speed tests, average heritabilities are .28, .24, and .20, respectively. Heritability is negligible for the memory tests, which consist of digit span (recall and recognition) and paired associates.

Although memory tests are less reliable than tests of other cognitive abilities, as indicated by the lower correlations for identical twins, these results agree with the results of other studies in suggesting that individual differences in memory may be less influenced by heredity than are other specific cognitive abilities. Vandenberg conducted extensive analyses of cognitive abilities in high-school twins in Michigan (Vandenberg, 1962) and in Kentucky (Vandenberg, 1968). The Michigan study is particularly impressive because 17 Primary Mental Abilities (PMA) tests, 18 other cognitive tests, 17 "perceptual" tests of Gestalt concepts, 10 motor skills, and numerous personality scales involving a total testing time exceeding 14 hours, were administered to about 45 identical twin pairs and 40 fraternal twin pairs. For the PMA tests, the memory scale and the

TABLE 11.2
Twin Correlations for Tests of Specific Cognitive Abilities in
Adolescence (from Wictorin, 1952)

| Test | Twin Correlations | |
	Identical 141 pairs	Fraternal 128 pairs
Verbal		
Verbal Analysis (comprehension)	.63	.53
Number Series (numerical reasoning)	.74	.49
Number Analysis (numerical reasoning)	.69	.57
Numerical Classification (numerical reasoning)	.70	.58
Numerical Reasoning (verbal arithmetic)	.87	.73
Spatial		
Form Perception (paper formboard)	.65	.53
Perceptual Speed		
Picture perception	.69	.61
Number perception	.83	.69
Routine simple arithmetic	.81	.74
Memory		
Memory for 2-digit numbers (recall)	.62	.58
Memory for 3-digit numbers (recognition)	.49	.45
Paired associates (word-number)	.43	.53

two tests comprising the scale score showed no significant genetic influence, although other PMA group factors such as verbal, spatial, and word fluency showed significant heritability. Twin correlations are not presented in Vandenberg's reports; the significance of genetic influence was evaluated by an F test based on the ratio of the variances of twin intrapair differences for fraternal twins and identical twins. Among the other cognitive tests, a test of memory for faces showed no significant heritability, although digit span from the Wechsler Intelligence Scale for Children suggested significant genetic influence. Vandenberg also administered 19 tests from the PMA to about 200 high-school twins in Kentucky (Vandenberg, 1968). Significant genetic influence was found for verbal and spatial tests but not for memory tests.

The Kentucky and Michigan PMA data sets together with twin data collected by the Thurstones on 48 identical and 55 fraternal twin pairs (Thurstone, Thurstone, & Strandskov, 1955) were submitted to multivariate analyses of twin intrapair differences on the PMA tests and scales (Loehlin & Vandenberg, 1968). Differences within pairs of identical twins can only be due to environmental factors, whereas both heredity and environment can cause differences within pairs of fraternal twins. For this reason, the factor structures derived from matrices of correlations of identical twin differences and of fraternal twin differences were explored in order to illuminate genetic and environmental contributions to the covariance among the abilities measured by the PMA. In general, the factor structures for twin differences were found to be similar for the two types of twins and both twin-difference factor structures were similar to the usual PMA phenotypic factor structure, thus suggesting that the structure of genetic effects on cognitive abilities is similar to the structure of environmental effects.

Heritability was also found to be low for digit span in a study of 120 pairs of twins from 13 to 18 years of age using the subtests of the WAIS (Block, 1968). Unfortunately, twin correlations were not reported for this study, which is one of the few that have used an individually administered test. Heritability was estimated from the within-pair variances for the two types of twins. Heritability estimates were equally high, about .70, for the verbal score, the performance score, and the total WAIS IQ score. Two of the 11 WAIS subtests showed no significant heritability; one was a spatial test, Object Assembly, and the other was a reasoning test, Picture Completion. Similar results were obtained in a parent-offspring study of 55 families with 10-year-old males (Williams, 1975). Correlations between parental WAIS scales and adolescents' WISC scores were greatest for Vocabulary (.37) and lowest for Digit Span (.09), Object Assembly (.01), and Picture Completion (-.07).

In another important study of specific cognitive abilities in high-school twins, a 2-day battery of 60 tests of information, aptitude, and achievement was administered to 337 pairs of identical twins and 156 pairs of fraternal twins (Schoenfeldt, 1968). The results of this Project TALENT study, shown in Table 11.3, point to substantial genetic influence on Verbal, Spatial, Perceptual Speed, and Memory factors. Heritability estimates average about .50, twice the average heritability of .25 found in the Swedish study by Wictorin (1952) which was described earlier. However, it should be noted that the average age of Wictorin's sample was 12, whereas Schoenfeldt's sample consisted of children in grades 9-12, approximately 14 to 17 years of age. Thus, together, these two studies suggest that the increase in heritability from childhood to adolescence might be

TABLE 11.3
Twin Correlations for Tests of Specific Cognitive Abilities in
Adolescence (Schoenfeldt, 1968)

Factor	Twin Correlations[a]	
	Identical 337 pairs	Fraternal 156 pairs
Verbal	.80	.48
Spatial Reasoning	.67	.41
Perceptual Speed	.67	.51
Memory	.43	.19

[a]Twin correlations averaged for males and females.

pinpointed to the period following early adolescence. The fact that Schoenfeldt's sample shows significant genetic influence on memory is not as contradictory to the results of the previous studies as it might at first appear because Schoenfeldt's Memory factor consists of two semantic tests, memory for words and memory for sentences. The other studies did not primarily assess semantic memory, which might reflect some of the strong genetic influence on verbal ability.

For IQ, fraternal twin correlations are greater than for nontwin siblings, suggesting that twins share more similar family environments than do other siblings. Results for specific cognitive abilities are similar. Instead of correlations of .50 as seen for fraternal twins, sibling correlations for specific cognitive abilities tend to be about .30. For example, the first family study of specific cognitive abilities in adolescence was reported in 1927 by Willoughby who administered 11 cognitive tests to 141 12- and 13-year-old children and to members of their families. For two verbal tests (vocabulary and antonyms), the average parent-offspring correlation was .30 and the average sibling correlation was .34. For two perceptual speed tests (digit symbol substitution and number and letter comparison), the correlations were .20 and .33, respectively. Thus, twin studies can be expected to overestimate the importance of shared environment for specific cognitive abilities as well as for IQ.

Adoption studies have had little information to offer concerning cognitive abilities in adolescence because they have generally focused on IQ and their samples have included a wide age range that usually encompasses both childhood and adolescence. Moreover, the designs used rely on parent-offspring comparisons that require genetic continuity from adolescence to adulthood as well as genetic influence both in adolescence and in adulthood. A major exception is the recent sibling adoption study mentioned in the previous section on IQ (Kent, 1985). The focus of the study was specific cognitive abilities; three tests were included in a telephone test battery to assess each of four factors: verbal, spatial, perceptual speed, and memory for 52 adoptive and 54 nonadoptive sibling pairs. Table 11.4 presents intraclass correlations for adoptive and nonadoptive siblings for these cognitive abilities. The most striking feature of the results is the negligible similarity for adoptive siblings which, as discussed in chapter 4, suggests that shared environment is of little importance for specific cognitive abilities as early as 13 years, the average age of the sample. Correlations for biological siblings are significant and correlations for adoptive siblings are low and even negative. For verbal and spatial abilities, the biological sibling correlation is substantially greater than the adoptive sibling correlation, suggesting substantial genetic influence. For perceptual speed and, especially, for memory, less genetic influence is implied. Test-retest reliabilities for the specific cognitive ability scores are .81, .73, .82, and .57, respectively, for verbal, spatial, perceptual speed, and memory.

These conclusions are supported by the results of a model-fitting multiple regression analysis (DeFries & Fulker, in press). The model-fitting yields

TABLE 11.4
Intraclass Correlations and Model-Fitting Regression Analysis for
Cognitive Abilities for Biological and Adoptive Siblings

	Intraclass Correlation		Model-Fitting Regression Analysis			
	Biological Siblings 54 pairs	Adoptive Siblings 52 pairs	h^2 (SE)	e^2_s (SE)	R	F
g Factor	.38	−.16	1.00*(.32)	−.17 (.11)	.32	4.4*
Verbal	.31	−.07	.62 (.32)	−.06 (.12)	.23	2.0
Spatial	.35	−.06	.81*(.34)	−.06 (.11)	.27	2.7*
Perceptual Speed	.21	−.10	.54 (.29)	−.13 (.10)	.27	2.7*
Memory	.29	.16	.30 (.40)	.15 (.14)	.29	3.1*

*$p < .05$.

parameter estimates of heritability (h^2) and shared environment (e^2_s) and their standard errors, which are shown in Table 11.4. The parameter estimates are very similar to those expected on the basis of the sibling correlations. The negative adoptive sibling correlations produce odd estimates such as a heritability of 1.0 for g and .81 for spatial ability and negative shared environment estimates. Of more interest, however, are the standard errors that indicate significant genetic influence for g and spatial and near significance for verbal ability.

Hierarchical multiple regressions, as described in chapter 3, were conducted to assess changes in these parameters during the 9- to 15-year age range. As described earlier for IQ, developmental change in shared environment was assessed by means of a two-way interaction between co-sibling score and age for the adoptive siblings; change in genetic influence was explored using a three-way interaction among co-sibling, age, and the coefficient of relationship (i.e., adoptive vs. biological sibling status). However, no significant interactions were detected for g or for specific cognitive abilities. In fact, with the exception of perceptual speed, none of the interactions accounted for more than 1% of the total variance. For perceptual speed, the interactions assessing shared family environment and genetic influence accounted for 1.5% of the variance; however, in both cases, the F was .85, indicating that the interaction was far from statistical significance.

In summary, this first sibling adoption study of specific cognitive abilities during adolescence found evidence for substantial genetic influence on verbal and spatial abilities as well as g. As expected, the biological sibling correlations are much lower than the fraternal twin correlations reported for children of similar ages by Wictorin (1952) and Fischbein (1979). On average, the biological sibling correlations are only about half the magnitude of the fraternal twin correlations, again suggesting that twins share much more family environment than do nontwin siblings. The biological sibling correlations are quite similar to those obtained by Willoughby (1927) for children of a similar age.

Scholastic Achievement

Several large studies of adolescent twins have employed measures of academic achievement and scholastic ability rather than traditional measures of specific cognitive abilities; however, the distinction between these domains is not at all clear. Given the educational importance of distinguishing between achievement and ability, it is surprising that the etiology of the relationship between academic achievement and cognitive abilities has not been explored using multivariate genetic analyses of the substantial phenotypic covariance between the two domains (Plomin & DeFries, 1979).

Husén (1959, 1960, 1963) has conducted several studies of scholastic achievement in Sweden. In one report (Husén, 1959), school grades were obtained for 352 pairs of identical and 668 pairs of fraternal 13-year-old twins. The identical and fraternal twin correlations were, respectively, .72 and .57 for reading, .76 and .50 for writing, .72 and .57 for reading, .81 and .48 for arithmetic, and .80 and .51 for history. These results imply substantial genetic influence. Similar results were obtained in another Swedish study of reading, writing, and arithmetic grades for 117 identical and 130 fraternal pairs in grades 2, 4, and 6 (Wictorin, 1952).

In another series of studies (Husén, 1960, 1963), academic achievement test scores were obtained when twins were 11 years old and again when they were 13 for over 300 twin pairs. Twin correlations for reading, writing, and arithmetic tests are presented in Table 11.5; they suggest substantial and roughly equal genetic influence for these three major scholastic subjects. Most interesting from a developmental behavioral genetic perspective is the finding that correlations for both types of twins increase by about .10 from 11 to 13. This suggests that shared environment—which in this case may be shared school environment—increases in its impact on scholastic achievement. This is a particularly interesting result because it is in the opposite direction from the results for specific cognitive abilities reviewed earlier that suggest decreasing influence of shared environment. However, this pattern of results might make sense if scholastic skills are influenced by the school environment to a greater extent than are specific cognitive abilities.

Two major twin studies of academic achievement have been conducted in the United States. One involved the National Merit Scholarship Qualifying Test (NMSQT) and combined data on a 1962 cohort of 692 identical and 482 fraternal twin pairs (Nichols, 1965) with data on a 1965 cohort for a total of 1,300 identical and 864 fraternal twin pairs (Loehlin & Nichols, 1976). The twin correlations for English usage, mathematics, social studies, natural sciences, and

TABLE 11.5
Twin Correlations for Scholastic Achievement Test Scores at
11 and 13 Years of Age (Husén, 1960, 1963)

| | Twin Correlations | | | |
| | 11 years | | 13 years | |
Tests	Identical 135 pairs	Fraternal 209 pairs	Identical 134 pairs	Fraternal 180 pairs
Reading	.77	.50	.89	.62
Writing	.76	.52	.88	.66
Arithmetic	.82	.61	.87	.52

TABLE 11.6
Twin Correlations for Subtests of the National Merit Scholarship
Qualifying Test (correlations averaged for males and females)

| | Twin correlations for raw scores (Loehlin & Nichols, 1976) | | Twin correlations for raw scores (Nichols, 1965) | | Twin correlations for residual scores[a] (Nichols, 1965) | |
Subtest	Identical 1300 pairs	Fraternal 864 pairs	Identical 687 pairs	Fraternal 482 pairs	Identical 687 pairs	Fraternal 482 pairs
English Usage	.72	.52	.74	.57	.44	.34
Mathematics	.71	.51	.72	.45	.46	.22
Social Studies	.69	.52	.78	.51	.31	.17
Natural Sciences	.64	.45	.68	.50	.29	.21
Vocabulary	.88	.62	.86	.64	.55	.32

[a]As explained in the text, residual scores are the subtest scores after the common variance among the tests has been removed.

vocabulary from the two cohorts are listed in Table 11.6. The tests generally show substantially greater correlations for identical twins than for fraternal twins. The average difference between the correlations for the two types of twins is .21, suggesting that over 40% of the variance of academic achievement is genetic in origin. The correlations for vocabulary—a traditional marker of verbal ability rather than academic achievement—are higher than for the other tests, but the difference between the identical and fraternal twin correlations is of the same magnitude.

The consistency of results across tests is less surprising when one realizes that the tests intercorrelate highly, .62 on average. In order to study the unique variance of each test, Nichols (1965) computed residual scores, removing the common variance among the tests represented by the unrotated first principal component. Twin correlations for the residual scores are listed in Table 11.6 for the 1962 cohort. The correlations are lower and fewer comparisons between identical and fraternal twin correlations yield significant differences. The mean difference between the identical and fraternal twin correlations for the raw scores is .22 for the 1962 cohort; for the residual scores, the mean difference is .16. These data suggest that—independent of general scholastic ability, which one would assume to be related to IQ—academic achievement nonetheless shows substantial genetic influence.

The data reported by Loehlin and Nichols (1976) were used in a multivariate analysis in which cross-correlations were compared for identical and fraternal twin pairs (Plomin & DeFries, 1979). Cross-correlations are the correlation, for example, between one twin partner's score on the English subtest and the other partner's score on mathematics. The results indicated that identical twin cross-correlations, although not as large as the phenotypic correlation between individuals, are substantial. The identical twin cross-correlations were consistently greater than the fraternal twin cross-correlations, thus suggesting some genetic mediation of the covariance among the five subtests of academic achievement. In addition, a factor analysis of the genetic covariance among the subtests indicated that one general genetic factor and one general environmental factor account for the phenotypic covariance among the subtests. In other words, the set of genes that affects one area of academic achievement largely overlaps with the set of genes that affects other academic areas. These findings were generally confirmed in a model-fitting approach to the same data (Martin, Jardine, & Eaves, 1984).

The other twin study of academic achievement is the Project TALENT study described in the previous section on specific cognitive abilities (Schoenfeldt, 1968). English tests involving capitalization and punctuation yielded average correlations of .63 for identical twins and .42 for fraternal twins, suggesting substantial genetic influence for these measures that would appear to assess achievement more than ability. However, mathematics tests produced results different from those in the NMSQT studies—the correlations were .62 and .55, respectively, for identical and fraternal twins. It should be noted that both the NMSQT studies (Loehlin & Nichols, 1976) and the Project TALENT study involved adolescents selected for above-average ability; results could differ for more representative samples.

A mathematics achievement test was also included in the only longitudinal twin study of academic achievement in adolescence (Fischbein, 1979). In this Swedish study of about 50 identical and 80 fraternal twin pairs from 10 to 13 years of age, identical and fraternal twin correlations for a mathematics test were .62 and .60, respectively, at 10 years of age. At 13 years, the twin correlations suggested greater genetic influence: .73 for identical twins and .55 for fraternal twins. Thus, as is the case for specific cognitive abilities, these longitudinal results suggest a possible increase in heritability from early to late adolescence.

In closing this section on scholastic skills, a new twin study of reading disability should be mentioned (Decker & Vandenberg, in press). Twenty pairs each of identical and fraternal twins were located in which at least one member of the pair was reading disabled; the twins ranged in age from 8 to 18 and had IQs of at least 90. The concordance for reading disability for identical twins was .80 and for fraternal twins the concordance was .45, suggesting substantial genetic influence on reading disability in adolescence.

Creativity

A domain related to cognitive abilities that has received only scant attention is creativity. In a study of 63 identical twin pairs and 54 fraternal twin pairs aged 13 to 19, a battery of 11 tests of creativity was administered (Reznikoff, Domino, Bridges, & Honeyman, 1973). The twin correlations, listed in Table 11.7, are substantial; however, differences between identical and fraternal twins average .13, a pattern of results suggesting somewhat less genetic influence for creativity than for cognitive abilities. An unusual feature of these results is that, in the case of three tests (Barron-Welsh, Franck Drawing Completion, and Obscure Figures), the correlations for fraternal twins exceed the correlations for identical twins.

Personality

In contrast to research in infancy and childhood, which has been spurred on by recent interest in temperament, behavioral genetic research on the topic of adolescent personality has been modest in quantity. In this section, behavioral

TABLE 11.7
Twin Correlations for Test of Creativity (Reznikoff et al., 1973)

	Twin Correlations	
Test	Identical 63 pairs	Fraternal 54 pairs
Alternate Uses	.72	.37
Associational Fluency	.66	.56
Barron-Welsh	.18	.42
Expressional Fluency	.71	.63
Franck Drawing Completion	.48	.59
Obscure Figures Test	.27	.48
Plot Titles	.49	.31
Possible Jobs	.56	.24
Quick Word	.83	.57
Remote Associates	.78	.43
Similes	.59	.22

genetic studies of adolescent personality are reviewed, again with a focus on the EAS traits of emotionality, activity, and sociability (Buss & Plomin, 1984). Before we begin to consider traditional scales of personality, one twin study of specific interest to adolescence should be mentioned. In a retrospective questionnaire study in which 200 pairs of adult twins reported age of first sexual intercourse, identical twin correlations were .40 and .41 for female and male pairs, respectively, and fraternal twin correlations were .20 and .11, suggesting moderate genetic influence on individual differences in age of first sexual intercourse (Martin, Eaves, & Eysenck, 1977). This may be due to genetic influence on sexual maturation—as noted earlier, maturational age as measured by peak height velocity or by age at menarche is strongly influenced genetically.

One of the first twin studies of personality, reported by Carter (1933, 1935), employed the then widely used 125-item Bernreuter Personality Inventory (Bernreuter, 1935), a questionnaire that assesses extraversion, neuroticism, self-sufficiency, and dominance and that also is scored for sociability and self-confidence (Flanagan, 1935). One problem with the questionnaire is that items are often scored on several scales, which results in substantial intercorrelations among the scales—on the average, the intercorrelation is .54. Correlations for high-school twins (40 identical twin pairs and 44 same-sex fraternal twin pairs) are listed in Table 11.8.

Three conclusions that emerge from this early twin study of personality continue to receive support from subsequent studies. First, identical and fraternal twin correlations for self-report questionnaires center around .50 and .30, respectively. Secondly, identical twin correlations are consistently greater than fraternal twin correlations for all measures, offering little evidence for differential heritability. One discrepancy between Carter's results and those of subsequent studies is that Carter's study suggests little genetic influence on extraversion, whereas subsequent studies have found strong evidence for heritability. However, the Bernreuter extraversion measure is not typical of extraversion

TABLE 11.8
Twin Correlations for the Bernreuter Personality Inventory
(Carter, 1935)

	Twin Correlations	
Scale	Identical 40 pairs	Fraternal 44 pairs
Neuroticism	.61	.32
Extraversion	.43	.40
Self-Sufficiency	.59	−.14
Dominance	.75	.34
Self-Confidence	.56	.20
Sociability	.54	.41

scales, and other researchers excluded the extraversion scale in analyses of the Bernreuter (e.g., Crook, 1937). Third, Carter found that correlations for adolescent twins were similar to those for older twins 20 to 65 years of age.

In terms of the EAS traits, neuroticism is similar to emotionality (Buss & Plomin, 1984) and sociability on the Bernreuter is similar to EAS sociability, although, as do nearly all other personality questionnaires, it mixes sociability and shyness items. Also similar to other self-report personality questionnaires, the Bernreuter does not assess activity level.

Differential Heritability

The surprising conclusion that personality traits do not appear to differ in heritability was emphasized by Loehlin and Nichols (1976) in their report of a study of 850 pairs of high-school twins. The median twin correlations for the 18 scales of the California Psychological Inventory were .50 for identical twins and .32 for fraternal twins. Loehlin and Nichols also examined twin correlations for 70 clusters of items obtained from the Objective Behavior Inventory, the Vocational Preference Inventory, and the Adjective Checklist. Details of the results of this study are presented in the next chapter because the twins were at least 17 years old; however, its relevance to the issue of differential heritability bears mention at this time. The magnitude of the twin correlations differed for the clusters, with specific activities showing higher correlations than self-concepts, occupational interests, or life goals; however, no consistent tendency was found for certain variables to show larger identical-fraternal correlation differences than others. The only exceptions seem to be political and social attitudes—such as opinions on God, racial integration, and federal welfare programs, which show little genetic influence and substantial family environmental influence. Nonetheless, Loehlin and Nichols' (1976) overall conclusion from these results is:

> Identical twins correlate about .20 higher than fraternal twins, give or take some sampling fluctuation, and it doesn't much matter what you measure—whether the difference is between .75 and .55 on an ability measure, between .50 and .30 on a personality scale, or between .35 and .15 on a self-concept composite. (p. 35)

This conclusion is shocking. Who would have expected all of the dozens of personality traits to show approximately equal heritabilities? Several important implications follow from this conclusion. One is that we should not be too surprised if questionnaires studies in adolescence yield evidence of genetic influence; it is difficult to devise a self-report questionnaire that does not show greater correlations for identical than for fraternal twins (Buss & Plomin, 1984).

Another implication is that huge sample sizes are needed to detect differential heritability if heritabilities for all personality traits tend to be moderate. For example, over 500 pairs of each type of twin are needed to demonstrate a significant difference between a heritability of .40 (based on an identical twin correlation of .50 and a fraternal twin correlation of .30) and a heritability of .60 (based on an identical twin correlation of .60 and a fraternal twin correlation of .30). Over 2,000 pairs of each type of twin are needed to demonstrate significant differential heritability when the heritabilities differ by .10.

A related implication is that large twin samples are needed to detect significant heritability if the expected identical twin correlation is .50 and the expected fraternal twin correlation is .30. For example, a sample of 250 identical and 250 fraternal twin pairs is needed to detect a significant ($p < .05$) correlational difference of this magnitude 80% of the time. Samples of 50 pairs of each type of twin have only 32% power to detect such a difference; this means that a significant difference between identical and fraternal twin correlations will be detected only about a third of the time. Thus, studies reporting that some personality dimensions are significantly heritable and others are not must be evaluated in terms of the power of their sample size to detect significant heritability. Furthermore, showing that some traits are significantly heritable and others are not does not imply that the traits differ significantly in their heritability.

An even more mischievous implication is that, in order for small twin samples to show significant heritability, the pattern of twin correlations must violate the twin model. For example, with 25 pairs of each twin type, if the identical twin correlation were .50, a *negative* fraternal twin correlation would be necessary to produce a significant difference in correlations. These problems are not obvious in the literature because the pattern of twin correlations is not always considered. Often studies report only the significance level of the difference between identical and fraternal twin correlations or the *F*-ratio of intrapair differences without presenting the correlations themselves.

The issue of differential heritability of personality traits has been debated, with some researchers gleaning hints of differential heritability. For example, a model-fitting analysis of Loehlin and Nichols' (1976) data suggested that the more heritable scales of the California Psychological Inventory (CPI) are those in the second-order domain of extraversion (Zonderman, 1982). An analysis combining data from three twin studies using the CPI also found that scales in the CPI extraversion domain showed the highest heritabilities (Carey, Goldsmith, Tellegen, & Gottesman, 1978). However, Loehlin (1978a) did not accept this conclusion because the analysis focused on identical and fraternal twin correlations rather than on *differences* between them.

To some extent, the lack of differential heritability for the CPI scales is due to item overlap; similar to the Bernreuter, some items are scored on several scales—38% of the 480 CPI items are scored on at least 2 of the 18 scales. In a study of adult twins, new CPI scales were created to eliminate overlapping items (Horn, Plomin, & Rosenman, 1976). The twin results for these new scales provided some evidence for differential heritability, with 2 of the 18 CPI scales, responsibility and femininity, showing heritabilities near zero.

With the exception of extraversion-related traits, no one disputes the consistency of the .20 difference between identical and fraternal twin correlations for diverse personality traits. Loehlin (1982) has developed a theory concerning differential heritability that might lead to a way out of the conundrum. His argument begins by noting that two major higher-order factors, extraversion and neuroticism, are measured by many personality questionnaires. Both traits apper to be substantially heritable. For example, in a study of nearly 13,000 adult twin pairs in Sweden—which is reviewed in the next chapter—heritabilities exceeding .50 emerged for these two traits. Loehlin also reanalzyed his NMSQT data to form seven orthogonal factors from the items of the CPI, two of which were extraversion and neuroticism. These two scales yielded the expected high heritabilities; other scales such as Stereotyped Masculinity, Intolerance of Ambiguity, and Persistence yielded much lower heritability estimates. Loehlin suggested that extraversion and neuroticism are such pervasive super-traits that they mask the differential heritability of other traits. This suggestion is relevant to the EAS approach to personality because sociability is the major component of extraversion and emotionality is central to neuroticism (Buss & Plomin, 1984).

Research on the topic of differential heritability has been limited to self-report personality questionnaires. Another possible explanation of the lack of evidence for differential heritability is that twins share perceptions of their general similarity and that identical twins generally view themselves as more similar than do fraternal twins. This could lead identical twins to respond more similarly to the items on self-report personality questionnaires than do fraternal twins, especially when the twins complete the questionnaire together. However, the lack of differential heritability also appears when parental ratings are employed, as discussed in chapter 10. One could argue that parents have general impressions of their twins' similarity that pervade ratings of their children. Although analyses of "cross-correlations" in which the mother rates one twin and the father rates the twin partner yield similar results, a critic could still make a case that parents share their perceptions of their children.

What is needed are data other than self-report or parental ratings and designs other than the twin method. Of course, most objective assessments entail tremendously greater costs in time and energy as compared to paper-and-pencil measures that can be administered via the mails. No studies using objective measures of personality in adolescence have been reported, although chapters 9 and 10 included infancy and early childhood studies that have employed objective assessments such as observer ratings of children's behavior in structured settings, teacher ratings, and observations involving behavior counts. Studies using objective measures tend to yield a diverse pattern of heritabilities, although the studies are not large enough to show that the heritabilities of various personality traits are significantly different (Plomin & Foch, 1980).

EAS Traits

In earlier chapters, a temperament theory was described that suggests that the most heritable aspects of personality are emotionality, activity, and sociability (EAS; Buss & Plomin, 1984). This approach does not conflict with the general finding of little differential heritability for personality measures if, as Loehlin (1982) suggests, the highly heritable "super-factors" of neuroticism and extraversion pervade such measures. Emotionality is the core of neuroticism, and sociability is the essence of extraversion; activity is simply not often assessed on self-report questionnaires.

In this section, behavioral genetic data relevant to the EAS theory in adolescence are reviewed, beginning with analyses of items from self-report personality questionnaires. In order to ward off disappointment, the reader is forewarned that few studies relevant to the EAS traits in adolescence have been reported and even fewer conclusions can be drawn. One reason for this state of affairs was noted by Vandenberg in 1967:

> A far more serious limitation hindering a rational evaluation is, in my opinion, based on the fact that most twin studies are small, isolated, one-shot affairs, which means that in effect their authors are amateurs, be they geneticists, anthropologists, or psychologists of whatever nationality. (p. 66)

This situation has improved somewhat during the past decade and a half, but not much.

Item Analyses. Carter's (1935) twin study of personality attempted to separate items into heritable and nonheritable categories. The author concluded that inspection of the two groups of items "leads to no clear-cut explanatory generalizations. If there is any distinctive quality characteristic of all the questions of either group, it is not apparent to the writer" (p. 72). Although no single quality summarizes the heritable items, sociability/shyness items appeared only in the heritable category:

Do you have difficulty in starting a conversation with a stranger?
Have books been more entertaining to you than companions?
Do you like to be with people a great deal?
Do you find it difficult to speak in public?
Are you very talkative at social gatherings?
Are you troubled with shyness?
Do you take the responsibility for introducing people at a party?

Although several neuroticism items appeared in the heritable group, other neuroticism items fell in the nonheritable category. As in other personality questionnaires, activity is not assessed by the Bernreuter Personality Inventory. Loehlin and Nichols (1976) conducted a similar analysis for items of the California Psychological Inventory and reached a conclusion similar to Carter's. However, again the data suggested more genetic influence for sociability/shyness than for other items. For example, among 16 CPI items showing high heritabilities, two are very similar to the heritable shyness items in Carter's study:

It is hard for me to start a conversation with strangers.

I am likely not to speak to people until they speak to me.

In addition, the high heritable classification included several items possibly related to extraversion such as showing off, talking before groups of people, wanting to be an actor, and being a leader. In the low heritable group of items, the only item that may be related to extraversion was a retrospective report concerning difficulty in talking before the class in school.

Even stronger results emerged from a study of adult twins (Horn, Plomin, & Rosenman, 1976). Cross-validation criteria were used to isolate 41 reliable CPI items that showed heritable influence. When these heritable items were submitted to factor analysis, the largest factor consisted mainly of shyness items—for example, "It is hard for me to start a conversation with strangers." More analyses at the item level are needed to clarify the heritable nature of personality scales.

Analyses of EAS Scales.   There are very few behavioral genetic data specifically involving EAS traits in adolescence. The early study by Carter (1935) described above yielded evidence for substantial genetic influence on neuroticism, with twin correlations of .61 and .32 for identical and fraternal twins, respectively. However, neither extraversion nor sociability as measured by the Bernreuter Personality Questionnaire showed much genetic influence.

One study of 262 pairs of twins from 7 to 17 years of age (Young, Eaves, & Eysenck, 1980) provides evidence for genetic influence on both extraversion and neuroticism, which can be viewed as complex versions of sociability and emotionality, respectively. No twin correlations were presented; however, model-fitting heritability estimates were about .50 for extraversion and .40 for neuroticism. An interesting aspect of this study was the inclusion of parental data. Model-fitting analyses suggested heritability estimates for the adults similar to those for the adolescents and covariance in genetic effects between adolescence and adulthood; however, because these results depend upon a parent-offspring family design in which family environment as well as heredity is shared by parents and their offspring, they must be viewed with considerable caution.

Five studies of high-school twins employed Cattell's High School Personality Questionnaire (Cattell, Blewett, & Beloff, 1955; Gottesman, 1963; Klein & Cattell, reported in Cattell, 1982; Osborne, 1980; Vandenberg, 1962). Second-order factors derived from Cattell's personality questionnaires assess extraversion and neuroticism; however, these twin studies reported results only for the primary factors, and those are difficult to relate to the EAS traits. Two traits appear to be related to emotionality: Factor Q_4, Nervous Tension vs. Autonomic Relaxation, and Factor C, Emotional Stability. Both dimensions yielded greater resemblance in identical twins than in fraternal twins in all studies with the exception of one (Gottesman, 1963). It is not possible to summarize the twin results because twin correlations were reported for only one study.

Interesting exceptions to the use of self-report questionnaires are two studies that assessed neuroticism in adolescents using objective measures such as flicker fusion that, although lacking in face validity as measures of neuroticism, have been shown to relate factorially to other neuroticism measures. In a study of 25 pairs each of identical and fraternal twins from 13 to 15 years of age, Eysenck and Prell (1951) found twin correlations of .85 and .21 for identical and fraternal twins, respectively. Although they did not report twin correlations, Cattell, Stice, and Kristy (1957) found significantly greater resemblance for identical twins than for fraternal twins on the neuroticism factor of Cattell's Objective Analytic Test Battery in a study of 104 identical and 30 fraternal twin pairs from 10 to 15 years of age. A summary of Cattell's recent work with laboratory measures can be found in his book (Cattell, 1982). The personality system assessed by Cattell's questionnaires appears to have no dimension of activity level; however, two dimensions might be related to sociability. Factor A (Cyclothymia vs. Schizothymia) is outgoingness. This scale is more complex than EAS sociability and emphasizes an individual's reserve in social interactions; perhaps for this reason, the scale displays little evidence of genetic influence in the five twin studies. A Cattell factor that appears to assess shyness is Factor H (Threctia vs. Parmia) which is described as "shy, timid, restrained, threat-sensitive vs. adventurous, 'thick-skinned,' socially bold" (Cattell, Eber, & Tatsuoka, 1970, p. 9l). In all five studies, identical twins were found to be more similar than fraternal twins for this factor. Cattell's manual states that "present evidence indicates [Factor H] to be one of the two or three most highly inherited of personality factors" (Cattell et al., 1970, p. 92).

Vandenberg's study of Michigan high-school twins (45 identical pairs and 35 fraternal pairs) included the Thurstone Temperament Schedule (TTS). Unlike other personality questionnaires, the TTS includes a scale to assess activity, and the Activity scale yielded twin correlations of .55 and -.06, respectively, for identical and fraternal twins. The large difference between the identical and fraternal twin correlations suggests substantial genetic influence; the lower-than-expected fraternal twin correlation is reminiscent of a similar finding in childhood. Another TTS scale, Vigorous, appears to be related to activity level; however, this dimension is more complex, including masculinity and emotional stability. The TTS Sociable scale yielded a pattern of results similar to Activity: the identical and fraternal twin correlations were .50 and -.06. The TTS Stable scale, which is meant to assess emotional stability, suggested no genetic influence; identical and fraternal twin correlations were .10 and .08, respectively. However, this scale has nothing to do with EAS emotionality in that it includes only neurotic reactions such as, "Do you often fret about the little daily chores?" Interestingly, the TTS includes no typical emotionality items such as being easily angered or frightened. Vandenberg (1967) also reports administering an abbreviated version of Comrey's (1965) personality and attitude questionnaires to high-school twins (111 identical pairs and 90 fraternal pairs). Although twin correlations were not reported, significant genetic influence was found for shyness but not for neuroticism.

Vandenberg (1967) also described a German study in which Gottschaldt (1960) analyzed adult and adolescence data on 35 pairs of identical twins and 33 pairs of fraternal twins who had been studied intensively 15 years earlier at summer camps that were held for twins only. The only EAS-relevant ratings of the twins involved vitality (tempo and energy level) and mood (how easily the twins were upset). The data were presented in terms twin concordance, from no difference within pairs to large intrapair differences. For both traits, twin concordances were much greater for identical twins than for fraternal twins, both in adolescence and in adulthood. Unfortunately, longitudinal analyses were not conducted, even though this is one of the few longitudinal twin studies of personality.

A few other twin studies of high-school students have been reported; however, their relevance to the EAS traits is even more unclear than in the case of the studies described above. For example, a study of 1,221 boys from 12 to 18 who were members of twin, nontwin sibling, and adoptee pairs included such difficult-to-classify traits as capacity to mobilize, anxiety, narcistic ego, and asthenia (Cattell, Vaughan, Schuerger, & Rao, 1982). Other examples are studies that used the MMPI; nonetheless, MMPI data are interesting because so little is known about the etiology of psychopathology in adolescence. For this reason, MMPI results from twin studies will be mentioned in the next section.

Other twin and adoption studies relevant to the EAS theory primarily included either children or adults. For example, the large-scale NMSQT twin study (Loehlin & Nichols, 1976) obtained detailed personality data; however, questionnaires were sent to participants toward the end of their senior year in high school so that they were at least 17 years old. For this reason, the EAS results from this important study will be presented in the next chapter.

Psychopathology

Surprisingly few behavioral genetic studies of psychopathology in adolescence have been reported, even though it is during adolescence that most major forms of psychopathology begin to make themselves known. Gottesman (1963, 1965) reported two studies in which the MMPI was administered to high-school twins. The results of these studies have been combined with those of another small study (Reznikoff & Honeyman, 1967) in Table 11.9 (from Vandenberg, 1967). The results, based on a total of 120 identical and 132 fraternal twin pairs, suggest that some common forms of psychopathology such as depression and psychopathy may be influenced by heredity. As in studies of normal personality, the results for extraversion suggest substantial genetic influence.

A small parent-offspring study compared adolescents' scores on the MMPI with MMPI scores that their parents had received in ninth grade (Hill & Hill, 1973). Parent-offspring correlations for the "neurotic" scales of the MMPI were negligible; however, the "psychotic" scales yielded an average correlation of .22.

The MMPI results for psychopathy reported by Vandenberg (1967) were confirmed by a twin study of adolescent delinquency (Rowe, 1983). Delinquent behavior such as theft, aggression, vandalism, and minor delinquencies such as trespassing were assessed via questionnaire. For 168 identical and 97 fraternal high-school twin pairs, twin correlations for antisocial behavior suggest moderate genetic influence: The twin correlations were .70 and .48 for identical and fraternal twins, respectively. Model-fitting analyses confirmed a significant role for genetic influences; they also suggested a possible role for shared family environment, although Rowe argues that in this case shared family environment reflects the influence of one twin on the other rather than aspects of the home environment. In a subsequent analysis, Rowe and Osgood (1984) showed that the well known relationship between delinquency of an adolescent and delinquency of the adolescent's friends is primarily due to genetic factors.

TABLE 11.9
Twin results for the Minnesota Multiphasic Personality Inventory
(from Vandenberg, 1967)

| | Twin Correlations | |
Scale	Identical 120 pairs	Fraternal 132 pairs
Social Introversion	.45	.12
Depression	.44	.14
Psychasthenia	.41	.11
Psychopathic Deviate	.48	.27
Schizophrenia	.44	.24
Paranoia	.27	.08
Hysteria	.37	.23
Hypochondriasis	.41	.28
Hypomania	.32	.18
Masculinity-Femininity	.41	.35

Conclusions

As is much too often the case, our principal conclusion must be that more research is needed before firm conclusions can be reached concerning genetic influences in adolescence. In some ways, the situation is worse for adolescence than for other developmental periods; for example, there are fewer behavioral genetic studies of personality in adolescence than in infancy, childhood, or adulthood.

However, the twin data as they stand suggest an exciting possibility in the domain of cognition: For both IQ and specific cognitive abilities, genetic influence appears to increase from early to late adolescence. This is particularly striking because one might expect that the relative influence of heredity would decrease as children experience more varied environments as their lebenswelt expands beyond the confines of the family.

Another interesting result emerging from adolescence research is that the relative roles of nature and nurture are similar to those in adulthood even though adolescents undergo dramatic developmental changes. This can be seen most clearly in twin data for height and weight, but the point is just as relevant to behavioral characteristics.

Most needed are longitudinal behavioral genetic studies of adolescence that can assess genetic change during this important developmental era. As Schaie said in 1975: "While it may be of theoretical interest to know what the relative contribution of genetic and environmental variance might be at a given age for a particular point in time (and this is all the twin studies really tell us), it is of much more concern to what extent developmental *change* can be accounted for as a function of environmental and preprogrammed maturational factors" (p. 216). For example, there have been no analyses of age-to-age genetic correlations during adolescence. However, an extension of the amplification model of the developmental genetics (see chapter 3) to adolescence would predict continuing high genetic correlations from year to year and increasing genetic variance from childhood to adolescence.

As discussed in earlier chapters, behavioral genetic methods are as useful for studying the environment as they are for understanding the influence of heredity. Two examples of particular relevance to adolescence research are the importance of nonshared environment (chapter 4) and genetic involvement in ostensibly environmental relationships (chapter 8). Rife with implications for adolescence research are the recent findings that heredity influences the way in which adolescents view their experiences. Although behavioral geneticists have scarcely considered adolescence, it is likely that behavioral genetic research will come to play a major role in furthering our understanding of the development of individual differences in adolescence.

Two important resources for behavioral genetic studies in adolescence are step-families and adolescent adoptees. The high divorce rate has resulted in large numbers of step-parents who rear children who are not genetically related to them. Broken and mended homes also result in half-siblings and genetically unrelated children who are reared together. Although the step-family design is not as straightforward as an adoption design, its major advantage is the availability of large numbers of such families. Confounding factors such as the age at which the child is exposed to the step-parent can be studied empirically.

Adoption studies are needed to confirm the results of twin studies. Now is the time to conduct adoption studies of adolescence (Plomin & Fulker, in press). From the late 1950s to the early 1970s, nearly 1% of all infants were adopted by nonrelatives (Mech, 1973). Thus, large numbers of adolescent and young adult adoptees are currently available, and many of these have been reared with other adoptees as well as natural children of the adoptive parents. Adoptive parent organizations and progressive adoption agencies often are willing to contact adoptive parents concerning possible research participation. The sharp increase in contraception and abortion that began in the 1970s and continues to the present time has greatly curtailed the number of younger adoptees; thus, it is important that adoption studies of adolescence are begun soon.

12 Adulthood

It is surprising how little behavioral genetic research has been focused on adulthood, the developmental period in which we spend the vast majority of our lives, from the adolescent to the aging years. The need for more research is becoming a familiar refrain. Previous chapters have indicated that much more behavioral genetic research is needed in infancy, childhood, and adolescence as well. Part of the reason for the lack of such research is that it is difficult to do—large samples of special subjects are needed. Also, there are relatively few behavioral geneticists to do it. However, one practical consideration makes it more difficult to conduct behavioral genetic research on adulthood than on earlier developmental periods: No longer are the family members—parents and offspring, twin and nontwin siblings—together in the same home or the same school. Researchers cannot visit a single home or send questionnaires to a single address to collect information on members of the family. In our mobile society, adult family members are frequently scattered throughout the country; sometimes even finding them is difficult. This cloud has a silver lining in that difficulty in contacting adult family members has led to the use of national registers that results in more representative samples than are usually employed in behavioral genetic research.

Developmentalists have not shown nearly as much interest in adulthood as in earlier and later periods of development. However, important developmental changes occur in adulthood. Although these changes seem to be in slow motion compared to adolescence, adult developmental changes are as dramatic in the long run as changes during other developmental periods because they continue for half the life span. Life-span psychologists (e.g., Baltes, Reese, & Lipsitt, 1980) have described major life event changes that take place during

253

adulthood, changes such as becoming independent from one's family, entering the workplace, marriage and divorce, having children, and having the children grow up and leave the family. Life-span research clearly indicates that such life events change people on the average. It is also likely that these life events change adults in different ways depending on their genetic propensities. Genetic change also occurs in adulthood, as seen in such minor changes as decreasing quantity of hair and quality of eyesight and in such devastating changes as those wrought by Huntington and Alzheimer diseases.

Developmental behavioral genetic research on adulthood is needed because we spend over half of our life as adults; moreover, it is during this half of the life span that individuals make their greatest contributions to society. We need to understand the etiology of individual differences among adults in their functioning and in developmental changes in their functioning without assuming that the answers to these questions are the same answers found in research on childhood and adolescence. This chapter reviews behavioral genetic studies of this middle half of the life span, from the late teen years to the 60s.

Physical Characteristics

Height does not change much during adulthood; however, as is all too obvious to most of us, weight usually increases, as does the distribution of body fat and the texture of skin. An important series of twin and adoption studies of height, weight, and body mass in adulthood has been conducted by Albert Stunkard and his colleagues (Stunkard, Foch, & Hrubec, 1985; Stunkard et al., 1985) For 1,975 pairs of male identical twins and 2,097 pairs of male fraternal twins, height and weight were assessed during induction into the United States military at the average age of 20 and the twins again reported their height and weight 25 years later. During these 25 years, the men increased 4 centimeters in height and 12 kilograms in weight on the average. The correlations for height and weight over the 25 years were .89 and .65, respectively, indicating slight developmental change in individuals' rank ordering for height and substantial change for weight. A body mass index of obesity was constructed by dividing weight in kilograms by the square of height in centimeters; the stability of this measure of body mass over the 25 years was .54.

Twin correlations for height, weight, and body mass at the average ages of 20 and 45 are presented in Table 12.1. The twin correlations for height are quite similar at 20 and 45 years and suggest heritabilities of about 80% at both ages. Considerable confidence can be attached to these estimates of heritability because, in samples of this size and with twin correlations of this magnitude, standard errors of heritability estimates are only about .04. Heritabilities of about 80% are also suggested by the twin correlations for weight. For height and especially for weight, shared environment diminishes in importance from 20 to

TABLE 12.1
Twin Correlations for Physical Characteristics at 20 and 45 Years
(adapted from Stunkard, Foch, & Hrubec, 1985)

	20 years		45 years	
	Identical	Fraternal	Identical	Fraternal
Height	.91	.51	.88	.48
Weight	.85	.46	.74	.33
Body mass index	.81	.42	.66	.24
Number of pairs	1975	2097	1975	2097

45 as seen in the smaller correlations at age 45 for both identical and fraternal twins. The twin correlations for height and weight in adulthood suggest greater genetic influence and less family environmental influence than in adolescence (see Table 11.1 for comparison). The body mass index also shows heritabilities of about 80% and little influence of shared family environment. At 45 years, the fraternal twin correlation is less than half the identical twin correlation for the body mass index and for weight, suggesting the possible influence of nonadditive genetic effects.

Similar results emerged from analyses of overweight individuals. For individuals 25% overweight at 20 years, the concordances were 47% and 28% for 98 pairs of identical twins and 114 pairs of fraternal twins, respectively. At 45 years, five times as many individuals were overweight and the twin results suggest slightly greater genetic influence: The concordance for identical twins (580 pairs) and fraternal twins (625 pairs) were 54% and 26%. These results indicate that obesity, the high extreme of the normal weight distribution, occurs for reasons similar to those that affect the rest of the distribution of weight: substantial genetic influence and no influence of shared family environment. Other studies of adult twins have found similar results for obesity (e.g., Medlund, Cederlof, & Floderus-Myrhed, 1976).

Stunkard et al. (1985) also conducted a longitudinal twin analysis using the method discussed in chapter 3 to assess genetic and environmental contributions to change and continuity. Twin cross-correlations from 20 to 45 years were calculated, and the differences in cross-correlations for identical and fraternal twins were used to solve for genetic correlations between 20 and 45 years. For height, the genetic correlation between 20 and 45 years was .97, indicating that genetic effects on individual differences in height at 20 years covary completely with genetic effects on height at 45 years. The environmental correlation between 20 and 45 years also was high, .60. However, environmental variance scarcely affects height; thus, the phenotypic stability between 20 and 45 for height is mediated almost entirely by genetic continuity.

For weight and body mass, the genetic correlations between 20 and 45 are lower than for height—.74 and .70, respectively. This finding suggests that heredity exerts somewhat different effects at 20 and 45. The environmental correlations between the two ages were low for weight (.27) and not significantly different from zero for body mass (-.12). Thus, these data suggest genetic involvement in both change and continuity for weight and body mass.

The genetics of weight was also studied in a sample of 840 Danish adoptees aged 33 to 56 selected so that the age and sex distibution was the same in each of four weight categories: thin, medium, overweight, and obese (Stunkard et al., 1985). Biological and adoptive parents were contacted and their current weight and height were assessed. The authors interpret the results to suggest that heredity plays an important role in fatness but that family environment has little or no effect, an interpretation consistent with the twin data previously reviewed. This interpretation is derived from analyses of variance that showed a mean relationship between body mass scores for biological parents and the four weight categories of the adoptees; no relationship emerged between body mass for adoptive parents and the adoptees' weight categories. However, a closer examination of the results suggests a different interpretation. For the adoptees in the overweight and obese categories (body mass scores 25 or greater), 41% had overweight or obese biological mothers and 49% had overweight or obese biological fathers. In contrast, for the normal weight adoptees, the incidences of overweight or obese biological mothers or fathers were 35% and 38%, respectively. Similar results were obtained for the smaller sample of obese adoptees (body mass scores of 30 or greater): 14% had obese biological mothers and 10% had obese biological fathers, whereas 8% of the normal weight adoptees had obese biological mothers and 9% had obese biological fathers. Viewed in this light, these results suggest some genetic influence on overweight, but much less than that suggested by the twin study.

A likely explanation for the discrepancy between these adoption results and those from the twin study is the age difference between the adoptees and their parents—as noted above, the correlation for weight between 20 and 45 is only .65; the genetic correlation between the two ages was calculated to be .74. Using the approach described in chapter 3, the twin results would predict that the weight correlation between biological parents and their adopted-away offspring should only be .29 when parents and their offspring are 25 years apart in age.

One adoption study involving the contemporaneous relationship of twins, the Minnesota Study of Twins Reared Apart, also obtained some relevant data (Bouchard, 1984). For 30 pairs of identical twins reared apart—separated at less than a month and not reunited until the average age of 24, the twin correlation for height was .94 at the average age of 36. Comparison data for 274 pairs of identical twins reared together yielded a correlation of .93; for 146 pairs of fraternal twins reared together, the correlation was .50. All of these results are consistent with the conclusion that the heritability of height in adulthood is greater than 80%. For weight, however, the correlation for identical twins reared apart was only .51; the comparison correlations were .83 for identical twins and .43 for fraternal twins. The separated identical twin correlation of .51 for weight is puzzling because it suggests a heritability of 51%, which conflicts with the twin study estimate of 80%. The answer probably lies in the small size of the sample of identical twins reared apart, as suggested by the results of a larger study conducted in Sweden.

The Swedish Early Separated Twins project (Pedersen, Friberg, Floderus-Myrhed, McClearn, & Plomin, 1984) identified 698 same-sex pairs of twins separated by the age of 10; half were separated by 12 months. At the average age of 43, the correlations for height (corrected for age and age at separation) were .87 for identical twins reared apart (168 pairs) and .67 for fraternal twins reared apart (438 pairs); for weight, the correlations are .78 and .46, respectively. The correlations for identical twins reared apart estimate heritabilities for height and weight similar to the estimates from twin studies. The correlations for fraternal twins reared apart are too high; however, the method used to diagnose zygosity by means of physical similarity in childhood is likely to have resulted in the misclassification of identical twins as fraternal twins, as suggested by the fact that there are 2.5 times the number of fraternal twins as identical twins, whereas approximately equal numbers of the two types of twins are to be expected. Additional information concerning zygosity is being collected as part of the ongoing study.

IQ

The classic longitudinal behavioral genetic studies of IQ, the Louisville Twin Study (Wilson, 1983) and the adoption study by Skodak and Skeels (1949), continued to follow subjects only as far as adolescence. There are no longitudinal behavioral genetic studies of IQ from adolescence to adulthood or during adulthood; thus, the following review is limited to cross-sectional analyses and the developmental comparisons and conclusions therefore are tenuous. Even more troublesome is the fact that extant studies of adulthood are primarily limited to young adults.

The previous chapter's review of IQ data on adolescence led to the hypothesis that genetic influence on individual differences in IQ increases from childhood to adolescence. The most elemental developmental behavioral genetic question that can be asked in adulthood is whether genetic influence on IQ changes—for example, does genetic influence continue to increase? More interesting developmental questions involve genetic change and continuity; however, these questions require longitudinal data.

Family Studies

The largest family study of cognition in adulthood is the Hawaii Family Study of Cognition (HFSC) which included 830 Caucasian families and 305 families of Japanese ancestry (DeFries et al., 1976; DeFries et al., 1979). Although the focus of the study was specific cognitive abilities, the test battery included a shortened version of Raven's Progressive Matrices, regarded as one of the best single measures of culture-fair abstract reasoning. For Caucasian families, the mean correlation between parents (aged 35 to 55) and their children (aged 13 to 33) is .26. Because the HFSC is a family study and family members share family environment as well as heredity, parent-offspring resemblance for scores on Progressive Matrices could be due solely to family environment. However, doubling this correlation provides an upper-limit estimate of heritability of about .50; that is, heredity can account for no more than 50% of the variance even if all of the familial resemblance is due to heredity and none to shared environment. This single parent-offspring estimate of familial resemblance can be inflated by assortative mating. However, another estimate of familiality, the regression of offspring on midparent, would not be affected by assortative mating. In the HFSC, the regression of offspring on midparent is .52, which suggests that assortative mating does not noticeably affect the single parent-offspring estimate.

Another measure of general cognitive ability from the HFSC is a composite score based on the common variance among 15 tests of specific cognitive abilities administered in the study to offspring as well as parents. This composite, called the first principal component, correlates .73 with the WAIS full-scale IQ, a correlation that is comparable to those reported between WAIS IQ and other standard tests of intelligence. The average single parent-offspring correlation for this general cognitive factor in the Caucasian families is .35. The regression of offspring on midparent is .60. Thus, the HFSC data are compatible with an upper-limit estimate of about .50 to .70 for heritability of IQ.

The large sample permitted analysis of the offspring-midparent regressions separately by age of the offspring. For the unrotated first principal component index of general intelligence, the regressions of offspring on midparent are .51, .64, .63, .59, .66, and .58, respectively, for six age groups: 13-14, 15, 16, 17, 18-19, and greater than 19 (DeFries et al., 1979). The increase in familial resemblance from 13-14 to 15 is not statistically significant, and familial resemblance hovers around .60 thereafter. It is difficult to interpret these age changes and continuities in a family study: As indicated in the previous chapter, we might expect to see increases in the effects of heredity and decreases in the effects of shared environment over the age range of the offspring in this study. These counterbalancing effects would leave familial correlations unchanged. The HFSC found lower levels of parent-offspring resemblance in the families of Japanese ancestry. The regression of offspring on midparent for Raven's Progressive Matrices is .24, much lower than the comparable regression of .52

in the Caucasian families. For the general composite, it is .42 rather than .60. Lower parent-offspring resemblance in the Japanese families could be due to genetic or environmental factors. However, an analysis of ethnic group-by-generation interactions revealed large increases in general cognitive ability for Japanese and Chinese families and large decreases for Caucasian families, a finding which suggests that cultural factors are important (DeFries, Corley, Johnson, Vandenberg, & Wilson, 1982).

Sibling resemblance as well as parent-offspring resemblance has been assessed in the HFSC. For 455 pairs of Caucasian siblings, the correlation for general intelligence is .31 on average for brother-brother, brother-sister, and sister-sister pairs. This correlation suggests that the upper limit of heritability is about .60, which is similar to the estimate based on parent-offspring regression. Because siblings are close in age and parents and offspring are 20 years apart on average, similar results for siblings and for parents and offspring are interesting from a developmental behavioral genetic perspective. However, they offer no simple interpretation in a family study—as just mentioned, it is possible that genetic variance increases from young adulthood to middle adulthood, while the influence of shared environment decreases. The possibility of cross-sectional developmental change in sibling resemblance was explored using hierarchical multiple regression techniques described in chapter 3 (Corley, 1985). Similar to the parent-offspring results, no significant changes in sibling resemblance emerged.

Although parent-offspring resemblance is less in Japanese than in Caucasian families, the sibling correlations are similar for the two groups. For 147 pairs of Japanese siblings, the correlation is .33; for the Caucasian siblings, the correlation was .31. This suggests that genetic and environmental influences shared by siblings is about the same for Caucasians and Japanese even though the parent-offspring results indicate greater familial influence for Caucasian families than for Japanese families.

An interesting analysis of the HFSC data (Johnson & Nagoshi, 1985) was inspired by Jensen's (e.g., 1985) work suggesting that loadings of cognitive tests on a first unrotated principal component (representing g or general cognitive ability) are related to the magnitude of genetic influence on the test. The g loadings of the 15 HFSC tests were correlated with the HFSC familial correlations for the tests. The correlation between the g loadings and tests for the various parent-offspring and sibling gender combinations was .51 on average, suggesting that the g-loading of a particular test is related positively to familial resemblance on the test.

The HFSC estimates of parent-offspring and sibling resemblance are lower than those cited in general reviews of the IQ literature (Bouchard & McGue, 1981; Erlenmeyer-Kimling & Jarvik, 1963). For example, for 8,433 pairs of parents and offspring in 32 studies, the median IQ correlation is .39; for 26,473 pairs of siblings in 69 studies, the median correlation is .45 (Bouchard &

McGue, 1981). It has been suggested that recent studies show less familial resemblance than do older studies (Plomin & DeFries, 1980). This difference has been tentatively ascribed to greater restriction of range in the more recent studies (Caruso, 1983), although other reasons are possible—for example, newer studies show less assortative mating than do older studies. However, in these reviews, no attention has been paid to the age of the subjects. Most of the family studies, for example, involve children and adolescents and, as suggested in previous chapters, it is likely that shared environmental influence is greater for children who continue to live in the same home with their parents and their siblings than it is for older individuals who no longer share the same family environment. The lower familial correlations in the HFSC may be due to the fact that it is one of the few studies in which the offspring included young adults (average age of 17 years).

Twin Studies

A major twin study of IQ in adulthood was conducted in Sweden using data on 19-year-old military recruits who completed a group intelligence test (Husén, 1959). Twin correlations for 538 pairs of identical twins and 1,070 pairs of fraternal twins were .90 and .70, respectively. These results suggest a heritability of about 40% and substantial shared environmental influence (about half of the total variance); the estimate of heritability is lower and the estimate of family environmental influence is higher than estimates based on studies of adolescence. These twin results conflict sharply with those of the HFSC in that the correlation for HFSC siblings is only about .30, whereas the fraternal twin correlation in the Swedish study was .70. Because fraternal twins are no more similar genetically than are nontwin siblings, the difference in correlations suggests that twins share substantially more similar family environments than do siblings who are not twins.

A study of adult twins in Norway employed the individually administered Wechsler Adult Intelligence Scales (Tambs, Sundet, & Magnus, 1984). For 40 pairs each of identical and fraternal twins from 30 to 57 years of age (average age of 41), the twin correlations were .88 and .47 for identical and fraternal twins, respectively. Thus, these Norwegian results suggest greater heritability, about 80%, and less shared environmental influence than does the Swedish study, although the correlation of .47 for fraternal twins is still substantially larger than the sibling correlation of .30 found in the HFSC.

A study of adult twins in England yielded yet another pattern of results (Canter, 1973). Raven's Progressive Matrices test was administered to 40 identical twin pairs and 45 fraternal twin pairs from 16 to 55 years of age (average age of 21). The identical and fraternal twin correlations were .68 and .46, respectively. The estimate of 44% heritability is similar to the estimate from the Swedish study, although the twin correlations in the English study are much lower.

The lack of consistency in the results of these three studies could be due to the use of different measures of intelligence, to differences in the ages of the two samples, or to differences between Swedish, Norwegian, and English populations. Nonetheless, the results are so discrepant that it is impossible to draw any conclusions about the genetics of adult intelligence on the basis of extant twin studies.

Data from the HFSC suggested that the degree of familial resemblance for a particular test is related to the test's g loading. Jensen (1985) has shown that twin estimates of heritability of WAIS subtests are also related to g-loadings—.55 in the study by Tambs et al. and .62 in the study by Block (1968) which was described in the previous chapter.

Adoption Studies

Adoption studies add substantially to our knowledge about the genetics of intelligence in adulthood. One adoption study of IQ compared resemblance in adoptive families to resemblance in nonadoptive families in which the children were from 16 to 22 years of age (Scarr & Weinberg, 1978b). The IQ correlation for 270 nonadoptive parents and their children was .40. In about 184 adoptive familes, the parent-offspring correlation was .12. Thus, these data imply substantial genetic influence, about 60% heritability. The adoptive parent-adoptee correlation of .12 suggests that shared family environment plays only a minor role in parent-offspring IQ resemblance when the offspring are adults. In other words, by the time they are adults, offspring resemble their parents in IQ primarily for hereditary reasons and only slightly for reasons related to the fact that they shared a family environment with their parents.

A particularly important discovery in Scarr and Weinberg's study is that the IQ correlation for 84 pairs of genetically unrelated adult individuals who had been reared together was -.03. This agrees with the results of a study of adolescent adoptees discussed in the previous chapter (Kent, 1985) and both studies contrast sharply with the correlation of about .30 found in studies of younger adoptee pairs. These two studies suggest the possibility that the influence of shared environment on IQ diminishes to negligible levels during adolescence, as discussed in chapter 4. This hypothesis also brings the data from the HFSC in line with results of twin and adoption studies in suggesting substantial genetic influence and little influence of shared family environment after adolescence.

Much has been written about the relatively few cases of identical twins reared apart, in part because this particular adoption design is so easy to understand (e.g., Farber, 1982). If pairs of genetically identical individuals are reared in uncorrelated environments, their correlation directly estimates heritability. However, use of this design is severely hampered by the rarity of such twins—only 69 pairs have been reported. Moreover, the usefulness of the major studies of identical twins reared apart is diminished from the perspective of developmental behavioral genetics by their inclusion of exceptionally wide age ranges: 11 to 59 years (Newman, Freeman, & Holzinger, 1937); 8 to 59 years (Shields, 1962); and 22 to 77 years (Juel-Nielsen, 1965). In addition, separation in these studies was not complete—the average age at separation was 16 months (with a range from 0 to 108 months) and the average age at reunion was 12 years. The data from a fourth study (Burt, 1966) are suspect (Hearnshaw, 1979) and are no longer included in summaries of behavioral genetic data (Rowe & Plomin, 1978).

The average IQ correlation for 69 pairs in the three studies is .74. There are few twin studies of comparably aged twins reared together; the three studies reviewed earlier yield an average weighted identical twin correlation of .88. Comparing the correlation of .74 for identical twins reared apart with the identical twin correlation of .88 provides dramatic evidence for the importance of genetic influence on IQ in adulthood. It is likely that the occurrence of selective placement in these studies caused the correlation of .74 to be inflated. In fact, many of the pairs were reared by biologically related individuals; typically, one was reared by the mother and the other by the mother's sister. For example, in Shields' study, only 14 of 44 pairs of separated twins were reared in unrelated families. Correcting the heritability estimate of .74 downward would make it fit better with the estimates from the other family, twin, and adoption studies in which IQ heritability in adulthood appears to be about .40 to .60. The comparison of the correlations for identical twins reared together and identical twins reared apart suggests the possibility that shared environment (including selective placement) affects twin resemblance in adulthood, although, as mentioned earlier, this modest influence of shared environment may be limited to twins.

Studies of twins reared apart are currently being conducted in the United States (the Minnesota Study of Twins Reared Apart; Bouchard, 1984) and in Sweden (Pedersen, Friberg, Floderus-Myrhed, McClearn, & Plomin, 1984). These newer studies promise to add substantially to the quantity and quality of the literature on twins reared apart. A preliminary analysis of the Minnesota study data on 29 pairs of identical twins reared apart, whose average age at testing was 36, yielded a twin correlation of .58 for Raven's Progressive Matrices. Comparison data for 71 pairs of identical twins and 42 pairs of fraternal twins yielded correlations of .66 and .19, respectively.

In the Swedish study, cognitive data have been analyzed for 34 pairs of fraternal twins whose average age was 59 and who had been separated before the age of 10 (76% were separated by 5 years; Pedersen, McClearn, Plomin, & Friberg, 1985). A measure of general cognitive ability, an unrotated first principal component score based on 12 cognitive tests, yielded a twin correlation of .52 for the fraternal twins reared apart, after the effects of age, age at separation, and differences in the twins' degree of separation (e.g., amount of post-separation contact) were partialed out. This correlation is similar to the correlation for fraternal twins reared together and suggests substantial genetic influence on IQ in middle age, although conclusions concerning the precise amount of genetic influence cannot be made because the 95% confidence interval for a correlation of .52 is from .19 to .75 for this small sample. An additional finding of interest is that the index of degree of separation, as well as age at separation, is not related to twin differences—this implies that sharing the same environment for a longer time early in life has little impact on individual differences in IQ in middle age.

Individual cases of identical twins reared apart are sometimes used to argue for the importance of environmental influences. Most often cited in this regard is the case of Gladys and Helen from the Newman et al. (1937) study. Their rearing environments were strikingly different, and the twins differed by 24 IQ points on the Stanford-Binet test. However, it is seldom noted that they differed by only eight points on the Otis IQ test. Also rarely considered is the fact that substantial IQ differences are sometimes found for pairs living in quite similar circumstances; these cases speak just as strongly for environmental influence on IQ. For example, Mabel and Mary were both brought up on farms in Ohio and visited each other frequently, and yet they differed by 17 IQ points on the Stanford-Binet and 14 IQ points on the Otis. Undoubtedly, the environment can make a difference in IQ—differences within pairs of identical twins provide some of the best evidence for this. If environmental variation accounts for about half of the IQ variance on the average, we would expect that environments that differ in their IQ-relevant characteristics by two standard deviations could produce a difference of 15 IQ points between the members of an identical twin pair reared apart in these two environments. However, the substantial influence of heredity on IQ variation is not denied when environmental influence is found.

Specific Cognitive Abilities

As indicated in the previous chapter, it appears that genetic influence increases during adolescence for specific cognitive abilities as well as for IQ. The data on childhood and adolescence suggest less genetic influence on tests of memory than on measures of other specific cognitive abilities such as verbal and spatial skills. Are similar trends seen in the data on specific cognitive abilities in adulthood?

Family Studies

An early family study of vocabulary and arithmetic computation included 108 families with test data on both parents and one or more children from late adolescence through early adulthood (Carter, 1932a). Mean parent-offspring correlations were .22 for vocabulary and .13 for arithmetic; correlations for 111 sibling pairs were .34 and .21, respectively. However, the author suggested that restriction of range lowered the familial correlations for these two tests. The vocabulary tests showed greater familial resemblance than did the arithmetic test, a finding that has emerged from later family studies as well. However, because this was a family study, family environment rather than heredity could be responsible for the greater familial resemblance for verbal tests.

The Hawaii Family Study of Cognition.   The most important family study of specific cognitive abilities is the Hawaii Family Study of Cognition (DeFries et al., 1976, 1979) which was introduced in the previous section on IQ. Fifteen tests of cognitive abilities assessing four major factors of cognition—verbal, spatial, perceptual speed, and memory—were administered to 6,581 individuals in 1,816 intact nuclear families in Hawaii. The families consisted of both biological parents (35 to 55 years old) and one or more children (13 to 33 years old).

Regressions of offspring on midparent for the four factors and for the 15 constituent tests that load on these factors are described in Fig. 12.1 separately for 830 Caucasian families and 305 Japanese families (DeFries et al., 1979). The most obvious fact is that familial resemblance differs for the various tests and factors. These data were corrected for test unreliability so that the differences in familiality are not caused by reliability differences among the tests. For both ethnic groups, the verbal and spatial factors show more familial resemblance than do the perceptual speed and memory factors.

Insufficient attention has been given to the fact that cognitive tests involve unique variance not explained by IQ or by major ability factors. That is, although spatial tests, for example, intercorrelate with other spatial tests, the correlations do not account for the majority of the reliable variance of the spatial tests. From a behavioral genetic perspective, the important point is that the low-level phenotypic correlations among spatial tests that lead us to talk about a spatial factor steals the spotlight from the majority of the variance that is unique and that might involve different etiologies. Figure 12.1 shows dramatic differences in familial resemblance for tests within each factor. For example, one test of spatial ability, Paper Form Board, yields one of the highest midparent-offspring regressions of all of the cognitive tests in both ethnic groups. However, another spatial test, Elithorn Mazes, shows a midparent-offspring regression that is only half the size of the regression for Paper Form Board. When such different results are averaged on a spatial ability factor, the familiality for spatial ability appears moderate. The divergence of results for spatial tests may be responsible for the lack of agreement among studies in the level of familiality for spatial ability (DeFries, Vandenberg, & McClearn, 1976). In contrast, the three major HFSC tests of verbal ability—Vocabulary, Word Beginnings and Endings, and

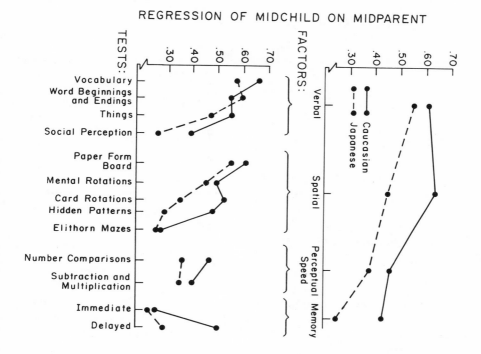

FIG. 12.1.   Regressions of midchild on midparent for four cognitive factors and 13 tests from the Hawaii Family Study of Cognition (data from DeFries et al., 1979).

Things—show substantial familiality. This may be the reason why most studies indicate that the greatest familial similarity occurs for verbal ability.

The midparent-offspring regressions for the composite scores for spatial, verbal, perceptual speed, and memory have been reported separately by age of the offspring (DeFries et al., 1979), as shown in Table 12.2. It is interesting that spatial ability shows an increase in familial resemblance that could be due to increased genetic influence or, less likely, to increased shared family environmental influence. However, this age trend in parent-offspring resemblance for spatial ability was not found to be statistically significant when the trend was tested using hierarchical multiple regression procedures described in chapter 3. There is a hint of decreasing familial resemblance for verbal ability after adolescence—the average parent-offspring regression from 13 to 16 is .54, whereas the average regression for offspring 17 and older is .45. However, perceptual speed and memory show little change in familial resemblance during this time frame.

Parent-offspring cross-correlations among the tests were analyzed in order to

TABLE 12.2
Regressions of Single Offspring on Midparent in the Hawaii
Family Study of Cognition as a Function of Offspring Age
(DeFries et al., 1979)

Composite	Age of Offspring					
	13–14	*15*	*16*	*17*	*18–19*	*20 +*
Spatial	.50	.51	.59	.69	.76	.67
Verbal	.50	.57	.56	.39	.52	.43
Perceptual Speed	.42	.36	.44	.48	.45	.47
Memory	.25	.34	.39	.26	.39	.36
Number of families	240	303	239	200	180	175

explore whether familial factors (either genetic or environmental) have broad, systematic influences across a wide range of specific cognitive abilities or whether different factors affect different abilities (DeFries, Kuse, & Vandenberg, 1979). That is, rather than calculating parent-offspring correlations for their scores on the same tests, correlations between parental scores on each of the 15 tests, and offspring scores on the other 14 tests were calculated. When this matrix of parent-offspring cross-correlations was submitted to factor analysis, the same four cognitive ability factors emerged: verbal, spatial, perceptual speed, and memory. These findings suggest that the genetic and family environmental influences salient to specific cognitive abilities are neither very broad nor idiosyncratic in their effect. Rather, there are several sets of familial influences that to some extent are grouped according to verbal, spatial, perceptual speed, and memory skills. Multivariate analysis of the covariance among traits represents an important direction for future behavioral genetic research in order to explore the etiology of the covariance among traits rather than merely analyzing the variance of traits considered one at a time (Plomin & DeFries, 1979).

Sibling correlations are also available for 455 Caucasian pairs and 147 Japanese pairs in the HFSC. The sibling correlations for the 15 tests and four composites are presented in Table 12.3. Correlations between single parents and single offspring are also included in the table for purposes of comparison with the sibling correlations and with results of other studies, which are usually reported in terms of single parent-offspring correlations. (Figure 12.1 depicts midparent-midoffspring regressions corrected for unreliability.) The sibling correlations are remarkably similar to the parent-offspring correlations. For the Caucasian families, the average parent-offspring correlation for the 15 tests is .22 and the average sibling correlation is .21. For the Japanese families, the parent-offspring and sibling correlations are .19 and .21, respectively. Siblings will be more similar than parents and offspring if nonadditive genetic variance is important or if siblings share family environment to a greater extent than do parents and their

TABLE 12.3
Correlations Between Single Parent and Single Child and Between Siblings for
Cognitive Tests and Factors in Two Ethnic Groups from the Hawaii Family Study
of Cognition (DeFries et al., 1979)

Tests and Factors	Caucasian		Japanese	
	Parent–Offspring	Sibling	Parent–Offspring	Sibling
Vocabulary	.32	.34	.36	.36
Word Beginnings and Endings	.23	.28	.22	.27
Things	.22	.20	.19	.25
Social Perception	.13	.12	.15	.26
Paper Form Board	.31	.27	.24	.18
Mental Rotations	.21	.25	.18	.19
Card Rotations	.26	.25	.16	.29
Hidden Patterns	.27	.25	.16	.14
Elithorn Mazes	.13	.08	.14	.14
Number Comparisons	.22	.23	.19	.20
Subtraction and Multiplication	.22	.31	.16	.29
Immediate Visual Memory	.08	.09	.08	− .03
Delayed Visual Memory	.16	.15	.09	.06
Pedigrees	.29	.22	.28	.22
Progressive Matrices	.26	.18	.20	.29
Verbal Composite	.28	.28	.35	.40
Spatial Composite	.33	.30	.25	.28
Perceptual Speed Composite	.25	.30	.15	.28
Visual Memory Composite	.14	.17	.09	.02
Number of Pairs	2,715	455	970	147

children. Thus, neither of these factors appears to be important for adult cognition. Furthermore, the HFSC siblings would be more similar than parents and offspring if genetic change or changes in the influence of shared environment occured from early adulthood (the age of the offspring and siblings) to middle adulthood (the age of the parents). Thus, these findings suggest that change in these factors on cognitive abilities is minimal during adulthood unless one factor increases and the other decreases.

Other Family Studies. Specific cognitive ability factors similar to those in the HFSC were examined in a study of 192 families in Israel in which the offspring were 17 years old on average (Loehlin, Sharan, & Jacoby, 1978). Parent-offspring correlations for the factors were .24 for a composite of two verbal tests, .30 for a composite of four spatial tests, .17 for two perceptual speed measures, and .23 for two numerical computation tests. Memory was not assessed. For 192 sibling pairs, the correlations for the four composites were .36, .39, .35, and .31, respectively. The comparable single parent-offspring correlations in the HFSC for verbal, spatial, and perceptual speed factors are .28, .33, and .25, respectively; the comparable HFSC sibling correlations for these three factors are .28, .30, and .30. Thus, the results of the two studies are quite comparable, although the sibling correlations in the Israeli study tend to be higher than in the Hawaiian study. The congruence between the studies is particularly remarkable because the Israeli sample was highly selected in that several thousand families were invited to participate in order to obtain the sample of 192 families when the Arab-Israeli war was in progress. In both studies, the results for the composite scales show little evidence of differential familiality. However, memory, which shows the lowest familiality, was not assessed in the Israeli study; furthermore, the individual tests show a substantial range of familial resemblance.

Several family studies of spatial ability were inspired by a family study in the early 1960s (Stafford, 1961) that revealed a pattern of parent-offspring correlations suggestive of sex-linked, recessive inheritance. The fact that the average performance of males on spatial tests is better than that of females is consistent with this hypothesis because males have only one X chromosome. Phenotypic expression of a recessive allele located on the X chromosome requires that the same allele be present on both X chromosomes for females; however, males will display the trait if the allele is present on their single X chromosome. The hallmark of sex-linked, recessive inheritance is that father-son resemblance is low because fathers give their sons only the Y chromosome; the X chromosome comes from their mothers. In addition, a sex-linked, recessive characteristic should show the highest correlations for mother-son and father-daughter pairs; mother-daughter correlations should fall between the father-son and the other parent-offspring correlations. Similarly, for siblings, the pattern of correlations from lowest to highest should be brother-sister, brother-brother, and sister-sister. This is the pattern of parent-offspring correlations found by Stafford, and some support for the hypothesis has come from other studies (Bock & Kolakowski, 1973; Hartlage, 1970; Yen, 1975).

Just as this hypothesis of a major gene for spatial ability began to find its way into textbooks, the results of several large studies using a number of spatial tests failed to support the hypothesis. For example, for the spatial factor score in the HFSC, parent-offspring correlations for Caucasian families are .33, .38, .29, and .31 for father-son, mother-daughter, mother-son, and father-daughter comparisons, respectively. For the Japanese families, the correlations are .26, .22, .20, and .32, respectively. The brother-sister, brother-brother, and sister-sister correlations are .36, .29, and .25, respectively, for Caucasian families, and .39, .17, and .29 in Japanese families. When the same spatial test used in the original study by Stafford was administered to a subsample of the HFSC families, analyses revealed a similar lack of replication (Corley, DeFries, Kuse,

& Vandenberg, 1980). Other studies also have consistently failed to support the hypothesis that spatial ability is influenced by a major gene on the X chromosome (Bouchard & McGee, 1977; Loehlin et al., 1978). In retrospect, it seems unlikely that a single major gene will exert a noticeable effect in the population for a trait as complex as spatial ability.

These family studies are nonetheless useful in documenting strong familial resemblance for spatial ability. The weighted average parent-offspring correlation is .20 for 296 families in three of the early studies (Bock & Kolakowski, 1973; Hartlage, 1970; Stafford, 1961). In a study of 200 college students and their families, the average parent-offspring correlation was .19 (Bouchard & McGee, 1977), which is lower than the parent-offspring correlations found in the HFSC. The average correlation for siblings in the study by Bouchard and McGee was .35.

In summary, family studies yield evidence of familial resemblance for specific cognitive abilities. These studies, especially the Hawaii Family Study of Cognition, also suggest that verbal and spatial factors show greater familiality than do perceptual speed and memory factors. Moreover, at the level of individual tests rather than group factors, familial resemblance, independent of reliability, varies widely. Because familial resemblance can be brought about by heredity or by family environment, twin and adoption studies are needed to determine the extent to which genetic and environmental influences are responsible for differential familiality of specific cognitive abilities.

Twin Studies

As mentioned earlier, a study of adult twins in Norway used the individually administered Wechsler Adult Intelligence Scale (WAIS; Tambs, Sundet, & Magnus, 1984). The results for the WAIS scales are presented in Table 12.4. Heritability is substantially greater for verbal IQ than for performance IQ; shared family environment has a negligible effect on verbal IQ. The same pattern of results is seen for the individual verbal and performance tests. Verbal tests show large differences between identical and fraternal twin correlations—too large, in that the fraternal twin correlations are less than half the identical twin correlations, which suggests a possible influence of epistasis. Performance tests generally show smaller differences; for one subtest, Picture Completion, the difference between the correlations for identical and fraternal twins is nonsignificant. Unlike the studies reviewed previously, memory as assessed by the Digit Span test shows substantial genetic influence; however, with a sample size of 40 pairs of each type of twin, the heritability estimate of 60% entails a standard error of 34%.

A longitudinal Swedish study of twins (Fischbein, 1981) mentioned in chapter 11 assessed verbal ability and inductive reasoning at 12 and at 18 years of age. At 12 years, identical and fraternal twin correlations were .70 and .60,

TABLE 12.4
Twin Correlations for the Wechsler Adult Intelligence Scale
(Tambs et al., 1984)

| | Twin Correlations | |
	Identical 40 pairs	Fraternal 40 pairs
Information	.82	.46
Comprehension	.81	.33
Arithmetic	.67	.27
Similarities	.71	.34
Digit Span	.63	.33
Vocabulary	.87	.27
Digit Symbol	.80	.50
Picture Completion	.39	.30
Block Design	.69	.42
Picture Arrangement	.56	.26
Object Assembly	.69	.48
Verbal IQ	.88	.42
Performance IQ	.79	.51

respectively, for verbal ability; for inductive reasoning, the twin correlations were .60 and .45. At 18 years, the twin correlations were .85 and .50 for verbal ability and .80 and .55 for inductive reasoning. Thus, these data suggest increasing genetic influence from adolescence to early adulthood for inductive reasoning and, especially, for verbal ability. Also, the results in adulthood are similar to those of the Norwegian study in suggesting greater genetic influence for verbal than for nonverbal tests—the heritabilities in the Swedish study were .70 and .50, respectively.

In an earlier cross-sectional twin study in Sweden, three verbal tests—synonyms, concept discrimination, and following verbal directions—were administered to a sample of male military recruits whose average age was 19 (Husén, 1959). For 269 identical twin pairs and 532 fraternal twin pairs, respectively, the correlations were .83 and .68 for synonyms, .74 and .61 for concept discrimination, and .83 and .59 for following verbal directions. Compared to the other Swedish study, these results suggest lower average heritability (34%) for verbal tests. A nonverbal test of inductive reasoning, similar to Raven's Progressive Matrices, yielded twin correlations of .63 for identical twins and .52 for fraternal twins, indicating even lower heritability than for the verbal tests.

An English study mentioned earlier employed a vocabulary test and Raven's Progressive Matrices in a study of 40 pairs of identical twins and 45 pairs of fraternal twins whose ages ranged from 16 to 55 (Canter, 1973). For vocabulary, the identical and fraternal twin correlations were .85 and .68, respectively; for

Progressive Matrices, the correlations were .68 and .46. These results are similar to those of Husén, although the heritability for the vocabulary test is not greater than that for the nonverbal test. Twin correlations were also presented separately for twins younger than 21 and 21 and over. Although the results suggest that heritability declines for Progressive Matrices and remains unchanged for vocabulary, the small sample size (about 20 pairs in each group) attenuates the credibility of this analysis.

One of the best studies of specific cognitive abilities in young adults was conducted in Finland (Partanen, Bruun, & Markkanen, 1966). The sample, 157 pairs of identical twins and 189 pairs of fraternal twins, included all male twin pairs born between 1920 and 1929 who were military recruits at the average age of 19. The twin results presented in Table 12.5 suggest moderate genetic influence (about 50% heritability) and moderate shared family environmental influence (about 25% of the total variance). Spatial tests show substantial genetic influence, but family environment has little effect. The biggest discrepancy with family studies is for the memory tests. The Finnish study yields heritabilities of .68 and .58 for the two memory tests (and no influence of shared environment). In contrast, for example, the average HFSC parent-offspring and sibling correlations for memory tests are about .15, which suggests an upper limit heritability estimate of .30. As usual, it is difficult to interpret discrepant results because different designs, tests, and populations were employed. In this particular case, the two memory tests were immediate and delayed versions of a test of memory for names; this semantic content might involve more verbal ability than do other tests such as memory for digits or pictures. Similar results emerged in a study of adolescent twins (Schoenfeldt, 1968) described in chapter 11.

Adoption Studies

An adoption study of adults was conducted in Minnesota by Scarr and Weinberg (1978b). As described earlier, the results suggested substantial heritability for IQ. Only a minor role for shared environment was implied by the adoptive parent-adoptee correlation of .12, and no shared environment at all was suggested by the adoptive sibling correlation of -.03. Results of this important study were reported separately for four subscales of the WAIS, as shown in Table 12.6. For all four subtests, the nonadoptive correlations are greater than the adoptive correlations, suggesting genetic influence. For vocabulary, significant adoptive family correlations suggest some shared environmental influence, although shared environment appears to be of negligible importance for the other WAIS subscales. This latter finding suggests that, although shared environment generally appears to play a minor role in cognitive abilities after adolescence, cognitive measures that rely heavily on vocabulary skills may show evidence of shared environmental influence. However, the study of adolescent adoptive

TABLE 12.5
Twin Correlations for Tests of Specific Cognitive Abilities
(Partanen et al., 1966)

| | | Twin Correlations | |
| | | Identical 157 pairs | Fraternal 189 pairs |
Cognitive Ability	Test		
Verbal	Verbal Opposites	.75	.51
	Word Fluency	.81	.54
Spatial	Rotated Squares	.58	.33
	Paper Form Board	.60	.39
Perceptual Speed	Addition/Subtraction	.73	.55
	Find Largest Number	.72	.45
Memory	Memory for Names	.69	.35
	Delayed Memory	.58	.29

TABLE 12.6
Correlations for Four WAIS Subscales for Adoptive and Nonadoptive
Families (Scarr & Weinberg, 1978)

| | Adoptive Family Correlation | | | Nonadoptive Family Correlation | | |
WAIS Subscale	Father–Offspring	Mother–Offspring	Sibling	Father–Offspring	Mother–Offspring	Sibling
Arithmetic	.07	−.03	−.03	.30	.24	.24
Vocabulary	.24	.23	.11	.39	.33	.22
Block Design	.02	.13	.09	.32	.29	.25
Picture Arrangement	−.04	−.01	.04	.06	.19	.16
Number of Pairs	175	184	84	270	270	168

siblings described in the previous chapter (Kent, 1985) showed no more shared environment for verbal tests including vocabulary than for other cognitive tests. Moreover, the Norwegian twin study (Tambs et al., 1984) revealed no influence of shared environment for WAIS vocabulary. Another discrepancy exists between the two studies: The Norwegian study suggests substantial genetic influence for Picture Arrangement, whereas the Minnesota study does not. However, it is not too surprising to find different results given the different ages (30 to 57 years in the Norwegian study and 16 to 22 in the Minnesota study), the different designs (twin vs. adoption), and the different countries (Norway vs. the United States).

The ongoing Minnesota study of identical twins separated in infancy has obtained twin correlations for Raven's Progressive Matrices and a vocabulary test for 29 pairs tested at the average age of 36 (Bouchard, 1984). The separated

TABLE 12.7
Correlations for Separated Fraternal Twins for Cognitive Abilities
with Age, Age at Separation and Degree of Separation Partialed Out
(Pedersen, McClearn, Plomin, & Friberg, 1985)

Cognitive Ability	Factor Score or Test	Twin Correlation 29 pairs
Verbal/		
Perceptual Speed	Factor score	.18
	Word Beginnings	.38
	Pedigrees	.14
	Identical Pictures	.27
	Vocabulary	.28
	Number Comparisons	.24
Spatial	Factor score	.30
	Mental Rotations	.29
	Card Rotations	.21
	Progressive Matrices	.44
Memory	Factor score	.31
	Figure Memory/Immediate	.31
	Figure Memory/Delayed	.29
	Picture Memory/Immediate	.28
	Picture Memory/Delayed	.15

identical twin correlations were .58 for Progressive Matrices and .78 for vocabulary. The Swedish study of separated fraternal twins described earlier focused on specific cognitive abilities (Pedersen, McClearn, Plomin, & Friberg, 1985). Table 12.7 lists twin correlations for 34 pairs of twins separated at 9 years of age or earlier and tested at the average age of 59 on 12 cognitive tests. Effects of degree of separation (including age at separation) were removed from these twin correlations so that twin similarity is not due to these environmental factors. Three factors rather than the usual four were found: Verbal and perceptual speed tests merged on a single factor for these middle-aged individuals. The correlation for the spatial factor, and the memory factor suggest substantial genetic influence. The verbal/perceptual speed factor and its tests yield evidence for moderate genetic effects.

One of the few conclusions that can be drawn from these scattered studies using different designs, different measures, and different populations is that genetic factors account for a substantial amount of genetic variance in specific cognitive abilities in adulthood. If anything, genetic influence increases during adulthood, which is noteworthy given that a simple environmental model would predict less genetic influence as individuals are subjected to ever-increasing experiential differences during their progression through the life span. Whether some specific cognitive abilities are more heritable than others is a question that remains for future research; however, individual tests should be examined as well as composite scores. A possible age trend suggested by the large-scale Hawaii Family Study of Cognition is increasing familial resemblance for spatial ability from adolescence through early adulthood; also, some evidence suggests that shared environment continues to influence vocabulary scores (but little else) in early adulthood. The fact that the Hawaii study yields sibling correlations that are virtually identical to parent-offspring correlations implies that developmental changes from early adulthood to middle age may not be dramatic—unless, as seems possible, increasing genetic influence is counterbalanced by decreasing influence of shared environment.

Other Cognitive Skills

Information-processing variables have rarely been included in behavioral genetic studies of cognition. However, the Minnesota Study of Twins Reared Apart incorporated three classic information-processing tasks in its study of 34 pairs of identical twins reared apart whose average age at testing was 36: Posner letter identification, Sternberg memory search, and Shepard-Metzler cube rotation. As reported by McGue, Bouchard, Lykken, and Feuer (1984), a principal component analysis of 12 scores obtained from these three tasks suggested three factors: overall speed of response, speed of information processing, and spatial processing. The three factors correlated -.31, -.32, and -.14 with WAIS IQ. The three correlations for the identical twins reared apart were .46, .13, and .20, respectively, suggesting substantial genetic influence on overall speed of response. Individual measures of speed of response also indicated substantial genetic influence. The correlations for physical identity and name identity on the Posner letter identification task and for positive and negative intercept measures were .56, .60, .32, and .37, respectively. It is noteworthy that none of the measures of speed of cognitive processing, measures that are of primary theoretical concern in the information-processing tasks, showed significant correlations for identical twins reared apart. Although these results could be interpreted to mean that the genetic component in information-processing tasks merely involves motor speed, the fact that the speed of response factor correlates as highly with IQ as does the speed of information processing factor suggests that the speed of response factor assesses more than motor speed. Others have argued that speed factors in information-processing tasks are essentially cognitive (Sternberg & Gardner, 1982).

Another aspect of cognition that has received little attention is creativity. As indicated in the previous chapter, a few twin studies of adolescence suggest that heredity has little effect on individual differences in creativity. A study of adult twins from 16 to 55 years (44 identical and 51 fraternal twin pairs) employed five tests of creativity (Canter, 1973). Only one of the five tests, Word Associations, showed a significantly greater correlation for identical than for fraternal twins.

Word Associations involves a list of 25 words with multiple meanings; the subject lists as many meanings as possible. Although this is a type of divergent thinking that is the hallmark of creativity, the task appears to be linked to verbal fluency and vocabulary. Indeed, of the five creativity tests, Word Associations correlates most highly with IQ. For all five tests of creativity, the higher the correlation with IQ, the more evidence is found for genetic influence, leading to the conclusion that creativity tests display little evidence of genetic influence independent of IQ. The same study included tests of "conceptual thinking"—tests in which subjects are asked to arrange, classify, or select stimulus material according to a number of concepts—in order to assess cognitive processes such as overinclusion and overexclusion that are characteristic of abnormal thought processes found in schizophrenia. Little evidence of genetic influence emerged for these measures.

Vocational Interests

In between cognition and personality lies the domain of vocational interests. Carter (1932b) found median correlations of .50 and .28 for identical and fraternal twins, respectively, for the Strong Vocational Interest Blank. Similar results suggestive of substantial influence of heredity and little influence of shared environment also emerged in a study by Vandenberg and Kelly (1964).

Three recent studies are especially noteworthy. Scholastic achievement data for twins from the National Merit Scholarship Qualifying Test (Loehlin & Nichols, 1976) were discussed in the previous chapter because the tests were given when the twins were juniors and seniors in high school. However, extensive questionnaire data were obtained during the year after graduation from high school when the twins were at least 17 years old. Among these questionnaires was the Holland Vocational Preference Inventory. A cluster analysis of the 160 items yielded 22 clusters of occupational interests. Median correlations for these clusters for over 800 twin pairs were .36 for identical twins and .19 for fraternal twins; none of the individual scales yielded results much different from these averages. An even larger sample of twins (over 1,500 pairs) from the same NMSQT population was administered the Strong Vocational Interest Blank (Roberts & Johansson, 1974). In this study, the twin correlations—.51 for identical twins and .27 for fraternal twins—were greater than those for the Holland measure reported by Loehlin and Nichols (1976).

In Table 12.8, the results of these two twin studies are summarized in terms of Holland's (1966) six interest styles. Although both studies suggest significant genetic influence on vocational interests, the studies do not agree concerning relative heritabilities. For example, Realistic Orientation yields the lowest heritability estimate in the study by Loehlin and Nichols and the highest heritability in the study by Roberts and Johansson. Because the samples are so

TABLE 12.8
Vocational Interest Correlations for Twins (Loehlin & Nichols, 1976;
Roberts & Johansson, 1974) and for Adoptive and Nonadoptive
Parents and Offspring (Scarr & Weinberg, 1978a)

| Vocational Type | Twin Correlations | | | | Parent-Offspring Correlations | |
| | Loehlin | | Roberts | | Scarr | |
	Identical	Fraternal	Identical	Fraternal	Nonadoptive	Adoptive
Realistic	.32	.28	.53	.21	.20	.12
Intellectual	.45	.31	.52	.28	.14	.06
Social	.43	.19	.50	.26	.22	.08
Enterprising	.41	.22	.42	.27	.19	.05
Conventional	.33	.16	.55	.30	.17	.07
Artistic	.41	.22	.55	.31	.10	.08
Number of pairs	507	328	979	607	120	115

large, these differences are important and are apparently due to the use of different measures of vocational interest.

Table 12.8 also compares the twin results to vocational interest results from the Minnesota study of adoptees aged 16 to 22 years (Scarr & Weinberg, 1978a). The results for the Strong Vocational Interest Blank are similar for the six Holland vocational types in suggesting moderate genetic influence and negligible influence of shared family environment. The adoption data suggest a lower estimate of heritability than do the twin data, and they do not agree with either twin study in terms of which interests show greater genetic influence. For example, in both twin studies, the correlations for Artistic Interest suggest substantial genetic influence; the adoption study, however, finds the lowest heritability estimate for Artistic Interest. All three studies agree that shared family environment is unimportant. The adoption study provides a direct estimate: The average correlation in adoptive families is .08, suggesting that shared family environment accounts for less than 10% of the variance in vocational interests.

Personality

In his book, *English Men of Science: Their Nature and Nurture*, Galton (1874) rated such personality traits as energy, perseverance, truthfulness, and even "taste for science," although his abiding interest was in the study of abilities. Galton saw evidence of familial resemblance for personality characteristics;

however, half a century passed before scientifically adequate research on personality was conducted.

As discussed in the previous chapter on adolescence, the few studies of personality as assessed by self-report questionnaires consistently point to moderate heritability. However, findings of significant genetic influence on all personality traits raise the issue of lack of differential heritability. It was suggested that the failure to find differential heritability may be due to the pervasiveness of the superfactors of neuroticism and extraversion. These two traits are related to emotionality and sociability, respectively. Together with activity level, which is seldom assessed in personality questionnaires, they constitute the EAS traits, the focus of our review of personality research. Although there have not been many behavioral genetic studies of personality in adulthood, a few large studies have been reported.

Family Studies

The first family study of personality traits in adults was reported by Starch in 1917. In one of the best early studies (Crook, 1937), college students, their siblings, and their parents were administered the Bernreuter Personality Inventory. Three scales of the Bernreuter were scored: neuroticism, dominance, and self-sufficiency. The average parent-offspring correlations for the three scales were .29, .22, and .15, respectively, for 267 pairs. Parent-offspring correlations were not noticeably different for younger and older offspring. The average sibling correlations for the three scales were .23, .15, and .17, respectively. Considered together, these data suggest that the average correlation for first-degree relatives is about .20. Of course, familial resemblance could be mediated environmentally or genetically; however, as we shall see, twin data suggest that about 40% of the variance on self-report personality measures is genetic. This implies that the correlation of .20 for first-degree relatives for personality comes about because of shared heredity, not shared environment.

The results of these early studies are similar to those obtained more recently. Most notable are the personality results from the Hawaii Family Study of Cognition (HFSC), which employed several personality questionnaires (Ahern, Johnson, Wilson, McClearn, & Vandenberg, 1982). Fifty-four scales from four personality questionnaires (Adjective Checklist, Eysenck Personality Inventory, the Comrey Personality Scales, and Cattell's Sixteen Personality Factor Questionnaire) were administered to various subsamples of the HFSC varying from 3,121 individuals in 669 families to 395 individuals in 100 families. The average age of the offspring was 17. Results of this study are summarized in Table 12.9 according to the probable placement of scales in the EAS system. This summary points to a major problem in the study of personality: its diversity. Of the 54 scales, only 7 appear relevant to the EAS categorization. Scales not listed in

Table 12.9 include a bewildering array of interesting traits such as heterosexuality, abasement, deference, rebelliousness, empathy, happy-go-lucky, suspicious, imaginative, anomie, and sensation-seeking. For the 54 scales, the average parent-offspring correlation was .12 and the average sibling correlation was also .12. The EAS correlations in Table 12.9 center around this average, thus providing little evidence that the EAS traits show greater familial resemblance than do other measures. Even if the HFSC familial resemblance were due entirely to heredity rather than to shared environment, the family data would suggest an upper-limit estimate of only 24% heritability. However, it should be kept in mind that familial resemblance primarily involves additive genetic variance, whereas twin study estimates of genetic influence include nonadditive genetic variance as well.

A few surprising exceptions to the general rule of low familial resemblance emerged from the HFSC data. The Lie scale of the EPI yielded the greatest familial resemblance, .50 for parents and offspring and .38 for siblings. This is unexpected because the Lie scale is usually used merely to assess whether individuals are ''faking good,'' and the results for the scale are seldom reported. One twin study suggests that familial resemblance for a lie scale is due to shared environment (Wilde, 1964). Another factor that showed greater than usual familial resemblance is social conformity as assessed by the CPS; the parent-offspring correlation was .23 and the sibling correlation was .37.

Familial resemblance in the HFSC is somewhat lower than that found in other

TABLE 12.9
Familial Correlations for Personality from the Hawaii Family Study
of Cognition (Ahern, Johnson, Wilson, McClearn, &
Vandenberg, 1982)[a]

Personality Test and Scale	Parent–Offspring	Sibling
Emotionality		
EPI neuroticism	.17	.07
CPS neuroticism	.07	.13
16 PF emotional stability	.17	.17
Activity		
CPS activity	.20	.03
Sociability		
ACL need for affiliation	.11	.08
EPI extraversion	− .05	.25
CPS extraversion	.25	.03
16 PF outgoing	.10	.01
16 PF shy	.13	.09

[a]ACL = Adjective Checklist (N = 1,710 parent-offspring and 556 sibling pairs); EPI = Eysenck Personality Inventory (N = 1,183 parent-offspring and 404 sibling pairs); CPS = Comrey Personality Scales (N = 321 parent-offspring and 90 sibling pairs); 16 PF = Cattell's Sixteen Personality Factor Questionnaire (N = 275 parent-offspring and 77 sibling pairs).

studies. For example, a study of 589 individuals in 98 families in England with offspring whose median age was 17 years found parent-offspring correlations of .21 and .24 for neuroticism and extraversion, respectively, using an earlier version of the EPI; sibling correlations were .34 and .27 (Insel, 1974). Data on second-degree relatives are quite rare for personality, but this study found grandparent-grandchild correlations of .21 and .12 for the two scales. Despite the higher correlations than in the HFSC, data from this study confirm the HFSC finding of substantial familiality for the Lie scale, yielding correlations of .31 for parents and offspring and .30 for siblings. A conservatism scale included in this study yielded parent-offspring and sibling correlations of .57 and .42, respectively. Assortative mating correlations are typically low for personality— near zero in this study for extraversion and neuroticism: however, for conservatism, the spouse correlation was .66. This result may be related to the HFSC finding with regard to social conformity and deserves further attention.

It should be noted that both of these studies involved offspring who were young adults. There have been no family studies in which all family members were middle-aged.

Twin Studies

It is possible that nonadditive effects of genes are responsible for the low familial personality correlations for first-degree relatives. If nonadditive genetic variance is important, siblings—who share a quarter of nonadditive genetic variance due to dominance and small portions of other higher-order genetic interactions— should be more similar than are parents and offspring, who share only additive genetic variance. However, this is not a powerful test of nonadditive genetic variance because siblings scarcely resemble each other for genetic interactions that involve more than two loci. Identical twins, however, will be identical for any genetic interaction, no matter how complex. For this reason, twin studies are needed to detect nonadditive genetic variance: If genetic variance is nonadditive, fraternal twin correlations will be less than half the magnitude of identical twin correlations. In other words, an estimate of heritability obtained by doubling the difference between identical and fraternal twin correlations will exceed the correlation for identical twins. However, environmental factors could account for this phenomenon as well. For example, fraternal twins might be contrasted to a greater extent than are identical twins.

The most important twin study of adulthood (Floderus-Myrhed, Pedersen, & Rasmusson, 1980) involved the traits of neuroticism (emotionality) and extraversion (sociability) in a Swedish sample of 4,987 identical twin pairs and 7,790 fraternal twin pairs from 17 to 49 years of age. For the entire sample, the identical and fraternal twin correlations were .50 and .23 for neuroticism and .51 and .21 for extraversion. These results suggest that about half of the variance in emotionality and sociability is due to genetic variance, which implies that the

TABLE 12.10
Twin Correlations for Neuroticism and Extraversion for Three Age
Groups (Floderus-Myrhed, Pedersen, & Rasmusson, 1980)

	17–29 years		30–39 years		40–49 years	
	Identical	Fraternal	Identical	Fraternal	Identical	Fraternal
Neuroticism	.58	.27	.45	.22	.41	.17
Extraversion	.55	.23	.44	.18	.49	.18
Number of Pairs	2290	3536	1584	2391	1113	1863

familial resemblance described in the previous section is due exclusively to
genetic resemblance. The fact that the fraternal twin correlations were slightly
less than half the magnitude of the identical twin correlations, suggests some
nonadditive genetic variance.

Twin results were reported separately for three age groups in the Swedish
study, as shown in Table 12.10. For both neuroticism and extraversion, twin
correlations are slightly greater for the youngest group than for the two older
groups. A model-fitting approach to these data (Eaves & Young, 1981) did not
achieve a satisfactory fit with simple models, probably because the sample is so
large that slight perturbations in the data are overinterpreted. In every case, the
fraternal twin correlation is less than half the identical twin correlation, which is
consistent with the hypothesis that nonadditive genetic variance affects adult
personality.

A Finnish twin study of young adult males (157 identical and 189 fraternal
pairs) using a different questionnaire found similar results for extraversion
(identical and fraternal twin correlations of .51 and .26, respectively); but the
results for neuroticism were quite different—identical and fraternal twin were
.28 and .21, respectively (Partanen, Bruun, & Markkanen, 1966). However, the
neuroticism questions emphasized neurotic symptoms, such as perspiring and
trembling hands, rather than emotionality.

British researchers have focused on neuroticism and extraversion because of
Eysenck's extensive research on these two traits (e.g., Eysenck, 1981). For
example, a study of 40 identical and 45 fraternal twin pairs from 16 to 55 years
with a mean age of 21 included the Eysenck Personality Inventory as well as
Cattell's Sixteen Personality Factor Questionnaire (Canter, 1973). The results for
both neuroticism and extraversion were different from those of the Swedish
study: For neuroticism, identical and fraternal twin correlations were .37 and
.23, respectively; for extraversion, the correlations were .34 and .29. However,
a sociability scale derived from the extraversion items suggested substantial
heritability: The identical twin correlation was .67 and the fraternal twin
correlation was .25. Cattell's 16 PF yielded more consistent evidence of genetic

influence: The identical and fraternal twin correlations were .36 and .06 for 16 PF neuroticism, .43 and .08 for 16 PF extraversion, .37 and .15 for 16 PF stability, and .58 and .30 for 16 PF shyness. Although most studies find evidence of genetic influence on extraversion, another study of 88 identical pairs and 42 fraternal pairs aged 13 to 69 years yielded correlations of .37 and .35 for the two types of twins (Wilde, 1964). In terms of the EAS theory, it is particularly noteworthy that the sociability component of extraversion showed substantial genetic influence in the study by Canter.

In a study of twins from 16 to 86 years of age (mean of 31 years), twin correlations for neuroticism were .47 and .07, respectively, for identical twins (303 pairs) and fraternal twins (172 pairs); the correlations for extraversion were .55 and .19 (Eaves & Young, 1981). The results for extraversion are quite similar to those of the Swedish study; however, both traits yielded a fraternal twin correlation that is much less than half the identical twin correlation, thus suggesting a substantial role for nonadditive genetic variance. The British work by Eaves and his colleagues has emphasized model fitting and generally has found little effect of shared environment.

One study is particularly noteworthy in that it involved, in addition to adult twins, other first-degree and second-degree family members (Eaves, 1978). On the basis of model-fitting analyses (no correlations were reported), it was concluded that age-related changes in genetic influence are important for neuroticism. In another report mentioned in the previous chapter, these data were combined with data on adolescent twins and singletons (7 to 17 years with a mean of 11 years) and their parents (Young, Eaves, & Eysenck, 1980). Using the twin data to estimate heritability in adolescence and adulthood and the parent-offspring data to estimate familial resemblance from adolescence to adulthood, model-fitting analyses suggested that consistency from adolesence to adulthood is substantially genetic in origin for neuroticism and moderately so for extraversion. However, this analysis is problematic unless one assumes that parent-offspring familiality is exclusively genetic in origin.

Analyses of the sociability component of extraversion indicate greater heritability than for the non-EAS component of extraversion, impulsivity (Eaves & Eysenck, 1975), a result similar to Canter's (1973) finding mentioned earlier. The identical and fraternal twin correlations were .49 and .18 for sociability and .35 and .15 for impulsivity for 451 pairs of identical twins and 257 pairs of fraternal twins. In a similar analysis of components of neuroticism for 316 pairs of identical twins and 196 pairs of fraternal twins (Eaves & Young, 1981), most of the components (such as depression, insomnia, and paranoia) were not relevant to the EAS conception of emotionality. However, identical and fraternal twin correlations for "worry" were .52 and .07; for a shyness component of neuroticism, the twin correlations were .39 and .00. These results suggest substantial nonadditive genetic variance.

In an interesting analysis of neuroticism assessed twice over a 2-year interval, it was found that changes in neuroticism over the 2 years, as assessed by the interaction of subjects' scores with time of testing, were due to nonshared environmental influences (Eaves & Eysenck, 1976a). However, a cross-sectional analysis of the effects of age indicated that intrapair differences in neuroticism correlate -.02 with age for identical twins and .19 with age for fraternal twins (Eaves & Eysenck, 1976b). This analysis of age changes in heritability is related to the general approach outlined in chapter 3; the fact that fraternal twins become more different with age, whereas identical twins do not, suggests increasing genetic variance for neuroticism during adulthood.

Analyses of subject × item interactions for the neuroticism items suggests that significant genetic effects on personality can be specific to items rather than to scales:

> First and foremost, [the results] suggest that genetic effects can be highly specific, even down to influencing features of an individual's response profile to items of a test. They thus challenge the view that the primary genetic effects on behaviour are organized along trait lines to the exclusion of more specific effects. In other words, it should not surprise us if there are quite distinct heritable behaviour profiles. Genes do not exercise just an undifferentiated "predisposing" effect at the gross level. (Eaves & Young, 1981)

As mentioned earlier, the NSMQT twin sample questionnaire data were obtained after the senior year of high school when the twins were at least 18 years old. For the California Psychological Inventory (CPI), the median twin correlations were .50 for identical twins (490 pairs) and .32 for fraternal twins (317 pairs). Only one of the 18 CPI scales is related to the EAS traits. CPI Sociability yielded twin correlations of .53 and .29 for identical and fraternal twins, respectively, which is not too different from the average twin correlations for the other personality traits. Several other personality questionnaires were administered in addition to the CPI, and 70 cluster scores were obtained from these items. Still, only three of these 70 clusters involved the EAS traits: The identical and fraternal twin correlations were .46 and .01 for a general shyness scale and .35 and .09 for a shyness scale specific to interactions with strangers. These correlations suggest substantial genetic influence, although the low fraternal twin correlations suggest the presence of nonadditive genetic variance. A similar pattern of results was found for the other EAS-relevant cluster—one that assessed tenseness, which might be related to emotionality; the correlations were .35 for identical twins and .09 for fraternal twins. An appendix in the monograph reporting these results lists twin results for 1,610 items included in the study (Loehlin & Nichols, 1976), which makes it useful for additional analyses. A reanalysis of items related to extraversion and neuroticism yielded evidence for greater than average heritability: The identical and fraternal twin correlations were, respectively, .61 and .25 for extraversion and .54 and .22 for neuroticism (Eaves & Young, 1981).

A study of middle-aged male twins yielded average CPI correlations of .44 and .19 for identical twins (99 pairs) and fraternal twins (99 pairs), respectively (Horn, Plomin, & Rosenman, 1976). These twin correlations are only slightly less than those for the young adults in the NMSQT sample despite the fact that the older twins were between 45 and 55 years of age and had been living apart for about 25 years. These authors also noted that one reason for the lack of differential heritability for the CPI scales is that about a quarter of the 480 CPI items are scored on more than one scale; eliminating these items yields greater evidence of differential heritability, with some scales such as Responsibility and Femininity showing zero heritability. Furthermore, item analyses, discussed later, indicated that the most heritable items are distributed evenly across the 18 CPI scales; thus, it is not surprising that twin studies using the CPI scales have found no evidence of differential heritability.

Although other twin studies of adults have not assessed EAS traits, interesting measures have been employed. For example, a newly developed omnibus personality questionnaire, Tellegen's Differential Personality Questionnaire (DPQ), has been subjected to twin analyses in a study of 231 identical and 106 fraternal twin pairs in young adulthood (Lykken, Tellegen, & DeRubeis, 1978). The 11 scales of the DPQ assess interesting traits such as well-being, stress reaction, and alienation and yield twin results similar to those of other personality questionnaires; however, the DPQ includes no analogs of the EAS traits.

A clear trend in adult twin research is the use of questionnaires focused on specific traits rather than omnibus measures of personality. For example, Zuckerman's Sensation-Seeking Scale was employed in a study of 233 identical twins and 138 fraternal twins with the average age of 31 (Fulker, Eysenck, & Zuckerman, 1980); twin correlations for sensation-seeking were .60 and .21, respectively, for identical twins (233 pairs) and fraternal twins (138 pairs). Another example is the use of the Internal-External Locus of Control scale in a study of college student twins and their families that yielded twin correlations of .46 for 50 pairs of identical twins and .18 for 59 pairs of fraternal twins; parent-offspring and sibling resemblance was similar to that of fraternal twins (Miller & Rose, 1982). Four other examples are twin analyses of Snyder's Self-Monitoring Scale (Dworkin, 1979); of Spence and Helmreich's Personal Attributes Inventory, which assesses masculinity and femininity (Rowe, 1982); of Block's measure of ego resiliency and ego control (Lykken, Tellegen, & Thorkelson, 1974); and of measures of Type A behavior (Rahe, Hervig, & Rosenman, 1978).

Another trend in twin research on personality in adulthood is the use of behavioral genetic methods to address current theoretical questions about the nature of personality. The major theoretical question during the 1970s and 1980s has been the trans-situational consistency of personality. In the 1970s, the very existence of personality was questioned—personality was thought to be lost in a tangle of situational variance. The extensive evidence of genetic influence on personality questionnaire measures should have slowed acceptance of this view; however, more to the point are studies of situational variance. An observational study of children described in chapter 10 indicated that heredity can affect profiles of responding across different situations (Matheny & Dolan, 1975). With adults, an S-R inventory that examines the effects of different situations and different modes of response was employed in a twin study of 54 pairs of identical twins and 34 pairs of fraternal twins whose average age was 30 (Dworkin, 1979). The results indicated significant genetic influence on "situation profiles" for anxiety, that is, the person-situation interactions as indexed by individuals' patterns of scores across situations. Twin correlations for situation profiles were .36 and .19, respectively, for identical and fraternal twins.

One non-EAS trait, conservatism, was singled out in the previous section on family studies because it showed the greatest familiality. The results of three twin studies (Eaves & Young, 1981) are remarkably consistent in suggesting only modest genetic influence and substantial influence of shared environment: Summarizing over the three studies, the average identical twin correlation is .67 for 894 pairs and the average fraternal twin correlation is .52 for 523 pairs. Strong familiality for lie scales also appears to be due primarily to shared environment.

Item Analyses

Personality scales constructed from phenotypic correlations among items are likely to contain items differing in heritability. For this reason, behavioral genetic analyses at the level of items are interesting. Data from an early twin study (Carter, 1935), presented in chapter 11, suggest that the most heritable items involve shyness. Similar results can be gleaned from two twin studies of adults. The NMSQT sample was used to conduct analyses of CPI items (Loehlin & Nichols, 1976). Among 16 CPI items showing high heritabilities, two are very similar to the shyness items found to be most heritable in Carter's (1935) twin study of adolescents:

"It is hard for me to start a conversation with strangers."
"I am likely not to speak to people until they speak to me."

In addition, several items that may be related to extraversion—such as showing off, talking before groups of people, wanting to be an actor, and being a leader— showed high heritabilities. Items of this type were not present in the low heritable group of items, with the possible exception of a retrospective report concerning difficulty in talking before the class in school.

Even stronger results emerged from a study of 50-year-old male twins (Horn, Plomin, & Rosenman, 1976). Cross-validation criteria were used to isolate 41 reliable CPI items that showed heritable influence. When these heritable items were submitted to factor analysis, the largest factor, accounting for 28% of the variance of the most heritable items, consisted mainly of shyness items—for example, "It is hard for me to start a conversation with strangers."

Longitudinal Analyses

Given the relative ease of administering self-report questionnaires, it is surprising to find so few longitudinal studies. A two-year follow-up study (Eaves & Eysenck, 1976a) was mentioned earlier.

The only long-term longitudinal study is a study following up 12 years later on twins tested in adolescence using the Minnesota Multiphasic Personality Inventory (MMPI) and the California Psychological Inventory (CPI; Dworkin, Burke, Maher, & Gottesman, 1976). Unfortunately, it is difficult to interpret the results of this study because the sample in adulthood included a total of only 43 pairs; few of the scales showed similar heritability in adolescence and in adulthood. Another set of analyses of these data focused on changes from adolescence to adulthood for CPI and MMPI profile scores (Dworkin, Burke, Maher, & Gottesman, 1977). The results suggested that changes in profile elevations for both the CPI and MMPI are influenced by heredity—the correlations for identical and fraternal twins, respectively, for the trend correlations were .36 and .13 for the CPI and .23 and .21 for the MMPI. Longitudinal change in profile contour, however, showed little similarity for twins. A 5-year longitudinal study of young adult twins who completed the MMPI (Pogue-Geile & Rose, 1985) is described later in this chapter.

Adoption Studies

Only two adoption studies of adult personality have been reported. Neither study obtained direct estimates of genetic influence from comparisons between biological parents and their adopted-away offspring; instead, they compared familial resemblance in adoptive and nonadoptive families. The Minnesota adoption study of adult adoptees from 16 to 22 years of age included several measures of personality for 115 adoptive families and 120 nonadoptive families (Scarr, Webber, Weinberg, & Wittig, 1981). The personality measures were chosen to assess extraversion (sociability) and neuroticism (emotionality). Midparent-offspring results (single parent-offspring results were not reported) and sibling results for adoptive and nonadoptive families are presented in Table 12.11. The results are mixed. For neuroticism and extraversion, the greater parent-offspring correlations in nonadoptive than in adoptive families suggest substantial genetic influence; the sibling results suggest similarly strong genetic influence for neuroticism but not for extraversion. Surprisingly, the social anxiety scale, which is related to shyness, shows no genetic influence for parents and offspring or for siblings; physical anxiety, however, yields evidence of genetic influence for both family relationships.

TABLE 12.11
Midparent-Offspring and Sibling Correlations in Adoptive and
Nonadoptive Families (Scarr, Webber, Weinberg, & Wittig, 1981)

Personality Measure[a]	Midparent-Offspring		Sibling	
	Adoptive	Nonadoptive	Adoptive	Nonadoptive
Emotionality				
EPI Neuroticism	.05	.25	.05	.28
APQ Social Anxiety	.17	.03	.36	.17
APQ Physical Anxiety	.06	.21	.04	.24
Sociability				
EPI Extraversion	.00	.19	.07	.06
DPQ Social Closeness	.00	.28	.13	.10

[a]EPI = Eysenck Personality Inventory; APQ = Activities Preference Questionnaire; DPQ = Differential Personality Questionnaire.

Over all the scales in this study, the median single parent-offspring correlations were .04 in adoptive families and .15 in nonadoptive families; the median sibling correlations are .07 and .20, respectively. Doubling the difference between the adoptive and nonadoptive correlations estimates heritability, which therefore is about 20% to 25%. The twin data yield fraternal twin correlations comparable to those for the nonadoptive siblings; however, identical twin correlations tend to be about .50, thus yielding estimates of heritability that are closer to 50% than 25%:

> The estimated heritabilities for the personality measures were much lower than those obtained in studies of identical and fraternal twins, which suggests that twin studies have exaggerated the degree of genetic variation in personality. (Scarr et al., 1981, p. 885)

However, another possibility is that nonadditive genetic variance is important for personality: Twin studies include nonadditive genetic variance, whereas family studies are essentially limited to revealing the effects of additive genetic variance. Scarr et al. (1981) also point out that their findings emphasize the importance of nonshared environment: "Individuals within families are vastly different in the personality characteristics we measured, and psychology has no theory to explain that individuality" (p. 897).

In this adoption study, the results for the Lie scale of the Eysenck Personality Inventory yield substantially lower familial correlations than in the studies reviewed earlier. Although the parent-offspring data suggest the possibility of genetic influence (the correlations in adoptive and nonadoptive families were .06 and .20, respectively), the sibling data agree with the twin data in suggesting that the variance is due to shared environment—sibling correlations were .26 and .18, respectively, in adoptive and nonadoptive families.

Family studies suggest that conservatism is strongly familial, and twin studies assign this familiality partly to heredity but mostly to shared environment. However, the Minnesota adoption study found strong genetic influence and little influence of shared environment for this trait (Scarr & Weinberg, 1978). A measure of authoritarian attitudes based on the California F-Scale, which assesses rigidity of belief and prejudice, was included in the study because it was assumed that it would primarily show shared environmental influence; however, the parent-offspring correlations were .07 for adoptive families and .40 for nonadoptive families. The adoptive sibling sample was too small for analysis; the nonadoptive sibling correlation was .41. The authors suggest that the reason for this surprising result is that the F- Scale correlates -.41 with vocabulary, a test that consistently yields evidence of genetic influence. Genetic influence on this dimension of authoritarianism is also suggested by data from the Minnesota study of twins reared apart; the correlation for 28 pairs of adult identical twins reared apart since infancy was .66 for authoritarianism as measured by the Differential Personality Questionnaire (Bouchard, 1984).

Similar results emerged from a recent adoption study in Texas (Loehlin, Willerman, & Horn, 1985). Data from an earlier study of adopted children of an average age of 7 years were discussed in chapter 10. The Thurstone Temperament Schedule and the California Psychological Inventory were administered to members of 220 families in which the adopted and nonadopted children were at least 14 years old. The average age of the adopted and nonadopted offspring was 18, with a range from 14 to 45 years. Average correlations of about .05 were found for adoptive parents and their adopted children as well as for adoptive siblings; correlations for nonadoptive parents and their children and for nonadoptive siblings were about .15. The results for EAS-relevant scales are presented in Table 12.12. Except for the Thurstone scale of stability, which appears to be related to emotionality, these data suggest moderate heritability for the EAS traits, about 30% on the average. The low correlations in adoptive families again point to the familiar finding that shared environment counts for little in the development of personality. Although only one of the 18 CPI scales relates to the EAS dimensions, the extraversion cluster of the CPI also yielded evidence of genetic influence: The average adoptive parent-adopted offspring correlation was .07 and the average nonadoptive parent-offspring correlation was .24. As expected from the Thurstone results for the stability scale, an emotional adjustment cluster from the CPI showed little evidence of genetic influence. Across all scales, adoptive sibling correlations averaged .02 for 123 pairs—data on only 15 pairs of nonadoptive siblings were available, so adoptive and nonadoptive sibling correlations cannot be compared. When the results of the Texas study were analyzed separately for adoptees from 14 to 19 years of age and for those from 20 to 29, no age-related difference in parent-offspring correlations could be discerned.

The most dramatic evidence for genetic influence on adult personality comes from adoption studies involving identical twins adopted apart. In two older

TABLE 12.12
Parent–Offspring Correlations in Adoptive and Nonadoptive Families
(Loehlin, Willerman, & Horn, 1985)

Personality Scale[a]	Adoptive	Nonadoptive
TTS Stable (Emotionality)	.04	.04
TTS Active	.03	.16
TTS Vigorous	.06	.33
TTS Sociable	.02	.18
CPI Sociability	.05	.18

[a]TTS = Thurstone Temperament Survey; CPI = California Psychological Inventory.

studies, identical twins reared apart were as similar as identical twins reared together for extraversion and neuroticism (Newman, Freeman, & Holzinger, 1937; Shields, 1962), which is consistent with the hypothesis that growing up in the same family with a sibling has little effect on personality resemblance. In the ongoing Minnesota Study of Twins Reared Apart, the median correlation for 28 pairs of twins reared apart is .65 for Tellegen's Differential Personality Questionnaire as compared to a correlation of .53 for identical twins reared together and .27 for fraternal twins reared together (Bouchard, 1984). A second-order factor called "negative affect" is similar to neuroticism and yields a correlation of .64 for the separated identical twins.

The study of Swedish separated twins (Pedersen et al., 1984), described earlier, is currently collecting extensive personality (as well as other biomedical and behavioral information) on its twins reared apart and matched twins reared together. However, extraversion and neuroticism questionnaires obtained earlier for a subsample of the twins reared apart yielded interesting results: For extraversion, the correlations for identical twins (36-59 pairs) and fraternal twins (121-159) reared apart were .54 and .29, respectively. A matched sample of twins reared together yielded correlations of .44 and .26—thus, again, the correlation for identical twins reared apart exceeds the correlation for identical twins reared together. For neuroticism, the correlations for both identical and fraternal twins reared apart were much lower, .18 and .01, in contrast to correlations of .37 and .18 for matched twins reared together.

Summary

The welter of personality traits, the scarcity of studies of adults, and the wide age range in adulthood combine to suggest caution in drawing any conclusions concerning genetic influence on adult personality. One thing that can be said with certainty is that familial resemblance is low, correlations of about .20 for first-degree relatives, with the exception of the attitudinal dimension of conservatism and "lie" scales. Twin studies suggest genetic influence greater than the upper-limit estimates provided by family studies; however, fairly consistent evidence emerges for the possibility of nonadditive genetic variance in that fraternal twin correlations are less than half the magnitude of identical twin correlations. Parent-offspring comparisons involve additive genetic variance alone and sibling comparisons include only a small portion of nonadditive genetic variance. Most impressive are the results of studies of identical twins reared apart, which yield correlations similar to (actually slightly greater than) the correlation for identical twins reared together. Thus, the adoption data on separated twins, although based on small samples, tend to agree with the classical twin design in pointing to substantial genetic influence, about 50% heritability. If one accepts all the data as equally valid, the best conclusion that explains the discrepancies between twin and adoption data is that nonadditive genetic variance is important for adult personality.

Shared family environment is of negligible importance, again with the possible exception of conservatism (which shows strong family environmental influence in twin studies but negligible amounts from the more direct test of the adoption design). Thus, for the most part, familial resemblance—meager as it is—is due to nature not nurture.

Concerning the EAS theory, existing evidence suggests that the sociability/shyness component of extraversion is more heritable than the impulsivity component and may be the most heritable dimension of personality. Emotionality has been primarily studied in the guise of neuroticism. These results concerning heritability are mixed, perhaps because neurotic symptoms are less heritable than is emotionality per se. Activity is rarely included in these studies.

Finally, some research suggests that it would be profitable to conduct more analyses at the level of items rather than scales.

Psychopathology

Adulthood is the only era of the life span in which there have been extensive behavioral genetic studies of psychopathology. Most of this research has focused on the psychoses, for which the age of onset occurs after adolescence. Increasingly, however, research is being conducted at the borderline between normal personality traits and psychopathology—"soft" psychopathology, including such neurotic traits as obsessions, phobias, and psychosomatic complaints.

Neuroses

A 5-year longitudinal study that employed the MMPI was conducted with a sample of 71 identical twins and 62 fraternal twins at ages 20 and 25 (Pogue-Geile & Rose, 1985). Scales derived from the MMPI items included social maladjustment, psychopathy (which, in normal samples, assesses aggressiveness and adventurousness), schizophrenia (creativity, sensitivity, and moodiness), overall adjustment (anxiety, self-confidence, and defensiveness), depression, and religiosity (included as a "control" scale expected to show shared family environmental influence). The average stability correlation over the 5 years for these six scales was .57. Twin results are presented in Table 12.13. The religiosity scale shows the expected effect of strong shared environmental influence. The other scales yielded results fairly typical of self-report personality questionnaires: The average identical and fraternal twin correlations at 20 years are .40 and .16, respectively; at 25 years, the correlations are .45 and .01. The fraternal twin correlations are lower than expected, which could be due to several factors—one of the most interesting from a genetic viewpoint is nonadditive genetic variance. A twin analysis of signed and absolute change scores over the 5-year period yielded no evidence of genetic influence; the twin correlations for change scores were low, suggesting that change is governed by nonshared environmental influences.

An interesting model-fitting multivariate analysis explored the relationship between obsessional traits and neuroticism in a study of 404 pairs of twins from 16 to 70 years of age with the average age of 31 (Clifford, Fulker, & Murray, 1981). Although twin correlations were not reported, model-fitting analyses indicated heritability estimates of about .35 for four scales assessing different aspects of obsessional behavior. Using maximum-likelihood confirmatory factor analysis adapted for use with genetic and environmental covariance matrices, the authors found a component of obsessional behavior that is genetically independent of general neuroticism.

In a study of psychoneurotic and psychosomatic complaints, the Amsterdam Biographical Questionnaire was administered to 88 pairs of identical twins and 42 pairs of fraternal twins aged 13 to 69 (Wilde, 1964). Identical and fraternal twin correlations were .53 and .11, respectively, for psychoneurotic complaints and .67 and .34 for psychosomatic complaints. Both of these results suggest

TABLE 12.13
MMPI Twin Correlations at 20 and 25 Years of Age (Pogue-Geile
& Rose, 1985)

MMPI Scale	20 years		25 years	
	Identical	Fraternal	Identical	Fraternal
Social maladjustment	.74	.28	.57	.15
Psychopathy	.47	.15	.23	.20
Schizophrenia	.50	.23	.34	−.07
Overall adjustment	.33	.12	.51	−.18
Depression	.43	.01	.61	−.06
Religiosity	.83	.65	.73	.67
Number of pairs	101	102	71	62

substantial genetic influence on these neurotic disorders; the results for psychoneurotic complaints also suggest nonadditive genetic variance.

Fears and phobias are also in the realm of "soft" psychopathology. Some research has suggested that anxiety neurosis, sometimes called panic disorder, shows familial resemblance (Pauls, Bucher, Crowe, & Noyes, 1985). An interesting study from a developmental perspective is an investigation of fears in college twins and their families (Rose & Ditto, 1983). For seven fear factors in a sample of 222 pairs of identical twins and 132 pairs of fraternal twins who were 20 years old on average (from 14 to 34 years), twin correlations were similar to those for other personality questionnaires, with an average identical twin correlation of about .50 and fraternal twin correlation of .30.

Of special interest in the Rose and Ditto (1983) study are cross-sectional analyses of the type described in chapter 3 to assess age changes in twin resemblance and in differential resemblance for identical and fraternal twins, that is, changes in heritability during early adulthood. Two fear factors—fear of death of a loved one and fear of one's own death—exhibited significant three-way interactions between twin resemblance, age, and zygosity, which indicates a differential influence of genetic factors over ages 14 to 34 in the acquisition or maintenance of fears related to dying. In order to interpret this significant interaction, the twin sample was divided at the median age of 20. For the scale involving fear of death of a loved one, data on twins under 20 yielded correlations of .45 for identical twins and .47 for fraternal twins, suggesting no hereditary influence and substantial influence of shared environment. Correlations for twins 20 and older were .60 for identical twins and .22 for fraternal twins. The same pattern of results was found for the scale involving fear of one's own death. Increasing identical twin resemblance and decreasing fraternal twin resemblance suggests an increase in genetic influence on fears related to dying. As Rose and Ditto (1983) indicate:

> Whatever the explanation, increased salience of shared genes in adult fear of death is an intriguing heuristic result of our analysis. To our knowledge, it provides the first demonstration of significant changes in heritability across age in social behaviors or attitudes. (Rose & Ditto, 1983, p. 367)

Criminal Behavior and Psychopathy

Behavioral genetic studies of criminal behavior are bound to raise even more hackles than the study of genetic influence on IQ; at the outset, it should be emphasized that the demonstration of genetic influence on criminality does not mean that crime is destined. Criminal behavior is multiply determined, and possible effects of genes on behavior labeled as criminal could include genetic influence on diverse characteristics such as body build, abnormal EEG patterns, IQ differences, and psychopathology (Wilson & Herrnstein, 1985).

The first twin studies of criminal behavior was described in a book with the unfortunate title *Crime as Destiny* (Lange, 1931). Lange identified 30 pairs of same-sex twins in which at least one member of the pair was a known criminal. The concordance for identical twins was 10 of 13 pairs, whereas only two of 17 fraternal twin pairs were concordant. Nine twin studies including 301 identical twin pairs and 335 fraternal twin pairs yield an average weighted concordance of 44% for identical twins and 20% for fraternal twins for criminality, defined as registered criminal offenses—as summarized by Christiansen (1977a), with the addition of data from Christiansen's (1977b) Danish study of criminality. These twin results suggest very substantial genetic influence on the phenotype of registered crime; as usual, fraternal twin resemblance is less than half the resemblance for identical twins, which is consistent with the hypothesis of nonadditive genetic variance.

The registers in Denmark have been used in adoption studies of criminality and psychopathy. Biological and adoptive parents of 4,065 male adoptees born between 1924 to 1947 were screened for criminal records (Mednick, Gabrielli, & Hutchings, 1984). The results, presented in a 2 × 2 design in Table 12.14, suggest little influence of family environment. Of the adopted males who had neither adoptive nor biological parents with criminal convictions, 13.5% had at least one conviction. If adoptive parents are criminal, the rate rises only slightly, to 14.7%. However, if biological parents are criminal, 20% of adopted males have at least one conviction. The highest percentage of criminal convictions, 24.5%, was found for adopted males with both adoptive and biological criminal parents. Most interestingly, some evidence of a genotype-environment interaction emerged (24.5% − 20.0% > 14.7% − 13.5%), which suggests that a criminal environment is especially influential for those with a genetic predisposition toward criminality. In addition, a relationship was found between the number of biological parent convictions and the incidence of criminality in their adopted-away offspring—adoptees were three times more likely to have been convicted for a criminal offense when the biological parents had three or more convictions than were adoptees whose biological parents had no convictions.

The results also suggest that the genetic disposition toward crime is general, that is, not specific as to type of offense. The study included other family relationships and these data also suggest genetic influence on criminal convictions: Half-siblings separated by adoption showed 12.9% concordance for convictions; full siblings reared apart yielded a concordance of 20.0%; and unrelated siblings reared together in the same adoptive home yielded a concordance of 8.5%. The highest concordance, 30.8%, occurred for siblings who, although reared apart, had a criminal biological father. The results of a large Swedish adoption study generally confirm the Danish data (Bohman, Cloninger, Sigvardsson, & von Knorring, 1982).

Psychiatric interview data concerning psychopathy were also obtained for the same sample (Schulsinger, 1972). Of the 305 biological relatives of 57

TABLE 12.14
Registered Criminality in Sons of Criminal and Noncriminal
Biological and Adoptive Fathers (Mednick, Gabrielli, & Hutchings, 1984)

Biological fathers	Adoptive fathers	
	Noncriminal	Criminal
Noncriminal	13.5% (of 2,492)	14.7% (of 204)
Criminal	20.0% (of 1,226)	24.5% (of 143)

psychopathic adoptees, 4% were psychopathic; 1% of the 285 biological relatives of matched control adoptees were psychopathic. No more than a chance incidence of psychopathy was found in the adoptive relatives of the psychopathic adoptees (1%). Expanding the construct of psychopathy to "psychopathic spectrum" (including psychopathy plus criminality, drug abuse, alcoholism, and hysterical character disorder) yielded similar results. Fourteen percent of the biological relatives of psychopathic adoptees were diagnosed as in the psychopathic spectrum; 7% of the biological relatives of the control adoptees were so diagnosed. Only 2% of the adoptive relatives of the psychopathic adoptees were diagnosed in the psychopathic spectrum. These data suggest that genetic influences are important for both classifications of psychopathy and that rearing environment does not appear to be influential.

Another adoption study of criminality was conducted in the United States with a sample of adopted-away offspring of 41 female offenders (90% felons) in correctional institutions (Crowe, 1972, 1974). Using incarceration as an index, six of the adopted-away offspring had been incarcerated as compared to 0% for a control group of matched adoptees. Psychiatric records were also used to study antisocial personality; 13% of the adopted offspring of criminal mothers and 0% of the control adoptees had been diagnosed as antisocial.

Unlike schizophrenia, for which genetic influence appears to spring *de novo* in late adolescence and adulthood, there is some evidence for precursors of criminal behavior before adulthood. Both retrospective and prospective longitudinal studies suggest that criminal adults tend to be more aggressive, have disciplinary problems, and are low achievers in school (Kirkegaard-Sørensen & Mednick, 1977a); they also tend to have slightly lower IQs on average (Kirkegaard-Sørensen & Mednick, 1977b).

Alcohol Use and Abuse

Aristotle declared that drunken mothers "bring forth children like themselves," and Plutarch said that "One drunkard begets another" (Burton, 1906). That alcoholism runs in families has been shown without exception in numerous family studies (reviewed by Cotton, 1979; Goodwin, 1976). In most studies, at least 25% of the male relatives of alcoholics are themselves alcoholic, as compared with 3% to 5% of males in the general population. This family affair is a polygenic one: Although more than a score of studies have attempted to locate single major genes related to alcoholism, reports of associations between such markers and alcoholism have not been replicated (Goodwin, 1979).

Twin Studies. Questionnaire studies of twins who are normal drinkers suggest that drinking patterns are influenced by heredity (Gabrielli & Plomin, 1985b; Loehlin, 1972; Partanen, Bruun, & Markkanen, 1966). One of these studies (Gabrielli & Plomin, 1985b) included 46 pairs of identical twins, 44 fraternal pairs, 37 nontwin sibling pairs, and 46 pairs of adoptive siblings from 20 to 60 years of age with an average age of 29. Detailed questions were asked concerning amount, frequency, and rate of alcohol consumption during the preceding year. Two factors, quantity and rate, were the focus of analysis. Scores corrected for age and weight yielded identical and fraternal twin correlations of .27 and .14, respectively, for quantity consumed and twin correlations of .50 and .17 for rate. Thus, both quantity and rate of alcohol consumption appear to be significantly influenced by heredity. However, two of the most societally relevant measures, heavy drinking and maximum amount drunk, showed the least evidence for genetic influence. Correlations for pairs of nontwin siblings were lower than the fraternal twin correlations—indeed, the sibling correlations were zero for both quantity and rate. This suggests that twins are more similar than nontwin siblings and that nonadditive genetic variance might be important. This first study of adoptive siblings' similarity for drinking behavior found correlations of zero for quantity and rate, indicating that shared environment (except for the special common twin environment) does not influence similarity in drinking behavior.

The same sample was used to assess anticipation of alcohol sensitivity, which may be as important as actual responses to alcohol in determining patterns of alcohol use. Genetic influence was suggested for anticipated sensitivity to physical symptoms and coordination but not for other effects of alcohol such as thinking problems, mood, or driving ability (Gabrielli & Plomin, 1985a). Another twin study also found that heredity is not involved in perceived changes in mood and personality following alcohol use (Clifford, Hopper, Fulker, & Murray, 1984).

A Finnish study included 172 identical and 557 fraternal male twins from 28 to 37 years of age who answered questions concerning 13 drinking variables that clustered as quantity, frequency, and ability to stop drinking (Partanen, Bruun, & Markkanen, 1966). The results are quite similar to those of the previously described study. Identical and fraternal twin correlations were, respectively, .38 and .11 for quantity, .61 and .32 for frequency, and .35 and .27 for the ability to stop drinking. Although the age range is narrow, an analysis of data on younger and older twins suggested that the ability to stop drinking was more influence by heredity in the younger group. Twin correlations for the other two factors were similar for younger and older twins.

A third twin study of normal drinking is especially interesting from a developmental perspective because it involved very young adults, 17 years old on average, whose drinking patterns are just beginning to be formed (Loehlin, 1972). Twins participating in the National Merit study described earlier answered questions about alcohol use and response; data on 490 identical twin pairs and 317 fraternal twin pairs were analyzed. Five of the six items indicative of heavy drinking yielded the highest heritabilities. For example, one such item, "had a hangover," yielded an identical twin correlation of .55 and a fraternal twin correlation of .24. Another item, "used alcohol excessively," yielded twin correlations of .24 and .04.

A Swedish twin study of 58 identical and 138 fraternal pairs (Kaij, 1960) employed a 5-point scale to measure degree of alcoholism, ranging from total abstention to chronic alcoholism (defined as a pathological desire for alcohol, regular blackouts, and withdrawal symptoms). The results were presented in terms of exact matches for categories—53% of the identical twins and 28% of the fraternal twins were concordant in this way. Although these results could be due to matches for the nonalcoholic end of the 5-point scale, the data suggest that concordance for identical twins but not fraternal twins is higher for the alcoholic end of the scale.

No twin studies of alcoholism per se have been reported, and the relationship between alcohol use and abuse is not understood (Murray & Gurling, 1980). However, medical histories of nearly 16,000 middle-aged male pairs of twins were examined for liver cirrhosis and alcoholic psychosis in a study by Hrubec and Omenn (1981). For liver cirrhosis, identical and fraternal twin concordances were 14.6% and 5.4%, respectively; for alcoholic psychosis, the concordances were 21.1% and 6.0%.

Adoption Studies.   No twin studies of alcoholism per se have been reported; twin studies have focused on drinking in the normal range. In contrast, adoption studies have focused on alcoholism. The sole adoption study that reported results for alcohol use in the normal range is the Swedish study of twins reared apart, which was described earlier (Pedersen et al., 1984). With age and age at separation partialled out, twin correlations for total alcohol consumed per month were .71 for identical twins reared apart (120 pairs) and .31 for fraternal twins reared apart (290 pairs). Matched twins reared together yielded correlations of .64 and .27, which are higher than those for a classical twin study described earlier (Gabrielli & Plomin, 1985b). The results for the separated twins and their matched controls suggest substantial genetic influences on individual differences in amount of alcohol consumed.

Several adoption studies of alcoholism indicate genetic influence. The Danish registers were used to find male adoptees with a biological parent who had been hospitalized for alcoholism and to select matched controls (Goodwin, Schulsinger, Hermansen, Guze, & Winokur, 1973). The 55 index adoptees and 78 control adoptees, 30 years old on average, were interviewed by a psychiatrist concerning alcohol use. The results showed that 18% of the adoptees with an alcoholic biological parent were themselves alcoholic; 5% of the control adoptees were alcoholic (Goodwin, 1976). Because there was no difference between the two groups for moderate, heavy, or problem drinking, it has been suggested that alcoholism is genetically distinct from problem drinking and even from heavy drinking. However, such a conclusion based on the results of a single study must be regarded with caution. A continuum of genetic influence would be expected on the basis of polygenic inheritance. That is, 25% of the sons of alcoholic parents are alcoholic; the same multifactorial influences that predispose these individuals to alcoholism should also affect other individuals to a lesser extent, thus leading to an increased frequency of individuals who drink heavily and experience drinking-related problems. A recent review of genetics and alcohol use (Murray & Gurling, 1980) and a recent adoption study (Cloninger, Bohman, & Sigvardsson, 1981) indicate that this issue is unresolved. Regardless of the relationship between alcohol use and abuse, the widespread use of alcohol and the prevalence of heavy drinking and its associated problems in our society indicate that research on the causes and effects of human alcohol use is of the utmost importance.

The same investigators (Goodwin et al., 1974) discovered that 20 of the adopted-away sons of alcoholic parents had 30 brothers who had been reared by an alcoholic biological parent. These males were interviewed in the same manner and compared to their brothers reared in nonalcoholic adoptive families. This design tests the importance of rearing environment by comparing two groups of males who are equally genetically related to alcoholics; the two groups differ in that members of one group share genes but not environment with an alcoholic parent, whereas the other group shares both genes and rearing environment. There was no significant difference between the two groups in alcoholism or in other categories of drinking, which suggests that parental rearing environment may not be important in the etiology of alcoholism.

A Swedish study of 50 adopted-away sons of alcoholic males found that 20% were also alcoholic compared to a 7% rate of alcoholism for males in the general population (Bohman, 1978). Subsequent analyses of this data set indicated a 22.4% rate of alcoholism for 259 adopted-away sons of biological fathers who abused alcohol; for 285 adopted-away daughters, 3.5% were alcoholic (Bohman, Sigvardsson, & Cloninger, 1982; Cloninger, Bohman, & Sigvardsson, 1981). The data led these researchers to suggest two types of alcoholism, a milieu-limited form which affects both men and women and depends upon nurture more than nature and a male-limited form that is highly heritable from father to son. Goodwin (1979) has also distinguished familial and nonfamilial alcoholism, the former characterized by a family history of alcoholism, early onset, and severe symptoms requiring treatment at an early age.

Two other adoption studies should be mentioned. The first one, a small study conducted in the 1940s in which 27 adoptees with a biological parent described as a heavy drinker were compared to 22 control adoptees, found that neither group of adoptees had adult drinking problems (Roe, 1944). The other study is a half-sibling study in which 69 alcoholic probands and 164 of their half-siblings were studied at the average age of 40 (Schuckit, Goodwin, & Winokur, 1972). Although this was not a true adoption study, because not all of the rearing parents were adoptive parents, the results indicated that it did not matter whether the children were reared with alcoholic or nonalcoholic parents. What did matter was whether their biological parent was alcoholic. When the biological parent was not alcoholic, 14% of the children were alcoholic when reared by an alcoholic parent and 8% were alcoholic when reared by a nonalcoholic parent. However, when the biological parent was alcoholic, the percentages were 46% and 50%, respectively. Similarly, alcoholism in half-siblings was not a function of whether they were reared with the alcoholic probands; rather, it was related to whether or not their biological parent was alcoholic.

Alcohol use and abuse serves as a useful example of what it means to say that genes influence behavior. No matter how strong the genetic propensity towards alcoholism, no one will become alcoholic unless they drink alcohol and lots of it. Furthermore, it is unlikely that genes drive us to drink; what is inherited is probably an absence of brakes:

> To summarize, large numbers of people are more or less "protected" from becoming alcoholic because of genetically determined adverse physical reactions to alcohol. Possibly, if anything is inherited in alcoholism, it is a *lack of intolerance* for alcohol. (Goodwin, 1979, p. 60)

Psychoses

So much behavioral genetic research has been reported for schizophrenia and the affective psychoses that it is not possible to provide a thorough review. (For more detail, consult Gottesman & Shields, 1982; Plomin et al., 1980; Rosenthal, 1970; Vandenberg, Singer, & Pauls, in press). An obvious but important point from the perspective of developmental behavioral genetics is that this research has been conducted solely in adulthood because that is the age of onset for these disorders. If genetic factors are important in the psychoses, it is possible that they become important only in adulthood.

Schizophrenia.   Most of the early work on psychoses involved schizophrenia, in part because of the severity of the disorder and in part because patients were usually hospitalized on a permanent basis and thus readily accessible. It is clear that schizophrenia runs in families. In 14 studies involving over 8,000 parents of schizophrenics, 5.6% of the parents were found to be schizophrenic (Gottesman & Shields, 1982). The risk in the general population is about 1%. In 13 studies involving nearly 10,000 siblings of schizophrenics, the risk was 10.1%. The risk for children of schizophrenics from seven studies of over 1,500 offspring of schizophrenics was 12.8%. The weighted average risk for first-degree relatives is 8.4%, more than eight times the risk for individuals chosen randomly from the population. However, it is important to note that over 90% of schizophrenics do not have a schizophrenic first-degree relative.

Twin studies indicate that this familial resemblance is due to heredity rather than shared family environment. For six older studies, concordance for 340 pairs of identical twins was found to be 65%, and fraternal twin concordance was 12% for 467 pairs (Gottesman & Shields, 1982). In five more recent studies totalling 210 identical twins and 309 fraternal twins, concordances were 46% and 14%, respectively. Again, genetic influence is substantial and nonadditive genetic variance appears to be important. Twin concordance is positively related to the severity of the cases (Gottesman & Shields, 1977).

Although twin data have for a long time suggested that familial resemblance for schizophrenia is genetic in origin, it was a single adoption study that turned the tide of environmentalism in this area (Heston, 1966). Adopted-away offspring of hospitalized chronic schizophrenic women were interviewed at the average age of 36 and compared to matched adoptees whose birth parents had no known psychopathology. Of 47 adoptees whose mothers were schizophrenic, 5 had been hospitalized for schizophrenia. None of the adoptees in the control group was schizophrenic. In addition, four other adopted-away offspring of schizophrenic mothers were regarded as schizophrenic or borderline schizo-phrenic by one or two of the three psychiatric raters. Nearly half of these adoptees demonstrated some diagnosable psychopathology. This led Heston to propose that the definition of schizophrenia should be broadened to include schizoid dimensions, the so-called "soft schizophrenic spectrum." These findings have generally been confirmed in adoption studies in Denmark by Rosenthal and co-workers (1968, 1971, 1972). The Danish researchers also studied adoptive and biological relatives of schizophrenic adoptees and found greater resemblance for biological relationships than for adoptive relationships (Kety, Rosenthal, Wender, & Schulsinger, 1975; Kety, Rosenthal, Wender, Schulsinger, & Jacobsen, 1976).

These and other adoption studies of schizophrenia provide 211 first-degree biological relatives of schizophrenic adoptees and 185 control individuals (DeFries & Plomin, 1978). The incidence of schizophrenia among the biological relatives of schizophrenics is 13%, whereas that in the control group is 1.6%. This summary result is consistent with the findings of each individual study. In addition, 12 pairs of identical twins reared apart have been identified in which at least one member of the pair was schizophrenic—7 of these pairs are concordant for schizophrenia (Gottesman & Shields, 1982). Thus, an overall view of the adoption study data on schizophrenia clearly allows us to reject the hypothesis of no genetic influence.

These studies also point to substantial influence of the environment; for example, concordance for first-degree relatives is a long way from 50%. One of the most important findings, however, is that shared family environment is unimportant: Familial resemblance is just as great when biological relatives are adopted apart as when they live together in the same family. Studies of identical twins discordant for schizophrenia have not been successful in identifying the source of these within-family environmental influences (Gottesman & Shields, 1982). It has been suggested that "the 'culprits' may be nonspecific, time-limited in their effectiveness, and idiosyncratic" (Gottesman & Shields, 1976, p. 379):

> So far, *no* specific environmental source of liability is known; the most likely environmental contributor, stress, may come from many sources and, apparently, may come during any stage of development. Prenatal or birth complications, early deprivations, broken homes, censuring parents, the death of someone close, failures in school, poor work or social relations, childbirth, a bad drug trip, as well as all kinds of *good* fortune may have effects on a predisposed individual that are obvious only in retrospect. In prospect, it will be impossible to prophesy the events themselves, let alone their effects. (Gottesman & Shields, 1982, p. 241-242)

Affective disorders.   Cyclical affective psychoses are etiologically distinct from schizophrenia: There is no more schizophrenia in relatives of affective psychotics than in the general population (Rosenthal, 1970). However, the ill-defined category of schizoaffective disorders appears to be related to affective psychoses, not schizophrenia (Angst, Felder, & Lohmeyer, 1979).

Familial resemblance for the affective disorders is as great as for schizophrenia: In nine studies of nearly 6,000 first-degree relatives of affected individuals, the risk is 9%, more than nine times the risk in the general population (Rosenthal, 1970). Eight family studies have been published since 1975 and they also suggest familial influence (Nurnberger & Gershon, 1981). In seven studies involving a total of 146 pairs of identical twins and 278 fraternal twin pairs, the overall concordance for identical twins is 65% and that for fraternal twins is 14% (Nurnberger & Gershon, 1981).

Only one adoption study has been reported. The adoptive parents and birth parents of 29 bipolar manic-depressive adoptees and 22 unaffected adoptees were included in the study (Mendlewicz & Rainer, 1977). The incidence of affective disorder was much greater in the birth parents of the probands (31%) than in the birth parents of unaffected adoptees (2%). A group of 31 bipolar probands reared by their natural parents was also studied and the incidence of affective disorders of these parents was 26%. Thus, parents who rear children who later develop an affective psychosis have no greater incidence of affective disorder than do birth parents of such probands who are adopted away at birth. The incidence of affective disorders in adoptive parents is the same whether or not their adopted child is affected. Also, an adoption study of suicide (Kety, 1979) suggests genetic involvement—3.9% of the biological relatives of 71 adoptees with affective disorders, but only 0.6% of 168 adoptive relatives of these adoptees, had committed suicide. For control adoptees with no known affective disorder, only 0.5% of their biological or adoptive relatives had committed suicide.

Heterogeneity.   Currently, the major focus of behavioral genetic studies of the psychoses is to search for etiologically distinct syndromes (e.g., Winokur, 1975). For example, this is the focus of the Iowa 500 project, a 35-year follow-up study of about 500 psychotic index cases and their 5,000 relatives (Tsuang, Crowe, Winokur, & Clancy, 1977). The classical symptomatological types of schizophrenia—paranoid, catatonic, hebephrenic, and simple—do not appear to "breed true"; not much is known about other diagnostic divisions such as process/reactive or mild/severe. Some genetic evidence, including Heston's study just described, suggests that lumping rather than splitting is needed— that is, a genetic vulnerability extends to a spectrum of schizophrenic disorders extending as far as schizoid characteristics such as antisocial personality (e.g., Shields, Heston, & Gottesman, 1975). The issue of heterogeneity remains unresolved for schizophrenia:

> It is far from clear to what extent schizophrenia is etiologically genetically heterogeneous or homogeneous. . . . We can pose two opposing hypotheses. One is that the components of the so-called spectrum of schizophrenic disorders comprise a genetic unity in the sense . . . that they represent differing (lesser) amounts of liability in the schizophrenia liability distribution. . . . The lumpers would prefer this hypothesis, and the splitters an opposite one. For them, the myriad of classifications and subtypes based on symptom homogeneity, or type of onset, course, or outcome, or type of premorbid personality or pre-Kraepelinian category would each have a different etiology. (Gottesman & Shields, 1982, p. 214-216)

Although schizophrenia has been slow to yield any secrets concerning heterogeneity, research on the affective psychoses has led to more clues for unravelling heterogeneity. Most work has focused on the distinction between unipolar depression and bipolar manic-depressive psychosis. Early family studies suggested that the two types breed true; however, recent studies paint a mixed picture. Overall, 12 family studies involving 3,563 first-degree relatives of bipolar probands yield an average weighted risk of 8.9% for bipolar affective illness; the risk for unipolar disorder is actually higher, 10.2% (Nurnberger & Gershon, 1981). However, in five studies involving 2,041 first-degree relatives of unipolar probands, the risk for unipolar illness is 6.9%, whereas the risk that the relatives of the unipolar probands will show bipolar illness is only 0.4%. In addition, a twin study of bipolar and unipolar disorders (Bertelsen, Harvald, & Hauge, 1977) and an adoption study of bipolar manic-depressive psychosis (Mendlewicz & Rainer, 1977) suggest that there is considerable overlap between the two types of affective disorders. However, there is enough support for unipolar and bipolar illness that the distinction warrants further exploration. Some evidence suggests that a dominant sex-linked gene is involved in the bipolar, but not in the unipolar, type (Mendlewicz & Fleiss, 1974). Furthermore, the types seem to respond differently to drugs (e.g., Baron, Gershon, Rudy, Jonas, & Buchsbaum, 1975). Further subdivision has been suggested. For example, the bipolar type can be subdivided on the basis of degree of mania (Dunner, Gershon, & Goodwin, 1976) and the unipolar type can be subdivided according to age of onset (Winokur, Cadoret, Baker, & Dorzab, 1975).

Conclusions

The basic questions of developmental behavioral genetics have scarcely been asked, let alone answered, with respect to adulthood: Does heritability change during adulthood? (Most studies have only involved young adults.) What is the genetic contribution to change and continuity during adulthood? (Hardly any longitudinal studies have been conducted in adulthood.)

Studies of adulthood are particularly difficult to boil down to their essence because of the welter of measures—seldom is the same measure used in more than one study, the large slice of the life span that we call adulthood, and the many countries from which the studies emanate. In general, results for adulthood are not strikingly different from those for adolescence. For cognition, studies reviewed in the last chapter indicate that genetic influence increases from early to late adolescence. Heritability appears to continue to be high in adulthood—if there are any changes in heritability, it increases. All of the estimates of heritability of IQ in adulthood range between 40% and 80%; most estimates are between 50% and 70%. Family studies, especially the Hawaii Family Study of Cognition, suggest that verbal and spatial abilities show greater familiality than do perceptual speed and memory; however, twin and adoption studies are too few in number to provide much insight into the relative contributions of nature and nurture to differential familiality. Several lines of evidence suggest that shared environment has little effect after adolescence. As in adolescence, creativity tests show little evidence of genetic influence; vocational interests suggest moderate genetic influence and little influence of shared environment.

The bewildering array of personality questionnaires and scales makes it particularly difficult to form conclusions concerning adult personality. With most to least confidence, research suggests: (a) First-degree relatives are not very similar for personality with the exception of a few scales such as conservatism, "lie" scales, and religiosity; correlations for first-degree relatives center around .20; (b) Nearly all of this familial resemblance is due to genetic similarity, not shared environment; (c) Sociability/shyness is among the most heritable of personality traits; (d) Nonadditive genetic variance appears to be important in the domain of personality. Most impressive are the results of studies of identical twins reared apart that consistently yield correlations similar to those for identical twins reared together.

The variety of measures, ages, and samples makes it impossible to say whether the heritability of personality changes during adulthood.

Questionnaire studies of psychopathology yield results similar to those for personality—moderate genetic influence (including nonadditive genetic variance) and no influence of shared environment. Data were reviewed for neuroses such as obsessions and phobias, criminal behavior and psychopathy, alcohol use and abuse, and schizophrenic and affective psychoses. Genetic influence is pervasive throughout psychopathology in adulthood. One of the few developmental analyses suggested increasing genetic influence for fears related to dying.

13 Senescence

The director of the National Institute on Aging noted the major reason why aging has become such an important area for research:

> In the twentieth century, life expectancy of the average American has increased by more than 50%. Basic improvements in sanitation, immunization, and medical care have resulted in a decrease in the number of deaths during infancy, childhood, and, for women, the childbearing years. Only 20% of all newborns in 1776 lived into their sixties, compared with over 80% in 1980. Life expectancy at birth for the total population has jumped from 48.2 years at the turn of the century to 73.2 years in 1978. . . . By the year 2030 as much as 20% of the United States' population will be 65 years of age or older. (Butler, 1981, pp. 1-4)

Of the 26 million men and women in the United States over the age of 65, only 5% live in nursing homes and only 15% live with their families. Thus, 80% are living independently. However, as B. F. Skinner points out in an interesting essay on aging, "It is good that old people are living longer and suffering less from poverty and illness than they once did, but if they are not enjoying their lives, they have not gained a great deal" (Skinner & Vaughan, 1983, p. 20). There is a great need to understand individual differences in functioning and adjustment late in the life span. As the age distribution shifts steadily upward, describing these individual differences and understanding their genetic and environmental origins will become increasingly important. As yet, however, so few behavioral genetic studies of elderly individuals have been conducted that a separate chapter is scarcely warranted. Nonetheless, this chapter on senescence is included to serve as a bookmark for what eventually will be a major area of developmental behavioral genetics.

Although elderly individuals are often caricatured with stereotypes of "the elderly," differences among individuals during senescence are as marked as in any other developmental era. Elderly individuals differ greatly in standard psychological measures of cognition, personality, and psychopathology, and vast variability also exists in daily functioning, independence, and productivity. Moreover, the quality of life in the last fifth of the life span is enormously variable from person to person. Some individuals retain functional competence to the very end of long lives, whereas others display a decline in competence when they are much younger.

Variance for elderly individuals is probably even greater than variance earlier in the life span. For example, a cross-sectional study of 1,955 individuals from 5 to 99 years of age assessed smell identification throughout the life span (Doty et al., 1984). Average declines in this ability are not seen until after 70 years. An important normative finding is that more than 60% of persons between 65 and 80 years experience major olfactory impairment and nearly 50% of individuals over 80 years are anosmic. This suggests an explanation for the facts that many elderly individuals complain that their food lacks flavor and that accidental gas poisonings are more frequent in the elderly. However, most interesting for developmental behavioral genetics is the change in variance: The interquartile range approximately doubles each decade from the 50s to the 70s. For cognition as well, increases in phenotypic variance are frequently noted. Future research in developmental behavioral genetics, especially longitudinal studies, can assess the extent to which increasing phenotypic variance among elderly individuals is due to increasing genetic or environmental variation. The reasonableness of a genetic hypothesis comes from frequently heard comments such as the following by an 87-year-old individual in a therapy session: "It seems that the older I get, the more I can't escape being me" (Blum & Weiner, 1979, p. 169). Perhaps earlier genetic differences among individuals continue to be amplified as the years go by, although it is also possible that decreased pressure to conform permits us to see behavioral individuality to a greater degree.

So little is known about behavioral genetic issues during senescence that it is not possible to organize this chapter in the same way as the preceding four chapters on infancy, childhood, adolescence, and adulthood. For example, there appear to be no behavioral genetic studies of physical characteristics such as height and weight for individuals beyond 65 years of age. A longitudinal study from 20 to 45 years that suggested considerable heritability for height, weight, and body mass at both ages was reviewed in chapter 12. However, phenotypic stability and genetic correlations from early adulthood to middle adulthood were found to be greater for height than for weight and body mass. Do these trends in heritabilities and genetic correlations continue beyond 65 years?

One's guess on such matters is likely to be influenced by opinions concerning the genetic processes involved in aging. The most common view could be called *coasting*. Because natural selection has only been concerned about the reproductive years, one could argue that, for the rest of our lives, we coast downhill with the genetic goods collected during the earlier years. Viewed in this way, aging would not appear to be very interesting, just more of the same. Even if this were an accurate reflection of the genetics of aging, changing environmental contingencies could nonetheless change heritabilities later in life. As discussed in the next chapter, it has been suggested that idiosyncratic, individual experiences accumulate throughout the lifespan, which should lead to lower heritabilities in studies of elderly individuals. Another element of change is implicated by one of the major demographic changes during the 20th century, the stretching of life expectancy by more than 50% during the twentieth century. In part, this change is due to cultural advances that allow greater genetic variability later in life than has been tolerated previously by natural selection. In addition, a developmental behavioral genetic perspective would be open to the possibility of dynamic genetic change actively governing rates of senescence. So far, little is known about these issues except that genetics probably plays a major role in sensecence: The only major twin study of physical aspects of aging suggests that individual differences in longevity and general functioning in old age are largely due to genetic variation, as described in the next section.

The possible relationships between genetics and senescence have been described eloquently by McClearn and Foch (1985):

> At a systems level, a principal issue of the genetics of aging concerns whether the aging process is positively controlled by the continued unfolding of a genetic program, or whether the phenomena of aging begin to occur when the genetic program that has operated through the embryonic and fetal periods, through infancy, childhood and adolescence to adulthood simply runs out. If the former, then is it the case that there are senescing genes that are turned on, or is it that anti-senescing genes which have been in play throughout life are turned off? (p. 129)

Many molecular mechanisms such as accumulation of transcription errors (DNA mutations), accumulation of translation errors (defective proteins), or determination of mechanisms that repair damaged DNA have been proposed to account for aging. Genetic research on the aging process has by and large involved a molecular level of investigation (e.g., Bergsma & Harrison, 1978; Schneider, 1978). A few single-gene disorders are relevant. One rare, presumably single-gene, effect of note is progeria. Progeria victims appear to undergo premature aging (for example, balding and diminished subcutaneous fat) beginning at the end of the first year of life, with death occurring during the second decade. It is not clear, however, that aging in fast-forward truly occurs for this disease, or for Werner's disease—which begins in the 30s or 40s and has a different set of symptoms (for example, premature graying and diabetes). Neither of these diseases involves neurological dysfunction, which is the hallmark of presenile dementias including Huntington's disease, Alzheimer's disease, and Pick's disease. For these three diseases, the first morbid signs appear in middle age.

Hardly any behavioral genetic data on behavioral aging have been reported. Only one twin study of cognitive abilities in elderly individuals has been conducted even though cognitive functioning occupies a central position in both behavioral genetic and aging research. Almost all cognitive research on aging has been normative in orientation, asking whether certain cognitive abilities show average changes as a function of age, although there are signs of greater interest in individual differences (Baltes, Dittman-Kohli, & Dixon, 1984; Schaie, 1983).

Kallman's Study

In the 1940s, Franz Kallman and Gerhard Sander (1948, 1949) organized a survey of twins in New York who were at least 60 years old. Over 1,000 pairs were studied biennially. Intrapair differences for longevity, diseases (including cancer), and general adjustment to aging were consistently smaller for identical twins than for fraternal twins (Jarvik & Falek, 1963; Kallman, 1957). For example, the average intra-pair difference in life span was 37 months for identical twins and 78 months for fraternal twins (Kallman & Sander, 1948, 1949). These results led to the conclusion that genetic influences are primarily responsible for individual differences in physical aspects of aging.

Psychological tests were administered to 75 identical and 45 fraternal twin pairs between the ages of 60 and 89 years (mean age = 69 years) who were selected for psychological testing on the basis of concordance for relatively good health, noninstitutionalization, and literacy (Kallmann, Feingold, & Bondy, 1951). The results for several Wechsler-Bellevue scales, Stanford-Binet vocabulary, memory tests, and a tapping test to evaluate hand-eye coordination and speed are presented in Table 13.1. Identical twins show significantly smaller intra-pair differences than fraternal twins with the exception of the memory tests involving simple recall of recent material. These results confirm the general trend noted in the previous chapter towards less genetic influence for memory tests than for other measures of specific cognitive abilities. The authors summarize their work as follows:

> In conclusion it may be said, therefore, that the similarities in the intellectual performances, adaptive potentialities and adjustive patterns of senescent one-egg twins generally exceed those observed in two-egg pairs. The manner in which genetically determined variations in aging and longevity correspond with those in intellectual and adaptational abilities is conclusive evidence of the considerable extent to which genic elements influence a person's variable capacity for maintaining a state of physical and mental health throughout life. (Kallman, Feingold, & Bondy, 1957, pp. 72-73)

TABLE 13.1
Intra-Pair Differences for 75 Identical and 45 Fraternal Twin Pairs
Whose Average Age Was 69 Years (Kallmann, Feingold,
& Bondy, 1951)

	Intra-Pair Differences	
Test	Identical	Fraternal
Verbal		
Stanford-Binet Vocabulary	2.3	4.3
Wechsler-Bellevue Similarities	2.6	3.6
Spatial		
Wechsler-Bellevue Block Design	3.4	6.5
Perceptual Speed		
Wechsler-Bellevue Digit Symbol	4.9	8.1
Memory		
Wechsler-Bellevue Digit Span Forward	1.0	1.1
Wechsler-Bellevue Digit Span Backward	0.8	1.0
Reproduction of Designs (memory)	2.3	3.5
Directions (memory for verbal)	4.8	5.5
Hand-Eye Coordination		
Tapping	10.1	16.1

Small samples of surviving twins were studied again in 1955 (Jarvik, Kallmann, Falek, & Klaber, 1957) and 1967 (Jarvik, Blum, & Varma, 1972). In 1967, when the surviving intact pairs were from 77 to 88 years of age, 19 pairs—13 identical and 6 fraternal—were studied again using seven tests of cognitive abilities. Although the sample is extremely small, twin correlations are presented in Table 13.2 for the 1947 testing (63 years average age) and for the 1967 testing (83 years) for these 19 twin pairs.

At both 63 and 83, identical twin correlations are high, especially for the verbal tests. As would be expected from the small sample size, the fraternal twin correlations vary widely and are often negative; however, taken at face value, the results suggest substantial genetic variance on the verbal measures at both ages. Block design shows no genetic influence and substantial influence of shared environment at both ages; both of these results are at odds with the results from the large sample reported in Table 13.1. The results for the perceptual speed measure are compatible with a hypothesis of genetic influence, although the large negative correlation for fraternal twins for the 1967 testing makes this finding questionable. The identical twin correlations are relatively lower for the memory tests. Although some genetic influence is suggested at both ages, the larger sample of 60-year-olds reported in Table 13.1 showed no evidence for significant genetic influence on memory tests. Further analyses of these data led to the concept of *critical loss*—a decline in non-speeded tasks that is associated with impending mortality (Jarvik & Falek, 1963; Jarvik & Blum, 1971). The

TABLE 13.2

Twin Correlations for 13 Identical and 6 Fraternal Pairs Tested in
1947 and Again in 1967 at the Average Age of 83 Years
(Jarvik, Blum, & Arman, 1972)

Test	1947 Twin Correlations		1967 Twin Correlations	
	Identical	Fraternal	Identical	Fraternal
Verbal				
Vocabulary	.89	− .31	.87	.29
Similarities	.76	− .02	.71	.38
Spatial				
Block design	.77	.86	.56	.68
Perceptual speed				
Digit symbol	.87	.27	.46	− .38
Memory				
Digits forward	.23	.09	.42	.24
Digits backward	.59	− .47	.52	.19
Tapping	.77	.47	.33	.55

researchers suggest that identical twin pairs are more often concordant for the absence of critical loss than are fraternal pairs, although with so few pairs it is impossible to have much confidence in this conclusion.

Swedish Twin Study

As mentioned in chapter 12, a large-scale study of older adults has been initiated in Sweden with a sample of twins reared apart and matched twins reared together (Pedersen, Friberg, Floderus-Myrhed, McClearn, & Plomin, 1984). The first phase of the project, which involves questionnaire data on over 200 pairs of twins reared apart and matched pairs of twins reared together whose age range is from 50 to 80, is nearly completed (McClearn, Nesselroade, Pedersen-Ottoson, Friberg, Plomin, & de Faire, 1984). The questionnaires assess personality, health, attitudes, and rearing environment. The second phase will involve individual testing of 50 pairs each of identical and fraternal twins reared apart and matched pairs of identical and fraternal twins reared together. The identical and fraternal twins reared apart who will be selected for testing are those whose age at separation and completeness of separation make them most appropriate for intensive study. This phase of the project will include measures of cognitive abilities (with systematic sampling of fluid and crystallized intelligence); current health status; specific biomarkers, including blood pressure and forced vital capacity; family and social environments; and significant life events. This cross-sectional study—and especially longitudinal follow-up studies—will provide valuable information concerning developmental behavioral genetic questions about the elderly.

Fluid and Crystallized Cognitive Abilities

Future behavioral genetic research on cognitive abilities in the elderly should assess the dimensions of fluid and crystallized intelligence in addition to the standard specific cognitive abilities. The fluid-crystallized distinction emerged in the context of aging, although it may be useful earlier in life as well. The two types of cognitive ability are defined as follows by John Horn, who has continued to promote this distinction first described in his work with Cattell (Cattell, 1963; Horn & Cattell, 1966):

> Crystallized intelligence, Gc, an indicator of one's appropriation of the intelligence of a culture, [refers to the] organization of basic processes brought about by acculturation, as realized through influences associated with selection/deselection, positive transfer, avoidance learning, the configurations of interpersonal groupings of significant others, and the climate for inquiry, as well as physiological factors. . . . A second major dimension represents an organization of mental resources produced by incidental learning and physiological influences that operate largely independently of those of acculturation. This is fluid intelligence (Gf). (Horn, 1982, p. 212)

WAIS Vocabulary and Information subtests are examples of crystallized tests; WAIS Digit Span and Block Design are closer to the fluid end of the fluid-crystallized dimension. However, it has been argued that fluid intelligence is equivalent to g, general cognitive ability, and that crystallized ability is a minor factor arising from general cultural knowledge (Gustafsson, 1984; Jensen, 1985).

The fluid-crystallized distinction has been emphasized in aging research because it has been hypothesized that, with age, crystallized abilities increase and fluid abilities decline:

> Abilities that reflect this expansion of knowledge base, intricacy of structuring and automation (as roughly recorded in Gc) increase with age throughout life. Abilities that reflect loss of physiological substrate and rigidities brought on by expansion and systematization of knowledge systems (as accumulated in Gf) decline with age, most noticeably in adulthood. (Horn, 1982, p. 212)

The predicted developmental changes in crystallized and fluid intelligence are average changes and thus cannot be addressed by the methods of behavioral genetics. However, the statements that crystallized intelligence is "brought about by acculturation" and that fluid intelligence involves factors "that operate largely independently of those of acculturation" provide testable hypotheses for behavioral genetics, if they are applied to individual differences. The etiologies of mean differences and individual differences can differ. For example, an average developmental increase in crystallized abilities could be due to acculturation, whereas differences among elderly individuals in such abilities could be largely genetic in origin. Nonetheless, in terms of individual differences, if crystallized intelligence is "brought about by acculturation," it would be reasonable to expect that crystallized abilities would show substantial and increasing environmental influence; fluid abilities should show substantial heritability. Although these predictions concerning individual differences in crystallized and fluid abilities have not been tested, relevant data do not augur well for the verification of these predictions. Vocabulary, a prototypic crystallized ability, is one of the most heritable cognitive tests in adulthood (chapter 12) and in Kallman's study of elderly twins. Some fluid ability tests, of which Raven's Progressive Matrices is an exemplar, show genetic influence in adulthood. On the other hand, tests of immediate memory such as WAIS Digit Span, also viewed as an example of fluid intelligence, suggest little genetic influence.

Dual-Process Theory

Another approach to cognition that has been proposed in the literature on aging and should be considered in future behavioral genetic research is known as the dual-process model of adult intellectual development (Baltes, Dittman-Kohli, & Dixon, 1984). The dual processes are cognition *qua* cognition in the context-free way that it is usually measured in cognitive tests, and the application of intelligence to real-life situations. The latter process "represents the contextual and functional elaboration of intelligence in terms of knowledge systems and procedural skills" (Baltes et al., 1984, p. 55). The relevance of this conceptualization for aging research in particular is that average decreases are hypothesized for the first type of process, whereas the second process is thought to increase on the average, a distinction similar to that of fluid and crystallized intelligence. Procedurally, this research utilizes a novel strategy especially useful in gerontological research—"testing the limits"—in which maximum performance or power is assessed rather than speeded or average performance. This strategy appears to show fewer average declines among the elderly than does more traditional testing. Even after the 70s, the average decline for such tests is only about half a standard deviation. Individual differences are much more impressive: About half of the population show no change in cognitive scores from middle age to old age; about one-sixth show an increase and about one-third show a decrease in performance.

A major branch of research of this type demonstrates average improvement of performance on cognitive tests by brief training (e.g., Baltes & Willis, 1982). Of course, mean changes induced by training are not related to questions concerning individual differences. Specifically, these results do not imply that genetic influences are unimportant in the etiology of individual differences in cognitive ability. In other words, the etiologies of means and variances are not necessarily related; in this case, it is likely that they are independent because the rank-order of individual differences is similar before and after training.

Beyond Cognition

There is more to life than cognitive abilities. Indeed, I doubt that cognitive ability plays a very important role in the well-being and general adjustment to daily life of older individuals. For example, consider intimacy, love, and sex. Some data suggest that intimacy and love decline on the average; however, individual differences in these characteristics are strongly related to mental and physical health (Traupmann & Hatfield, 1981). What about sex? A widespread stereotype about the elderly is that they are asexual. However, the work of Masters and Johnson (1966, 1970) has demonstrated a lifelong potential for sexual response. Moreover, a longitudinal study suggests that patterns of sexual activity remain relatively stable in middle and late life (Weiler, 1981). Over 500 men and women between the ages of 46 and 71 were studied at 2-year intervals for 6 years. Of these individuals, 278 completed all four rounds of data collection and remained married.

> To summarize these data: During the 6 years of the study period, for individuals between the ages of 46 and 71 at the start of the study, 62% had stable or increasing levels of sexual activity, 7% had continuously absent sexual activity, 11% ceased having sexual activity, and 8% had decreasing levels of sexual activity. Combining these data in a different way, 65% of the subjects had a stable pattern (either present and stable or continuously absent) and 19% had a decreasing pattern (decreasing from some levels to a lower level or to no activity). (Weiler, 1981, p. 323)

One of the best predictors of sexual activity in old age is the level of sexual activity earlier in life. This is usually interpreted environmentally, along the lines of "use it or lose it." However, a genetic hypothesis is just as reasonable: Perhaps genetic factors are responsible for individual differences in sexual activity earlier in life and these differences covary genetically with inter-individual differences in sexual activity late in life. Longitudinal behavioral genetic studies that can estimate age-to-age genetic and environmental correlations are needed to answer such questions, as explained in chapter 3.

Other aspects of individual differences during senescence may be even more important: Functional capabilities, adjustment, and enjoyment are examples.

Cicero said that life is a play with a badly written last act. In his excellent essay on enjoying old age, Skinner responds to this thought:

> Perhaps that is why giving a really great performance is so hard. When played with skill the part of Old Person is marked by tranquility, wisdom, freedom, dignity, and a sense of humor. Almost everyone would like to play it that way, but few have the courage to try. Most would feel that they were badly cast. But are these the character traits of a few exceptional old people or the traits of ordinary people under exceptional circumstances? If the latter, can the circumstances not be changed in such a way that everyone who plays Old Person will give a better performance? (Skinner & Vaughan, 1983, p. 141)

If the former, what? Skinner, always the environmentalist, implies that there is nothing that can be done. To the contrary, knowledge of genetically induced differences among individuals may be critically important in improving the quality of later life. At the least, it is crucial to begin to understand the causal factors underlying individual differences in functioning and adjustment late in the life span because that is the path that will lead to primary prevention. If it is found that genetic differences lead to differences that we observe among elderly individuals, a first step is to recognize such differences and to realize that these differences cannot be eliminated merely through emulation of the life styles of people who continue to function well in old age. Risk studies are needed to identify individuals likely to be at risk for specific problems so that we can begin to prevent or at least alleviate these problems. For example, elderly individuals who are depressed can be helped to enjoy old age as Skinner suggests; however, the time for intervention might be earlier, perhaps at retirement or perhaps earlier still, for individuals particularly at risk for depression in reaction to the changes of later life. Because people are so different, we cannot expect to find a single prevention or intervention technique that affects all the elderly; we will be lucky to find environmental factors that have an effect for some people. A genetic perspective could be useful at a more personal level as well: Part of knowing what to expect and what to do is knowing who we are, and in this heredity plays a major role.

Psychopathology

Older people are subject to most of the mental health problems that afflict younger people; in addition, the elderly are at risk for the dementias. However, only 2% of psychiatric clinic outpatients are over age 65, even though about 10% of the population is in that age group—this discrepancy is thought to be due to greater tolerance of mild psychopathology by older people, their families, and mental health practioners (Kaplan, 1979).

Psychoses

Schizophrenia and the major affective disorders have an average onset long before senescence and, for this reason, genetic studies of the psychoses have not focused on the elderly. Paranoid psychoses may be the mode of expression of schizophrenia in late life (Roth, 1955). The risk of schizophrenia in first-degree relatives of patients with late-life paranoia is about 5%, which is lower than the risk for relatives of patients with earlier-appearing schizophrenias but considerably higher than the risk in the general population (Kay, 1959). On the basis of data such as these, it has been suggested that genetic factors play a lesser role in the etiology of late-life paranoid psychosis and affective disorders (Ford & Jarvik, 1979). This hypothesis would run counter to the general finding that heritability increases rather than decreases during development. Although late life could be an exception to this rule, the evidence upon which the hypothesis is based involves the relationship between mental illness in the elderly and mental illness in younger family members. No studies of familial resemblance specifically for late-life psychopathology have been reported. Because the etiologies of early and late forms of illness could well differ, it is not surprising that familial resemblance appears to be lower when late-life psychopathology is related to early-life psychopathology of relatives.

Dementias

The category of psychopathology specific to senescence is the dementias. Dementias affect only about .5% of individuals at age 70 and about 4% of individuals at age 85; thus, the vast majority of elderly individuals are not affected by dementia. Nonetheless, the number of senile individuals more than doubled between 1940 and 1970, and a sharp increase is expected by the turn of the century because the most rapidly increasing age group includes people over 80, the group most vulnerable to dementia (Kaplan, 1979). No effective measures exist for preventing or treating these diseases.

A major genetic advance in recent years in a related area has been the use of recombinant DNA linkage techniques to locate the gene for Huntington's disease on chromosome 4 (Gusella et al., 1983). Huntington's disease, not usually considered as a dementia because it is initially marked by motoric disturbances, involves selective neuronal cell death, primarily in the basal ganglia. Its first signs are usually seen in the 30s and 40s, and the disease progresses inexorably until it ends in physical immobility and death after about 15 to 20 years. Previously, genes could be cloned only after the primary protein deficit had been discovered; for Huntington's disease and many other neurological disorders, the primary protein deficit is not known. The importance of the mapping of the gene for Huntington's disease is that restriction-fragment-length polymorphisms

(RFLP's, pronounced riff-lipps), chopped up DNA cut by the restriction nucleases described in chapter 2, were used to isolate a DNA marker linked to Huntington's disease as part of an attempt to clone the Huntington's gene and then determine the protein for which the gene codes. In comparison to the traditional 30 protein markers typically used in linkage studies, RFLP's are far more numerous; although only three were known in 1980, there are now more than 150 and the number increases weekly. The major advantage of using RFLP's is that a DNA sequence need not be expressed as a protein to be useful as a marker. Although Huntington's disease is relatively rare—its incidence is about 5 per 100,000 in the in the United States and Europe (Heathfield, 1973), this technique is of great value because it can be applied to other single-gene diseases (Gusella et al., 1984).

Creutzfeldt-Jakob disease, an even more rare neurological disease of vascular origin, has been the subject of intense interest because of the likelihood that it may involve, in addition to hereditary influence, a virus-like agent. Similar to the demonstration of the infectious nature of Kuru transmitted by cannibalism of the Fore natives of New Guinea (Gajdusek, 1977), intracerebral innoculation in chimpanzees and other animals of brain material from a patient with Creutzfeldt-Jakob disease leads to neurological disease (Traub, Gajdusek, & Gibbs, 1977). Unlike Huntington's disease, for which there is an average life span of about 16 years from onset, 90% of individuals affected by Creutzfeldt-Jakob disease die within 2 years.

Two major dementias are Pick disease and Alzheimer's disease, both of which involve marked loss of neurons. The two diseases are difficult to distinguish clinically—both involve insidious memory defects and lead to severe dementia, neurological defects, and death. However, Pick disease is characterized by cerebral atrophy primarily in the frontal and temporal lobes and by the structurally distinct Pick neuronal cell, whereas Alzheimer's disease is marked by neurofibrillary tangles and granulovacular degeneration (Corsellis, 1976). Neuropathology findings suggest that most cases of dementia involve symptoms similar to Alzheimer's. For this reason, most cases of senile psychosis with chronic brain syndrome now tend to be called Alzheimer's disease.

Kallmann's twin study (1950, 1955) yielded the following risk estimates for relatives of senile index cases: 3% for parents, 7% for siblings, 8% for fraternal twins, and 43% for identical twins. A large Swedish study found that the risk for primary relatives was 4.3 times that for the general population—2% up to age 70 and 16% up to age 85 (Larsson, Sjogren, & Jacobson, 1963). In a study of severe dementia in Sweden, sibling risk was found to be 18% (Akesson, 1969). Finally, in a study of the families of 30 well-documented cases of Alzheimer's disease, the morbidity risk was 23% for parents and 10% for siblings (Heston & Mastri, 1977). In addition, Alzheimer's patients themselves were at increased risk for Down's syndrome, which relates to earlier findings that surviving patients with Down's syndrome eventually develop Alzheimer's disease and suggests that the two diseases are genetically correlated. The common defect may be the spatial organization of microtubules (Heston & Mastri, 1977).

Pick disease and Alzhemier's disease involve destruction of brain neurons. Although dementias are no longer thought to be secondary to cerebral arterio-sclerosis, a major form of senile dementia, repeated infarct dementia, is thought to be caused by the occurrence of multiple strokes. The disease affects perhaps as many as 4% of individuals over 65 years and shows some evidence of familial resemblance (Ford & Jarvik, 1979).

Although these studies point to strong familial influence for the dementias, it cannot be assumed that familial resemblance is due to heredity. Twin and adoption studies are needed to determine whether the observed familiality is genetic in origin.

Drug Abuse

Increasing attention is being paid to alcoholism and drug abuse among the elderly. Alcoholism may affect 20% of the elderly in nursing homes; in the general population of individuals over 65, 10% to 20% are said to be alcoholic (Schuckit & Pastor, 1979). Some of these individuals are young alcoholics grown old; however, at least a third begin abusing alcohol after the age of 60. Concerning drug abuse, persons over 60 years of age presently constitute 10% of the United States population, yet they receive 25% of all prescribed drugs; the sheer quantity of drugs prescribed presents a risk for drug abuse (Schuckit & Moore, 1979). The leading drugs of abuse in the elderly, in order of decreasing frequency, are diazepam (Valium), barbiturate mixtures, phenobarbital, and propoxyphene (Darvon). Elderly individuals are particularly prone to side effects of such drugs. No behavioral genetic studies have considered problems of drug abuse in later life.

Neuroses

What about neuroses in the elderly? Old age is viewed as a stressor and myriad patterns of adaptation can be seen among elderly individuals (Blum & Weiner, 1979). However, there are no behavioral genetic studies of anxiety reactions, reactive depression, hypochondriasis, obsessive-compulsive reactions, or hysteria late in the life span.

Summary and Prospects

Senescence will undoubtedly become a major focus of developmental behavioral genetics; this chapter merely serves as an indication of its potential importance. The likelihood of substantial genetic influence on functioning, adjustment, and cognitive abilities is suggested by the sole twin study of normal senescent individuals. Some new directions for developmental behavioral genetic research on cognitive functioning in the last fifth of the life span include the distinction between fluid and crystallized abilities and the dual-process theory that distinguishes between context-free cognition and the pragmatics of intelligence as applied to real-life situations. However, perhaps more important than cognitive abilities are functional capabilities, adjustment, enjoyment, intimacy, love, and sex. Nothing is known about these domains from a behavioral genetic perspective. Nor is anything known about the genetics of neuroses, drug abuse, and psychoses during senescence, although the dementias do appear to show familial resemblance.

In an excellent chapter on behavioral genetics and aging, McClearn and Foch (1985) describe the exciting prospects for research on this important and nearly unexplored epoch of development. They suggest that cognitive functioning, which has been at the forefront of research in both geronotology and behavioral genetics, will increasingly share the spotlight with other psychological domains, especially domains such as sensory and motoric processes that affect functional capabilities. They also suggest that a multivariate, multidisciplinary perspective that includes behavioral, biological, and biomedical variables will characterize future gerontological genetic research.

14

Life-Span Developmental Behavioral Genetics

Data from human behavioral genetic research on infancy, childhood, adolescence, adulthood, and senescence were reviewed separately in the previous five chapters for the purpose of highlighting developmental changes in genetic and environmental influences. In this chapter, these pieces are brought back together in a life-span perspective on developmental behavioral genetics. This chapter relies heavily on a description of developmental behavioral genetics published in a volume on life-span developmental psychology (Plomin & Thompson, in press).

Life-Span Developmental Psychology

The essence of life-span developmental psychology is its focus on continuing development throughout life:

> Life-span developmental psychology is concerned with the description, explanation, and modification (optimization) of developmental processes in the human life course from conception to death. Like other developmental specialities such as child development or gerontology, life-span developmental psychology is not a theory but an orientation. (Baltes, Reese, & Lipsitt, 1980, p. 66)

The major contribution of life-span developmental psychology is its insistence that development occurs beyond adolescence. As obvious as that sounds, developmental psychologists have been so preoccupied with infancy, childhood, and adolescence that developmental textbooks until recently included no discussion of later development. Because maturity is attained by early adulthood, the other 70% of the life span is seen as decline, a winding-down of earlier developmental processes, rather than development in a positive sense. Thus, the emphasis of life-span developmental psychologists on development as a lifelong process has redressed this imbalance in developmental psychology. The life-span orientation is of special importance for developmental behavioral genetic research because, as indicated in the previous two chapters, so little is known about the etiology of individual differences in adults, at least beyond early adulthood, and next to nothing is known about individuality during senescence.

This life-long view of development implies that developmental processes differ during the life span in terms of onset, duration, termination, and directionality: "Behavior-change processes associated with life-span development do not always extend across the entire life span; novel behavior-change processes can emerge at many points in the life course including old age" (Baltes et al., 1980, p. 74). In contrast, for many developmental psychologists, development is viewed essentially as growth—that is, unidirectional and cumulative changes such as the unfolding of Piagetian stages of development. Although the central theme of developmental behavioral genetics is change throughout the life span, it is important to recognize that neither genetic nor environmental change is necessarily unidirectional or cumulative.

In addition to its major emphasis on lifelong development, other emphases of the life-span perspective provide a novel orientation for developmental behavioral genetics. Three examples follow. First, the long-term view of development of life-span developmental psychology extends beyond the life span of the individual to consider historical change such as cohort effects. As discussed later, the possibility of historical change has rarely been considered in behavioral genetics.

A second example is an emphasis on life events rather than chronological age. The hegemony of chronological age in developmental research is understandable in that chronological age is a convenient marker for the developmental changes that occur, especially early in development. For example, infants walk alone at 12 months on average and they say two words by 14 months. However, as development proceeds, the importance of chronological age as a marker of developmental change is diminished. For example, in gerontology, it is widely recognized that chronological age bears only a weak relationship to biological aging. Life events become more important markers of development later in life. Even in adolescence, the rapid changes of early adolescence might be better understood if studied in the context of stages of physical maturation rather than chronological age. In adulthood, important life events such as career changes, marriage, childrearing, and divorce are not highly correlated with age. Behavioral genetic research will profit from considering these life events and behaviors relevant to the life context. As indicated in the previous chapters, the substance of behavioral genetic research tends to be nondevelopmental in that traits are selected that are thought not to change importantly during development such as personality traits and cognitive abilities. Instead, developmental behavioral geneticists will begin to study changes in behavior in the context of important life events.

Another heuristically valuable contribution of life-span developmental psychology is its model of developmental processes throughout the life span, discussed in the following section. It should be noted that these contributions of life-span developmental psychology are more theoretical than empirical. In the first life-span developmental psychology chapter in the *Annual Review of Psychology*, Baltes et al. (1980) conclude:

> The speed and intensity of the growth of the field during the last decade has been impressive. Yet it is also obvious that much of the work has been conceptual and methodological rather than empirical. Although this is perhaps a natural stage in any rapidly developing field, we believe that a stronger infusion of empirical life-span work is now imperative. (p. 101)

Developmental behavioral geneticists will surely profit by considering the conceptual and methodological advances of life-span developmental psychology. At the same time, developmental behavioral genetics will also contribute empirically to life-span developmental psychology.

Hypothetical Life-Span Profile of Influences

Life-span theorists have considered normative and non-normative influences as well as biological and environmental influences throughout the life span (e.g., Baltes, 1979). Two types of normative factors have been emphasized. *Normative age-graded* influences are those environmental and biological influences that are strongly related to chronological age. A novel emphasis of the life-span approach is *normative history-graded* influences, such as cohort effects, that are associated with historical time rather than chronological age. *Non-normative* influence refers to "biological and environmental determinants that do not occur in any normative age-graded or history-graded manner for most individuals" (Baltes et al., 1980, p. 76). Although the word "biological" is included in the definition of non-normative influences, the examples used to describe such influences are environmental life events such as career changes, divorce, and accidents (Callahan & McCluskey, 1983). Like Freud, many developmentalists assume that biological influences regulate normative maturation, whereas environmental influences are responsible for individual differences. However, most of behavioral genetics lies hidden in the non-normative category, a point discussed in detail later.

Baltes (1979; Baltes et al., 1980) has suggested a prototypical pattern of the roles played by age-graded, history-graded, and non-normative life events, as shown in Fig. 14.1. Normative age-graded influences are thought to peak in childhood and show a second lesser peak in advanced old age. The hypothesized

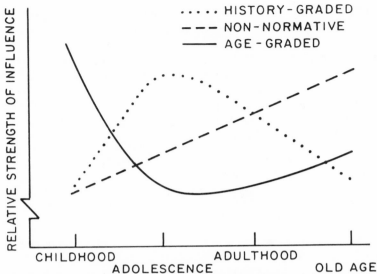

FIG. 14.1. Hypothetical life-course profiles representing the relative impact of normative age-graded, normative history-graded, and non-normative influences on life-span development. (From Baltes, Reese, & Lipsitt, 1980. Reprinted by permission.)

peak in childhood is predicted by the view that species-typical canalization weakens as children develop (McCall, 1979). For example, it is difficult to detect differences in mental development among normal children, retarded children, and primates during infancy, although the differences are apparent by early childhood (Scarr, 1976). The hypothesized secondary peak of normative age-graded influence in advanced old age is quite speculative, emerging from notions of "a genetically based program of dying" (Baltes et al., 1980, p. 78).

History-graded factors are hypothesized to be most influential in adolescence and early adulthood when societal and intergenerational factors have their greatest impact. Non-normative life events are thought to increase throughout the life span as "significant life events take on a more and more important role in determining the course of human development" (Baltes et al., 1980, p. 78).

In the following two sections, each of these components of Baltes' model of life-span influences is considered from the perspective of developmental behavioral genetics.

Developmental Behavioral Genetics and Normative Influences

Because developmental behavioral genetics addresses issues of individual differences rather than species-typical development, it has little to offer in terms of understanding normative influences. However, it could be argued that the only truly normative event is death; everything else, including birth, can contribute to differences among individuals. Nonetheless, variance analyses of behavioral genetic data would profit by considering average effects of age and history. In terms of age-graded influences, the major goal of developmental behavioral genetics is to address the effect of age throughout the life span on behavioral genetic analyses.

History-graded effects also need more careful attention in behavioral genetics, especially because behavioral genetic research has a longer history than nearly any other area of psychology. Although it is a standard caveat that behavioral genetic analyses are sample-specific, cohort effects on behavioral genetic data that extend back to the beginning of the century have not been systematically examined. It would be surprising if the dramatic changes in our society even during the past three decades did not have some effect on the genetic and environmental influences underlying variance of psychological variables. The introduction of radio and television and greater access to higher education are obvious examples of environmental changes. Possible genetic changes in the population should also be considered. For example, the United States is not just a cultural melting pot, it is also a genetic melting pot in which genetically diverse populations are blended.

Behavioral genetic data on IQ from the last half-century suggest a possible cohort effect (Plomin & DeFries, 1980). IQ data before 1960 are compatible with a high heritability, perhaps .70, whereas the newer data suggest a heritability closer to .50. Possible explanations other than cohort effects include differences in sample size and representativeness, in the tests employed, and in methods of test administration and analysis such as adjustment for age. However, the difference could be a real cohort effect attributable to environmental or genetic change in the population. One attempt to examine these possibilities suggested that newer studies show less variance than older studies (Caruso, 1983). However, restriction of range could be a cohort effect rather than a statistical artifact—for example, genetic variance would be decreased if assortative mating declined or if genetic differences among ethnic groups were broken down through intermarriage. Cohort effects have not been considered in behavioral domains other than IQ.

Schaie (1975) has proposed that quantitative genetic designs and analyses be extended to include combinations of cross-sectional and longitudinal data in order to assess cohort effects separately from age effects. The cohort-sequential method is the best design for this purpose; this method replicates the traditional longitudinal design over a succession of cohorts by sampling two or more cohorts at two or more times of measurement. One ongoing research program, the LaTrobe Twin Study—a mixed longitudinal study of 1,356 twins and their siblings and cousins, who are studied several times between the ages of 3 and

15—has been designed with the purpose in mind of assessing short-term cohort changes (Hay & O'Brien, 1983).

Developmental Behavioral Genetics and Non-Normative Influences

The usefulness of behavioral genetics lies primarily in its contributions to the study of non-normative influences. As a first step in outlining life-span profiles of non-normative influences, developmental behavioral genetics would urge consideration of genetic sources of non-normative influence, not just life events, because genetic variance usually accounts for significant and often substantial amounts of variance.

Figure 14.2 summarizes behavioral genetic data relevant to genetic and environmental influences on IQ throughout the life span. The strength of these influences is depicted in terms of variance explained rather than "relative strength" as in Fig. 14.1, which describes normative as well as non-normative influences. Figure 14.2 indicates that genetic influence increases dramatically from infancy to childhood, and there is some evidence for continuing increases during adolescence. Genetic effects account for about 15% of the variance in infant mental test scores and increase in importance to explain about 50% of the variance during adolescence. Even for IQ, the most frequently studied trait, the variance accounted for in adulthood and, especially, in old age is estimated on the basis of considerable guesswork.

Even when heritability does not change during development, this does not imply that the same genetic mechanisms are involved at each age. The same heritability at different ages could mask markedly different genetic mechanisms. As explained in chapter 3, the critical issue for developmental behavioral genetics is the study of genetic sources of change and continuity. This requires longitudinal behavioral genetic studies, and such studies are rare. Nonetheless, the seminal research described in chapter 3 suggests that age-to-age genetic correlations are high. However, to the extent that genetic correlations are less than unity, age-to-age genetic change is implied.

Because of its balanced view that considers both environmental and genetic influences, behavioral genetics represents a powerful approach to the study of non-normative environmental influences. As emphasized throughout this book, behavioral genetic research provides the best available evidence for the importance of environmental influences. A novel and important distinction made in behavioral genetics is the subdivision of environmental influence into influences shared by family members—those that make members of family similar to one another—and nonshared environmental influences that do not contribute to familial resemblance, as explained in chapter 4.

For IQ, the importance of shared environmental factors appears to decline sharply during adolescence, as indicated in Fig. 14.2. Although twin data

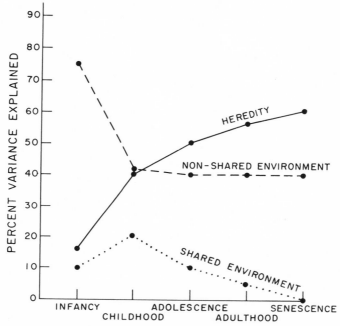

FIG. 14.2.   Life-span profiles of non-normative genetic and environmental influences on individual differences in mental development.

suggest substantial shared environmental influence from birth through the first 2 or 3 years, this apparently is a perinatal effect peculiar to twins. Figure 14.2 discounts the twin estimate of shared environmental influence in infancy and reflects the more likely hypothesis that shared environmental influences increase in importance during infancy and early childhood. The empirical support for these conclusions is presented in chapter 4.

In Fig. 14.2, nonshared environmental influence is shown to be responsible for variance not explained by heredity or by shared environment. Because neither heredity nor shared environmental influences account for much variance in infancy, nonshared environmental factors are responsible for the majority of variance on infant mental tests. As genetic factors and shared environment begin to account for greater amounts of variance in childhood, nonshared environmental influences decline in importance and continue to explain about 40% of the variance as genetic influence increases and shared environmental influence decreases in importance during adolescence and adulthood. The nonshared environmental component includes error variance, which, in the case of IQ, accounts for about 10% of the variance.

For other domains such as specific cognitive abilities and personality, not enough is known even to begin such a summary illustration. For specific cognitive abilities, the best guess is that verbal and spatial abilities follow a developmental profile roughly similar to that of general mental development. However, verbal ability appears to show greater genetic influence early in life than does spatial ability or even general mental development. Genetic influence on verbal ability remains high throughout adolescence and early adulthood. There is some suggestion in the literature that genetic influence on spatial ability increases during adulthood. Although perceptual speed and, especially, memory show less genetic influence than do verbal and spatial abilities, these specific cognitive abilities are rarely studied before early adolescence so that it is not possible to glean even a tentative life-span profile of influence. In terms of environmental influences, verbal ability, especially vocabulary, appears to show some influence of shared environment, even in adulthood.

The picture for personality is even less clear. For the EAS temperaments of emotionality, activity, and sociability, heritability appears to be substantial and relatively unchanging from infancy through childhood. Data from self-report questionnaires in adolescence and adulthood show substantial genetic involvement for these three traits—perhaps accounting for as much as 50% of the variance—and a hint of increasing genetic influence in adulthood. For the myriad other personality traits, much less is known, although it is likely that they will show varied patterns of genetic influence and perhaps developmental changes in the extent of genetic influence. In terms of environmental influence, perhaps the most surprising result in human behavioral genetics is that, for most aspects of personality and psychopathology, nonshared environmental influences account for all of the relevant environmental variance: Growing up in the same family contributes nothing to siblings' similarity.

In summary, developmental behavioral genetic research suggests some refinements with regard to non-normative influences on life-span developmental profiles. The major differences between Fig. 14.1 and Fig. 14.2 include the following: Figure 14.1 addresses normative as well as non-normative influences, whereas Fig. 14.2 focuses only on non-normative influences; Figure 14.1 does not specify genetic sources of non-normative influence, whereas Fig. 14.2 indicates that genetic sources of non-normative influence are increasingly important throughout the life span; and life events or experiences of the nonshared environmental variety are shown to increase sharply in Fig. 14.1, whereas Fig. 14.2 shows them to explain about 40% of the variance of IQ scores throughout most of the life span.

Principles of Life-Span Developmental Behavioral Genetics

It is useful to step back from the welter of research findings to consider general principles that can be drawn from developmental behavioral genetics. The principles are phrased as broadly as possible rather than being presented as a lengthy list of specific statements. As we proceed down the list of principles, the data base becomes increasingly spotty; however, I am less concerned about being correct in the details of these principles than I am in beginning a list of what we know about developmental behavioral genetics at this time, to be used as a yardstick against which progress in the field can be evaluated in years to come.

As indicated in chapter 3, the two main questions of developmental behavioral genetics involve variance at different ages and covariance between ages. The first question addresses the relative contributions of genetic and environmental factors to variance at each age, not assuming that the findings at one age will generalize to any other age. The second question addresses the extent to which genetic and environmental factors at one age covary with those at another age. More is known about the first question because it can be answered with cross-sectional data, whereas longitudinal data are required to answer the second question.

Principle One: Heredity Is Influential Throughout the Life Span

The influence of heredity on individual differences in development is nearly ubiquitous. So far, only a handful of traits apparently are not much influenced by heredity. For example, measures of creativity show little genetic influence; in the domain of personality, a few traits such as conservatism and religiosity appear to be only slightly influenced by heredity. However, for the vast majority of characteristics, heredity is not only significant but also substantial in its impact. Genetic influence sometimes accounts for as much as 50% of the observed variance. This relationship between genes and behavior is remarkably strong— perhaps unparalleled in the behavioral sciences, where observed relationships between independent and dependent variables often account for only 1% of the variance and rarely more than 10%.

Principle Two: When Heritability Changes During Development, It Increases

One surprising principle that emerges from research in developmental behavioral genetics is that if developmental changes in the magnitude of genetic influence are observed, the changes are in the direction of increased influence. This can be seen most clearly for mental development: As illustrated in Fig. 14.2, heritability is less than 20% in infancy, increases to 40% in childhood and about 50% in adolescence, and continues to increase slightly through adulthood, although the evidence becomes less clear later in the life span. It should be emphasized that this finding does not address the processes that lead to these IQ outcomes. For example, increasing genetic variance for IQ could be due to measurement artifacts rather than to developmental changes in genetic influence on cognitive processes. Nonetheless, it is noteworthy that IQ, as we measure it, shows sharply increasing genetic variance from infancy through adolescence.

For many characteristics, heritability does not seem to change very much during development; at least, sufficient data are not available to detect changes in heritability. For example, the EAS temperaments do not show striking developmental changes in heritability. Nonetheless, whenever any change is seen, it is in the direction of increasing heritability. For instance, activity level appears to show an increase in heritability during infancy, and the heritabilities of extraversion and neuroticism appear to increase slightly during adulthood.

It would be incredible if this principle of increasing heritability were literally true for all domains—exceptions are bound to be observed. However, it is interesting that extant data point so consistently in this direction. This trend is especially interesting because no one seems to have anticipated it. Indeed, as mentioned in chapter 3, most developmentalists would probably guess that the reverse would be true: As children develop and experience more diverse environments, environmental variance would increasingly account for phenotypic variance and heritability would decrease. This is explicitly the view among Soviet developmentalists (Mangan, 1982). Developmental increases in heritability merely indicate that genetic variance comes to account for larger portions of phenotypic variance, not the process by which that change occurs. Increasing heritability could be caused by an increase in genetic variance, perhaps due to the influence of genes expressed only later in development, or to the amplification of genetic effects expressed early in development. Another possibility that seems less likely is that environmental variance decreases during development—one example, however, is the damping of perinatal effects during infancy and early childhood.

Principle Three: Environment Is Influential Throughout the Life Span

Although genetic influence is significant and often substantial, behavioral genetic data provide the best available evidence for the importance of the environment. There is no psychological characteristic and there is no period of development for which genetic variance accounts for all of the phenotypic variance. In fact, heritability rarely exceeds 50%. The rest of the variance is nongenetic in origin, although the specific environmental factors responsible for this major portion of phenotypic variance have rarely been isolated.

Principle Four: Most Environmental Influence Is of the Nonshared Type

One important lead for finding specific environmental influences is that, whatever these influences may be, they operate in such a way as to make two children in the same family as different from each other as are children reared in different families. This is the topic of chapter 4. The research reviewed in chapters 9 through 14 indicates that, throughout the life span, shared environment has little effect on personality and psychopathology. One of the most dramatic developmental findings on this topic concerns IQ. Although shared environment accounts for as much as 25% of the variance of IQ in childhood, its importance wanes to negligible levels by late adolescence. Thus, even for cognition, nonshared environmental influences are of major importance.

Principle Five: Nature Is Involved in Nurture

An important direction for future research in developmental behavioral genetics is the study of the developmental interface between nature and nurture. So far, research indicates no striking genotype-environment interactions within the normal range of genotypes and environments. Genotype-environment correlation is more promising: Although it is not yet possible to abstract any general principles from this work, Scarr and McCartney's theory that the passive form of genotype-environment correlation diminishes in importance during childhood and that reactive and active forms become more important should serve to guide research on this important topic.

A recent advance in understanding the interface between nature and nurture is the demonstration that heredity affects measures of the environment (chapter 7) and that it mediates relationships between measures of the environment and measures of development (chapter 8). At least in infancy, over half of the relationship between environmental measures and developmental measures in nonadoptive families is mediated genetically on average.

Principle Six: Genetic Correlations Across the
Life Span Are Substantial

The previous statements are based on analyses of cross-sectional data that assess genetic and environmental components of variance. As discussed in chapter 3, however, the most interesting issues in developmental behavioral genetics involve age-to-age genetic and environmental covariance. For example, to what extent do genetic effects on development in infancy correlate with genetic effects on development in childhood? For heritable characteristics, low genetic correlations from age to age indicate genetic change, whereas high age-to-age genetic correlations imply genetic continuity. Genetic correlations can be high even though heritability is low—that is, even if genetic deviations at two ages make only a small contribution to phenotypic variance at each age, genetic deviations at the two ages could correlate perfectly.

Questions of continuity and change must be addressed by analyses of longitudinal behavioral genetic data, and these are quite rare. However, data that have been obtained using the parent-offspring adoption design—which can be thought of us an instant longitudinal study from childhood (offspring) to adulthood (parents)—suggest that genetic correlations from infancy to adulthood are substantial. In other words, when genetic effects on behavior are observed in infancy, this genetic variance covaries highly with genetic variance on that behavior in adulthood. As explained in chapter 3, substantial genetic correlations from age to age do not necessarily imply substantial phenotypic continuity from age to age: Phenotypic stability depends on the heritability at each age as well as on the genetic correlation between the ages.

Principle Seven: Genetic Effects Are Amplified During Development

The juxtaposition of Principles Two and Six leads to an intriguing hypothesis concerning developmental genetics. If genetic covariance from age to age is very high and yet heritability increases, this implies that genetic effects are amplified during development. In other words, slight genetic effects early in development are magnified as development proceeds, creating increased genetic variance while genetic covariance remains high. For example, slight differences in neuroanatomy or neurophysiology early in life could cascade into increasingly larger behavioral differences among children as life goes on.

This statement concerning age-to-age covariance is based on a small amount of data. However, the novelty of the model of genetic amplification and its import for understanding the processes by which heredity affects development make this a worthy heuristic for future research. The amplification model makes some strong and testable predictions. For example, it predicts that as the children in the Colorado Adoption Project grow older, the genetic correlations from childhood to adulthood as estimated from parent-offspring correlations will continue to approach unity even though heritability increases. The model also predicts that longitudinal twin data will show a similar pattern of high age-to-age genetic correlations and increasing heritability during childhood. A related prediction from the amplification model is that increasing stability of IQ during childhood comes about because the high age-to-age genetic correlation begins to account for more of the phenotypic variance. That is, heritability increases and the high genetic correlation from age to age shows up in increasing phenotypic stability. This could explain the apparent relationship between heritability and stability in development.

Principle Eight: Genes Produce Change as Well as Continuity in Development

Although the magnitude of genetic continuity is surprisingly high, to the extent that age-to-age genetic correlations throughout the life span are less than 1.0, genetic change is implied. Genetic change, even in the midst of considerable genetic continuity, is likely to be interesting and important. Furthermore, genetic change is suggested by the principle that heritability increases during development, even though the amplification model suggests that increased genetic variance later in development might be attributable to the amplification of genetic differences earlier in life.

Development, Genetics, and Psychology

Combining developmental psychology and behavioral genetics enriches both fields. It gives to developmental psychology a powerful theory and methodology for the study of individual differences in development. To behavioral genetics, it presents a new set of questions concerning genetic and environmental change and continuity throughout the life span.

The most urgent need in the field of developmental behavioral genetics is longitudinal studies. Longitudinal research is much more valuable than cross-sectional studies in this area because only longitudinal studies can address the etiologies of age-to-age change and continuity, the essential question of developmental behavioral genetics. However, longitudinal behavioral genetic studies demand enormous dedication and delay of gratification, not to mention money. Nonetheless, without such studies, developmental behavioral genetics will not begin to achieve its potential.

In the future, the field will continue to fill in the gaping holes in the matrix of psychological domains and developmental periods. In his presidential address to the Behavior Genetics Association in 1983, John DeFries indicated that some domains and developmental periods have been completely neglected by behavioral geneticists. Table 14.1 provides an update on the matrix of psychological domains and developmental periods. This overview makes it clear that much developmental behavioral genetic research is needed even in the traditional domains of cognition, personality, and psychopathology. In the table, a zero indicates that no studies have been conducted at that intersection of developmental period and substantive domain; one asterisk means that only one study has been conducted; and a double asterisk denotes two or more studies. A double asterisk is not meant to imply that we know all that needs to be known about a particular cell in the matrix: To the contrary, questions outnumber answers even for IQ and personality, the most frequently studied domains. Cross-sectional studies with wide age ranges are entered in the table at the average age of their samples. Longitudinal studies, however, are entered at each age, and the three major longitudinal studies (Skodak and Skeels' adoption study, the Louisville Twin Study, and the Colorado Adoption Project) therefore are responsible for filling in much of the matrix. "At-risk" studies, although an important approach for developmental behavioral genetics, are not included in the table because they

TABLE 14.1

Developmental Behavioral Genetic Studies in Major Developmental
Periods and Major Substantive Domains[a]

Period Years	IQ	Specific Cognitive Abilities	Scholastic Abilities	Personality/ Temperament	"Hard" Psycho- Pathology	"Soft" Psycho- Pathology
Infancy						
0–1	**	0	—	**	0	0
2	**	*	—	**	0	*
Childhood						
3–5	**	**	0	**	*	**
6–8	**	**	*	**	0	*
Adolescence						
9–11	**	**	**	**	0	0
12–15	**	**	**	**	0	**
Adulthood						
16–29	**	**	0	**	**	**
30–49	**	*	0	**	**	**
50–69	*	*	0	*	0	0
Senescence						
70+	*	*	0	0	0	0

[a]Key: 0 = no studies; * = one study; ** = more than one study; — = not applicable.

are not typically used to assess genetic variance at any one age or age-to-age covariance.

The biggest gaps in the matrix occur for middle age and senescence. Also, psychopathology has received little attention in most periods of the life span other than adulthood. An asterisk or double asterisk in the table could refer to family, twin, or adoption studies. Many more zeros would be observed if the table displayed the number of studies separately by design because few family studies and adoption studies have been conducted. Furthermore, each domain other than IQ and each age period could be examined in a more refined manner. This would lead to an epidemic of zeros in the table. Zeros would also be pandemic if we were to ask about longitudinal studies that can address the most important question of developmental behavioral genetics: the etiology of age-to-age change and continuity.

Moreover, the table lists only the major domains of cognition, personality, and psychopathology, because these areas have received the most attention from behavioral geneticists. Other important dimensions of behavior have not yet been considered, and these represent rich territory for future behavioral genetic exploration. Some possibilities include neonatal development, motoric development, information-processing and other experimental approaches to cognition, vulnerability and invulnerability to stress, interests and attitudes, social cognition, familial and nonfamilial relationships, life satisfaction, and functional capacities. In addition to these dimensions of behavior seen throughout the life span, behaviors important in the context of life events and developmental transitions represent an outstanding opportunity for future research in developmental behavioral genetics. The possibilities are limitless, including children's relationships with siblings and parents, the stresses of beginning school, the physical and social transitions of early adolescence, entrance into the adult world of work and marriage, childrearing behavior, and adjustment to the changes of later life.

Although there is much to do, developmental behavioral genetics has already made substantial progress, especially considering the newness of the field. Two of the most important discoveries, the twin themes of this book, are that genes are involved in change as well as continuity in development and that the best way to study nurture is through the study of nature. If nothing else, the young interdiscipline of developmental behavioral genetics has made it clear that there is much to be learned at the intersection of development, genetics, and psychology.

References

Abramovitch, R., Pepler, D., & Corter, C. (1982). Patterns of sibling interaction among preschool-age children. In M. Lamb & B. Sutton-Smith (Eds.), *Sibling relationships: Their nature and significance across the lifespan* (pp. 61-68). Hillsdale, NJ: Lawrence Erlbaum Associates.

Adams, B., Ghodsian, M., & Richardson, K. (1976). Evidence for a low upper limit of heritability of mental test performance in a national sample of twins. *Nature, 263*, 314-316.

Ahern, F. M., Johnson, R. C., Wilson, J. R., McClearn, G. E., & Vandenberg, S. G. (1982). Family resemblances in personality. *Behavior Genetics, 12*, 261-280.

Akesson, H. O. (1969). A population study of senile and arteriosclerotic psychoses. *Human Heredity, 19*, 545-566.

Ambros, V., & Horvitz, H. R. (1984). Heterochronic mutants of the nematode Caenorhabditis elegans. *Science, 226*, 409-416.

Anastasi, A. (1958). Heredity, environment, and the question "How?" *Psychological Review, 65*, 197-208.

Anava, S. G., Jonas, V., Rosenfeld, M. G., Ong, E. S., & Evans, R. M. (1982). Alternative RNA processing calcitonin gene expression. *Nature, 298*, 240-244.

Angst, J., Felder, W., & Lohmeyer, B. (1979). Schizo-affective disorders: Results of a genetic investigation. *Journal of Affective Disorders, 1*, 137-153.

Baker, L. A. (1983). *Bivariate path analysis of verbal and nonverbal abilities in the Colorado Adoption Project*. Unpublished doctoral dissertation, University of Colorado, Boulder.

Bakwin, H. (1973). Reading disability in twins. *Developmental Medicine and Child Neurology, 15*, 184-187.

Baltes, P. B. (1979). Life-span developmental psychology: Some converging observations on history and theory. In P. B. Baltes & O. G. Brim, Jr. (Eds.), *Life-span development and behavior* (Vol. 1, pp. 255-279). New York: Academic Press.

Baltes, P. B., Dittman-Kohli, F., & Dixon, R. A. (1984). New perspectives on the development of intelligence in adulthood: Toward a dual-process conception and a model of selective organization with compensation. In P. B. Baltes & O. G. Brim, Jr. (Eds.), *Life-span development and behavior* (Vol. 6, pp. 33-76). New York: Academic Press.

Baltes, P. B., Reese, H. W., & Lipsitt, L. P. (1980). Life-span developmental psychology. *Annual Review of Psychology, 31*, 65-110.

Baltes, P. B., & Willis, S. L. (1982). Plasticity and enhancement of intellectual functioning in old age: Pennsylvania State's Adult Development and Enrichment Project (ADEPT). In F. I. M. Craik & S. E. Trehub (Eds.), *Aging and cognitive processes*. New York: Plenum.

Baron, M., Gershon, E. S., Rudy, V., Jonas, W. Z., & Buchsbaum, M. (1975). Lithium carbonate response in depression. *Archives of General Psychiatry, 32*, 1107-1111.

Baskin, Y. (1984, December). Doctoring the genes. *Science 84*, 52-60.

Bayley, N. (1949). Consistency and variability in the growth of intelligence from birth to eighteen years. *Journal of Genetic Psychology, 75*, 165-196.

Bayley, N. (1954). Some increasing parent-child similarities during the growth of children. *Journal of Educational Psychology, 45*, 1-21.

Bayley, N. (1955). On the growth of intelligence. *American Psychologist, 10*, 805-818.

Bayley, N. (1969). *Manual for the Bayley Scales of Infant Development.* New York: Psychological Corporation.

Beckwith, L. (1971). Relationships between attributes of mothers and their infants' IQ scores. *Child Development, 42*, 1083-1097.

Bell, R. Q. (1968). A reinterpretation of the direction of effects in socialization. *Psychological Review, 75*, 81-95.

Belmont, L., & Marolla, F. A. (1973). Birth order, family size, and intelligence. *Science, 182*, 1096-1101.

Berbaum, M. L., & Moreland, R. L. (1980). Intellectual develpment within the family: A new application of the confluence model. *Developmental Psychology, 16*, 506-515.

Bergsma, D., & Harrison, D. E. (1978). *Genetic effects on aging* (The National Foundation—March of Dimes, Birth Defects: Original article series). New York: Liss.

Bernreuter, R. G. (1935). *Manual for the personality inventory.* Stanford: Stanford University Press.

Bertelsen, A., Harvald, B., & Hauge, M. (1977). A Danish study of manic-depressive disorders. *British Journal of Psychiatry, 130*, 330- 351.

Bessman, S. P., Williamson, M. L., & Koch, R. (1978). Diet, genetics, and mental retardation interaction between phenylketonuric heterozygous mother and fetus to produce nonspecific diminution of IQ: Evidence in support of the justification hypothesis. *Proceedings of the National Academy of Sciences U.S.A., 78*, 1562-1566.

Block, J. B. (1968). Hereditary components in the performance of twins on the WAIS. In S. G. Vandenberg (Ed.), *Progress in human behavior genetics* (pp. 221-228). Baltimore: Johns Hopkins Press.

Blum, J. E., & Weiner, M. B. (1979). Neurosis in the older adult. In O. J. Kaplan (Ed.), *Psychopathology of aging* (pp. 167-195). New York: Academic Press.

Bock, R. D., & Kolakowski, D. (1973). Further evidence of sex-linked major-gene influence on human spatial visualizing ability. *American Journal of Human Genetics, 25,* 1-14.

Bohman, M., Cloninger, C. R., Sigvardsson, S., & von Knorring, A. L. (1982). Predisposition to petty criminality in Swedish adoptees. I. Genetic and environmental heterogeneity. *Archives of General Psychiatry, 39,* 1233-1241.

Bohman, M. (1978). Some genetic aspects of alcoholism and criminality: A population of adoptees. *Archives of General Psychiatry, 35,* 269- 276.

Bohman, M., Sigvardsson, S., & Cloninger, C. R. (1982). Maternal inheritance of alcohol abuse: Cross-fostering analysis of adopted women. *Archives of General Psychiatry, 38,* 965-969.

Bouchard, T. J., Jr. (1984). Twins reared together and apart: What they tell us about human diversity. In S. W. Fox (Ed.), *Individuality and determinism* (pp. 147-178). New York: Plenum.

Bouchard, T. J., Jr., & McGee, M. G. (1977). Sex differences in human spatial ability: Not an X-linked recessive gene effect. *Social Biology, 24,* 332-335.

Bouchard, T. J., Jr, & McGue, M. (1981). Familial studies of intelligence: A review. *Science, 212,* 1055-1059.

Breland, H. M. (1974). Birth order, family configuration, and verbal achievement. *Child Development, 45,* 1011-1019.

Brenner, S. (1974). The genetics of Caenorhabditis Elegans. *Genetics, 77,* 71-94.

Brinster, R. L., Chen, H. Y., Warren, R., Sarthy, A., & Palmiter, R. D. (1982). Regulation of metallothionein-thymidine kinase fusion plasmids injected into mouse eggs. *Nature, 296,* 39-42.

Broman, S. H., Nichols, P. L., & Kennedy, W. A. (1975). *Preschool IQ: Prenatal and early development correlates.* Hillsdale, NJ: Lawrence Erlbaum Associates.

Burks, B. (1928). The relative influence of nature and nurture upon mental development: A comparative study of foster parent-foster child resemblance and true parent-true child resemblance. *Twenty-Seventh Yearbook of the National Society for the Study of Education, 27* (1), 219-316.

Burt, C. (1966). The genetic determination of differences in intelligence: A study of monozygotic twins reared together and apart. *British Journal of Psychology, 57,* 137-153.

Burton, R. (1906). *The anatomy of melancholy.* London: William Tegg.

Buss, A. H., & Plomin, R. (1975). *A temperament theory of personality development.* New York: Wiley-Interscience.

Buss, A. H., & Plomin, R. (1984). *Temperament: Early developing personality traits.* Hillsdale, NJ: Erlbaum.

Butler, R. N. (1981). Overview on aging: Some biomedical, social, and behavioral perspectives. In R. W. Fogel, E. Hatfield, S. B. Kiesler, & E. Shanas (Eds.), *Aging: Stability and change in the family* (pp. 1-8). New York: Academic Press.

Caldwell, B. M., & Bradley, R. H. (1978). *Home Observation for Measurement of the Environment.* Little Rock: University of Arkansas.

Callahan, E. J., & McCluskey, K. A. (1983). *Life-span developmental psychology: Nonnormative life events.* New York: Academic Press.

Canter, S. (1973). Personality traits in twins. In G. Claridge, S. Canter, & W. I. Hume

(Eds.), *Personality differences and biological variations* (pp. 21-51). New York: Pergamon Press.

Cantwell, D. P. (1975). Genetic studies of hyperactive children: Psychiatric illness in biologic and adopting parents. In R. R. Fieve, D. Rosenthal, & H. Brill (Eds.), *Genetic research in psychiatry* (pp. 273-280). Baltimore: Johns Hopkins University Press.

Carey, G., Goldsmith, H. H., Tellegen, A., & Gottesman, I. I. (1978). Genetics and personality inventories: The limits of replication with twin data. *Behavior Genetics*, *8*, 299-314.

Carter, H. D. (1932a). Family resemblance in verbal and numerical abilities. *Genetic Psychology Monographs*, *12*, 3-10.

Carter, H. D. (1932b). Twin similarities in occupational interests. *Journal of Educational Psychology*, *23*, 641-655.

Carter, H. D. (1933). Twin similarities in personality traits. *Journal of Genetic Psychology*, *43*, 312-321.

Carter, H. D. (1935). Twin similarities in emotional traits. *Character and Personality*, *4*, 61-78.

Caruso, D. (1983). Sample differences in genetics and intelligence data: Sibling and parent-offspring results. *Behavior Genetics*, *13*, 453- 458.

Casler, L. (1976). Maternal intelligence and institutionalized children's developmental quotients: A correlational study. *Developmental Psychology*, *12*, 64-67.

Cassada, R., Isnenghi, E., Denich, K., Radnia, K., Schierenberg, E., & Smith, K. (1980). Genetic dissection of embryogenesis in Caenorhabditis elegans. In D. B. Brown (Ed.), *Developmental biology using purified genes* (pp. 209- 227). New York: Academic Press.

Cattell, R. B. (1963). Theory of fluid and crystallized intelligence: A critical experiment. *Journal of Educational Psychology*, *54*, 1-22.

Cattell, R. B. (1973). *Personality and mood by questionnaire*. San Francisco: Jossey-Bass.

Cattell, R. B. (1982). *The inheritance of personality and ability*. New York: Academic Press.

Cattell, R. B., Blewett, D. B., & Beloff, J. R. (1955). The inheritance of personality: A multiple-variance analysis of approximate nature-nurture ratios for primary personality factors in Q-data. *American Journal of Genetics*, *7*, 122-146.

Cattell, R. B., Eber, H., & Tatsuoka, M. M. (1970). *Handbook for the Sixteen Personality Factor Questionnaire (16 PF)*. Champaign, IL: IPAT.

Cattell, R. B., Stice, G. F., & Kristy, N. (1957). A first approximation to nature-nurture ratios for eleven primary personality factors in objective tests. *Journal of Abnormal and Social Psychology*, *54*, 143-159.

Cattell, R. B., Vaughan, D. S., Schuerger, J. M., & Rao, D. C. (1982). Heritabilities, by the multiple abstract variance analysis (MAVA) model and objective test measures, of personality traits U.I.23, capacity to mobilize, U.I.24, anxiety, U.I.26, narcistic ego, and U.I.28, asthenia, by maximum-likelihood methods. *Behavior Genetics*, *12*, 361-378.

Cech, T. R., Zaug, A. J., & Grabowski, P. J. (1981). In vitro splicing of the ribosomal RNA precursor of Tetrahymena: Involvement of a guanosine nucleotide in the excision of the intervening sequence. *Cell*, *27*, 487-496.

Chambon, P. (1981). Split genes. *Scientific American*, *244*, 60-71.

Christiansen, K. O. (1977a). A review of studies of criminality among twins. In S. A. Mednick & K. O. Christiansen (Eds.), *Biosocial bases of criminal behavior* (pp. 45-88). New York: Gardner.

Christiansen, K. O. (1977b). A preliminary study of criminality among twins. In S. A. Mednick & K. O. Christiansen (Eds.), *Biosocial bases of criminal behavior* (pp. 89-108). New York: Gardner.

Clifford, C. A., Fulker, D. W., & Murray, R. M. (1981). A genetic and environmental analysis of obsessionality in normal twins. In L. Gedda, P. Parisi, & W. E. Nance (Eds.), *Twin research 3: Intelligence, personality, and development* (pp. 162-168). New York: Liss.

Clifford, C. A., Hopper, J. L., Fulker, D. W., & Murray, R. M. (1984). A genetic and environmental analysis of a twin family study of alcohol use, anxiety, and depression. *Genetic Epidemiology, 1*, 63-79.

Cloninger, C. R., Bohman, M., & Sigvardsson, S. (1981). Inheritance of alcohol abuse: Cross-fostering analysis of adopted men. *Archives of General Psychiatry, 38*, 861-869.

Cohen, D. J., Dibble, E., & Grawe, J. M. (1977). Fathers' and mothers' perceptions of children's personality. *Archives of General Psychiatry, 34*, 480-487.

Cohen, J. (1977). *Statistical power analysis for the behavioral sciences.* New York: Academic Press.

Cohen, J., & Cohen, P. (1975). *Applied multiple regression/correlation analysis for the behavioral sciences.* New York: Halstead Press.

Comrey, A. L. (1965). Scales for measuring compulsion, hostility, neuroticism, and shyness. *Psychological Reports, 16*, 697-700.

Conneally, P. M., & Rivas, M. L. (1980). Linkage analysis in man. *Advances in Human Genetics, 10*, 209-266.

Cooper, R. M., & Zubek, J. P. (1958). Effects of enriched and restricted early environments on the learning ability of bright and dull rats. *Canadian Journal of Psychology, 12*, 159-164.

Corley, R. (1985). *Developmental analysis of sibling correlations in the Hawaii Family Study of Cognition.* Manuscript submitted for publication.

Corley, R. P., DeFries, J. C., Kuse, A. R., & Vandenberg, S. G. (1980). Familial resemblance for the Identical Blocks Test of spatial ability: No evidence for X linkage. *Behavior Genetics, 10*, 211-215.

Corsellis, J. A. N. (1976). Aging and the dementias. In W. Blackwood & J. A. N. Corsellis (Eds.), *Greenfield's neuropathology* (pp. 796-848). London: Edward Arnold.

Costantini, F., & Lacy, E. (1981). Introduciton of a rabbit B-globin gene into the mouse germ line. *Nature, 294*, 92-94.

Cotton, N. S. (1979). The familial incidence of alcoholism: A review. *Journal of Studies in Alcohol, 40*, 89-116.

Cowan, W. M. (1979). The development of the brain. *Scientific American, 241*, 121-133.

Crick, F. H. C. (1979). Split genes and RNA splicing in evolution of eukaryotic cells. *Science, 204*, 264-271.

Cronbach, L. J., & Snow, R. E. (1975). *Aptitudes and instructional methods: A handbook for research on interactions.* New York: Irvington.

Crook, M. N. (1937). Intra-family relationships in personality test performance. *Psychological Record, 1*, 479-502.

Crowe, R. R. (1972). The adopted offspring of women criminal offenders: A study of their arrest records. *Archives of General Psychiatry, 27*, 600-603.

Crowe, R. R. (1974). An adoption study of antisocial personality. *Archives of General Psychiatry, 31*, 785-791.

Cytryn, L., McKnew, D. H., Zahn-Waxler, C., Radke-Yarrow, M., Gaensbauer, T. J., & Harmon, R. J. (1984). Affective disturbances in the offspring of affectively ill parents—a developmental view. *The American Journal of Psychiatry, 141*, 219-222.

Daniels, D. (in press). Sibling personality differences and differential experience of siblings in the same family, *Journal of Personality and Social Psychology.*

Daniels, D. (1985). *Understanding the family environment: A study of adoptive and nonadoptive infant siblings.* Unpublished doctoral dissertation, University of Colorado, Boulder.

Daniels, D., Dunn, J., Furstenberg, F. F., Jr., & Plomin, R. (1985). Environmental differences within the family and adjustment differences within pairs of adolescent siblings. *Child Development, 56*, 764-774.

Daniels, D., & Plomin, R. (1985). Differential experience of siblings in the same family. *Developmental Psychology, 21*, 747-760.

Darwin, F. (1892). *The autobiography of Charles Darwin and select letters.* New York: Dover.

Decker, S. N., & Vandenberg, S. G. (1985). Colorado twin study of reading disability. In D. B. Gray & D. Pearl (Eds.), *Dyslexia: The study of the science.* New York: York.

DeFries, J. C. (1979). Comment. In J. R. Royce & L. P. Mos (Eds.), *Theoretical advances in behavior genetics* (pp. 381-383). Alphen aan den Rijn, The Netherlands: Sijthoff & Noordhoff.

DeFries, J. C. (1983, July). *Behavior genetics: As you like it.* Presidential address, presented at the meeting of the Behavior Genetics Association, London, England.

DeFries, J. C., Ashton, G. C., Johnson, R. C., Kuse, A. R., McClearn, G. E., Mi, M. P., Rashad, M. N., & Vandenberg, S. G. (1976). Parent-offspring resemblance for specific cognitive abilities in two ethnic groups. *Nature, 261*, 131-133.

DeFries, J. C., Corley, R. P., Johnson, R. C., Vandenberg, S. G., & Wilson, J. R. (1982). Sex-by-generation and ethnic group-by-generation interactions in the Hawaii Family Study of Cognition. *Behavior Genetics, 12*, 223- 230.

DeFries, J. C., & Fulker, D. W. (1985). Multiple regression of twin data. *Behavior Genetics, 15*, 467-473.

DeFries, J. C., Gervais, M. C., & Thomas, E. A. (1978). Response to 30 generations of selection for open-field activity in laboratory mice. *Behavior Genetics, 8*, 3-13.

DeFries, J. C., Johnson, R. C., Kuse, A. R., McClearn, G. E., Polovina, J., Vandenberg, S. G., & Wilson, J. R. (1979). Familial resemblance for specific cognitive abilities. *Behavior Genetics, 9*, 23-43.

DeFries, J.C., Kuse, A. R., & Vandenberg, S. G. (1979). Genetic correlations, environmental correlations, and behavior. In J. R. Royce & L. P. Mos (Eds), *Theoretical advances in behavior genetics* (pp. 389-421). Alphen aan den Rijn, The Netherlands: Sijthoff & Noordhoff.

DeFries, J. C., & Plomin, R. (1978). Behavioral genetics. *Annual Review of Psychology*, *29*, 473-515.

DeFries, J. C., Plomin, R., & LaBuda, M. C. (1985). *Genetic stability of cognitive development from childhood to adulthood.* Manuscript submitted for publication.

DeFries, J. C., Plomin, R., Vandenberg, S. G., & Kuse, A. R. (1981). Parent-offspring resemblance for cognitive abilities in the Colorado Adoption Project: Biological, adoptive, and control parents and one-year-old children. *Intelligence*, *5*, 245-277.

DeFries, J. C., Vandenberg, S. G., & McClearn, G. E. (1976). The genetics of specific cognitive abilities. *Annual Review of Genetics*, *10*, 179-207.

DeFries, J. C., Vogler, G. P., & LaBuda, M. C. (in press). Colorado Family Reading Study: An overview. In J. L. Fuller & E. C. Simmel (Eds.), *Behavior genetics: Principles and applications II*. Hillsdale, NJ: Lawrence Erlbaum Associates.

Dixon, L. K., & Johnson, R. C. (1980). *The roots of individuality: A survey of human behavior genetics.* Belmont, CA: Wadsworth.

Doty, R. L., Shaman, P., Appelbaum, S. L., Giberson, R., Siksorski, L., & Rosenberg, L. (1984). Smell identification ability: Changes with age. *Science*, *226*, 1441-1443.

Dunn, J. (1980). Feeding and sleeping. In M. Rutter (Ed.), *The Scientific foundations of developmental psychiatry* (pp. 119-128). London: Heinemann Medical Books.

Dunn, J. (1983). Sibling relationships in early childhood. *Child Development*, *54*, 787-811.

Dunn, J., & Kendrick, C. (1982). *Siblings: Love, envy, and understanding.* London: Grant McIntyre.

Dunn, J., Plomin, R., & Daniels, D. (in press). Consistency and change in mothers' behavior towards two-year-old siblings. *Child Development*.

Dunn, J. F., Plomin, R., & Nettles, M. (1985). Consistency of mothers' behavior towards infant siblings. *Developmental Psychology*, *21*, 1188-1195.

Dunner, D. L., Gershon, E. S., & Goodwin, F. K. (1976). Heritable factors in the severity of affective illness. *Biological Psychiatry*, *11*, 43-51.

Duyme, M. (1981). Les enfants abandonnes: Role des familles adoptives et des assistantes maternelles. *Monographies Francaises de Psychologie, Whole No. 56.*

Dworkin, R. H. (1979). Genetic and environmental influences on person-situation interactions. *Journal of Research in Personality*, *13*, 279-293.

Dworkin, R. H., Burke, B. W., Maher, B. A., & Gottesman, I. I. (1976). A longitudinal study of the genetics of personality. *Journal of Personality and Social Psychology*, *34*, 510-518.

Dworkin, R. H., Burke, B. W., Maher, B. A., & Gottesman, I. I. (1977). Genetic influences on the organization and development of personality. *Developmental Psychology*, *13*, 512-521.

Eaves, L. J. (1978). Twins as a basis for the causal analysis of personality. In W. E. Nance (Ed.), *Twin research: Psychology and methodology* (pp. 151-174). New York: Liss.

Eaves, L. J., & Eysenck, H. J. (1975). The nature of extraversion: a genetical analysis. *Journal of Personality and Social Psychology*, *32*, 102-112.

Eaves, L. J., & Eysenck, H. J. (1976a). Genetical and environmental components of inconsistency and unrepeatability in twins' responses to a neuroticism questionnaire. *Behavior Genetics*, *6*, 145-160.

Eaves, L. J., & Eysenck, H. J. (1976b). Genotype x age interaction for neuroticism. *Behavior Genetics, 6*, 359-362.

Eaves, L. J., & Young, P. A. (1981). Genetical theory and personality differences. In R. Lynn (Ed.), *Dimensions of personality*. Oxford: Pergamon Press.

Edgar, R. S. (1980). The genetics of development in the Nematode Caenorhabditis elegans. In T. Leighton & W. F. Loomis (Eds.), *The molecular genetics of development* (pp. 213-235). New York: Academic Press.

Ehrman, L., & Parsons, P. A. (1981). *The genetics of behavior*. Sunderland, Ma: Sinauer Associates.

Eichorn, D. H. (1969, August). *Developmental parallels in the growth of parents and their children*. Presidential address (Division 7) presented at the meeting of the American Psychological Association, Washington, DC.

Elardo, R., & Bradley, R. H. (1981). The Home Observation for Measurement of the Environment (HOME) scale: A review of research. *Developmental Review, 1*, 113-145.

Elderton, E. M. (1922). A summary of the present position with regard to the inheritance of intelligence. *Biometrika, 14*, 378-408.

Emmons, S., Klass, M. R., & Hirsch, D. (1979). Analysis of the constancy of DNA sequences during development and evolution of the nematode Caenorhabditis elegans. *Proceedings of the National Academy of Sciences U.S.A., 76*, 1333-1337.

Erlenmeyer-Kimling, L., & Jarvik, L. F. (1963). Genetics and intelligence: A review. *Science, 142*, 1477-1479.

Erlenmeyer-Kimling, L., Marcuse, Y., Cornblatt, B., Friedman, D., Rainer, J. D., & Rutschmann, J. (1984). The New York High-Risk Project. In N. F. Watt, E. J. Anthony, L. C. Wynne, & J. E. Rolf (Eds.), *Children at risk for schizophrenia: A longitudinal perspective* (pp. 169-189). Cambridge: Cambridge University Press.

Ernst, L., & Angst, J. (1983). *Birth order: Its influence on personality*. Springer-Verlag.

Eysenck, H. J. (1981). *A model for personality*. Berlin: Springer-Verlag.

Eysenck, H. J., & Prell, D. B. (1951). The inheritance of neuroticism: An experimental study. *Journal of Mental Science, 97*, 441-465.

Eysenck, S. B. G. (1965). *Manual of the Junior Eysenck Personality Inventory*. London: University of London Press.

Fagan, J. F., III (1985). A new look at infant intelligence. In D. Detterman (Ed.), *Current topics in human intelligence: Research methodology* (pp. 223-246). Norwood, NJ: Ablex.

Falconer, D. S. (1981). *Introduction to quantitative genetics* (2nd ed.). London: Longman.

Farber, S. L. (1982). *Identical twins reared apart: A reanalysis*. New York: Basic Books.

Finucci, J. M. (1978). Genetic considerations in dyslexia. In H. R. Myklebust (Ed.), *Progress in learning disabilities* (Vol. IV, pp. 41-63). New York: Grune and Stratton.

Finucci, J. M., Guthrie, J. T., Childs, A. L., Abbey, H., & Childs, B. (1976). The genetics of specific reading disability. *Annals of Human Genetics, 40*, 1-23.

Fisch, R. O., Bilek, M. K., Deinard, A. S., & Chang, P. N. (1976). Growth, behavioral, and psychologic measurements of adopted children: The influences of genetic and socioeconomic factors in a prospective study. *Behavioral Pediatrics, 89*, 494-500.

Fischbein, S. (1977a). Intra-pair similarity in physical growth of monozygotic and dizygotic twins during puberty. *Annals of Human Biology, 4*, 417-430.

Fischbein, S. (1977b). Onset of puberty in MZ and DZ twins. *Acta Geneticae Medicae et Gemellologiae, 26*, 151-158.

Fischbein, S. (1979). *Heredity-environment influences on growth and development during adolescence: A longitudinal study of twins.* Lund: CWK/Gleerup.

Fischbein, S. (1981). Heredity-environment influences on growth and development during adolescence. In L. Gedda, P. Parisi, & W. E. Nance (Eds.), *Twin research 3: Intelligence, personality, and development* (pp. 211- 226). New York: Liss.

Fischbein, S., & Nordqvist, T. (1978). Profile comparisons of physical growth for monozygotic and dizygotic twin pairs. *Annals of Human Biology, 5*, 321-328.

Fisher, R. A. (1918). The correlation between relatives on the supposition of Mendelian inheritance. *Transactions of the Royal Society of Edinburgh, 52*, 399-433.

Flanagan, J. C. (1935). *Factor analysis in the study of personality.* Stanford: Stanford University Press.

Floderus-Myrhed, B., Pedersen, N., & Rasmuson, I. (1980). Assessment of heritability for personality, based on a short form of the Eysenck Personality Inventory: A study of 12,898 twin pairs. *Behavior Genetics, 10*, 153-162.

Foch, T. T., & Plomin, R. (1980). Specific cognitive abilities in 5- to 12- year-old twins. *Behavior Genetics, 10*, 507-520.

Folstein, S., & Rutter, M. (1977). Infantile autism: A genetic study of 21 twin pairs. *Journal of Child Psychology and Psychiatry, 18*, 297- 321.

Ford, C. V., & Jarvik, L. F. (1979). Genetic aspects of psychopathological disorders in later life. In O. J. Kaplan (Ed.), *Psychopathology of aging* (pp. 7-33). New York: Academic Press.

Freedman, D. G. (1974). *Human infancy: An evolutinary perspective.* Hillsdale, NJ: Lawrence Erlbaum Associates.

Freeman, F. N., Holzinger, K. J., & Mitchell, B. (1928). The influence of environment on the intelligence, school achievement, and conduct of foster children. *Twenty-Seventh Yearbook of the National Society for the Study of Education, 27* (1), 103-217.

Fulker, D. W., & DeFries, J. C. (1983). Genetic and environmental transmission in the Colorado Adoption Project: Path analysis. *British Journal of Mathematical and Statistical Psychology, 36*, 175-188.

Fulker, D. W., Eysenck, S. B. G., & Zuckerman, M. (1980). A genetic and environmental analysis of sensation seeking. *Journal of Research in Personality, 14*, 261-281.

Fuller, J. L. (1964). Physiological and population aspects of behavior genetics. *American Zoologist, 4*, 101-109.

Fuller, J. L., & Thompson, W. R. (1978). *Foundations of behavior genetics.* St. Louis: Mosby.

Furstenberg, F. F., Jr., Winquist-Nord, C., Peterson, J. L., & Zill, N. (1983). The life course of children of divorce. *American Sociological Review, 48*, 656-668.

Gabrielli, W. F., Jr., & Plomin, R. (1985a). Individual differences in anticipation of alcohol sensitivity. *The Journal of Nervous and Mental Disease, 173*, 111-114.

Gabrielli, W. F., & Plomin, R. (1985b). Drinking behavior in the Colorado Adoptee and Twin Sample. *Journal of Studies on Alcohol, 46*, 24- 31.

Gajdusek, D. C. (1977). Unconventional viruses and the origin and disappearance of Kuru. *Science, 197*, 943-960.

Galbraith, R. C. (1982). Sibling spacing and intellectual development: A closer look at the confluence models. *Developmental Psychology, 18*, 151-173.

Galton, F. (1874). *English men of science: Their nature and nurture*. London: Macmillan.

Galton, F. (1875). The history of twins as a criterion of the relative powers of nature and nurture. *Journal of the Anthropological Institute, 6*, 391-406.

Garcia-Coll, C., Kagan, J., & Reznick, J. S. (1984). Behavioral inhibition in young children. *Child Development, 55*, 1005-1019.

Garfinkle, A. S., & Vandenberg, S. G. (1981). Development of Piagetian logicomathematical concepts and other specific cognitive abilities. In L. Gedda, P. Parisi, & W. E. Nance (Eds.), *Twin research 3: Intelligence, personality, and development* (pp. 51-60). New York: Liss.

Gehring, W. J. (1985). The Homeo Box: A key to understanding of development? *Cell, 40*, 3-5.

Gluzman, Y., & Shenk, T. (1983). *Enhancers and eukaryotic gene expression*. Cold Spring Harbor: Cold Spring Harbor Laboratory.

Gold, L., Pribnow, D., Schneider, T., Shinedling, S., Singer, B. S., & Stormo, G. (1981). Translational initiation in prokaryotes. *Annual Review of Microbiology, 35*, 365-403.

Goldsmith, H. H. (1983a, June). *Emotionality in infant twins: Longitudinal results*. Paper presented at the Fourth International Congress on Twin Studies, London, England.

Goldsmith, H. H. (1983b). Genetic influences on personality from infancy to adulthood. *Child Development, 54*, 331-355.

Goldsmith, H. H. (1984). Continuity of personality: A genetic perspective. In R. N. Emde & R. J. Harmon (Eds.), *The development of attachment and affiliative systems*. New York: Plenum.

Goldsmith, H. H., & Campos, J. J. (1982a). Genetic influence on individual differences in emotionality. *Infant Behavior and Development, 5*, 99.

Goldsmith, H. H., & Campos, J. J. (1982b). Toward a theory of infant temperament. In R. N. Emde & R. Harmon (Eds.), *The development of attachment and affiliative systems: Psychological aspects* (pp. 161-193). New York: Plenum.

Goldsmith, H. H., & Gottesman, I. I. (1981). Origins of variation in behavioral style: A longitudinal study of temperament in young twins. *Child Development, 52*, 91-103.

Goodwin, D. W. (1976). *Is alcoholism hereditary?* New York: Oxford University Press.

Goodwin, D. W. (1979). Alcoholism and heredity. *Archives of General Psychiatry, 36*, 57-61.

Goodwin, D. W., Schulsinger, F., Hermansen, L., Guze, S. B., & Winokur, G. (1973). Alcohol problems in adoptees raised apart from alcoholic biological parents. *Archives of General Psychiatry, 28*, 238-243.

Goodwin, D. W., Schulsinger, F., Moller, N., Hermansen, L., Winokur, G., & Guze, S. B. (1974). Drinking problems in adopted and nonadopted sons of alcoholics. *Archives of General Psychiatry, 31*, 164-169.

Gordon, J. W., Scangos, G. A., Plotkin, D. J., Barbos, J. A., & Ruddle, F. H. (1980). Genetic transformation of mouse embryos by microinjection of purified DNA. *Proceedings of the National Academy of Sciences U.S.A., 77*, 7380-7384.

Gottesman, I. I. (1963). Heritability of personality: A demonstration. *Psychology Monographs*, *77* (Whole No. 572).

Gottesman, I. I. (1965). Personality and natural selection. In S. G. Vandenberg (Ed.), *Methods and goals in human behavior genetics* (pp. 63-80). New York: Academic Press.

Gottesman, I. I. (1974). Developmental genetics and ontogenetic psychology: Overdue detente and propositions from a matchmaker. In A. D. Pick (Ed.), *Minnesota symposia on child psychology* (pp. 55-80). Minneapolis: University of Minnesota Press.

Gottesman, I. I., & Shields, J. (1976). A critical review of recent adoption, twin, and family studies of schizophrenia: Behavioral genetics perspectives. *Schizophrenia Bulletin*, *2*, 360-401.

Gottesman, I. I., & Shields, J. (1977). Twin studies and schizophrenia a decade later. In B. A. Maher (Ed.), *Contributions to the psychopathology of schizophrenia* (pp. 253-266). New York: Academic Press.

Gottesman, I. I., & Shields, J. (1982). *Schizophrenia: The epigenetic puzzle*. Cambridge: Cambridge University Press.

Gottfried, A. W. (1984). *Home environment and early cognitive development: Longitudinal research*. New York: Academic Press.

Gottfried, A. W., & Brody, N. (1975). Interrelationships between and correlates of psychometric and Piagetian scales of sensorimotor intelligence. *Developmental Psychology*, *11*, 379-387.

Gottfried, A. W., & Gottfried, A. E. (1984). Home environment and cognitive development in young children of middle-socioeconomic-status families. In A. W. Gottfried (Ed.), *Home environment and early cognitive development: Longitudinal research* (pp. 57-115). New York: Academic Press.

Gottschaldt, K. (1960). Das problem der phanogenetik der personlichkeit. In P. Lersch & H. Thomae (Eds.), *Personlichkeitsforschung und personlichkeitstheorie, Handbuck der psychologie* (pp. 222-280). Gottingen: Hogrefe.

Gould, S. J. (1985, November). Geoffrey and the homeobox. *Natural History*, 12-23.

Grotevant, H. D., Scarr, S., & Weinberg, R. A. (1977). Intellectual development in family constellations with adopted and natural children: A test of the Zajonc and Markus model. *Child Development*, *48*, 1699-1703.

Guilford, J. P., & Fruchter, B. (1973). *Fundamental statistics in psychology and education*. New York: McGraw-Hill.

Gusella, J. F., Tanzi, R. E., Anderson, M. A., Hobbs, W., Gibbons, K., Raschtchian, R., Gilliam, T. C., & Wallace, M. R. (1984). DNA markers for nervous system diseases. *Science*, *225*, 1320-1326.

Gusella, J. F., Wexler, N. S., Conneally, P. M., Naylor, S. L., Anderson, M. A., Tanzi, R. E., Watkins, P. C., & Ottina, K. (1983). Apolymorphic DNA marker genetically linked to Huntington's disease. *Nature*, *306*, 234-238.

Gustafsson, J. E. (1984). A unifying model for the structure of intellectual abilities. *Intelligence*, *8*, 179-203.

Hall, G. S. (1904). *Adolescence: Its psychology and its relations to physiology, anthropology, sociology, sex, crime, religion, and education*. New York: Appleton.

Hanson, D. R., & Gottesman, I. I. (1976). The genetics, if any, of infantile autism and childhood schizophrenia. *Journal of Autism and Childhood Schizophrenia, 6*, 209-233.

Hardy-Brown, K. (1981). An analysis of environmental and genetic influence on individual differences in the communicative development of fifty adopted one-year-old children (Doctoral dissertation, University of Colorado, Boulder, 1980). *Dissertation Abstracts International, 41*, 3025B.

Hardy-Brown, K. (1982). Communicative development in the first year of life: Genetics and environmental influences. *Behavior genetics, 12*, 587. (Abstract)

Hardy-Brown, K. (1983). Universals and individual differences: Disentangling two approaches to the study of language acquisition. *Developmental Psychology, 19*, 610-624.

Hardy-Brown, K., & Plomin, R. (1985). Infant communicative development: Evidence from adoptive and biological families for genetic and environmental influences on rate differences. *Developmental Psychology, 21*, 378-385.

Hardy-Brown, K., Plomin, R., & DeFries, J. C. (1981). Genetic and environmental influences on rate of communicative development in the first year of life. *Developmental Psychology, 17*, 704-717.

Hartlage, L. C. (1970). Sex-linked inheritance of spatial ability. *Perceptual and Motor Skills, 31*, 610.

Hay, D. A. (1984, June). *Do the genetic determinants of cognition change at adolescence?* Paper presented at the meeting of the Australian Psychological Society.

Hay, D. A. (1985). *Essentials of behaviour genetics*. Oxford: Blackwells.

Hay, D. A., & O'Brien, P. J. (1983). The La Trobe Twin Study: A genetic approach to the structure and development of cognition in twin children. *Child Development, 54*, 317-330.

Hearnshaw, L. S. (1979). *Cyril Burt, psychologist*. Ithaca, NY: Cornell University Press.

Heathfield, K. W. G. (1973). Huntington's chorea: A centenary review. *Postgraduate Medical Journal, 49*, 32-45.

Hedrick, D. L., Prather, E. M., & Tobin, A. R. (1975). *Sequenced Inventory of Communication Development*. Seattle: University of Washington Press.

Henderson, N. D. (1967). Prior treatment effects on open field behaviour of mice: A genetic analysis. *Animal Behaviour, 15*, 364-376.

Henderson, N. D. (1970). Genetic influences on the behavior of mice can be obscured by laboratory rearing. *Journal of Comparative and Physiological Psychology, 73*, 505-511.

Henderson, N. D. (1972). Relative effects of early rearing environment on discrimination learning in housemice. *Journal of Comparative and Physiological Psychology, 79*, 243-253.

Hentschel, C. C., & Birnstiel, C. C. (1981). The organization and expression of histone gene families. *Cell, 25*, 301-313.

Herrman, L., & Hogben, L. (1932-1933). The intellectual resemblance of twins. *Proceedings of the Royal Society of Edinburgh, 53*, 105-129.

Herskowitz, I., Blair, L., Forbes, D. Hicks, J., Kassir, Y., Kushner, P., Rine, J., Sprague, G., & Strathern, J. (1980). Control of cell type in the yeast Saccharomyces cerevisiae and a hypothesis for development in higher eukaryotes. In T. Leighton &

W. F. Leighton (Eds.), *The molecular genetics of development* (pp. 79-118). New York: Academic Press.

Heston, L. L. (1966). Psychiatric disorders in foster home reared children of schizophrenic mothers. *British Journal of Psychiatry, 112,* 819-825.

Heston, L. L., & Mastri, A. R. (1977). The genetics of Alzheimer's disease: Associations with hematologic malignancy and Down's syndrome. *Archives of General Psychiatry, 34,* 976-981.

Hildreth, G. H. (1925). *The resemblance of siblings in intelligence and achievement.* New York: Columbia Teachers College.

Hill, J. P. (1982). Guest editorial for special issue on early adolescence. *Child Development, 53,* 1409-1412.

Hill, M. S., & Hill, R. N. (1973). Hereditary influence on the normal personality using the MMPI. *Behavior Genetics, 3,* 133-144.

Ho, H. Z., Foch, T. T., & Plomin, R. (1980). Developmental stability of the relative influence of genes and environment on specific cognitive abilities in childhood. *Developmental Psychology, 16,* 340-346.

Holland, J. L. (1966). *The psychology of vocational choice.* Waltham: Blaisdell.

Honzik, M. P., MacFarlane, J. W., & Allen, L. (1948). Stability of mental test performance between 2 and 18 years. *Journal of Experimental Education, 17,* 309-322.

Hoopes, J. L. (1982). *Prediction in child development: A longitudinal study of adoptive and nonadoptive families.* New York: Child Welfare League of America.

Horn, J. L. (1982). The aging of human abilities. In B. B. Wolman (Ed.), *Handbook of developmental psychology* (pp. 847-870). Englewood Cliffs, NJ: Prentice-Hall.

Horn, J. L., & Cattell, R. B. (1966). Refinement and test of the theory of fluid and crystallized intelligence. *Journal of Educational Psychology, 57,* 253-270.

Horn, J. M. (1983). The Texas Adoption Project: Adopted children and their intellectual resemblance to biological and adoptive parents. *Child Development, 54,* 268-275.

Horn, J. M., Loehlin, J. C., & Willerman, L. (1979). Intellectual resemblance among adoptive and biological relatives: The Texas Adoption Project. *Behavior Genetics, 9,* 177-207.

Horn, J. M., Loehlin, J. C., & Willerman, L. (1982). Aspects of the inheritance of intellectual abilities. *Behavior Genetics, 12,* 479-516.

Horn, J. M., Plomin, R., & Rosenman, R. (1976). Heritability of personality traits in adult male twins. *Behavior Genetics, 6,* 17-30.

Hrubec, Z., & Omenn, G. S. (1981). Evidence of genetic predisposition to alcohol cirrhosis and psychosis: Twin concordances for alcoholism and its biological end points by zygosity among male veterans. *Alcoholism: Clinical and Experimental Research, 5,* 207-215.

Husén, T. (1959). *Psychological twin research: A methodological study.* Stockholm: Almqvist & Wiksell.

Husén, T. (1960). Abilities of twins. *Scandinavian Journal of Psychology, 1,* 125-135.

Husén, T. (1963). Intra-pair similarities in the school achievements of twins. *Scandinavian Journal of psychology, 4,* 108-114.

Hutchings, B., & Mednick, S. A. (1975). Registered criminality in the adoptive and biological parents of registered male criminal adoptees. In R. R. Fieve, D.

Rosenthal, & H. Brill (Eds.), *Genetic research in psychiatry* (pp. 105–116). Baltimore: Johns Hopkins University Press.

Hutchings, B., & Mednick, S. A. (1977). Criminality in adoptees and their adoptive and biological parents: A pilot study. In S. A. Mednick & K. O. Christiansen (Eds.), *Biosocial bases of criminal behavior* (pp. 127–142). New York: Gardner.

Insel, P. (1974). Maternal effects in personality. *Behavior Genetics, 4*, 133-144.

Jacob, F., & Monod, J. (1961). On the regulation of gene activity. *Cold Spring Harbor Symposia on Quantitative Biology, 26*, 193-209.

Jacobs, B. S., & Moss, H. A. (1976). Birth order and sex of sibling as determinants of mother-infant interaction. *Child Development, 47*, 315-322.

Jahner, D., Stuhlmann, H., Stewart, G. L., Harbers, K., Lohler, J., Simon, I., & Jaenisch, R. (1982). De novo methylation and expression of retroviral genomes during mouse embryogenesis. *Nature, 298*, 623-628.

Jarvik, L. F., & Blum, J. E. (1971). Cognitive decline as predictors of mortality in twin pairs: A twenty-year longitudinal study of aging. In E. Palmore & F. C. Jeffers (Eds.), *Prediction of life span* (pp. 199-211). Lexington, MA: Heath Lexington.

Jarvik, L. F., Blum, J. E., & Varma, A. O. (1972). Genetic components and intellectual functioning during senescence: A 20-year study of aging twins. *Behavior Genetics, 2*, 159-171.

Jarvik, L. F., & Falek, A. (1963). Intellectual stability and survival in the aged. *Journal of Gerontology, 18*, 289-294.

Jarvik, L. F., Kallmann, F. J., Falek, A., & Klaber, M. M. (1957). Changing intellectual functions in senescent twins. *Acta Genetica et Statistica Medica, 7*, 421-430.

Jenkins, S., Owen, C., Bax, M., & Hart, H. (1984). Continuities of common behavior problems in preschool children. *Journal of Child Psychology and Psychiatry, 25*, 75-89.

Jensen, A. R. (1971). A note on why genetic correlations are not squared. *Psychological Bulletin, 75*, 223-224.

Jensen, A. R. (1976). The problem of genotype-environment correlation in the estimation of heritability from monozygotic and dizygotic twins. *Acta Geneticae Medicae et Gemellologiae, 25*, 86-99.

Jensen, A. R. (1985, April). *The g beyond factor analysis.* Paper presented at Buros-Nebraska Symposium on Measurement and Testing, University of Nebraska, Lincoln.

Jinks, J. L., & Fulker, D. W. (1970). Comparison of the biometrical genetical, MAVA, and classical approaches to the analysis of human behavior. *Psychological Bulletin, 73*, 311-349.

Johnson, R. C., & Nagoshi, C. J. (1985). The ubiquity of g. *Behavioral and Brain Sciences, 8*, 232-233.

Johnston, A., DeLuca, D., Murtaugh, K., & Diener, E. (1977). Validation of a laboratory play measure of child aggression. *Child Development, 48*, 324-327.

Juel-Nielsen, N. (1965). Individual and environment: A psychiatric-psychological investigation of monozygous twins reared apart. *Acta Psychiatrica et Neurologica Scandinavica Monograph, 183* (Supplement).

Kagan, J. (1982). Comments on the construct of difficult temperament. *Merrill-Palmer Quarterly, 28*, 21-24.

Kagan, J., Reznick, J. S., Clarke, C., Snidman, N., & Garcia-Coll, C. (1984). Behavioral inhibition to the unfamiliar. *Child Development*, *55*, 2212-2225.

Kaij, L. (1960). *Alcoholism in twins*. Stockholm: Almqvist & Wiksell.

Kallmann, F. J. (1950). The genetics of psychoses: An analysis of 1232 twin index families. *Congres international de Psychiatrie, Rapports*, *6*, 1-27.

Kallmann, F. J. (1953). *Heredity in health and mental disorder*. New York: Norton.

Kallmann, F. J. (1955). Genetic aspects of mental disorders in later life. In O. J. Kaplan (Ed.), *Mental disorders in later life* (pp. 26-46). Stanford, CA: Stanford University Press.

Kallmann, F. J. (1957). Twin data on the genetics of aging. In G. E. Wolstenhoime & C. M. O'Connor (Eds.), *Methodology of the study of aging* (pp. 131-143). London: J. & A. Churchill.

Kallmann, F. J., Feingold, L., & Bondy, E. (1951). Comparative adaptational, social, and psychometric data on the life histories of senescent twin pairs. *American Journal of Human Genetics*, *3*, 65-73.

Kallmann, F. J., & Roth, B. (1956). Genetic aspects of preadolescent schizophrenia. *American Journal of Psychiatry*, *112*, 599-606.

Kallmann, F. J., & Sander, G. (1948). Twin studies on aging and longevity. *Journal of Heredity*, *39*, 349-357.

Kallmann, F. J., & Sander, G. (1949). Twin studies on senescence. *American Journal of Psychiatry*, *106*, 29-36.

Kaplan, O. J. (1979). Introduction. In O. J. Kaplan (Ed.), *Psychopathology of aging* (pp. 1-6). New York: Academic Press.

Kay, D. (1959). Observations on the natural history and genetics of old age psychoses: Stockholm material 1931-1937. *Proceedings of the Royal Society of Medicine*, *52*, 791-794.

Kenny, D. A. (1979). *Correlation and causality*. New York: Wiley-Interscience.

Kent, J. (1985). *Genetic and environmental contributions to cognitive abilities as assessed by a telephone test battery*. Unpublished doctoral dissertation, University of Colorado, Boulder.

Kety, S. S. (1979). Disorders of the human brain. *Scientific American*, *241*, 202-218.

Kety, S. S., Rosenthal, D., Wender, P. H., & Schulsinger, F. (1976). Studies based on a total sample of adopted individuals and their relatives: Why they were necessary, what they demonstrated and failed to demonstrate. *Schizophrenia Bulletin*, *2*, 413-428.

Kety, S. S., Rosenthal, D., Wender, P. H., Schulsinger, F., & Jacobsen, B. (1975). Mental illness in the biological and adoptive families of adopted individuals who have become schizophrenic: A preliminary report based on psychiatric interviews. In R. R. Fieve, D. Rosenthal, & H. Brill (Eds.), *Genetic research in psychiatry* (pp. 147-166). Baltimore: Johns Hopkins University Press.

Kirkegaard-Sorensen, L., & Mednick, S. A. (1977). A prospective study of predictors of criminality: 4. School behavior. In S. A. Mednick & K. O. Christiansen (Eds.), *Biosocial bases of criminal behavior* (pp. 254-266). New York: Gardner.

Kirkegaard-Sorensen, L., & Mednick, S. A. (1977). A prospective study of predictors of criminality: 5. Intelligence. In S. A. Mednick & K. O. Christiansen (Eds.), *Biosocial bases of criminal behavior* (pp. 267-274). New York: Gardner.

Knaack, R. (1978). A note on the usefulness of the Coloured Progressive Matrices (CPM) with preschool children. *Psycol. Erziehung Unterricht, 25*, 159-167.

Koch, H. L. (1966). *Twins and twin relations.* Chicago: University of Chicago Press.

LaBuda, M. C., DeFries, J. C., Fulker, D. W., & Plomin, R. (in press). Longitudinal stability of cognitive ability from infancy to early childhood: Genetic and environmental etiologies. *Child Development.*

Lange, J. (1931). *Crime as destiny.* London: Allen & Unwin.

Larsson, T., Sjogren, T., & Jacobson, G. (1963). Senile dementia: A clinical sociomedical and genetic study. *Acta Psychiatrica Scandinavica, 39* (Suppl. 167), 1-259.

Leahy, A. M. (1935). Nature-nurture and intelligence. *Genetic Psychology Monographs, 17*, 236-308.

Leighton, T., & Loomis, W. F. (1980). *The molecular genetics of development.* New York: Academic Press.

Lerner, R. M. (1984). *On the nature of human plasticity.* Cambridge: Cambridge University Press.

Lewin, R. (1984). Why is development so illogical? *Science, 224*, 1327-1329.

Lewis, M. (1983). What do we mean when we say "infant intelligence scores"? In M. Lewis (Ed.), *Origins of intelligence: Infancy and early childhood* (pp. 1-17). New York: Plenum.

Li, C. C. (1975). *Path analysis: A primer.* Pacific Grove, CA: Boxwood Press.

Loehlin, J. C. (1972). An analysis of alcohol-related questionnaire items from the National Merit Twin Study. *Annals of the New York Academy of Science, 197*, 117-120.

Loehlin, J. C. (1978a). Are CPI scales differently heritable: How good is the evidence? *Behavior Genetics, 8*, 381-382.

Loehlin, J. C. (1978b). Heredity-environment analyses of Jencks's IQ correlations. *Behavior Genetics, 8*, 415-436.

Loehlin, J. C. (1979). Combining data from different groups in human behavior genetics. In J. R. Royce & L. P. Mos (Eds.), *Theoretical advances in behavior genetics* (pp. 303-334). Alphen aan den Rijn, The Netherlands: Sijthoff and Noordhoff.

Loehlin, J. C. (1982). Are personality traits differentially heritable? *Behavior Genetics, 12* 417-428.

Loehlin, J. C. (1983). John Locke and behavior genetics. *Behavior Genetics, 13*, 117-121.

Loehlin, J. C., & DeFries, J. C. (1985). *Genotype-environment correlation revisited.* Manuscript submitted for publication.

Loehlin, J. C., Horn, J. M., & Willerman, L. (1981). Personality resemblance in adoptive families. *Behavior Genetics, 11*, 309-330.

Loehlin, J. C., & Nichols, R. C. (1976). *Heredity, environment and personality.* Austin: University of Texas Press.

Loehlin, J. C., Sharan, S., & Jacoby, R. (1978). In pursuit of the "spatial gene": A family study. *Behavior Genetics, 8*, 27-41.

Loehlin, J. C., & Vandenberg, S. G. (1968). Genetic and environmental components in the covariation of cognitive abilities: An additive model. In S. G. Vandenberg (Ed.), *Progress in human behavior genetics* (pp. 261-285). Baltimore: Johns Hopkins University Press.

Loehlin, J. C., Willerman, L., & Horn, J. M. (1982). Personality resemblances between unwed mothers and their adopted-away offspring. *Journal of Personality and Social Psychology*, *42*, 1089-1099.

Loehlin, J. C., Willerman, L., & Horn, J. M. (1985). Personality resemblance in adoptive families when the children are late adolescents and adults. *Journal of Personality and Social Psychology*, *48*, 376-392.

Longstreth, L. E., Davis, B., Carter, L., Flint, D., Owen, J., Rickert, M., & Taylor, E. (1981). Separation of home intellectual environment and maternal IQ as determinants of child IQ. *Developmental Psychology*, *17*, 532- 541.

Lykken, D. T. (1982). Research with twins: The concept of emergenesis. *Psychophysiology*, *19*, 361-373.

Lykken, D. T., Tellegen, A., & DeRubeis, R. (1978). Volunteer bias in twin research: The rule of two-thirds. *Social Biology*, *25*, 1-9.

Lykken, D. T., Tellegen, A., & Thorkelson, K. (1974). Genetic determinants of EEG frequency spectra. *Biological Psychology*, *1*, 245-259.

Lytton, H., Martin, N. G., & Eaves, L. (1977). Environmental and genetical causes of variation in ethological aspects of behavior in two-year-old boys. *Social Biology*, *24*, 200-211.

Maccoby, E. E., & Jacklin, C. N. (1974). *The psychology of sex differences*. Stanford: Stanford University Press.

Maccoby, E. E., & Martin, J. A. (1983). Socialization in the context of the family: Parent-child interaction. In P. H. Mussen (Ed.), *Handbook of child psychology (4th ed): Vol. 4. Socialization, personality, and social development* (pp. 1-101). New York: Wiley.

Mangan, G. (1982). *The biology of human conduct: East-West models of temperament and personality*. Oxford: Pergamon.

Martin, N. G., Eaves, L. J., & Eysenck, H. J. (1977). Genetical, environmental and personality factors influencing the age of first sexual intercourse in twins. *Journal of Biosocial Science*, *9*, 91-97.

Martin, N. G., Jardine, R., & Eaves, L. J. (1984). Is there only one set of genes for different abilities? A reanalysis of the National Merit Scholarship Qualifying Test (NMSQT) data. *Behavior Genetics*, *14*, 355-370.

Masters, W. H., & Johnson, V. E. (1966). *Human sexual response*. Boston: Little, Brown & Co.

Masters, W. H., & Johnson, V. E. (1970). *Human sexual inadequacy*. Boston: Little, Brown & Co.

Matheny, A. P., Jr. (1975). Twins: Concordance for Piagetian-equivalent items derived from the Bayley Mental Test. *Developmental Psychology*, *2*, 224-227.

Matheny, A. P., Jr. (1980). Bayley's Infant Behavior Record: Behavioral components and twin analyses. *Child Development*, *51*, 1157-1167.

Matheny, A. P., Jr. (1983). A longitudinal twin study of stability of components from Bayley's Infant Behavior Record. *Child Development*, *54*, 356-360.

Matheny, A. P., Jr., & Dolan, A. B. (1975). Persons, situations and time: A genetic view of behavioral change in children. *Journal of Personality and Social Psychology*, *14*, 224-234.

Matheny, A. P., Jr., & Dolan, A. B. (1980). A twin study of personality and temperament during middle childhood. *Journal of Research in Personality*, *14*, 224-234.

Matheny, A. P., Jr., Dolan, A. B., & Wilson, R. S. (1976). Within-pair similarity on Bayley's Infant Behavior Record. *Journal of Genetic Psychology*, *128*, 263-270.

Matheny, A. P., Jr., & Wilson, R. S. (1981). Developmental tasks and rating scales for the laboratory assessment of infant temperament. *JSAS Catalog of Selected Documents in Psychology*, *11*, 81-82.

Matheny, A. P., Jr., Wilson, R. S., Dolan, A. B., & Krantz, J. Z. (1981). Behavior contrasts in twinships: Stability and patterns of differences in childhood. *Child Development*, *52*, 579-588.

Maxwell, J., & Pilliner, A. E. G. (1960). The intellectual resemblance between siblings. *Annals of Human Genetics*, *24*, 23-32.

Mayr, E. (1982). *The growth of biological thought*. Cambridge, MA: Harvard University Press.

McCall, R. B. (1970). IQ pattern over age: Comparisons among siblings and parent-child pairs. *Science*, *170*, 644-648.

McCall, R. B. (1972). Similarity in developmental profile among related pairs of human infants. *Science*, *178*, 1004-1005.

McCall, R. B. (1977). Challenges to a science of developmental psychology. *Child Development*, *48*, 333-344.

McCall, R. B. (1979). The development of intellectual functioning in infancy and the prediction of later IQ. In J. D. Osofsky (Ed.), *Handbook of infant development* (pp. 707-741). New York: Wiley-Interscience.

McCall, R. B. (1981). Nature-nurture and the two realms of development: A proposed integration with respect to mental development. *Child Development*, *52*, 1-12.

McCarthy, B. J., & Hoyer, B. H. (1964). Identity of DNA and diversity of messenger RNA molecules in normal mouse. *Proceedings of the National Academy of Science U.S.A.*, *52*, 915-922.

McClearn, G. E., & Foch, T. T. (1985). Behavioral genetics. In J. E. Birren & K. W. Schaie (Eds.), *Handbook of the psychology of aging* (2nd ed., pp. 113-143). New York: Van Nostrand Reinhold.

McClearn, G. E., Nesselroade, J. R., Pedersen-Ottoson, N. P., Friberg, L. T., Plomin, R., & de Faire, U. H. (1984). *Genetic and environmental influences in behavioral aging*. Grant proposal funded by the National Institute of Aging.

McClintock, B. (1957). Controlling elements and the gene. *Cold Spring Harbor Symposia on Quantitative Biology*, *21*, 197-216.

McGue, M., Bouchard, T. J., Jr., Lykken, D. T., & Feuer, D. (1984). Information processing abilities in twins reared apart. *Intelligence*, *8*, 239-258.

McKusick, V. A. (1983). *Mendelian inheritance in man* (7th ed.). Baltimore: Johns Hopkins University Press.

Mech, E. V. (1973). Adoption: A policy perspective. In B. M. Caldwell & H. N. Ricciuti (Eds.), *Reviews of child development research: Child development and social policy* (pp. 467-508). Chicago: University of Chicago Press.

Medlund, P., Cederlof, R., & Floderus-Myrhed, B. (1976). A new Swedish twin registry. *Acta Medica Scandinavica*, (Supp. 600).

Mednick, S. A., Gabrielli, W. F., Jr., & Hutchings, B. (1984). Genetic influences in criminal convictions: Evidence from an adoption cohort. *Science*, *224*, 891-894.

Mendlewicz, J., & Fleiss, J. L. (1974). Linkage studies with X-chromosome markers in bipolar (manic-depressive) and unipolar (depressive) illnesses. *Biological Psychiatry*, *9*, 261-294.

Mendlewicz, J., & Rainer, J. D. (1977). Adoption study supporting genetic transmission in manic-depressive illness. *Nature*, *268*, 327-329.

Merriman, C. (1924). The intellectual resemblance of twins. *Psychological Monographs*, *33*, (Whole No. 152).

Miller, J. Z., & Rose, R. J. (1982). Familial resemblance in locus of control: A twin family study of the internal-external scale. *Journal of Personality and Social Psychology*, *42*, 535-540.

Mittler, P. (1969). Genetic aspects of psycholinguistic abilities. *Journal of Child Psychology and Psychiatry*, *10*, 165-176.

Mittler, P. (1971). *The study of twins*. Harmondsworth, England: Penguin Books.

Moos, R. H. (1974). *Preliminary manual for Family Environment Scale, Work Environment Scale, and Group Environment Scale*. Palo Alto, CA: Consulting Psychologists Press.

Moos, R. H., & Moos, B. S. (1981). *Family Environment Scale manual*. Palo Alto, CA: Consulting Psychologists Press.

Morrison, J. R., & Stewart, M. A. (1973). The psychiatric status of the legal families of adopted hyperactive children. *Archives of General Psychiatry*, *28*, 888-891.

Munsinger, H. (1975). The adopted child's IQ: A critical review. *Psychological Bulletin*, *82*, 623-659.

Munsinger, H., & Douglass, A. (1976). The syntactic abilities of identical twins, fraternal twins, and their siblings. *Child Development*, *47*, 40-50.

Murray, R. M., & Gurling, H. M. D. (1980). Genetic contributions to normal and abnormal drinking. In M. Sandler (Ed.), *Psychopharmacology of alcohol*. New York: Raven.

Nance, W. E. (1976). Genetic studies of the offspring of identical twins. *Acta Geneticae Medicae et Gemellologiae*, *25*, 103-113.

Newman, J., Freeman, F., & Holzinger, K. (1937). *Twins: A study of heredity and environment*. Chicago: University of Chicago Press.

Nichols, P. L., & Broman, S. H. (1974). Familial resemblance in infant mental development. *Developmental Psychology*, *10*, 442-446.

Nichols, R. C. (1965). The National Merit Twin Study. In S. G. Vandenberg (Ed.), *Methods and goals in human behavior genetics* (pp. 231-244). New York: Academic Press.

Nurnberger, J. I., & Gershon, E. S. (1981). Genetics of affective disorders. In E. Friedman (Ed.), *Depression and antidepressants: Implications for courses and treatment*. New York: Raven.

O'Connor, M., Foch, T. T., Sherry, T., & Plomin, R. (1980). A twin study of specific behavioral problems of socialization as viewed by parents. *Journal of Abnormal Child Psychology*, *8*, 189-199.

Orvaschel, H. (1983). Maternal depression and child dysfunction: Children at risk. In B. B. Lahey & A. E. Kazdin (Eds.), *Advances in clinical child psychology* (Vol. 6, pp. 169-197). New York: Plenum.

Osborne, R. T. (1980). *Twins: Black and white*. Athens, GA: Foundation for Human Understanding.

Osofsky, J. D. (1979). *Handbook of infant development*. New York: Wiley-Interscience.

Paigen, K. (1980). Temporal genes and other developmental regulators in mammals. In T. Leighton & W. F. Loomis (Eds.), *The molecular genetics of development* (pp. 419-470). New York: Academic Press.

Palmiter, R. D., Brinster, R. L., Hammer, R. E., Trumbauer, M. E., Rosenfeld, M. G., Birnberg, N. C., & Evans, R. M. (1982). Dramatic growth of mice that develop from eggs microinjected with metallothionein-growth hormone fusion genes. *Nature, 300*, 611-615.

Palmiter, R. D., Chen, H. Y., & Brinster, R. L. (1982). Differential regulation of metallothionein-thymidine kinase fusion genes in transgenic mice and their offspring. *Cell, 29*, 701-710.

Partanen, J., Bruun, K., & Markkanen, T. (1966). *Inheritance of drinking behavior*. Helsinki: Finnish Foundation for Alcohol Studies.

Pauls, D. L., Bucher, K. D., Crowe, R. R., & Noyes, R. (in press). A genetic study of panic disorder pedigrees. *American Journal of Human Genetics*.

Pedersen, N. L., Friberg, L., Floderus-Myrhed, B., McClearn, G. E., & Plomin, R. (1983, June). *Swedish early separated twins: Identification and characterization*. Paper presented at the Fourth International Congress on Twin Studies, London, England.

Pedersen, N. L., Friberg, L., Floderus-Myrhed, B., McClearn, G. E., & Plomin, R. (1984). Swedish early separated twins: Identification and characterization. *Acta Geneticae Medicae et Gemellologiae, 33*, 243-250.

Pedersen, N. L., McClearn, G. E., Plomin, R., & Friberg, L. (1985). Separated fraternal twins: Resemblance for cognitive abilities. *Behavior Genetics, 15*, 407-419.

Pelton, P. A., & Plomin, R. (in press). Genetic mediation of environmental influences in early childhood. *Behavior Genetics*. (Abstract)

Pfouts, J. H. (1980). Birth order, age-spacing, IQ differences, and family relations. *Journal of Marriage and the Family, 43*, 517-531.

Plomin, R. (1974). *A temperament theory of personality development: Parent-child interactions*. Unpublished doctoral dissertation, University of Texas, Austin.

Plomin, R. (1981). Heredity and temperament: A comparison of twin data for self-report questionnaires, parental ratings, and objectively assessed behavior. In L. Gedda, P. Parisi, & W. E. Nance (Eds.), *Twin research 3: Intelligence, personality, and development* (pp. 269-278). New York: Liss.

Plomin, R. (1983). Childhood temperament. In B. Lahey & A. Kazdin (Eds.), *Advances in clinical child psychology* (Vol. 6, pp. 45-92). New York: Plenum.

Plomin, R. (1983). Developmental behavioral genetics. *Child Development, 54*, 253-259.

Plomin, R. (1985). Behavioral genetics. In D. Detterman (Ed.), *Current topics in human intelligence: Research methodology* (pp. 297-320). Norwood, NJ: Ablex.

Plomin, R. (in press-a). Multivariate analysis and developmental behavioral genetic analyses of change and continuity. *Behavior Genetics*.

Plomin, R. (in press-b). Developmental behavioral genetics and infancy. In J. D. Osofsky (Ed.), *Handbook of infant development* (2nd ed.). New York: Wiley-Interscience.

Plomin, R., & Daniels, D. (in press). Developmental behavioral genetics and shyness. In W. H. Jones, J. M. Cheek, & S. R. Briggs (Eds.), *A sourcebook on shyness: Research and treatment*. New York: Plenum.

Plomin, R., & DeFries, J. C. (1979). Multivariate behavioral genetic analysis of twin data on scholastic abilities. *Behavior Genetics, 9*, 505-517.

Plomin, R., & DeFries, J. C. (1980). Genetics and intelligence: Recent data. *Intelligence, 4*, 15-24.

Plomin, R., & DeFries, J. C. (1981). Multivariate behavioral genetics and development: Twin studies. In L. Gedda, P. Parisi, & W. E. Nance (Eds.), *Twin Research 3: Intelligence, personality, and development* (pp. 25-33). New York: Liss.

Plomin, R., & DeFries, J. C. (1985a). *Origins of individual differences in infancy: The Colorado Adoption Project.* New York: Academic Press.

Plomin, R., & DeFries, J. C. (1985b). A parent-offspring adoption study of cognitive abilities in early childhood. *Intelligence, 9*, 341-356.

Plomin, R., DeFries, J. C., & Loehlin, J. C. (1977). Genotype-environment interaction and correlation in the analysis of human behavior. *Psychological Bulletin, 84*, 309-322.

Plomin, R., DeFries, J. C., & McClearn, G. E. (1980). *Behavioral genetics: A primer.* San Francisco: Freeman.

Plomin, R., & Deitrich, R. A. (1982). Neuropharmacogenetics and behavioral genetics. *Behavior Genetics, 12*, 111-121.

Plomin, R., & Foch, T. T. (1980). A twin study of objectively assessed personality in childhood. *Journal of Personality and Social Psychology, 39*, 680-688.

Plomin, R., & Foch, T. T. (1981). Sex differences and individual differences. *Child Development, 52*, 383-385.

Plomin, R., Foch, T. T., & Rowe, D. C. (1981). Bobo clown aggression in childhood: Environment, not genes. *Journal of Research in Personality, 15*, 331-342.

Plomin, R., & Fulker, D. W. (in press). Behavioral genetics and development in early adolescence. In R. M. Lerner & T. T. Foch (Eds.), *Biological-psychosocial interactions in early adolescence: A life-span perspective.* Hillsdale, NJ: Lawrence Erlbaum Associates.

Plomin, R., Loehlin, J. C., & DeFries, J. C. (1985). Genetic and environmental components of "environmental" influences. *Developmental Psychology, 21, 391-402.*

Plomin, R., & Rowe, D. C. (1979). Genetic and environmental etiology of social behavior in infancy. *Developmental Psychology, 15*, 62-72.

Plomin, R., & Thompson, L. (in press). Life-span developmental behavioral genetics. In P. B. Baltes, D. Featherman, & R. M. Lerner (Eds.), *Life-span developmental psychology*, Vol. 8. Hillsdale, NJ: Lawrence Erlbaum Associates.

Plomin, R., & Vandenberg, S. G. (1980). An analysis of Koch's (1966) Primary Mental Abilities test data for 5- to 7-year-old twins. *Behavior Genetics, 10*, 409-412.

Pogue-Geile, M. F., & Rose, R. J. (1985). Developmental genetic studies of adult personality. *Developmental Psychology, 21*, 547-557.

Rahe, R. H., Hervig, L., & Rosenman, R. H. (1978). Heritability of Type A behavior. *Psychosomatic Medicine, 40*, 478-486.

Raven, J. C. (1965). *Guide to using the Coloured Progressive Matrices.* London: Grieve the Printers.

Razin, A., Cedar, H., & Riggs, A. D. (1984). *DNA methylation: Biochemistry and biological significance.* New York: Springer-Verlag.

Reppucci, C. M. (1968). *Hereditary influences upon distribution of attention in infancy.* Unpublished doctoral dissertation, Harvard University.

Reznikoff, M., Domino, G., Bridges, C., & Honeyman, M. (1973). Creative abilities in identical and fraternal twins. *Behavior Genetics, 3,* 365-377.

Reznikoff, M. G., & Honeyman, M. S. (1967). MMPI profiles of monozygotic and dizygotic twin pairs. *Journal of Consulting Psychology, 31,* 100.

Rice, T., Corley, R., Fulker, D. W., & Plomin, R. (1985). *The development and validation of a test battery measuring specific cognitive abilities in four-year-old children.* Manuscript submitted for publication.

Richards, T. W., & Simons, M. P. (1941). The Fels Child Behavior Scales. *Genetic Psychology Monographs, 24,* 259-309.

Roberts, C. A., & Johansson, C. B. (1974). The inheritance of cognitive interest styles among twins. *Journal of Vocational Behavior, 4,* 237-243.

Rodgers, J. L. (1984). Confluence effects: Not here, not now! *Developmental Psychology, 20,* 321-331.

Rodgers, J. L., & Rowe, D. C. (1985). Does contiguity breed similarity? A within-family analysis of nonshared sources of IQ differences between siblings. *Developmental Psychology, 21,* 743-746.

Roe, A. (1944). The adult adjustment of children of alcoholic parentage raised in foster homes. *Quarterly Journal of Studies on Alcohol, 5,* 378- 393.

Rogosa, D. (1979). Causal models in longitudinal research: Rationale, formulation, and interpretation. In J. R. Nesselroade & P. B. Baltes (Eds.), *Longitudinal research in the study of behavior and development* (pp. 263- 302). New York: Academic Press.

Rose, R. J., & Ditto, W. B. (1983). A developmental-genetic analysis of common fears from early adolescence to early adulthood. *Child Development, 54,* 361-368.

Rosenthal, D. (1970). *Genetic theory and abnormal behavior.* New York: McGraw-Hill.

Rosenthal, D. (1972). Three adoption studies of heredity in the schizophrenic disorders. *International Journal of Mental Health, 1,* 63-75.

Rosenthal, D., Wender, P. H., Kety, S. S., Schulsinger, F., Welner, J., & Ostergaard, L. (1968). Schizophrenics' offspring reared in adoptive homes. *Journal of Psychiatric Research, 6,* 377-391.

Rosenthal, D., Wender, P. H., Kety, S. S., Welner, J., & Schulsinger, F. (1971). The adopted-away offspring of schizophrenics. *American Journal of Psychiatry, 128,* 307-311.

Roth, M. (1955). The natural history of mental disorder in old age. *Journal of Mental Science, 101,* 281-301.

Rothbart, M. K., & Derryberry, D. (1981). Development of individual differences in temperament. In M. E. Lamb & A. L. Brown (Eds.), *Advances in developmental psychology* (pp. 37-86). Hillsdale, NJ: Lawrence Erlbaum Associates.

Rowe, D. C. (1981). Environmental and genetic influences on dimensions of perceived parenting: A twin study. *Developmental Psychology, 17,* 203-208.

Rowe, D. C. (1982). Sources of variability in sex-linked personality attributes. *Developmental Psychology, 18,* 431-434.

Rowe, D. C. (1983a). Biometrical genetic models of self-reported delinquent behavior: A twin study. *Behavior Genetics, 13,* 473-489.

Rowe, D. C. (1983b). A biometrical analysis of perceptions of family environment: A study of twin and singleton sibling kinships. *Child Development, 54,* 416-423.

Rowe, D. C., & Osgood, D. W. (1984). Heredity and sociological theories of delinquency: A reconsideration. *American Sociological Review*, *49*, 526-540.

Rowe, D. C., & Plomin, R. (1977). Temperament in early childhood. *Journal of Personality Assessment*, *41*, 150-156.

Rowe, D. C., & Plomin, R. (1978). The Burt controversy: A comparison of Burt's data on IQ with data from other studies. *Behavior Genetics*, *8*, 81-84.

Rowe, D. C., & Plomin, R. (1979). A multivariate twin analysis of within- family environmental influences in infants' social responsiveness. *Behavior Genetics*, *9*, 519-525.

Rowe, D. C., & Plomin, R. (1981). The importance of nonshared (E_1) environmental influences in behavioral development. *Developmental Psychology*, *17*, 517-531.

Safer, D. J. (1973). A familial factor in minimal brain dysfunction. *Behavior Genetics*, *3*, 175-186.

Sanchez, O., & Yunis, J. J. (1977). New chromosome techniques and their medical applications. In J. J. Yunis (Ed.), *New chromosomal syndromes* (pp. 1-54). New York: Academic Press.

Scarr, S. (1966). Genetic factors in activity and motivation. *Child Development*, *38*, 663-673.

Scarr, S. (1969). Social introversion-extraverson as a heritable response. *Child Development*, *40*, 823-832.

Scarr, S. (1976). An evolutionary perspective on infant intelligence: Species patterns and individual variations. In M. Lewis (Ed.), *Origins of intelligence* (pp. 165-197). New York: Plenum.

Scarr, S., & Kidd, K. K. (1983). Developmental behavior genetics. In P. H. Mussen (Ed.), *Handbook of child psychology (4th ed.): Vol. 2. Infancy and developmental psychobiology* (pp. 345-433). New York: Wiley.

Scarr, S., & McCartney, K. (1983). How people make their own environments: A theory of genotype → environment effects. *Child Development*, *54*, 424-435.

Scarr, S., Webber, P. I., Weinberg, R. A., & Wittig, M. A. (1981). Personality resemblance among adolescents and their parents in biologically related and adoptive families. *Journal of Personality and Social Psychology*, *40*, 885-898.

Scarr, S., & Weinberg, R. A. (1977). Intellectual similarities within families of both adopted and biological children. *Intelligence*, *1*, 170-191.

Scarr, S., & Weinberg, R. A. (1978a). Attitudes, interests, and IQ. *Human Nature*, April, 29-36.

Scarr, S., & Weinberg, R. A. (1978b). The influence of "family background" on intellectual attainment. *American Sociological Review*, *43*, 674- 692.

Schachter, F. F., Shore, E., Feldman-Rotman, S., Marquis, R. E., & Campbell, S. (1976). Sibling deidentification. *Developmental Psychology*, *12*, 418-427.

Schachter, F. F., & Stone, R. K. (1985). Difficult sibling, easy sibling: Temperament and the within-family environment. *Child Development*, *56*, 1335-1344.

Schaffer, H. R. (1971). *The growth of sociability*. Harmondsworth: Penguin.

Schaie, K. W. (1975). Research strategy in developmental human behavior genetics. In K. W. Schaie, V. E. Anderson, G. E. McClearn, & J. Money (Eds.), *Developmental human behavior genetics: Nature-nurture redefined* (pp. 205-219). Lexington, MA: Lexington Books.

Schaie, K. W. (1983). *Longitudinal studies of adult psychological development*. New York: Guilford.

Schmid, C. W., & Jelenik, W. R. (1982). The Alu family of dispersed repetitive sequences. *Science, 216*, 1065-1070.

Schneider, E. L. (1978). Cytogenetics of aging. In E. L. Schneider (Ed.), *The genetics of aging* (pp. 27-52). New York: Plenum.

Schoenfeldt, L. F. (1968). The hereditary components of the Project TALENT two-day test battery. *Measurement and Evaluation in Guidance, 1*, 130-140.

Schooler, C. (1972). Birth order effects: Not here, not now! *Psychological Bulletin, 78*, 161-175.

Schuckit, M. A., Goodwin, D. W., & Winokur, G. (1972). A study of alcoholism in half siblings. *American Journal of Psychiatry, 128*, 1132-1135.

Schuckit, M. A., & Moore, M. A. (1979). Drug problems in the elderly. In O. J. Kaplan (Ed.), *Psychopathology of aging* (pp. 229-241). New York: Academic Press.

Schuckit, M. A., & Pastor, P. A., Jr. (1979). Alcohol-related psychopatholgy in the aged. In O. J. Kaplan (Ed.), *Psychopathology of aging* (pp. 211- 227). New York: Academic Press.

Schulsinger, F. (1972). Psychopathy: heredity and environment. *International Journal of Mental Health, 1*, 190-206.

Segal, N. L. T. (in press). Monozygotic and dizygotic twins: A comparative analysis of mental ability profiles. *Child Development*.

Shapiro, J. (1983). *Mobile genetic elements*. New York: Academic Press.

Shields, J. (1962). *Monozygotic twins brought up apart and brought up together*. London: Oxford University Press.

Shields, J., Heston, L. L., & Gottesman, I. I. (1975). Schizophrenia and the schizoid: The problem for genetic analysis. In R. R. Fieve, D. Rosenthal, & H. Brill (Eds.), *Genetic research in psychiatry* (pp. 167-197). Baltimore: Johns Hopkins University Press.

Shine, J., & Dalgarno, L. (1974). Escherichia coli 16S ribosomal RNA: Complementarity to nonsense triplets and ribosome binding sites. *Proceedings of the National Academy of Sciences U.S.A., 71*, 1342- 1346.

Singer, S., Corley, R., Guiffrida, C., & Plomin, R. (1984). The development and validation of a test battery to measure differentiated cognitive abilities in three-year-old children. *Educational and Psychological Measurement, 49*, 703-713.

Skinner, B. F., & Vaughan, M. E. (1983). *Enjoy old age: A program of self-management*. New York: Norton.

Skodak, M., & Skeels, H. M. (1949). A final follow-up of one hundred adopted children. *Journal of Genetic Psychology, 75*, 85-125.

Snyder, S. H. (1980). Brain peptides as neurotransmitters. *Science, 209*, 976-983.

Snygg, D. (1938). The relation between the intelligence of mothers and of their children living in foster homes. *Journal of Genetic Psychology, 52*, 401-406.

Stabenau, J. R. (1975). Some genetic and family studies in autism and childhood schizophrenia. In D. V. S. Sankar (Ed.), *Mental health in children* (pp. 31-60). Westbury, NY: PJD Publications.

Stafford, R. E. (1961). Sex differences in spatial visualization as evidence of sex-linked inheritance. *Perceptual and Motor Skills, 13*, 428.

Sternberg, R. J., & Gardner, M. K. (1982). A componential interpretation of the general factor in human intelligence. In H. J. Eysenck (Ed.), *A model for intelligence* (pp.231-254). Heidelberg: Springer-Verlag.

Stocks, P. (1933). A biometric investigation of twins and their brothers and sisters. *Annals of Eugenics, 5*, 1-55.

Stunkard, A. J., Foch, T. T., & Hrubec, Z. (1985). *Genetics and human obesity: I. Results of a twin study*. Manuscript submitted for publication.

Stunkard, A., Sorensen, T. I. A., Hanis, C., Teasdale, T., Chakraborty, R., Schull, W. J., & Schulsinger, F. (1985). *Genetics and human obesity. II. Results of an adoption study*. Manuscript submitted for publication.

Svanum, S., & Bringle, R. G. (1980). Evaluation of confluence model variables on IQ and achievement test scores in a sample of 6- to 11-year-old children. *Journal of Educational Psychology, 72*, 427-436.

Tambs, K., Sundet, J. M., & Magnus, P. (1984). Heritability analysis of the WAIS subtests: A study of twins. *Intelligence, 8*, 283-293.

Tanner, J. M. (1978). *Fetus into man: Physical growth from conception to maturity*. Cambridge, MA: Harvard University Press.

Tanner, J. M., Healy, M. J. R., Lockhart, R. D., Mackenzie, J. D., & Whitehouse, R. H. (1956). The prediction of adult body measurements from measurements taken each year from birth to 5 years. *Archives of Diseases in Childhood, 31*, 372-381.

Taylor, C. E., & Condra, C. (1978). Genetic and environmental interaction in Drosophila pseudoobscura. *Journal of Heredity, 69*, 63-64.

Terman, L. M., & Merrill, M. A. (1973). *Stanford-Binet Intelligence Scale: 1972 norms edition*. Boston: Houghton-Mifflin.

Thomas, A., & Chess, S. (1977). *Temperament and development*. New York: Brunner/Mazel.

Thomas, A., & Chess, S. (1982). Temperament and follow-up to adulthood. In R. Porter & G. M. Collins (Eds.), *Temperamental differences in infants and young children* (pp. 168-175). London: Pitman.

Thomas, A., Chess, S., & Birch, H. G. (1968). *Temperament and behavior disorders in children*. New York: New York University Press.

Thompson, L. A., & Fagan, J. F., III. (1983). A family study of infant recognition memory. *Behavior Genetics, 13*, 555. (Abstract).

Thompson, L. A., Plomin, R., & DeFries, J. C. (1985). Parent-infant resemblance for general and specific cognitive abilities in the Colorado Adoption Project. *Intelligence, 9*, 1-13.

Thompson, L. A., (1985). *Multivariate genetic analysis of "environmental" influences on infant cognitive development*. Manuscript submitted for publication.

Thorndike, E. L. (1905). Measurement of twins. *Archives of Philosophy, Psychology, and Scientific Methods, 1*, 1-64.

Thurstone, T. G., Thurstone, L. L., & Strandskov, H. H. (1955). *Scores of one hundred and twenty-five pairs of twins on fifty-nine tests* (Report No. 12, Psychometric Laboratory). Chapel Hill, NC: University of North Carolina.

Tiisala, R., & Kantero, R. (1971). Some parent-child correlations for height, weight and skeletal age up to 10 years. *Acta Paediatrica Scandinavica*, (Suppl. 220), 42-48.

Torgersen, A. M. (1982). Influence of genetic factors on temperament development in early childhood. In R. Porter & G. M. Collins (Eds.), *Temperamental differences in infants and young children* (pp. 141-154). London: Pitman.

Torgersen, A. M., & Kringlen, E. (1978). Genetic aspects of temperamental differences in infants: A study of same-sexed twins. *Journal of the American Academy of Child Psychiatry, 17*, 433-444.

Traub, R., Gajdusek, D. C., & Gibbs, C. J. (1977). Transmissable virus dementia: The relation of transmissable spongiform encephalopathy to Creutzfeldt-Jakob disease. In W. L. Smith & M. Kinsbourne (Eds.), *Aging and dementia* (pp. 91-146). New York: Spectrum.

Traupmann, J., & Hatfield, E. (1981). Love and its effect on mental and physical health. In R. W. Fogel, E. Hatfield, S. B. Kiesler, & E. Shanas (Eds.), *Aging: Stability and change in the family* (pp. 253-274). New York: Academic Press.

Turner, G., & Opitz, J. M. (1980). Editorial comment: X-linked mental retardation. *American Journal of Medical Genetics, 7*, 407-415.

Uzgiris, I. C., & Hunt, J. M. (1975). *Assessment in infancy*. Urbana: University of Illinois Press.

Vale, J. R. (1980). *Genes, environment and behavior: An interactionist approach*. New York: Harper & Row.

Van den Daele, L. (1971). Infant reactivity to redundant proprioceptive and auditory stimulation: A twin study. *Journal of Psychology, 78*, 269-276.

Vandenberg, S. G. (1962). The Hereditary Abilities Study: Hereditary components in a psychological test battery. *American Journal of Human Genetics, 14*, 220-237.

Vandenberg, S. G. (1967). Hereditary factors in normal personality traits (as measured by inventories). In J. Wortis (Ed.), *Recent advances in biological psychiatry* (pp. 65-104). New York: Plenum.

Vandenberg, S. G. (1968). The nature and nurture of intelligence. In D. C. Glass (Ed.), *Genetics* (pp. 3-58). New York: Rockefeller University Press.

Vandenberg, S. G., Singer, S. M., & Pauls, D. L. (in press). *The heredity of behavioral disorders in adults and children*. New York: Plenum.

Wachs, T. D. (1983). The use and abuse of environment in behavior-genetic research. *Child Development, 54*, 416-423.

Wachs, T. D., & Gruen, G. (1982). *Early experience and human development*. New York: Plenum.

Waddington, C. H. (1957). *The strategy of the genes*. London: Allen & Unwin.

Wagner, M. E., Schubert, H. J. P., & Schubert, D. S. P. (1979). Sibship-constellation effects on psychosocial development, creativity and health. *Advances in Child Development and Behavior, 14*, 57-148.

Watson, J. D., Tooze, J., & Kurtz, D. T. (1983). *Recombinant DNA: A short course*. New York: Freeman.

Watt, N. F. (1984). In a nutshell: The first two decades of high-risk research in schizophrenia. In N. F. Watt, E. J. Anthony, L. C. Wynne, & J. E. Rolf (Eds.), *Children at risk for schizophrenia: A longitudinal perspective* (pp. 572-596). Cambridge: Cambridge University Press.

Watt, N. F., Anthony, E. J., Wynne, L. C., & Rolf, J. E. (1984). *Children at risk for schizophrenia: A longitudinal perspective*. Cambridge: Cambridge University Press.

Weiler, S. J. (1981). Aging and sexuality and the myth of decline. In R. W. Fogel, E. Hatfield, S. B. Kiesler, & E. Shanas (Eds.), *Aging: Stability and change in the family* (pp. 317-327). New York: Academic Press.

Wictorin, M. (1952). *Bidrag til raknefardighetens psykologi, en tvillingundersokning.* Goteborg: Elanders.

Wigler, M., Levy, D., & Perucho, M. (1981). The somatic replication of DNA methylation. *Cell, 24,* 33-40.

Wilde, G. J. S. (1964). Inheritance of personality traits: An investigation into the hereditary determination of neurotic instability, extroversion, and other personality traits by means of a questionnaire administered to twins. *Acta Psychologica, 22,* 37-51.

Willerman, L. (1973). Activity level and hyperactivity in twins. *Child Development, 44,* 288-293.

Williams, T. (1975). Family resemblance in abilities: The Wechsler scales. *Behavior Genetics, 5,* 405-409.

Willoughby, R. R. (1927). Family similarities in mental tests abilities. *Genetic Psychology Monographs, 2,* 239-277.

Wilson, J. Q., & Herrnstein, R. J. (1985). *Crime and human nature.* NY: Simon & Schuster.

Wilson, R. S. (1975). Twins: Patterns of cognitive development as measured on the WPPSI. *Developmental Psychology, 11,* 126-139.

Wilson, R. S. (1976). Concordance in physical growth for monozygotic and dizygotic twins. *Annals of Human Biology, 3,* 1-10.

Wilson, R. S. (1977). Mental development in twins. In A. Oliverio (Ed.), *Genetics, environment and intelligence* (pp. 305-336). Alphen aan den Rijn, The Netherlands: Elsevier.

Wilson, R. S. (1979). Analysis of longitudinal twin data. *Acta Geneticae Medicae et Gemellologiae, 28,* 93-105.

Wilson, R. S. (1983). The Louisville Twin study: Developmental synchronies in behavior. *Child Development, 54,* 298-316.

Wilson, R. S., Brown, A., & Matheny, A. P., Jr. (1971). Emergence and persistence of behavioral differences in twins. *Child Development, 42,* 1381-1398.

Wilson, R. S., & Matheny, A. P., Jr. (1976). Retardation and twin concordance in infant mental development: A reassessment. *Behavior Genetics, 6,* 353-358.

Wilson, R.S., & Matheny, A. P., Jr. (1986). Behavior-genetics research in infant temperament: The Louisville Twin Study. In R. Plomin & J. Dunn (Eds.), *The study of temperament: Changes, continuities, and challenges* (pp. 81- 97). Hillsdale, NJ: Lawrence Erlbaum Associates.

Wingfield, A. H. (1928). Twins and orphans. *Journal of Educational Psychology, 19,* 410-423.

Winokur, G. (1975). The Iowa 500: Heterogeneity and course in manic-depressive illness (bipolar). *Comprehensive Psychiatry, 16,* 125-131.

Winokur, G., Cadoret, R., Baker, M., & Dorzab, J. (1975). Depression spectrum disease versus pure depressive disease: Some further data. *British Journal of Psychiatry, 127,* 75-77.

Wright, S. (1931). Statistical methods in biology. *Journal of the American Statistical Association, 26,* 155-163.

Yarrow, L. J., Goodwin, M. S., Manheimer, H., & Milowe, I. D. (1973). Infancy experiences and cognitive and personality development at ten years. In J. L. Stone,

H. T. Smith, & L. B. Murphy (Eds.), *The competent infant: Research and commentary* (pp. 1274-1281). New York: Basic Books.

Yeates, K. O., MacPhee, D., Campbell, F. A., & Ramey, C. T. (1983). Maternal IQ and home environment as determinants of early childhood intellectual competence: A developmental analysis. *Developmental Psychology, 19,* 731-739.

Yen, W. M. (1975). Sex-linked major-gene influences on selected types of spatial performance. *Behavior Genetics, 5,* 281-298.

Young, P. A., Eaves, L. J., & Eysenck, H. J. (1980). Intergenerational stability and changes in the causes of variation in adult and juvenile personality. *Journal of Personality and Individual Differences, 1,* 35-55.

Youngman, P., Zuber, P., Perkins, J. B., Sandman, K., Igo, M., & Losick, R. (1985). New ways to study developmental genes in spore-forming bacteria. *Science, 228,* 285-291.

Zajonc, R. B. (1983). Validating the confluence model. *Psychological Bulletin, 93,* 457-480.

Zajonc, R. B., & Markus, G. B. (1975). Birth order and intellectual development. *Psychological Review, 82,* 74-88.

Zerbin-Rudin, E. (1967). Kongenitale wortblindheit oder spezifische dyslexie (congenital word-blindness). *Bulletin of the Orton Society, 17,* 47-56.

Zonderman, A. B. (1982). Differential heritability and consistency: A reanalysis of the National Merit Scholarship Qualifying Test (NMSQT) California Psychological Inventory (CPI) data. *Behavior Genetics, 12,* 193-208.

Zuckerman, M., & Oltean, M. (1958). Some relationships between maternal attitude factors and authoritarianism, personality needs, psychopathy, and self-acceptance. *Child Development, 30,* 27-36.

Author Index

A

Abbey, H., 212, *332, 339*
Abramovitch, R., 83, *332*
Adams, B., 230, *332*
Ahern, F. M., 72, 277, 278, *332*
Akesson, H. O., 314, *332*
Allen, L., 204, *344*
Ambros, 37, 41
Anastasi, A., 91, *332*
Anava, S. G., 35, *332*
Anderson, M. A., 313, 314, *342*
Angst, J., 299, *332*
Anthony, E. J., 223, *357*
Appelbaum, S. L., 304, *338*
Ashton, G. C., 258, 264, *337*

B

Baker, L. A., 179, *332*
Baker, M. M., 301, *358*
Bakwin, H., 212, *332*
Baltes, P. B., 253, 306, 310, 311, 317, 318, 319, 320, *332, 333*
Barbos, J. A., 30, *341*
Baron, M., *333*
Baskin, Y., 30, 301, *333*
Bax, M., 192, *345*
Bayley, N., 103, 153, 170, 172, 178, 182, 192, 204, 228, *333*

Beckwith, L., 148, *333*
Bell, R. Q., 87, 110, *333*
Belmont, L., 78, *333*
Beloff, J. R., 247, *335*
Berbaum, M. L., 78, *333*
Bergsma, D., 305, *333*
Bernreuter, R. G., 242, *333*
Bertelsen, A., 301, *333*
Bessman, S. P., 12, *333*
Bilek, M. K., 200, *339*
Birch, H. G., *356*
Birnstiel, C. C., 31, *342*
Blair, L., 39, *342*
Blewett, D. B., 247, *335*
Block, J. B., 230, 235, 261, *333*
Blum, J. E., 304, 307, 308, 315, *332, 345*
Bock, R. D., 268, 269, *334*
Bohman, M., 292, 296, *334*
Bondy, E., 306, 307, *346*
Bradley, R. H., 82, 102, 122, 127, 137, 152, 163, *334, 339*
Breland, H. M., 78, *334*
Brenner, S., 37, *334*
Bridges, C., 241, *353*
Bringle, R. G., 78, *356*
Brinster, R. L., 38, 39, *334, 351*
Brody, N., 176, *342*
Broman, S. H., 173, 174, *334, 350*
Brown, A., 186, 188, 217, *358*
Bruun, K., 271, 272, 280, 294, *351*

Nesselroade, J. R., 308, *349*
Nettles, M., 83, 137, *338*
Newman, J., 230, 262, 263, 288, *350*
Nichols, P. L., 173, 174, *350*
Nichols, R. C., 71, 131, 132, 238–240, 243, 244, 247, 249, 275, 276, 282, 284, *347, 350*
Nordgvist, T., 227, *340*
Noyes, R., 291, *351*
Nurnberger, J. I., 299, 300, *350*

O

O'Brien, P. J., 233, 322, *342*
O'Connor, M., 216, 217, 222, *350*
Oltean, M., 140, *359*
Omenn, G. S., 295, *344*
Ong, E. S., 35, *332*
Opitz, J. M., 13, *357*
Orraschel, H., 223, *350*
Osborne, R. T., 247, *350*
Osgood, D. W., 250, *354*
Osofsky, J. D., 170, *351*
Ottina, K., 313, *342*
Owen, C., 192, *345*
Owen, J., 151, *348*

P

Paigen, K., 41, 42, *351*
Palmiter, R. D., 38, 39, *334*
Parsons, P. A., 11, *339*
Partanen, J., 271, 272, 280, 294, *351*
Pastor, P. A., Jr., 315, *355*
Pauls, D. L., 291, 297, *357*
Pedersen, N. L., 72, 129, 257, 262, 273, 279, 280, 288, 295, 308, *340, 351*
Pederson-Ottoson, N. P., 308, *349*
Pelton, P. A., 157, *351*
Perkins, J. B., 25, 39, *359*
Perucho, M., 34, *358*
Peterson, J. L., 82, *340*
Pfouts, J. H., 78, *351*
Pilliner, A. E. G., 230, *349*
Plomin, R., 6, 10, 11, 13, 14, 15, 18, 20, 47, 50, 51, 52, 53, 54, 55, 56, 58, 59, 60, 61, 62, 72, 73, 77, 80–88, 89, 91, 94, 99, 100, 101, 102, 110, 114, 115, 120, 122, 123, 124, 129, 135, 136, 137, 140, 141, 144, 147, 152, 153, 155, 156, 157, 158, 159, 160, 163, 164, 165, 169, 170, 171, 174, 177, 178, 179, 180, 181, 182, 184, 186, 189, 192, 196, 197, 202, 203, 206, 207, 208, 209, 210, 211, 213, 214, 215,

216, 217, 218, 219, 223, 226, 232, 238, 240, 243, 244, 245, 246, 247, 252, 257, 260, 262, 266, 283, 284, 288, 294, 295, 297, 308, 317, 321, *334, 337, 338, 340, 344, 347, 349, 350, 351, 352, 353, 354, 355, 356*
Plotkin, D. J., 30, *341*
Pogue-Geile, M. F., 285, 289, 290, *352*
Polovina, J., 258, 264, 265, 266, 267, *337*
Prather, E. M., 153, 180, *342*
Prell, D. B., 248, *339*
Pribnow, D., 35, *341*

R

Radke-Yarrow, M., 223, *337*
Radnia, K., 37, *335*
Rahe, R. H., 283, *352*
Rainer, J. D., 223, 299, 301, *339, 350*
Ramey, C. T., 152, 165, *359*
Rao, D. C., 249, *335*
Raschtchian, R., 314, *342*
Rashad, M. N., 258, 268, *337*
Rasmusson, J., 72, 279, 280, *340*
Raven, J. C., 198, *352*
Razin, A., 34, *352*
Reese, H. W., 253, 317–320, *333*
Reppucci, C. M., 190, *353*
Reznick, J. S., 182, 295, *341, 346*
Reznikoff, M., 241, *353*
Reznikoff, M. G., 250, *353*
Rice, T., 209, 210, *353*
Richards, T. W., 219, *353*
Richardson, K., 230, *332*
Rickert, M., 151, *348*
Riggs, A. D., 34, *352*
Rine, J., 39, *342*
Rivas, M. L., 13, *336*
Roberts, C. A., 276, *353*
Rodgers, J. L., 78, 79, *353*
Roe, A., 297, *353*
Rogosa, D., 110, *353*
Rolf, J. E., 223, *357*
Rose, R. J., 283, 285, 289, 290, 291, *350, 352, 353*
Rosenberg, L., 304, *338*
Rosenfeld, M. G., 35, *332, 351*
Rosenman, R., 244, 247, 283, 284, *344, 352*
Rosenthal, D., 73, 297, 298, 299, *346, 353*
Roth, B., 191, *346*
Roth, M., 313, *353*
Rothbart, M. K., 182, *353*
Rowe, D. C., 77, 79, 82, 84, 85, 89, 130, 131,

Subject Index